The Silence of God

FAITH MEETS FAITH

An Orbis Series in Interreligious Dialogue

Paul F. Knitter, General Editor

In our contemporary world, the many religions and spiritualities stand in need of greater intercommunication and cooperation. More than ever before, they must speak to, learn from, and work with each other, in order to maintain their own identity and vitality and so to contribute to fashioning a better world.

FAITH MEETS FAITH seeks to promote interreligious dialogue by providing an open forum for the exchanges between and among followers of different religious paths. While the series wants to encourage creative and bold responses to the new questions of pluralism confronting religious persons today, it also recognizes the present plurality of perspectives concerning the methods and content of interreligious dialogue.

This series, therefore, does not want to endorse any one school of thought. By making available to both the scholarly community and the general public works that represent a variety of religious and methodological viewpoints, FAITH MEETS FAITH hopes to foster and focus the emerging encounter among the religions of the world.

Already published:

FAITH MEETS FAITH SERIES

The Silence of God

The Answer of the Buddha

Raimundo Panikkar

Translated from the Italian by
Robert R. Barr

ORBIS BOOKS

Maryknoll, New York 10545

Originally published as *El Silencio del Dios* by Guadiana De Publicaciones, Madrid © 1970 by Raimundo Panikkar

English translation © 1989 by Orbis Books

This English translation is based on the Italian version of the book, on which the author worked in dialogue and collaboration with Umâ Marina Vesci to whom thanks and gratitude are here expressed.

Published by Orbis Books, Maryknoll, NY 10545
Manufactured in the United States of America
Manuscript editor and indexer: William E. Jerman

Library of Congress Cataloging-in-Publication Data

Panikkar, Raimundo, 1918–
   [Silencio del Dios. English]
   The silence of God: the answer of the Buddha / Raimundo Panikkar; translated from the Italian by Robert R. Barr.
     p. cm. – (Faith meets faith series)
   Bibliography: p.
   Includes index.
   ISBN 0-88344-446-1. – ISBN 0-88344-445-3 (pbk.)
   1. Buddhism–Doctrines. 2. Buddhism–Relations–Christianity.
3. Christianity and other religions–Buddhism. I. Title.
II. Series: Faith meets faith.
BQ4150.P3813   1989   89–2950
294.3'42–dc19   CIP

To those who do not know how to read and write

attá hi attano natthi[1]

Namo tassa bhagavato
arahato sammāsambuddhassa[2]

For silence to be response,
a silent query must go before.
But any silent query
shelters, in silence, the very question.
Now, if there is no query,
there is no response:
there is only a glance,
a smile;
love,
and forgiveness;
all,
nothing,
yes,
no.
Absence.[3]

Contents

III
INTERPRETATION

Preface to the English Edition

Fortune has it that I know some of the languages into which my books have been translated. This has sometimes led to the temptation—to which I have succumbed on occasion—to revise translated texts again and again. In the present instance, I have gone through the translation and introduced some modifications here and there. But the credit for the difficult task of rendering the Italian text, along with the flavor and nuances of the Spanish original, goes to Dr. Robert R. Barr, who has done an excellent job. N. Shanta has also gone through the notes and put a certain order into what had been their somewhat loose structure in the previous two editions. I express here my gratitude to both of them.

This work in English is published by Orbis Books, widely known for the publication of front-line works on Latin American (and other) theologies of liberation. The present work, sui generis as it may appear at first sight, belongs very much to a similar, though enlarged, category. It suggests avenues for liberative processes in the human realm and in the realm of theology. It offers a wider horizon that may serve both to promote a deeper understanding of liberation theology (one of the most important phenomena of our times) and to a broader application of its insights. Liberation, after all, is the central concern of Gautama the Buddha. A theology of liberation has also to consider a possible liberation of theology.

This English edition comes three decades after the work was originally conceived. It represented an existentially new step in my life. I have not recanted my Buddhist conversion, just as I did not abjure previous commitments and involvements. I believe I have purified and enlarged them. But I have not ended the pilgrimage of my life.

Silvano Panunzio entitles an insightful review of the Italian edition "Il silenzio di Panikkar . . . e la risposta di Dio." He fears I have gone too far— at least from a Christian viewpoint. My rejoinder was that I would never have dared to give "God's answer." That would have been going too far, from *any* viewpoint. I have only related the Buddha's message to our modern predicament. I have neither rejected Christ nor denied allegiance to other traditions.

Why should we build walls of separation and feel jealous about constituencies? To extol one religious and human tradition does not mean to belittle the others. Synthesis may not seem likely. Perhaps no synthesis is possible. But that does not mean that the alternative is either one-sidedness or eclecticism. Why should everything be compatible, or even comparable? But this is not an argument for schizophrenia or irrationality.

The radius is not commensurate with the circumference—but both are real and mutually related. Each circumference *has* a radius, and yet it cannot be *measured* by it. The circumference is transcendent to the radius. Before numbers (like π) were called irrational, they were called *numeri surdi* (deaf) and even *ficti* (fictitious—that is, not true numbers). We cannot measure the circumference of God with the radius of Buddhism. But I am not attempting to do in the field of mathematics what the Cantors, Dedekinds, and Pincherles, and many others, did in the field of mathematics. I am certainly not advocating either a *mathesis universalis* or sheer irrationality. I am simply making room for incommensurability because there is no need to measure everything. The *Dhammapada* (XXIII, 4) refers to nirvana as the unreachable region, *agata disa*, the untrodden country. The radius will never reach the circumference!

Since the first edition of this book, much has been written on what is studied here. I have given new courses and seminars on topics treated here. But I have made no attempt to incorporate new data and thoughts into this edition. Every book has a certain unity, and the harmony of this one would suffer were I to stuff it with new materials. What is important in any given study of this type is not so much new information but the original insight. We should not fall prey to the modern scientific distortion of equating the latest discoveries and a given subject area. I am not defending atemporal truths, but I am saying that a quarter century of testing is a good criterion for the relevance of a topic.

Having resisted the temptation to write more, I shall also resist saying less, and so I entrust what I have written (*ho gegrapha*, John 19:22) to the reader, trusting in the theory of a creative discernment (*intus-legere*) by way of a courageous "ascending of the stream" (*uddhaṁsoto ūrdhvaṁsrotas*) (*Dhammapada*, XVI, 10) up to the Source.

•

A postscript on language: Because the English language does not attribute masculine or feminine gender to inanimate things and abstract concepts, it has a greater potential for sexist or patriarchal expressions. God should not be masculine; neither should "Man" (*anthropos*). In many other languages, there is a word for Man and another for male. The sad fact of history is that males have monopolized humanness. To use the word "humanity" for Man is too abstract; and "humankind" is an expression of Darwinistic ideology (as if Man were a species) which I do not accept. To say "man/woman" or "he/she" only deepens the lethal split of modern culture. Waiting for an *utrum,* a new gender that would include masculine and feminine without being neuter (*neutrum*: neither nor), I have decided, in many of my writings, to use "Man" with capital M when refering to *anthropos.* I would have preferred to follow such usage in this book.

Preface to the Original Edition

sabbapāpassa akaraṇam kusalassa upasampadā
sacittapariyodapanaṃ etaṃ buddhana sāsanam.[1]

This book is part of another, more complete and extensive work, which the uproar of life refuses to permit me to complete. It would be entitled *The Silent Messages*.

The occasion of the present breach of silence was my collaboration on the encyclopedia *L'ateismo contemporaneo*.[2] My contribution there, "Buddhismo e ateismo,"[3] here becomes an entire monograph.

I should like to underscore once and for all that I entertain no pretension to the proffering of solutions or the proposing of theses—let alone to engagement in any apologetics for Christianity, propaganda for Buddhism, or defense of atheism. I desire only to offer a series of suggestions and hypotheses, the result of philosophical and theological research (which for me is an integral part of my life), in the hope that these reflections may bear some fruit. At the same time, I hope to be faithful to Buddhist intuitions, Christian experience, and the contemporary cultural world—no slender ambition, to be sure, nor one that should be attempted without commensurate humility. The first act of fidelity—to Buddhist intuitions—will demand that the author simply vanish, to take his place at the feet of the Enlightened One. The second act of fidelity—to Christian experience, a filiation—will call for trinitarian experience, lived personally. The third act of fidelity—to contemporary culture, a vocation—will demand a sacrosanct respect for the concrete situation of contemporary humankind. The price of the audacity to attempt the braiding of such a cordage can only be the very life of the one making the attempt. And that one must immediately cease to regard his life to be of any value if he will dare to risk its loss.[4]

The pages to follow, then, are not a work of erudition, but the fruit of experience, and a manifestation of life. This experience and this manifestation, perhaps out of shyness, clothe themselves, breechcloth to overcoat, in culture and philosophy, in order to be seen in public.[5] What the author really wishes to say, he fails to utter. But silence, too, is communicative.

A book about silence can only be a contradiction. But it will be contradictory only as what is understood and what is asserted: the leap to reality is a *mortal* leap. No other testimony is possible than the witness of death. This was the lesson of the Buddha. Therefore did Christ die on the cross.

The *munis* of India, who spend years and years in absolute silence, do not speak, but very often put things in writing, and write their responses to disciples' questions. Just as no word says anything except in emerging from silence, so silence is silent only when it knows how to take flesh and manifest itself without thereby melting away. This would be my hope.

Introduction

Although it may not appear so at first sight, this book reflects a good portion of its author's spiritual journey over a quarter of a century. It is in some way an autobiography, in which the *autos* is typical of our age, the *bios* represents the life of the three major cultural forces of our time, and the *graphy* is not anecdote, but an echo of the common human condition.

AUTOS

I speak, then, not of the isolated individual (that modern Western dogma), but of the human person (that knot in a network of relationships woven ad infinitum). I speak of the *autos*: the "self" not locked up in the idiosyncratic solipsism of individuality, but expressing in a unique though limited way the whole of reality. The "self," the *ātman*, is not the *ego*. Nor is the *autos* the negation of the *other*, but the affirmation of what one *is*, of what I *am*.

I have said that the *autos* is typical, and therefore personal. When I began the work of writing this book, early in the 1960s, my odyssey had already included the experience of the confluence of Christianity and Hinduism. But my personal identity was not yet sufficiently worked out, nor had I as yet been freed from unassimilated circumstantial elements of secondary importance. I had yet to experience — in intellectual depth and existential intensity — both that great post-Christian phenomenon called atheism, and that great post-Hindu phenomenon called Buddhism. It was only some twenty-five years later that I came to be aware of the profound meaning of this odyssey.

Never have I consciously planned my personal adventure. Therefore I regard it, in its quintessence, as typical of our age. This book reflects something of that adventure. One need only change such generic nouns as Hinduism, Christianity, Buddhism, and atheism, to other, more concrete ones, in order to grasp what I seek to indicate here. We need only think of our disappointments in our own traditions, of the quest for our proper identity beyond traditional frontiers, of the disorientation consequent upon this quest, and of the almost forced renunciation of concern with transcendental problems — not only for lack of time, but often enough for want of interest in their strange forms and the estrangement from life in which they are presented in our times. We need only think of contemporary literature, the plastic arts, music, and so on — and their breach of every canon, issuing in the appearance of new styles. The contemporary world is at least partly characterized by internal laceration, rendered artificially painless by technological gadgetry.

The *autos* is personal, by all means. But it is not individual. If I have called it typical, it is not because I hold it forth as a model for imitation, but because it appears to me to be a characteristic paradigm of current generations, and perhaps of some coming ones as well — even in what it contains of imperfection, indeed of error. After all, what is truth, on the experiential level, but truthfulness?

The *autos* of this autobiography, then, is circumscribed by that considerable and ever-growing number of contemporary men and women, in North and South, East and West, who appear to have lost — or at least lost sight of — the myth that unifies life. Modern persons have had to toil to win their identity by subjecting the legacy of their respective traditional cultures to a radical critique. The state of affairs in Africa is different from that in Asia, and these in turn differ from what obtains in the West. But everywhere, tradition is threatened. And although the traditional often survives — by plunging into the more or less unconscious underground strata of the human psyche, individual as well as collective — humanity's musty traditions, for an enormous number of our contemporaries, are now divested of any capacity to confer personal identity. The traditional is in crisis, and the human being arrives at a full self-awareness only by subjecting tradition to a radical critique.

To subject something to a critique means to strain it through the sieve of our awareness, in order to arrive, by way of this discernment, at a certitude capable of orientating us in our thought and ultimately in our life. Now, the sieve of the modern critique of tradition is not so much the academician's den, or the thinker's brain, but the bustle of life itself, and the heart of the common person. It is contemporary human existence itself that does our filtering of the legacy of tradition. Democracy, science, technology, the modern state, exotic spiritualities, and so on, are but so many other names for this challenge to tradition. The impact is shattering. We are no longer in a position to accept, casually and confidently and in naive belief, what our elders teach. But neither are we able to leave off believing in something — even if that something is nothing. In a word: the old has gone rotten, and the new has no footing. Indeed, perhaps never in all past ages has modernity shown its character of being a mode, a fashion, a precarious impermanence, as much as it does today. But we have passed the point of no return.

The remedy lies not in some revolution — a capsizing of situations — but in a liberation from the situation itself and in creating something new. A revolution is always basically conservative. It sets a situation on its ear, it tears down institutions, but it preserves basic structures. In other words, the remedy does not consist in an iconoclastic behavior, but in a critical attitude. The former aspires to the destruction of that which it regards as evil. The latter strives for discernment of a suspected ambiguity, and its elimination. An iconoclastic attitude very often provokes a reaction in the opposite direction. The critical mind-set, on the other hand, stimulates change—and it may be radical change. To confound the two is lethal.

It goes without saying that I understand "critical" here not in the sense of what I commonly refer to as "criticism"—the subjection of something to an unfavorable, and often petty, judgment—nor even in the sense of a purely theoretical judgment, but as the praxis that shakes human actions through the existential sieve of theory. There is no criticism without that sieve, but the sieve must have hands to shake it.

Persons of common sense have often preferred to forego criticism, for fear of falling into an all-demolishing iconoclasm. And this fact has been exploited by the defenders of the status quo. Any criticism of Latin American policies, for example, is accused of "communism" in many Latin American countries, just as any attempt at a reform of socialism in the Second World is labeled "fascist." But there are even more striking examples of this phenomenon in the area of religion. What does it mean to be a Christian or Hindu today? What does it mean to be a "believer"? Is a Catholic who criticizes the papacy thereby exposed as a lukewarm Catholic? Must one venerate the *samgha* in order to be a good Buddhist? Is belief in God the only form of religion? Must one accept military service to be a good citizen? Must one believe in a hereafter in order to lead a moral life?

The passage or transition, the *pascha*, from one basic conception of reality to another is not achieved easily. Nor is this transition without its dangers, even traumas. Perhaps (fortunately?) it can never be achieved completely. As much as we may seek to dissimulate our origins, our archetypes betray us. Perhaps they save us, in forcing us to a realization that personal identity is not simply the upshot of some process of deliberated selection, but the ripe fruit of an all-inclusive situation. Although we seek to strip the karma of our traversed paths, some of them centuries-old, from our past and eject it from the body of our beliefs, it adheres to our very being. Language demonstrates this with a vengeance. We may wish to exalt our labor, for example, or convince ourselves that labor is simply the result of a force in motion. But our very words for our work recall our fatigue, our effort, even our torture—the "toilsome" and "laborious" aspect of that work. We may learn a new language, or even more than one, but our native tongue never loses its privileged status. My father, in the course of one whole period of his life, all but forgot his native Malayalam, having immersed himself in the world of Western languages. But it only took an illness, and restricted activity, and he was fluent in it once more.

Westerners today feel all the debility of theism. But they are equally skeptical of atheism as a response to the ultimate questions on the meaning of existence. In like manner, Asians, who have suffered so much from religious distensions of their traditions, nevertheless resist categorical acceptance of foreign solutions presented to them in the guise of a purely "scientific" view of reality. Africans suffer an inferiority complex imposed on them by long centuries of colonization and slavery. But when they adopt modern ways, they awaken to the fearful suspicion that the cure may be worse than the disease. Latin Americans suffer under their Christian tradition, but they mistrust Marxist messianisms.

We must all achieve our *ident*ity on the basis of a radical *authen*ticity. The typical is not the topical. The paradigmatic is not the commonplace. Symbol is not sign. And perhaps this is one of the values of this autobiography—to be a symbol for a good part of the destiny of contemporary humankind in its quest for an identity that will enable it to discover an *idem* that will be neither an *ego* nor an *other*, but a *non-ego*. The *ego* stifles, the *other* alienates. Atheism suffocates. Theism drives you mad.

The *autos*, I repeat, is neither the individual nor a sociologically relevant group of individuals. The *autos* is the human person understood as the microcosm constituting the locus for the drama of the universe. Now, person is thought as well as action. Theory alone, mere thinking, simple change of awareness—even "conscientization"—deprived of an accompanying praxis, is not only impotent, but myopic. It sees only what its limited situation permits it to see. At the same time, mere praxis, simple change of structures—even a revolution—without a concomitant theory, is not only blind, but also incapable of effectuating any meaningful transformation. It changes only the order of factors and the persons in charge. The underlying schemas abide. It is only in the real world of the person—neither singular nor plural—that the crucial factors influencing the course of the universe are at work.

And it is precisely contemporary awareness that is suffering a radical crisis of planetary proportions. Faith in *God*—fatherly, protective, good, and almighty—is on the decline. (Nor does a mother-God, despite certain advantages, resolve the crisis.) Confidence in the goodness, intelligence, and power of humankind is also weakening. Hope in a kind of wisdom in nature or natural spontaneity is no longer viable. Fissures begin to appear everywhere in the traditional concepts of God, human nature, and the world as separate entities. But nihilism, as the conclusion of a syllogism all of whose premises have been disproven, becomes another groundless ideology, resulting from impatient and provisional reactions.

The contemporary human *autos* is genuinely in crisis. Certain small groups still manage to believe themselves safe (or "saved," which explains the proliferation of certain sects), but not even they can ignore the fact that humanity as a whole has embarked on one and the same adventure. Despite the insistence of their proponents that partial solutions are only "first aid," the fact remains that partial solutions are only partial—that is, through-and-through heretical. We are all bound together in a common life. And it is of this *bios* that the present cryptic autobiography intends to speak.

BIOS

Yesterday the interconnection of human life was a theory. Today it is an existential fact. We are all related, and not only in the order of being, but in the order of eating and breathing as well, not to mention thinking and believing. It is impossible to isolate ourselves from the influences of the world around us, in all the senses of that expression. Nor do I refer only to the mass media, with their potential for manipulation. I refer as well to that more subtle factor that renders these media both possible and effective: the relentless human need to rely on something superior to the individual.

Modern life is characterized neither by immobility nor by peaceful reflection. We are subjected to cultural bombardments like those of the bombs that will kill or maim living beings but leave their buildings intact — to crumble, with the passage of time, for want of anyone to maintain them. Institutions, customs, and myths are gradually emptied of meaning, leaving only their empty shells. Then everything collapses in due time, and the just pay the price of sinners' misdeeds.

It is not our grandparents who threaten our lifestyle. If they ever tried, they have been defeated. It is our grandchildren who challenge the meaning of modern society, however strenuous (and, at times, correct) our efforts to justify ourselves. But the field of our crisis is neither the individual nor the generational, but the cultural. The crisis is being played out in the personal core of human existence. The problem is much deeper than might appear at first sight. It is more than a merely political, or economic, or merely institutional problem. Weighing in the balance are the past six thousand years of human experience. The significance of the collapse of ancient civilizations dwindles by comparison. After all, those civilizations bequeathed their legacy to their successors. This is no longer the present case. If current civilization, now attempting to become planetary, crumbles, there will be no generation to receive its legacy. No longer will there be conquerors or conquered.

No culture, and no religion, can solve the human problem all by itself. Humankind is not only white or Marxist or masculine. Human identification can no longer be made in terms of civilization, Christianity, education, or national citizenship. Hence the need for a mutual fertilization of human traditions, as I have been advocating for decades. We are mutually linked, and the solution to the human problem will not come from one direction alone. The *salus ex Judaeis* principle ("salvation is from the Jews" — John 4:22), may have been valid for the Samaritans of yore. But it is not a universal principle. Salvation comes from above, it comes from below, it comes from right and left, and from within and without. Any messianism is suspect.

Three great traditions meet and intersect in our time: the theistic, especially the monotheistic; the *nāstika* or nontheistic, especially the

Buddhist; and something like a third, with two heads: the secular and atheistic. Their inevitable encounter produces typhoons that can spell doom for particular vessels, and even tidal waves that submerge whole peoples. The traditional *homo religiosus*, who would include the first two groups, must come to terms with the *homo saecularis*, and the two together must explore the possibility of a meeting of minds and hearts in the acknowledgment of a reality that neither shifts the center of gravity toward transcendence (not even toward the transcendence known as immanent) nor shifts it toward the empirically given (not even if it is called future).

Are these distinct conceptions of the world compatible? How can we opt for any of them if we recognize that the others, too, contain elements of truth? Can they correct, perhaps even complement, one another? Is cross-fertilization feasible? A mere juxtaposition, were it possible, would only create more of that cultural schizophrenia of which we already see such abundant examples. To replace the "either-or" with the "as-well-as" is not the solution. We need to overcome both.

In a more or less conscious and direct way, a large portion of contemporary humanity is suffering the impact of these three great currents. The present volume seeks to express a fragment of the cultural *bios* of our century, by way of a description of a central case of the contemporary crisis, in light of the teachings of a centuries-old tradition.

The title of this work suggests the situation of a considerable portion of current humanity. God, in any of the possible acceptations of this symbol, including that of a more or less absolute Future, may or may not exist. But at all events, for many human beings God does not appear to be real. God seems ineffective, and deaf, or at least speechless, inasmuch as God permits all manner of holocaust, injustice, and suffering. The divine—or the superhuman, if one prefers—although subjected to different interpretations, has been an all but constant point of reference in human history. It is this point of reference that is in crisis today. This is the problem of God, by whatever name God be called: the question of the center of reality and the meaning of life.

Many still call on God, but few expect a response. The current crisis is manifested in a crisis of invocation. Theologians of manifold confessions and religions have been telling us for some time now that one cannot properly speak *of* God. But the believer continues to speak *to* God, in invocation, calling on God not only to send rain, or to heal persons dear to the petitioner, but that God's will be done as well, or that God's kingdom come, at least in the form of a beneficent shower of humaneness, justice, and peace.

If one cannot properly speak of God because God is a mystery; if one cannot call on God because God does not respond; if second causes are all monopolized by scientific explanations of the present or the future; if the sorrows of the heart are better remedied by human love than by the divine (volatilized by psychoanalysis) — then what function remains to that which so many traditions have called God? Is it true that, after all these centuries, humankind has finally managed to crucify God — or, more benignly, has eliminated God as a superfluous hypothesis? Or is it only the monotheists and their successors who will disappear from the face of the earth? Or indeed only those who hurl themselves into a holy war against all the "unbelievers"?

Invocation — the raising of the heart in a plea for true love, the raising of the mind in a quest for salvific knowledge, and the raising of the life of the individual in a cry for real help — is becoming more and more necessary in the contemporary world, and at the same time more and more impossible.

First, it is becoming more and more *necessary*. We cannot bear up alone under the weight of existence. Modern life is becoming ever more precarious. The precarious leads to prayer: both of these English words derive from the medieval Latin *precaria*. The collapse of the hierarchical structure of society is rendering it less and less possible for a wife to look upon her husband as her god (as she continues to do in traditional India), or for children to accept their parents as models, or for students to accept their teachers as superior to themselves, or for laborers to accept their employers as more fit to be giving orders. We know too much psychology, sociology, and history to have failed to discover the errors, indeed the hypocrisies, of our "betters." Any intermediate steps on the "superior-inferior stairway" that have not altogether disappeared are cracking and splitting.

And yet the invocation of something above us becomes more necessary than ever. Individuals cannot know all things, or solve all problems, or control all the factors that mold their life. They can place no confidence in their peers, who are as fragile and fallible as themselves. They cannot rely on society, for society is precisely one of their greatest burdens. They feel the need to ascend higher, to cry for help, to reach out to something above, to trust in a love, or a goodness, or a someone. Invocation, as emergence from oneself in order to trust, or take refuge in, or at least to contact, something or someone superior to ourselves, becomes ever more imperative.

At the same time, such invocation is becoming *impossible*. The God to whom this invocation is directed, the God at the acme of the hierarchy of beings, appears impotent, and from that moment forward is silent. Human beings discover, with great pain, their own isolation, constrained, as they are, to live as individuals. They now seek to emerge from themselves lest they founder in the mass of their peers — lest they be lost. But there is nowhere for them to go. They emerge from themselves, yes, but only to tumble into the void. Their cry for help finds no response but its own echo or the mockery of their fellows. To be sure, many of our contemporaries swell the ranks of every sort of association or sect that claims to guarantee the genuineness and efficacy of invocation. But either these movements are soon abandoned, as fleeting fashion, or they are bureaucratized and calcified, or eventually they fall victim to the temptation of power and cynicism. In a word, sincere invocation becomes *impossible*. "To what God shall we pray with our oblations?" was the pregnant question of the Vedas themselves (*Rg Veda*, 10, 121, 1). "It may be that even he knows not," respond the Rishis (ibid., 129, 7), centuries before the Buddha subjected the query itself to the rigors of his critique. In any case, God seems not to hear, let alone respond. God is with the mightiest battalion, or the most advanced science. Sacrifice, even in the noblest and deepest sense of commerce with the divine, has fallen into desuetude, even in most of the traditional religions. The grand belief in the future, with its apogee in Marxism, has likewise vanished, and the historical (the political, economic, and cultural) horizon is too gloomy or nebulous to inspire the men and women of today.

The subtitle of this book might seem too ambitious, were it to be misinterpreted as saying that the Buddha gives *us* the "answer." That answer, whatever it may be, we shall have to forge ourselves, personally. But the Enlightened One does say to us something of importance for our world.

In the Vedic, the Mediterranean, and the African worlds, as well as elsewhere, we find belief in a reality of which the divine is an essential part. Reality includes the divine — ever infinite, mysterious, unreachable, ineffable, to be sure, but immanent in the world-as-total-reality. Theologies here are theologies within a cosmology. This is why there are theo-*logies*, work of the Logos. The divine is "part" of reality, to the point where, in some instances, it and it alone is precisely the true reality: human destiny is to become God, to discover human identity with *brahman*, to be the true people of God, to attain to a vision of God or a life in converse with God, and so on. The divine is the beginning and the end of the unfolding of the cosmos.

There is always a relationship between creature and creator, between order of appearance and order of being, between the many and the one, even between nothing and being. This relationship may be, in one sense, a *relatio rationis*. But in another sense it is quite constitutive. The Buddha, on the other hand, claims to overcome any cosmology. He makes a genuine leap into the void. The void does not exist. The void simply is not. The void is not devoid *of* anything. Transcendence — if one undertakes to speak of it — "is" so pure that it *is not*. The non-Buddhist world, in its very infinitude, is somehow spherical, somehow complete. Cosmology, in its most profound notion, is all that can be thought. It may well be thought of as open and "unthinkable": still it is within human experience. On the other hand, the Buddha denounces the very infinitude that is "thought" to be contained within such an infinite reality. He renounces any statement on the subject. And his renunciation is not that of utterance and cogitation upon *something* that stands beyond enunciation and cogitation. It is not even a renunciation of speech and thought, because there is precisely no object of which to speak or think — "nothing" to manifest or understand. The obstacle is not the failure of thought or meditation to constitute a catapult to transcendency. The obstacle lies in the fact that humankind, catapult, and transcendency all form a system — as "open" a system as you will — and the Buddha does not allow himself to be shut up in any system, no matter how infinite it is said to be. Neither cosmology nor theology, let alone anthropology, encompasses the mystery of reality, according to the Buddha.

The Buddha teaches that one must renounce the thirst (*tṛṣṇā, tanha*) for existence and nonexistence alike, that one must prescind from the quest for salvation, for *nirvāna*. The forbidden thirst includes not only desire, but will: the will to power, the will to being, as well as the will to nonbeing, the will that constitutes the quintessence of the spirit of the West all these past centuries. "*Das Urseyn ist Wollen*," said Schelling: "Primordial being is willing" (*Werke*, 2, 1, 338), capturing the spiritual history of the West in a nutshell. The Buddha's answer consists in giving no answer. After all, an answer would say "nothing."

Salvation cannot be sought. It cannot be desired. What is sought, what is desired, is transformed by this very fact, into the object of volition or desire. Such an object cannot be human salvation. No object can be. The human being is not, ultimately, a consuming animal. No object will render humans fully happy. The issue is the subject. The subject cannot be objectified without destroying it. Salvation may only be hoped for. Hope for something is not willing it, nor even desiring it. Hope is not desire. Hope, then, is not the thirst the Buddha combats. Hope is not the desire of anything, because hope is not a projection into the future. "Hope shows now, in hope itself, that fruition is certain," as Fray Luis de León put it (fruition is already here, and hence is certain). Hope is a basic attitude of the present — or, still better, of sempiternity — that is, of a presence embracing the "three times" (ultimately because it embraces the "three worlds"). Hope is not of the future, but of the invisible.

Hope is not an awaiting. Awaiting is precisely what the Buddha excoriates as self-centered ambition, whereas hope is precisely what leads the Blessed One to preach his doctrine. Hope can only be a gift, a boon, a thing bestowed — without it being necessary to postulate, in thought or imagination, any giver. Hope is grace, perhaps the very grace of existence.

But all of this can only be lived, not consigned to writing. And I have spoken of an autobiography.

GRAPHIA

The *graphia* (graphics, -graphy) of this autobiography is woven only of the cloth of the contemporary situation, without the embroidery of shapes and colors that cover its texture. Let me speak more clearly. Our times are accustomed to sociological studies, psychological reflections, and of course all manner of political treatises. On the interpenetration of diverse cultures we have, at most, anthropological essays, and precious little in the way of an approach to our problems with the radicality of a transcultural philosophical mentality. As I have said, what we are accustomed to are short narratives, draped though they may be in the chintz of statistics, or clad in the livery of socio-economic theories. It is seldom that one dares to delve down to the heart of the human condition — among other reasons, because something more than short narratives is indispensable for any further development of the topic at issue. But the narratives of this autobiography are those of the personal life of the readers. I shall remain in the paradigm.

Let readers expect nothing of mine, then. They may, however, come by a great deal of what is ours. To be sure, nothing of ours will be served up in flowery words, or reflected in statistics, or in responses to a questionnaire. It may even be something that we shall not wish to acknowledge, and we may go on intoxicating ourselves with work under the pretext of having to make a living.

This -*graphy*, then, is a piece of writing about the possible crossfertilization of the three great cultures, or groups of cultures, mentioned above. But it does not come to any conclusions or syntheses, for these are always premature in an autobiography.

In addition to its being a critique of those diminutive forms of orthodoxy that I have elsewhere called "microdoxies," this study has another ambition as well: to recover silence — the silence of things, and even the silence of God. But I do not enter upon a thematic explication of the relationship between silence and word, or being and thought, as I have attempted to do elsewhere. Not everything can be said, because not everything can be thought — and this not only because not everything is thinkable subjectively (on the part of the thinking subject, ourselves), but because not everything is thinkable intrinsically. Being and thought do not coincide, not even at their apex. Reality does not need to be transparent to itself. The monotheism that postulates a self-cognizant Being is a legitimate hypothesis. However, secularism has brought this hypothesis into a state of crisis, and Buddhism supplements it with another. But more on this below.

Perhaps I might introduce the subject matter of this book by returning to the role of thought in its relationship to reality. The ultimate characteristic of being is freedom. There is nothing arbitrary in being. But everything is free. Therefore nothing can be thought to its furthest depths. Everything moves and acts according to its own nature. Nothing occurs by chance, either in the physical, the intellectual, or the spiritual world. Everything follows its own nature. That is why one can discover a certain order among things. But the supreme characteristic is *freedom*.

In what does this freedom consist? Precisely in the primacy, and therefore the independence, of being — even where thought is concerned. What do I mean by this? I mean that each being *acts*, and at bottom *is*, as it is, and not as thought would force it or oblige it to be. I mean that each being contains a nucleus of freedom, which coincides with its *being*. Freedom is the physiognomy of *being*. This freedom renders being not only radically unthinkable, but also, and especially, *unthought*. Being is not thought about. It is being that thinks—among its other activities!

This is not the place for an elucidation of the extent to which all of this is compatible with the idea of substance, or whether I am instead advocating a Buddhist (and anatmic) conception of reality. For the moment, I wish to say only that when thought has found the solution to a problem, it is by dint of having dissolved it. If it thinks God, God becomes an object and dissolves. Thought corrodes. But its repression smothers. Thought cannot be repressed. Once a question arises, to hush it up is no answer. Nor is this the Buddha's answer. The answer that comes to us from Abrahamic traditions, including the Marxist, consists in telling us that there is no such God as the object of thinking, but that there does exist an objective transcendentalism wherein is situated a transcendent God, a transcendent Future. It is here, and only here, in this Abrahamic orbit, that the distinction between believers and nonbelievers has a certain meaning—right up to the absurdity of two military superpowers playing at an ideo-theological war that threatens the very life of the planet. There has been relatively little thinking about the theological roots of the politico-cultural situation of the present. Behind all the imperialistic and economic avatars is the cultural factor, "blackmailing" the world and obliging it to choose between God and not-God, to be either believing or unbelieving.

The -*graphy* of this book interprets the Buddha's message of the past twenty-five centuries as a possible key to overcome this dilemma, and as an encouragement to us to embrace a new innocence in which false alternatives will be bypassed. This will be done neither by way of a discovery of the critical power of our mind (as with the Vedanta against the "karmakandins" or Kant against the "dogmatists"), nor by way of a discovery of the destructive capacity of reason (as with the philosophy of feeling, and existentialisms of every sort), nor by way of philosophies of other kinds. It will be done by way of our recognition of the futility of any pretension to have an absolute language—whether such a symbol goes by the name of God or reason or science, or be structured in any other manner.

To explain reality is to transform it. To think reality is itself of the order of its manipulation. Not that there are things that cannot be uttered or thoughts that cannot be had, or that these particular things or thoughts are correct rather than those others. It is rather a matter of the Buddhist intuition of the via media between agnosticism and absolutism.

A large part of today's humanity lives under the impression that some inescapable dialectic is at work between the ideologies of the First and Second Worlds. No wonder that violence and war seem inevitable. There is no nonviolent way to resolve conflicts when each side believes itself to be in possession of the truth. The political consequences are obvious to everyone.

The twin ideologies struggling today for the hegemony of the world and of consciences represent the last phase of a historical dialectic that, unless it is transcended by the contributions of other human cultures, will end by destroying history itself.

All of this would be the *Sitz im Leben* of this autobiography, intended as a "writing of the life of humankind." Therefore I speak of God.

The Silence of God

Part I

The Problem

1

A Crime of Lèse Humanité

Ἐὰν ʽυμῖν εἴπω οʼυ μή πιστεύσητε[1]

An elementary rule of methodology proscribes formulating a judgment on anything in categories foreign to it. An anthropological maxim, on the other hand—and one just as elementary—would have it that no boundaries can be set to human thinking. Accordingly, although the problematic of contemporary atheism constitutes a cultural circumstance peculiar to the West, it is nevertheless possible that an investigation of the religious phenomenon of atheism will yield valuable elements for an elucidation of what is perhaps one of the most important problems of our time.

Of course, to label "atheistic" those conceptions of the world that fail to present a concept of God after the manner of the believing West would be as mistaken as to deny that there had ever been atheism in history. At bottom both opinions spring from the prejudice just cited—that of judging a phenomenon by categories foreign to it. And yet surely the unity of human nature is such that it must be possible to elaborate the intellectual coordinates needed for grasping a religious and cultural phenomenon distinct from one's own.

Unfortunately for both sides, this effort to grasp another cultural and religious world from within is a rather difficult task, because of the somewhat novel, integral asceticism it demands, and because of certain sociological conditionings.

The concrete problem I seek to address is whether it is possible to build a religio-cultural (or whatever it might be called) bridge, with an arch twenty-five centuries high and a span of thousands of miles, between the contemporary religious preoccupation with atheism and the message of the Buddha—a message at the basis of a way of life that, to all appearances, leaves no room for God.

Once the problem has been sketched out, I shall limit myself to a presentation of certain basic texts that have won Buddhism its reputation as atheistic. Then, in part 3, I shall proceed to a synthetic interpretation of these texts, in the light of Buddhistic principles and keeping in mind the categories of contemporary Western thought.

It is common knowledge that there is no such thing as "Buddhism" in the singular; that so-called primitive Buddhism is still problematic, and that the authentic teaching of the Buddha is very far from having been definitively identified.[2] Indeed, there has never been unanimity here, neither in antiquity, nor in the present state of Buddhistic research, nor even in the various religious schools of thought today that all claim to be following the Buddha.[3] All this is an example of the imprecision, if not arbitrariness, of the concept of religion as a compact body of orthodoxy.[4] I should like to make it clear from the outset, then, that I make no claim that all the texts that I shall cite have issued directly from the mouth of the Buddha. Many of them, indeed, date from a period much later than that of primitive Buddhist tradition. Still, in one way or another they all represent the authentic Buddhist spirit. It is quite remarkable that, despite the huge variety of sects and opinions within Buddhism, and despite the fact that "the age of Buddhist revelation was never closed,"[5] the basic intuitions of Buddhism have been completely preserved throughout the twenty-five centuries of its history. The Emperor Asoka commanded it to be sculpted in stone: "Whatever the blessed Buddha hath said, hath been well said."[6] The orthodox tradition has echoed ever after: "Whatever has been well said, has been said by the Buddha."[7]

However this may be — for my intent is not primarily historical — it cannot be denied that there is a "Buddhist fact," together with an impalpable something that could be called a Buddhist spirit.[8] It is this fact and this spirit to which I shall be referring in this study inasmuch as my aim is not that of philosophical archeology, but that of elucidating a historico-religious reality that, with its roots in the past, nonetheless retains its full strength in the present as well.

Let me emphasize yet again that the perspective of my undertaking is not historical, but philosophical. Were I to approach the "Buddhist fact" from a historical and chronological angle, I should have to "fine-tune" a great number of the notions here expressed. The numerous references in the notes are the tribute owed to the rigor of facts. But by relegating this material to notes I am reminding the reader that, although a historical study is indispensable, it does not preclude an effort of philosophical understanding that is neither antihistorical nor entangled in historicism.

The fact of such a variety of opinions ought not to be the occasion for our losing sight of a "something" transcending the notional world that comes down to us through such a long human tradition. We need only recall, for example, the phenomenology of opinions concerning Christ, which yield a spectrum of judgments including imposture, Docetist apparition, and the status of the only-begotten of God.

In undertaking the task I set before myself — and having to straddle East and West in the attempt, as I seek to be faithful both to Buddhism and to Christianity — it does not seem to me an exaggeration or mere rhetoric to speak of Christian-Buddhist mutual misunderstanding in terms of a "lèse humanité." That two spiritual "facts" of the scope of Christianity and Buddhism, coexisting for some twenty centuries now, and together comprising about a third of humankind, could be ignorant of one another, and that when they do meet they lack even a common language in which to engage in dialogue—that the opinion each has formed of the other generally represents only the grossest approximation—is an ongoing absurdity, not to say scandal.[9] Nor is the situation only one of the past.[10] Even in our age of the "global village" it persists.[11]

The current notion of Buddhism in the West is that of an atheistic, nihilistic, negative "religion," yoked with a polytheistic, rather superstitious or magical, popular faith. Some see it as a more or less profound, universalistic "mystique." For others it is a simple "philosophy," understanding the word in the restricted sense it has taken on in recent centuries in the Western world.[12] Buddhism, and Zen in particular, with the recent fashionability of "Eastern spirituality," may appear to be a technique or method for attaining personal integration or psychological peace, and thus the Buddha comes to be considered a "saint" rather than the bearer of a sacred charism to found a religious movement.[13] On the Buddhist side, misunderstanding is just as great. For example, Christ has been seen as the victim of a sadistic God.[14] And the mutual misunderstanding abides, although at last there are some gladdening signs that it may be overcome.

The reasons for such misunderstanding, it seems to me, are easy to list. In the first place, until recently there were no sociological categories available in either culture adequate to encounter, to know, and to evaluate the other. Secondly, when an opportunity did finally present itself, it was vitiated by the "uneven ground" of the encounter, as well as by many other historical factors—conquest and resistance, conversion and counterattack, political questions and their economic corollaries, and so on. Thirdly, even a minimal philosophical and theological basis for a dialogue was wanting.[15] A nonreligious dialogue will never strike to the root of the question; and yet there cannot be religious communication until there is true sacral communion.[16]

Indifference and a "superiority complex" have of course played a role on the Buddhist side. On the Christian side, an exclusivistic, not to say disdainful, interpretation of Buddhism, has been such that, where positive values could not be denied, they have been attributed to "natural human goodness," or to a theory of plagiarism, or to primitive Christian influences. Here let us recall the long-held Western notion that the Buddha must have lived some time after Christ, because undeniable similarities were otherwise inexplicable.[17] To be sure, the same error has been committed on the other side.[18]

The present study seeks to make a contribution to the correction of this misunderstanding, albeit not by a direct study of it, but by a demonstration of the possibility (without slipping into an amorphous syncretism) of the cross-fertilization of a problematic of the modern West with the ancient Buddhist tradition.[19] What I seek to achieve is basically a positive integration of both traditions. It goes without saying, of course, that my pursuit of such a cross-fertilization will necessitate use of a special language.

2

A Surfeit of Opinions

An analysis of the fate of Buddhism at the hands of Western scholars delivers up an almost dizzying diversity of opinion with respect to the major part of even the basic points.[1] To limit myself to the theme of this study, Buddhism has been labeled pantheistic,[2] polytheistic,[3] theistic,[4] agnostic,[5] and atheistic.[6] Again, whereas some seek to defend it as a pure agnosticism,[7] others regard it as simply pragmatism in its refusal to take a position on problems of a purely theoretical nature.[8] Still others praise (or condemn) Buddhism as the most radical, consistent nihilism.[9] Finally, there are even authors for whom the Buddha is a mythical personage,[10] and Buddhism a mythology,[11] by and large of a magical character.[12] Today it is gradually becoming recognized that Buddhism is neither theistic nor atheistic,[13] but the notion of an "atheistic religion" is still paradoxical for a whole sector of humanity.[14] Accordingly, there are those who deny Buddhism any religious character whatever,[15] and those who, on the contrary, deem it the purest of religions.[16]

It can scarcely be denied that the phenomenon of Buddhism is sufficiently extensive and complex for all these opinions to enjoy some de facto foundation.[17] Nevertheless, up to the present there has been precious little agreement in the interpretation of Buddhism.[18] Historical monographs fail to resolve the problem; they confirm the heterogeneity of Buddhism in time and space. And yet today there is an incipient convergence of opinion, precisely in the area of philosophical interpretation.

Order among the various opinions held regarding the Buddha's faith in an ultimate reality may be introduced as follows.

CYNICISM

According to this interpretation, the Buddha was an authentic cynic, concealing an answer to the fundamental question posed by persons in his time and in every successive generation.

7

Within this first interpretation, there is a subdistinction to be made between a cynicism of *simulation* and one of *dissimulation*.[19] According to the former explanation, the Buddha himself did not know which side to take: he had no precise notion when it came to ultimate issues. Silence,[20] then, and simulation, became his only recourse.[21] In other words the Buddha was an impostor, and simply took advantage of the good faith of others. Today there would no longer seem to be anyone to maintain such an erroneous position.

The second position, on the other hand, seeks to save appearances at least, holding that the Buddha must certainly have been personally convinced of one solution or another — generally thought to be the nihilistic alternative — but that he felt constrained to dissimulate his conviction lest he limit too severely the number of his followers.[22] Here too, then, the Buddha turns out to be a charlatan of sorts, although of some good will. Obviously our times cannot admit such a thesis, altogether bereft as it is of any textual basis, and simply proceeding from an a priori bias against religion in general or Buddhism in particular.

Not only is there not the slightest evidence for doubting the Buddha's radical genuineness and honesty, but there is no apparent reason for attributing to him such distorted intentions in the first place. Someone like the Buddha, had he wished to deceive, could surely have found some more expeditious means of doing so than to preach a doctrine that excludes the slightest concession to the human instinct of self-assertion. Further, the Buddha explicitly denies that he has followed the esoteric practice of the "master's closed hand" with his disciples[23] — that is, that he has concealed from them anything necessary for their salvation.[24] The Buddha shared all that he had to share.[25]

NIHILISM

According to a second interpretation, the Buddha was an out-and-out atheist. He preached an absolute nihilism. *Nirvāṇa* is total annihilation. In the "beyond" there is nothing, neither a God nor anything else. The Buddha refused to speak of God because he did not believe in God. His denial of God was so radical that he refused the issue any place in his system, even for the purpose of denying God's existence. In this conception, Buddhism would be atheism pure and simple.[26]

It would be difficult to find a buddhologist today to maintain the thesis of nihilism, propounded principally, and in varying degrees of subtlety,[27] by French orientalists in the middle of the last century.[28] Here again it would be a simple matter to demonstrate that texts are being read against a background of a "metaphysical" system whose values are foreign to the spirit and intentions of Buddhism.[29]

Vis-à-vis a negative, contingent notion of existence — with or without justification, it matters little for our case — its denial, even the assertion of its annihilation, will scarcely be the equivalent of what we term nihilism, or even atheism, today. An adequate analysis will be arrived at not by playing with words, but by interpreting intuitions.

There is also the familiar thesis that Buddhistic atheism — or better, nihilism — was a later aberration. According to this conception, primitive, authentic Buddhism was not nihilistic; later Buddhism, by contrast, especially that of the philosophers, represents the adventitious construction of a radical nihilism.[30]

AGNOSTICISM

The only adequate reason found by some authors for the Buddha's refusal to take a position vis-à-vis ultimate issues is a personal agnosticism on his part, coupled with a prudent reserve with respect to its expression.[31] On this view, the Buddha had come to the realization that there was nothing that could be known with certainty — that the human mind simply lacked a capacity for knowing truth. He thereupon made a virtue of necessity by adopting his characteristic attitude of refusing to allow himself to be caught in metaphysical or philosophical disquisitions.[32]

The celebrated parable in the *pāli* canon of the leaves in the Buddha's hand — so few in comparison with all those of the thicket — has been, from ancient times, the orthodox rejoinder to the theory of the Buddha's agnosticism:

> Once the Buddha was abiding in the *simsapā* wood, in the region of *Kosambī*. Taking some *simsapā* leaves in his hand, he put this question to his disciples: "Where, think ye, are there surely more leaves — here in my hand, or on all of the trees of the wood?"
>
> But his disciples replied: "Few are the leaves in thy hand, whilst in the forest are many more."
>
> But he said to them: "Thus it is with my teaching: what I know, but have not taught ye, is altogether more than what I have taught ye. But why have I not taught ye these things? Because they are of no utility for the end."[33]

One need not, to be sure, fly to the diametrically opposite position, and hold that the Buddha claimed to be omniscient, that he knew everything, but that he did not wish to reveal it to his disciples. Besides postulating a rather extravagant act of faith in the person of the Buddha, this interpretation would contradict the explicit assertion on his part that he did not follow the custom of the "closed hand."[34]

On the other hand, agnosticism is quite a straightforward doctrine, and it would have cost the Buddha nothing at all to declare that he did not know, or that human beings could not know, the answer to the ultimate puzzles of existence. But the Buddha never stated that he was an agnostic.

On the contrary, his whole comportment was that of the "Enlightened One," indeed, the one who knows, who has seen, who has "arrived." The Buddha never entertained the least doubt as to his own position and solution. The Buddha knows. He knows, and makes manifest, the road of salvation. Nothing could be further removed from the attitude of an agnostic.

PRAGMATISM

Pragmatism may not be the best term for the fourth interpretation. Today the word implies a certain utilitarianism that would have been foreign to the Buddha's mentality. But it has been used, and so I shall use it as well—to denote a certain eminently practical, indeed we might say existential, attitude on the Buddha's part.[35] On the "pragmatistic" view, then, the reason why the Buddha said nothing of God or the afterlife was simply that he deemed the question to be of little moment. Indeed, it could be an obstacle along the path to one's ultimate end. Here the Buddha would be the prototype of the religious prophet who comes not to preach a doctrine or teach a theory, but to point out a path and fulfill a mission.[36] Here, Buddhistic "annihilation" would be but the annihilation of hatred, lust, sloth, and so on.[37]

This position has also been termed "positivistic."[38] But once again we have a term with specific connotations that would be inapplicable to the case of the Buddha. What is really meant by the expression in this context is a kind of prudent abstentionism, an attitude that would avoid complicating unnecessarily the personal question of salvation. The Buddha is reported to have cited the analogy of someone wounded by an arrow who would pause to engage in speculation upon the event rather than remove the arrow.[39] And indeed whenever the Buddha refuses a reply—and yet rejects a negative interpretation of his refusal—the reason that he invariably advances is that a theoretical response is not conducive to the end,[40] that it fails to advance the realization of the ideal:

> Wrongly, basely, falsely, and without foundation do certain ascetics and Brahmins accuse me, saying that Gautama the ascetic is a nihilist, and that he preaches annihilation, destruction, and nonexistence. Such I am not, such I do not assert. Today, monks, as before, I proclaim one thing alone: sorrow, sorrow's destruction. . . .[41]

This "pragmatism" on the Buddha's part has likewise been interpreted as a kind of silence of etiquette. That is, the silence of the Buddha would be nothing more than an elegant, traditional way of "saying" that the question is out of place.[42] Here, basically, the picture is that of a kind of superiority on the part of the Compassionate One: he simply does not deign to enter into questions weighing upon the rest of mortals.

To be sure, such an attitude is not altogether incompatible with the spirit of Buddhism; and of course any practical attitude, willy-nilly, demands a determinate theoretical conception of which it is ultimately the tributary. The very fact of considering the question of God to be irrelevant presupposes a determinate conception of the divinity, and certainly not one in which God would assume a central position even if only in order to be denied. Again, to assert that the important thing is salvation, without any concern for a speculative examination of salvation, surely presupposes a determinate conception both of salvation and of the human cognitive faculty. The theory of a "pragmatism" on the part of the Buddha, then, although containing a particle of truth, in the final analysis cannot be maintained, resting as it does on a presupposed, speculative basis.[43]

PROBLEMATICISM

A more subtle and more profound variant of the foregoing is the current of thought that interprets the silence of the Buddha concerning basic philosophical questions as a position of radical problematicism.[44]

If a question is ill posed, ill stated, if the premises from which it issues cannot be accepted—then a direct answer to it will automatically be tantamount to falling into error. In the theory of problematicism, it is for this reason, and not simply out of etiquette, that the Buddha refused to give a reply: neither the positive nor the negative answer satisfied him.[45]

This is an altogether plausible explanation, but scarcely a compelling one. The Buddha would have had merely to restate the question in correct fashion.

But problematicism goes a step further, and posits a more intimate relationship between query and response. It is not, we hear, a matter of formulation. What the theory of problematicism is at pains to underscore is that any question on problems of a certain type is automatically itself problematic. What we have here is Heisenberg's uncertainty principle applied to the distortion a question introduces into the problem it addresses. Anyone who poses such a question not only distorts the question, but renders impossible any response that does not accept the presuppositions of the question itself. In other words, the question is unanswerable because at bottom all intellectual inquiry violates the virginity of something that, precisely in being transformed into a question, sacrifices the only context in which a reply could be appropriate. According to the theory of problematicism, then, the Buddha's very intuition condemned him to silence. "If I declare that there is *ātman*," he says, "it will be thought of as eternal; if I declare that there is not *ātman,* it will be imagined utterly to perish at death."[46]

I shall make no attempt to conceal my sympathy for this line of solution. But I cannot help observing that, first, it would surely be something of a philosophical anachronism to interpret a problematic twenty-five centuries old by superimposing on it a philosophical grid predicated on a degree of awareness altogether peculiar to our own recent generations. And secondly, if this had really been the Buddha's solution, it is not clear why he should not have said so. Let us not overlook the fact that, unlike so many of our own contemporaries, the Buddha did not say that silence was the adequate answer.[47] He simply kept silent. "It is not for me to debate with the world but for the world to debate with me," tradition attributes to the Master.[48]

To be sure, it could be said that the Buddha envisaged the possibility of this solution, but that, for want of philosophical categories necessary to express it, he preferred to keep silence. It has even been said that he of course knew the solution, but because his contemporaries were not prepared to hear it, his only recourse was to be silent.

I shall not, then, enter upon a discussion either of the Buddha's omniscience, or of the possibility that he was perhaps several centuries ahead of human collective awareness. I grant, however, that these two theologico-religious explanations seem acceptable, once those of a strictly philosophical order have been exhausted.[49]

An explanation by way of problematicism, then, touches a most important point in the Buddha's outlook, and its pursuit could shed light on the parallel question in our own contemporary speculation. But it does not seem to me to correspond either to the Buddha's deepest intuition, which was religious, not epistemological, or to his simple, prophetic attitude, which is basically incompatible with any merely intellectual problematic.

DIALECTICS

In the minds of the most enthusiastic proponents of a dialectical interpretation, the honor of having been the first dialectician falls to the Buddha.[50] Other interpreters prefer to style his attitude a "critical" one.[51] The reason why the Enlightened One eschewed intellectual disquisitions on ultimate issues is precisely because they transcend the sphere of intellection and thought, and that it is only by a "quantum leap" that they can be adequately grasped. That is, they must simply be experienced.[52] If one would arrive at release and deliverance, one must transcend all antinomies.[53]

This solution, of venerable rootage in Buddhist tradition, nurturing as it does the whole of *mādhyamika*—touches on a central point in the consciousness of the Buddha—namely, on the transcendence of reality with respect to both the phenomenological and the conceptual orders.[54] If God can be imprisoned in a concept, if the afterlife can be thought of as an embellished prolongation of this one—if the purely conceptual order cannot be overcome—then evidently there is indeed neither God, nor an afterlife, nor reality. The Buddha cannot give an answer capable of transcending the rational categories of any kind of question whatsoever.

Now, in the first place, it would appear rather forced to call this position dialectical: if enlightenment is reached in virtue of a dialectical transcendence, then a conceptual structure is thereby accorded a causal importance and function that it is simultaneously denied. In the second place, it would seem rather presumptuous, and ultimately improbable, to suppose that none of those approaching the Buddha to seek his counsel appreciated such a distinction—that all of them were riveted to a rationalistic conception of reality. It is true, of course, that the formulation of any question must give it enough intellectual content to render it intelligible. Still, it would not seem that seekers who come with a vital, existential question will necessarily be looking only for satisfaction of their own intellectual curiosity. It seems to me that the position developed by *mādhyamika*—that no philosophical system is anything more than a rational, not to say rationalistic, "philosophism"—not only is a gratuitous, and rather condescending, presumption, but fails to do justice to the de facto approaches undertaken by a goodly number of the philosophical systems of East and West alike.[55]

Thus the dialectical account of the silence of the Buddha does not seem to me to be particularly satisfactory. I do not think it admissible that the Buddha was the only one, or the first, to have discovered that reality transcends concepts and thought.[56] Many others, both before and after him, have seen this and expressly maintained it, not having recourse to his silence.

Dialectics does enter into the Buddha's position, and the best evidence for this is in the later Buddhist tradition that developed it in a particular way. But it does not seem to me to represent the Tathagata's[57] basic intuition. It is too technically philosophical and contrary to the spirit of the great Compassionate One who was unwilling to write a single line. Let us keep in mind that this renunciation of writing represents a renunciation of any claim to be able to establish fixed principles or immutable laws valid for all times and intelligible to all readers. Here the Buddha reminds us not only of Socrates, but of Jesus himself.[58]

APOPHATICISM

Here I could have used the term "mysticism," but I have been dissuaded from its use by its so many and varied connotations.[59]

As we have seen, we cannot seriously regard the silence of the Buddha as proceeding from an ignoble pretense at knowledge he did not have, any more than from dishonest dissimulation of such knowledge. Its motives reach far deeper than this. Nor, surely, is the reason for his reticence reducible to a psychological inability to speak of reality or supply a correct answer to basic human questions. Nor, thirdly, does it seem to me that the depth of the Buddha's intuition is explained by laying his silence to the account of an epistemological exigency—that is, to the incapacity of the human mind to comprehend the ultimate mystery of reality. Incomprehensibility granted, it does not justify his silent message.[60] Still less is the Buddha's silence explained by a sort of anti-intellectual, or perhaps merely supra-intellectual, attitude, in which reality would be considered attainable by means of a faculty (if this is what we should have to call it) whose capacity outstripped that of the normal human intellect. There is nothing in the Buddha—indeed, if anything, the contrary would be the case—to incline one to suspect him of some sort of predilection for "supernatural," extraordinary phenomena. The ultimate reason for the Buddha's silence seems to me to be rooted neither in the inherent limitation of the human subject, nor in the imperfection of our cognition, nor in the mysterious, recondite nature of reality.[61]

Instead, it seems to me that the ultimate reason for the silence of the Buddha resides precisely in the fact that this ultimate reality *is* not. Let me hasten to explain.[62] The term "apophatic" is usually used in reference to an epistemological apophaticism, positing merely that the ultimate reality is *ineffable*—that human intelligence is incapable of grasping, of embracing it—although this ultimate reality itself may be represented as *intelligible,* even supremely intelligible, *in se.* A gnoseological apophaticism, then, comports an ineffability on the part of the ultimate reality only *quoad nos.* Buddhistic apophaticism, on the other hand, seeks to transport this ineffability to the heart of ultimate reality itself, declaring that this reality— inasmuch as its *logos* (its expression and communication) no longer pertains to the order of ultimate reality but precisely to the manifestation of that order—is ineffable not merely in our regard, but as such, *quoad se.* Thus Buddhistic apophaticism is an ontic apophaticism.[63] Ultimate reality is so supremely ineffable and transcendent that, strictly speaking, Buddhism will be constrained to deny it the very character of being.[64] Being, after all, is what is; but what is, by the very fact of being, is in some manner thinkable and communicable. It belongs to the order of manifestation, of being. And therefore it cannot be considered to be ultimate reality itself.[65]

When the Buddha refuses to respond, then, it is not for any subjective reason—neither his own, nor that of his hearer, nor that of human nature— but in virtue of an exigency of reality itself. His is not a methodological or a pedagogical silence, but an ontic silence.[66] His silence not only clothes the reply, it invades the question. He is not only silent, he reduces to silence.

Tradition recalls the Buddha's love for silence:[67] his concern for his own silence, his recommendations that his followers keep silence,[68] and the hush that was so characteristic of Buddhist gatherings.[69] *Noble silence* is part and parcel of the Buddhist spirit,[70] as it is of any monastic institution.[71] Not only does the Buddha proscribe every idle word—he proclaims every word idle that purports to bear on the ultimate mystery of reality.

His celebrated "audience" with Brahmā after his enlightenment is instructive here. (It is also interesting to note that orthodox commentators reject this myth as spurious, because it seems to militate against the Buddha's omniscience[72] after the experience of the *Budh-gāya.*) In this myth, the Buddha's first reaction to his enlightenment is an inclination to withdraw into absolute silence and to communicate his intuition to no one. Brahmā insists that he reconsider. Reluctant, the Buddha attempts to justify his resolve with his celebrated inquiry as to whether he, the Buddha, will find many disciples capable of grasping his message.[73] Brahmā reassures him; but still the Enlightened One determines to speak only of the way to reach the goal, and not of the goal itself — the ultimate and most sublime truth that is *nirvāṇa*.[74]

So seriously does Gautama take the incommunicability of the supreme experience that from this time forward he no longer seeks to communicate it or even speak of it. Ultimate reality, by virtue of its very ultimacy, has no need of our knowledge, our concern, or indeed that we should have any care for it at all.[75] To treat it as a "something" in some manner dependent on our cognition, our concern for it, our affirmation or negation of it, our apprehension of it, experience of it, or what you will — this would ineluctably be to consider it as something intramundane, one more being among beings, however earnest the protest of our lips and even of our heart that it is sublime, transcendent, and ineffable.

The Tathagata has "arrived," and there is no returning for him. He will show the path, but will say nothing of the goal, for he would thereby disfigure it, he would risk directing men and women toward what they think, wish, feel, and believe to be the goal, and not toward that in-effable, in-exsistent end that no one has seen,[76] where no one has entered and remained alive;[77] and where every word must withdraw and depart.[78]

It has not been my intent to offer an exhaustive catalogue of the various opinions of buddhologists on the silence of the Buddha with regard to ultimate reality, but only to categorize the opinions that seem to me to be the most important.[79] What I have said thus far will be enough to enable me to proceed with my examination of so-called Buddhist atheism.

3

Buddhism:
Atheistic Religion

"Atheism is a cruel undertaking. To carry it to its ultimate consequences costs dearly. And I think I have taken it to the very end."[1] Atheism, in this pregnant statement of Jean-Paul Sartre, is found at the end of a journey — at the terminus of a prolonged adventure — personal and collective — undertaken by a goodly part of the West — and is transformed by virtue of its very radicality into a religious attitude. Atheism is here a *religious atheism*.[2] With the Buddha, by contrast, atheism is present from the outset, at the very beginning of his reform. His is an *atheistic religion*.[3]

Buddhism's credentials as a religion have been called into question only by those who confound religion with a determinate doctrine concerning transcendent truths — in other words, by those who, in their ignorance of the dynamic nature of all religion (of its character as *orthopraxis*), seek to reduce it simply to *orthodoxy*.[4] But no religion is content to be mere doctrine. The task of religion is to lead human beings to their true end, and religion requires of them the holy comportment that will save them — however diverse the definitions of the end and the conceptualizations of holy comportment (even as mere openness or passivity). "Nothing that is not eternal is any occasion for gladness, deserves any salutation, or has any value worthy of our ambitioning," says the Buddhist scripture.[5]

It is precisely by reason of its eminently religious nature that Buddhism eschews all ties to doctrine and renounces all speculation. Thus in a certain sense the very fact of speculation is for the Buddha an indication that one has not attained the goal. As we have seen, the Buddha himself is credited with having originated the classic parable of the person wounded by an arrow, who would seek first to know what type of weapon it was, which direction it had come from, who had shot it, for what reason, and so on.[6] Our "metaphysician" will surely die without learning the answers. Men and women wounded by the arrow of suffering must first extract the suffering and be saved.

16

"The time is short" (1 Cor. 7:29; cf. Rom. 13:11);[7] It must be "made the most of" (Eph. 5:16; Col. 4:5),[8] nor should one dally with "empty, seductive philosophy" (Col. 2:8; cf. Eph. 5:6).[9] Thus Christian tradition, too, warns us not to love the world,[10] for the world may cause us to fall (1 John 2:15); the structure of this *kosmos* is a passing one (1 Cor. 7:31).[11]

THE FOUR NOBLE TRUTHS

It is in this context that the Four Noble Truths of the Buddha's first sermon in Vārāṇasī are to be situated.[12] Together with the Eightfold Path to the attainment of the end, they constitute the core of all Buddhism.[13] I here reproduce a translation of the apposite text in full, to afford the reader the opportunity to breathe in the climate of this "atheistic religion":[14]

Thus have I heard:[15] Once the Exalted One was dwelling near Benares, at Isipatana, in the Deer-Park.

Then the Exalted One thus spake unto the company of five monks:[16]

Monks, these two extremes should not be followed by one who has gone forth as a wanderer. What two?

Devotion to the pleasures of sense, a low practice of villagers, a practice unworthy, unprofitable, the way of the world (on the one hand); and (on the other) devotion to self-mortification, which is painful, unworthy and unprofitable.

By avoiding these two extremes the Tathāgata has gained knowledge of that middle path which giveth vision, which giveth knowledge, which causeth calm, special knowledge, enlightenment, Nibbāna.[17]

And what, monks, is that middle path which giveth vision . . . Nibbāna?[18]

Verily it is this Ariyan eightfold way, to wit: Right view, right aim, right speech, right action, right living, right effort, right mindfulness, right concentration. This, monks, is that middle path which giveth vision, which giveth knowledge, which causeth calm, special knowledge, enlightenment, Nibbāna.

Now this, monks, is the Ariyan truth about Ill:[19]

Birth is Ill, decay is Ill, sickness is Ill, death is Ill: likewise sorrow and grief, woe, lamentation and despair. To be conjoined with things which we dislike: to be separated from things which we like—that also is Ill. Not to get what one wants—that also is Ill. In a word, this body, this fivefold mass[20] which is based on grasping—that is Ill.

Now this, monks, is the Ariyan truth about the arising of Ill:[21]

It is that craving[22] that leads back to birth, along with the lure and the lust that lingers longingly now here, now there: namely, the craving for sensual pleasure, the craving to be born again, the craving for existence to end. Such, monks, is the Ariyan truth about the arising of Ill.

And this, monks, is the Ariyan truth about the ceasing of Ill:[23]

Verily it is the utter passionless cessation of, the giving up, the forsaking, the release from, the absence of longing for this craving.[24]

Now this, monks, is the Ariyan truth about the practice that leads to the ceasing of Ill:

Verily it is this Ariyan eightfold way, to wit: Right view, right aim, right speech, right action, right living, right effort, right mindfulness, right concentration.[25]

Monks, at the thought of this Ariyan truth of Ill, concerning things unlearnt before, there arose in me vision, insight, understanding: there arose in me wisdom, there arose in me light.

Monks at the thought: This Ariyan truth of Ill is to be understood — concerning things unlearnt before, there arose in me vision, insight, understanding: there arose in me wisdom, there arose in me light.

Monks, at the thought: This Ariyan truth about Ill has been understood (by me) — concerning things unlearnt before, there arose in me vision, insight, understanding: there arose in me wisdom, there arose in me light.

Again, monks, at the thought of this Ariyan truth about the arising of Ill, concerning things unlearnt before, there arose in me vision, insight, understanding: there arose in me wisdom, there arose in me light.

At the thought: This arising of Ill is to be put away — concerning things unlearnt before . . . there arose in me light.

At the thought: This arising of Ill has been put away — concerning things unlearnt before . . . there arose in me light.

Again, monks, at the thought of this Ariyan truth about the ceasing of Ill, concerning things unlearnt before . . . there arose in me light.

At the thought: This ceasing of Ill must be realized — concerning things unlearnt before . . . there arose in me light.

At the thought: This Ariyan truth about the ceasing of Ill has been realized — concerning things unlearnt before . . . there arose in me light.

Again, monks, at the thought of this Ariyan truth about the practice leading to the ceasing of Ill, concerning things unlearnt before . . . there arose in me light.

At the thought: This Ariyan truth about the practice leading to the ceasing of Ill must be cultivated — concerning things unlearnt before . . . there arose in me light.

At the thought: This Ariyan truth about the practice leading to the ceasing of Ill must be cultivated — concerning things unlearnt before . . . there arose in me light.

At the thought: This Ariyan truth about the practice leading to the ceasing of Ill has been cultivated — concerning things unlearnt before there arose in me vision, insight, understanding: there arose in me wisdom, there arose in me light.

Now, monks, so long as my knowledge and insight of these thrice revolved twelvefold[26] Ariyan truths, in their essential nature, was not quite purified—so long was I not sure that in this world, together with its Devas,[27] its Māras,[28] its Brahmās,[29] among the hosts of recluses and brahmins, of Devas and mankind, there was one enlightened with supreme enlightenment.[30]

I have cited this passage in extenso not only because of its capital importance for all Buddhism, but also because it will be of service in the elucidation of the precise point of my investigation, the atheism of the Buddha.[31]

I shall not stop to engage in a commentary on the content of this text. Let me simply note its eminently religious nature.[32] Neither the word "God" nor the corresponding concept occurs; and yet it can scarcely be said that this ineffable reality, so often and so facilely named, denominated, "God," is simply denied.

The entire text bathes in an aroma of salvation. There is concern to leave the absolute free and uncontaminated, and thus to exclude all contingent existence, or *saṃsāra*. (Hence the reference to the cycle of births improperly called "reincarnation.") Our experience is always an experience of contingency, and although there may be reasons that lead us to conclude that at the terminus of human experience is the absolute, even this concluded-to experience of the absolute will itself, as such, be a contingent experience. God is never strictly experienced *in se*.[33] Even were we to admit of an absolute object (which in the strict meaning of the terms would be a self-contradiction), the subject experiencing it would still be contingent, would not be self-sustaining, would not be, strictly speaking, an ultimate, genuine *sub-jectum*. What remains for the human being to do, then, is to consider the de facto situation, and to see in what its actual basic structure consists. According to our text, the basic structure of the concrete subject, the human being, is suffering. The elimination of contingency is the supreme object of human endeavor. It leads to the cessation of suffering.[34]

Let Christians not say that Buddhism ascribes too great an importance to suffering. The place of suffering is, if anything, even more central in Christian spirituality, as evinced by history and by Christian doctrine. The passion of Christ represents the supreme apotheosis of suffering, a suffering hypostatized in the divinity itself. It was necessary for Christ to suffer and die.[35] God did not spare his own Son,[36] but, as we see, delivered him up to death for love of the world.[37] The Son of Man gives himself up to suffering, against the instincts of his own will, in order to fulfill that of the Father.[38]

The theologian may well consider that the essence of the cross is love, not suffering—but the fact remains that the course of the life of the Redeemer was such that suffering came to occupy an altogether central place in

Christianity.[39] Indeed, whereas Hinduism seeks to eliminate pain and Buddhism to destroy it, Christianity clasps it to its heart, and seeks to bestow meaning upon it, pronouncing it a sharing in the suffering of Christ[40] (the ideal of *apatheia* is not only Stoic, but Christian as well).[41]

Nowhere has the Buddha said that being, as understood by the *astika*s, is suffering, or that nonbeing is felicity. To label him a pessimist, then, appears rather gratuitous. For him, suffering is not inherent in reality. Hence it can be eliminated.

Suffering is inherent only in *ex*-sistence — in the desire to be, in thirst in any of its forms. What is to be eliminated is not reality — this would be a meaningless proposition anywhere in India (reality that could ever not-be would not be genuine reality) — but rather suffering, the whole negative element of ex-sistence. Reality, for the Buddha, does not ex-sist, does not "stand (out) there," cannot have "there is" predicated of it, inasmuch as having and being are categories of contingency and hence shot through with limitation. The road to salvation is not that of speculation, but that of the concrete *praxis* of the elimination of suffering — and thereby of all limitation, contingency, and creatureliness (to avail myself of non-Buddhist categories).

Śākyamuni would have understood these words:

> I tell you, brothers, the time is short. From now on those with wives should live as if they had none; those who weep should live as though they were not weeping, and those who rejoice as though they were not rejoicing; buyers should conduct themselves as though they owned nothing, and those who make use of the world as though they were not using it, for the world as we know it is passing away. I should like you to be free from worries.[42]

THE MESSAGE OF THE BUDDHA

> That things have to be, Kaccāna, constitutes one extreme; that things have not to be, the other. These two extremes, Kaccāna, have been evaded by the Tathagata, and this is the middle path that he teaches.[43]

To paraphrase: it is as risky and false to take the extreme position that God exists (understanding existence in the only way we can understand it, unless enlightenment were to afford an immediate insight into the other side of the question) as to assert that God does not exist. But a Buddhist mentality will at once add: to deny that God exists is an equally false extreme as to deny that God does not exist. The Buddha's claim is precisely to be able to assent to all these propositions without falling into agnosticism.

The notion that God is beyond our normal means of comprehension, that God can be known only inadequately, is common to many religions.

Christianity, in order to express this difficulty in the knowledge of God, has recourse to the alternate use of a pair of opposites, knowledge and ignorance, precisely so as to evidence the inadequacy of our cognitive faculties.[44] The Buddha, with his concern to avoid extremes, proceeds differently. The passage just cited asserts that in the last analysis it is of no consequence whether or not we know if being or nonbeing is at the root of things. The Enlightened One keeps to the simple observation of the relativity of the degree of truth contained in either of these contrary propositions. Shortly before, according to Ānanda's account, the Sublime One had told Kaccānagotta:

> This world is generally laid to the account of either being or nonbeing. Surely, for the one who considers wisely and according to truth the processes of generation and apparition in this world, there really is not nonbeing in this world; for the one who considers wisely and according to truth the processes of destruction and disappearance in this world, there really is not being in this world.[45]

The Buddha's message can be summed up in what tradition records as his last words: "Work [realize, perform, act out] your salvation with diligence."[46] That is, abandon speculation and concentrate on the one thing needful for salvation.[47] This is what is all-important, and I have shown you the path: the way of the elimination of everything that places any limits upon us, the criterion and manifestation of these limits being pain and suffering.[48]

The Buddha has no theories.[49] But, as Buddhism has observed from ancient times, the renunciation of metaphysics is itself a metaphysics. To reject all philosophical systems is only to replace the concept of philosophy as *knowledge* of reality with that of philosophy as the path to the *attainment* of that same reality.[50] But when the way of salvation shifts from religion to philosophy, gnosticism is born.

On the other hand, the explicit renunciation of attachment to any theory comports a greater pluralism with respect to theories than does the acknowledgment of a determinate doctrine. This is why so few cultures in the world offer a greater and more varied flowering of schools than does Buddhism. It will not be out of place, then, to attempt to retranslate the Buddha's basic intuition in terms of a certain metaphysics.[51]

Salvation must be attained "with diligence." Now, this salvation cannot be attained if one remains strapped to the finite, for salvation is infinite. Hence the importance of a radical self-stripping, including total self-denial with respect to any and all conceptual formulation. Salvation consists in the elimination of suffering, for it is in suffering that our limitation is expressed and crystalized. When Christian scholasticism sees in felicity, in *beatitudo,* the essence of the life to come—that is, the essence of the human being's final end, and hence the anthropological dimension of union with God — it is only saying the same thing.[52]

Attainment of this *beatitudo* may be the goal, but the human being can never fully achieve it, or even know just what it is, in this life. By contrast, suffering falls altogether within the sphere of our experience, and it is precisely the path to its elimination that the Buddha proclaims — through the discovery of its origin in the thirst that is constitutive of created being. In other words, one must discover that the origin of unhappiness is precisely in the *ex-sistence* of that being. Indeed, existence not only constitutes the tension of being *extra causas*, it represents the very nature of the being that is not of itself, that is not *a se*.[53] So long as beings labor under the illusion that they are being itself, or even being at all — indeed, as long as they so much as desire to be being itself, or being at all — they suffer, because they are not, or not yet, being itself. The elimination of suffering as the Buddha proposes it is not alleviation after the fashion of an analgesic drug, but the radical extirpation of suffering, through the destruction of its cause — through the destruction of ex-sistence itself, not only such as we live it, but such as we cannot help but live and think it as we make our journey through this world.[54]

The thirst for attaining being, for *being*, or for *not being* — behold the threefold origin of pain and suffering. Only by uprooting the very appetite that is constitutive of contingent being (and this is tantamount to the elimination of contingency — that is, of existence) can that being's inherent limitation, which is the cause of its suffering, be destroyed.[55] Suffering produced by any appetite (the *thirst to attain to being*) can be overcome only by a *love* for transcending every object of desire. As long as there are objects loved, the pain abides. The pain of not being God (the *thirst to be*) cannot be slaked by the attainment of any *hope* less than that of being God. As long as hope perdures, the goal has not been reached, and the pain abides. The pain of existence (the *thirst not to be*) is eliminated only by *faith* in the transcending of all being. As long as we are sustained by faith, we are not self-sustaining, and therefore still "are" — and the pain goes on. There is no solution, then, so long as there is such a thing as the contingent individual.

Here the "old self" will raise an anguished objection, with all the thrust of the overpowering, autochthonous Occidental mind: Is the only remedy that the core of my self-identity disappear? And the Buddha will reply that the sooner the eliminable is eliminated, the better.

It is the very fear of disappearing that causes suffering, and until one finds relief and surcease in what cannot be feared to disappear, one is not even on the road to salvation. But, the objection will be raised, then there will no longer be anyone to find relief and surcease. And the Buddha can only rejoice that there is no longer anyone in need of relief. Reality has no need of any relief, nor any need of anything or anyone at all upon which or upon whom to recline. Reality sustains itself of and in itself — although the very expression becomes meaningless the moment we realize that "self-sustaining" can be the attribute only of that which indeed has need of being sustained. If we seek to mount to *nirvāṇa* weighed down with this burden, we shall never arrive there. Here we have the cause of the temporal cycle of all ex-sistences: the fear of losing what can be lost. Pure "sistence" does not ex-sist, nor is it afraid of being lost; it is beyond any anxiety, beyond any fear. It has no fear, because it dwells where pain has lost its meaning, abides in stark breach with the world of time and space, matter and spirit, essence and existence, human beings and the gods.[56]

Unless one loses one's own life. . . .[57]

Never did the Buddha deny *existentially* what convention has come to call ultimate reality.[58] He only rejected any name for it, any determination, whether that of "ultimate" or that of "reality."[59] He refused to accept any personification of it. For him, as for the whole of the tradition of India, personification was tantamount to anthropomorphism. The Buddha resists any intent to penetrate God by the force of our volitive and intellective formulas.

If ultimate reality were the God of whom the theists speak, then the Buddha replies that this reality must be responsible for all that transpires here below, including evil. Thus it is with a view to defending all the rights of this ultimate reality that the Buddha refuses to accept theism. To put it another way: it is in order to defend the absolute transcendence of divinity that the Buddha, reasonably enough, denies divinity.

Transcendence itself is actually an anthropocentric notion, inasmuch as the human being is its point of reference — which, it must quickly be added, must be transcended, of course. Precisely because the absolute does not transcend, it *is not* a transcendent being. Or, if you will: so utterly is the absolute *transcendent,* that, transcending itself in itself, it leaves all being behind, not excluding being itself, Very Being. The Buddha would say: If you cannot do without a concept or image of God, so be it; but the highest religion is atheistic, as well as apolytheistic and a-antitheistic.

Part II

The Texts

Assaddho akataññū ca sandhicchedo ca yo
naro hatāvakāso vantāso sa ve uttamaporiso[1]

The origin of the idea that Buddhism is atheistic is at least fourfold.[2] First is the common belief that Buddhism denies the existence of the soul, the *ātman* — conscious being or substance *(nairātmyavāda)*. Secondly there is the widespread notion that in Buddhism the human being's end is nirvana understood as total extinction and complete annihilation. Third is the Buddhistic discovery of a universal concatenation of all things *(pratītyasamutpāda)* that seems to exclude a transcendent cause. Finally, there is the negative interpretation put on the Buddha's silence in response to the human mind's most basic questions, especially that concerning an otherworldly existence — the Buddha's celebrated *avyakrta*.

With a view to developing my own solution to the problem of the Buddha's supposed atheism, I can do no better than to examine some of the principal texts upon which these four ideas are based.

4

Nairātmyavāda

Early twentieth-century Buddhist studies are at pains to distinguish a so-called primitive, or precanonical, Buddhism from the great Buddhistic systems of Theravada and Mahayana.[1] Many authors[2] hold that the central teaching of this primitive Buddhism corresponds to the actual ideas of the Buddha, among which the radical denial of the existence of the atman, or of any form of substantial self, is salient. There is no soul, there is no self, there is no conscious substance. This theory, we hear, stands in stark opposition to the great tradition of Indian wisdom, the *ātma-vāda,* or the doctrine of the atman, of which we read in the Upanishads. According to other authors,[3] this doctrine is not that of the Buddha himself, but a later development, and an interpolation in the texts attributed to the Enlightened One. According to this latter interpretation, the doctrine of the Buddha himself was altogether within the Upanishadic tradition, and his occasional denials of the existence of the soul were dictated by pedagogical considerations: the Buddha was simply seeking to put an end to abusive interpretations of that existence.[4]

Without entering into any purely exegetical discussions, it can scarcely be denied that a series of basic texts, as well as later Buddhist tradition, incline toward the first interpretation. To be sure, the *anātma-vada* can be interpreted in a rather different manner.[5] For my purposes, however, this is all but indifferent. Both original Buddhism and its later development place the conception of the *anātman* in a central position. The living tradition of Buddhism is "anatmic."

A first difficulty, and a more serious one than might appear at first sight, consists simply in how to translate the word *ātman.* Besides its meaning as a pronoun—demonstrative, indefinite, and even reflexive[6]— *ātman* has been translated as "soul,"[7] "substance,"[8] "I,"[9] "oneself," "self-hood," "self,"[10] and so on. Curiously, one cannot call these translations false, although they all fail to reflect either the background or the attributes of the original. The question is an important one, but I shall not address it, and shall simply use the original Sanskrit without attempting a translation.

Discussion of the correct interpretation of the mind of the Buddha on this point,[11] like a discussion of the problem itself,[12] is as old as Buddhism[13] and as recent as any philosophical, theological, or religious encounter with contemporary Buddhism. Indeed it is impossible to engage in a serious discussion of Buddhism even today without first establishing one's point of departure as either in *ātman* or in *anātman*.[14]

One point, however, is beyond all question. The Buddha's declared position is equidistant from both extremes. He espouses neither *śāśvatavāda* (eternalism) nor *ucchedavāda* (nihilism).[15] There is no *ātman,* to be sure. But neither *is* there an *anātman*. The latter cannot be dealt with as though it were a thing, a sort of negative atman or antisubstance. Buddhistic thought calls for new categories. It requires a manner of thinking that will have divested itself of the habit of hypostatization.

Leaving exegetical discussions and nominalistic disputes aside, we may define the atman that the Buddha will not accept as that imperishable, immortal substance, the subject of all changes, to whose perfection all acts of those who believe in it must needs tend.[16] There is no subject. There is no *empirical* subject: it is surely evident that an empirical subject cannot be a substrate, but rather stands in need of a foundation itself. There is no *absolute* subject either: from the moment anything becomes a substrate for anything else at all, it is deprived of its "absoluteness" and transcendence.[17]

The Buddha's intuition is one of pure contingency. It is the discovery of the absence of an ultimate subject of operation. It is the primary experience of transiency, and consequently of the pain inherent in all beings. By "there is no atman" the Buddha means that there is nothing that could be the ultimate object or primary subject of human experience, nothing to be posited as the ultimate, definitive fundament of everything else. Conversely we may say that the Buddha's conception is tantamount to the recognition that there are no privileged beings in this world. There are not substances here and accidents there. No, whatever comes within our experience is equally transitory, passing, and unstable — not only colors and feelings, but the subject experiencing them as well.

Let me attempt a brief synthesis of the basic proposition of the *anātma-vāda*. Of course, it will be methodologically inadmissible to criticize it from a point of departure in a doctrine that presupposes its contradiction. If we presuppose that substance, the ontological subject, is an indispensable condition for intelligibility, the effort to eliminate it will appear absurd. One may not, then, lodge the following objection against the anatmic view of things: if there is "nothing" to change, there can be no change. The Buddhist — besides raising exactly the same objection[18] — will reply that, precisely, there *is* no change, but only things that change.

It is not that there is no subject of intelligibility in the Buddhist position. Rather, there are as many as, at any given moment, sustain the constant flow of all things. That is, the subject of a given act of intelligibility is not some substrate that undergoes transformations adventitious to its outer shell. Rather this subject is itself in constant transmigration. Or, better, there is no "itself" to change skins: the "selves" are precisely dynamic points. That is, the totality of things is nothing but the manifestation of the cosmic symphony of the whole of existent reality, and no substrate is needed to underlie it. All is music, but no one is playing. This will become clearer as we examine other basic Buddhist concepts, all of which are intimately intermeshed:

Greet the Buddha, the Perfect One, best of all teachers. He has proclaimed the principle of (universal) Relativity [that all things coexist in mutual relatedness]; nirvana, the happy cessation of every plurality: the principle that nothing disappears and nothing appears, that nothing ends and nothing remains, that nothing is the same and nothing is different, that nothing moves, neither here nor there.[19]

The following texts give an appreciation of the Buddhist intuition.

NO PERMANENT SUBJECT

'Body, brethren, is not the Self. If body, brethren, were the Self, then body would not be involved in sickness, and one could say of body: "thus let my body be. Thus let my body not be." But, brethren, inasmuch as body is not the Self, that is why body is involved in sickness, and one cannot say of body: "thus let my body be; thus let my body not be."

Feeling is not the Self. If feeling, brethren, were the Self, then feeling would not be involved in sickness, and one could say of feeling "thus let my feeling be; thus let my feeling not be."

Likewise perception, the activities and consciousness are not the Self. If consciousness, brethren, were the Self, then consciousness would not be involved in sickness, and one could say of consciousness: "thus let my consciousness be; thus let my consciousness not be;" but inasmuch as consciousness is not the Self, that is why consciousness is involved in sickness: that is why one cannot say of consciousness: "thus let my consciousness be; thus let my consciousness not be."

Now what think ye, brethren. Is body permanent or impermanent?'

'Impermanent, lord.'

'And what is impermanent, is that weal or woe?'

'Woe, lord.'

'Then what is impermanent, woeful, unstable by nature, is it fitting to regard it thus: "this is mine; I am this; this is the self of me?" '

'Surely not, lord.'

'So also is it with feeling, perception, the activities and consciousness. Therefore, brethren, every body whatever, be it past, future or present, be it inward or outward, gross or subtle, low or high, far or near—every body should be thus regarded, as it really is, by right insight—"this is not mine; this am not I; this is not the Self of me."

Every feeling whatever, every perception whatever, all activities whatsoever (must be so regarded).

Every consciousness whatever, be it past, future or present, be it inward or outward, gross or subtle, low or high, far or near,—every consciousness, I say, must be thus regarded, as it really is, by right insight: "this is not mine; this am not I; this is not the Self of me."

So seeing, brethren, the well-taught Ariyan disciple feels disgust for body, feels disgust for feeling, for perception, for the activities, feels disgust for consciousness. So feeling disgust he is repelled; being repelled, he is freed; knowledge arises that in the freed is the freed thing; so that he knows: "destroyed is rebirth; lived is the righteous life; done is my task; for life in these conditions there is no hereafter." '

Thus spake the Exalted One, and the band of five brethren were pleased thereat, and welcomed what was said by the Exalted One. Moreover, by this teaching thus uttered the hearts of those five brethren were freed from the āsavas without grasping.[20]

THE ATMAN: NOT IDENTIFIABLE

"Or, in regard to the Ego, Ānanda, one holds the view, 'Verily, neither is sensation my Ego, nor does my Ego have no sensation. My Ego has sensation; my Ego possesses the faculty of sensation.'

"In the above case, Ānanda, where it is said, 'Sensation is my Ego,' reply should be made as follows: 'Brother, there are three sensations: the pleasant sensation, the unpleasant sensation, and the indifferent sensation. Which of these three sensations do you hold to be the Ego?'

"Whenever, Ānanda, a person experiences a pleasant sensation, he does not at the same time experience an unpleasant sensation, nor does he experience an indifferent sensation; only the pleasant sensation does he then feel. Whenever, Ānanda, a person experiences an unpleasant sensation, he does not at the same time experience a pleasant sensation, nor does he experience an indifferent sensation; only the unpleasant sensation does he then feel. Whenever, Ānanda, a person experiences an indifferent sensation, he does not at the same time experience a pleasant sensation, nor does he experience an unpleasant sensation; only the indifferent sensation does he then feel.

"Now pleasant sensations, Ānanda, are transitory, are due to causes, originate by dependence, and are subject to decay, disappearance, effacement, and cessation; and unpleasant sensations, Ānanda, are transitory, are due to causes, originate by dependence, and are subject to decay, disappearance, effacement, and cessation; and indifferent sensations, Ānanda, are transitory, are due to causes, originate by dependence, and are subject to decay, disappearance, effacement, and cessation. While this person is experiencing a pleasant sensation, he thinks, 'This is my Ego.' And after the cessation of this same pleasant sensation, he thinks, 'My Ego has passed away.' And while he is experiencing an indifferent sensation, he thinks, 'This is my Ego.' And after the cessation of this same indifferent sensation, he thinks, 'My Ego has passed away.' So that he who says, 'Sensation is my Ego,' holds the view that even during his lifetime his Ego is transitory, that it is pleasant, unpleasant, or mixed, and that it is subject to rise and disappearance.

"Accordingly, Ānanda, it is not possible to hold the view, 'Sensation is my Ego.'

"In the above case, Ānanda, where it is said, 'Verily sensation is not my Ego; my Ego has no sensation,' reply should be made as follows: 'But, brother, where there is no sensation, is there any "I am"?' "

"Nay, verily, Reverend Sir."

"Accordingly, Ānanda, it is not possible to hold the view, 'Verily, sensation is not my Ego; my Ego has no sensation.'

"In the above case, Ānanda, where it is said, 'Verily, neither is sensation my Ego, nor does my Ego have no sensation. My Ego has sensation; my Ego possesses the faculty of sensation,' reply should be made as follows: 'Suppose, brother, that utterly and completely, and without remainder, all sensation were to cease — if there were nowhere any sensation, pray, would there be anything, after the cessation of sensation, of which it could be said, "This am I"?' "

"Nay, verily, Reverend Sir."

"Accordingly, Ānanda, it is not possible to hold the view, 'Verily, neither is sensation my Ego, nor does my Ego have no sensation. My Ego has sensation; my Ego possesses the faculty of sensation.'

"From the time, Ānanda, a priest no longer holds the view that sensation is the Ego, no longer holds the view that the Ego has no sensation, no longer holds the view that the Ego has sensation, possesses the faculty of sensation, he ceases to attach himself to anything in the world, and being free from attachment, he is never agitated, and being never agitated, he attains to Nirvana in his own person; and he knows that rebirth is exhausted, that he has lived the holy life, that he has done what it behooved him to do, and that he is no more for this world.

"Now it is impossible, Ānanda, that to a mind so freed a priest should attribute the heresy that the saint exists after death, or that the saint does not exist after death, or that the saint both exists and does not exist after death, or that the saint neither exists nor does not exist after death.

"And why do I say so?

"Because, Ānanda, after a priest has been freed by a thorough comprehension of affirmation and affirmation's range, of predication and predication's range, of declaration and declaration's range, of knowledge and knowledge's field of action, of rebirth and what rebirth affects, it is impossible for him to attribute such a heretical lack of knowledge and perception to a priest similarly freed."[21]

ATMAN: A MERE NAME

Then drew near Milinda the king[22] to where the venerable Nāgasena was; and having drawn near, he greeted the venerable Nāgasena; and having passed the compliments of friendship and civility, he sat down respectfully at one side. And the venerable Nāgasena returned the greeting; by which, verily, he won the heart of king Milinda.

And Milinda the king spoke to the venerable Nāgasena as follows:

"How is your reverence called? Bhante, what is your name?"

"Your majesty, I am called Nāgasena; my fellow-priests, your majesty, address me as Nāgasena: but whether parents give one the name Nāgasena, or Sūrasena, or Vīrasena, or Sīhasena, it is, nevertheless, your majesty, but a way of counting, a term, an appellation, a convenient designation, a mere name, this Nāgasena; for there is no Ego here to be found."[23]

Then said Milinda the king,

"Listen to me, my lords, ye five hundred Yonakas, and ye eighty thousand priests! Nāgasena here says thus: 'There is no Ego here to be found.' Is it possible, pray, for me to assent to what he says?"

And Milinda the king spoke to the venerable Nāgasena as follows:

"Bhante Nāgasena, if there is no Ego to be found, who is it then furnishes you priests with the priestly requisites—robes, food, bedding, and medicine, the reliance of the sick? who is it makes use of the same? who is it keeps the precepts? who is it applies himself to meditation? who is it realizes the Paths, the Fruits, and Nirvana? who is it destroys life? who is it takes what is not given him? who is it commits immorality? who is it tells lies? who is it drinks intoxicating liquor? who is it commits the five crimes that constitute 'proximate karma'? In that case, there is no merit; there is no demerit; there is no one who does or causes to be done meritorious or demeritorious deeds; neither good nor evil deeds can have any fruit or result. Bhante Nāgasena, neither is he a murderer who kills a priest, nor can you priests, bhante Nāgasena, have any teacher, preceptor, or ordination. When you say, 'My fellow-priests, your majesty, address me as Nāgasena,' what then is this Nāgasena? Pray, bhante, is the hair of the head Nāgasena?"

"Nay, verily, your majesty."

"Is the hair of the body Nāgasena?"

"Nay, verily, your majesty."

"Are nails . . . teeth . . . skin . . . flesh . . . sinews . . . bones . . . marrow of the bones . . . kidneys . . . heart . . . liver . . . pleura . . . spleen . . . lungs . . . intestines . . . mesentery . . . stomach . . . faeces . . . bile . . . phlegm . . . pus . . . blood . . . sweat . . . fat . . . tears . . . lymph . . . saliva . . . snot . . . synovial fluid . . . urine . . . brain of the head Nāgasena?"

"Nay, verily, your majesty."

"Is now, bhante, form Nāgasena?"

"Nay, verily, your majesty."

"Is sensation Nāgasena?"

"Nay, verily, your majesty."

"Is perception Nāgasena?"

"Nay, verily, your majesty."

"Are the predispositions Nāgasena?"

"Nay, verily, your majesty."

"Is consciousness Nāgasena?"

"Nay, verily, your majesty."

"Are, then, bhante, form, sensation, perception, the predispositions, and consciousness unitedly Nāgasena?"

"Nay, verily, your majesty."

"Is it, then, bhante, something besides form, sensation, perception, the predispositions, and consciousness, which is Nāgasena?"

"Nay, verily, your majesty."

"Bhante, although I question you very closely, I fail to discover any Nāgasena. Verily, now, bhante, Nāgasena is a mere empty sound. What Nāgasena is there here? Bhante, you speak a falsehood, a lie: there is no Nāgasena."

Then the venerable Nāgasena spoke to Milinda the king as follows:

"Your majesty, you are a delicate prince, an exceedingly delicate prince; and if, your majesty, you walk in the middle of the day on hot sandy ground, and you tread on rough grit, gravel, and sand, your feet become sore, your body tired, the mind is oppressed, and the body-consciousness suffers. Pray, did you come afoot, or riding?"

"Bhante, I do not go afoot: I came in a chariot."

"Your majesty, if you came in a chariot, declare to me the chariot. Pray, your majesty, is the pole the chariot?"

"Nay, verily, bhante."

"Is the axle the chariot?"

"Nay, verily, bhante."

"Are the wheels the chariot?"

"Nay, verily, bhante."

"Is the chariot-body the chariot?"

"Nay, verily, bhante."

"Is the banner-staff the chariot?"

"Nay, verily, bhante."

"Is the yoke the chariot?"

"Nay, verily, bhante."

"Are the reins the chariot?"

"Nay, verily, bhante."

"Is the goading-stick the chariot?"

"Nay, verily, bhante."

"Pray, your majesty, are pole, axle, wheels, chariot-body, banner-staff, yoke, reins, and goad unitedly the chariot?"

"Nay, verily, bhante."

"Is it, then, your majesty, something else besides pole, axle, wheels, chariot-body, banner-staff, yoke, reins, and goad which is the chariot?"

"Nay, verily, bhante."

"Your majesty, although I question you very closely, I fail to discover any chariot. Verily now, your majesty, the word chariot is a mere empty sound. What chariot is there here? Your majesty, you speak a falsehood, a lie: there is no chariot. Your majesty, you are the chief king in all the continent of India; of whom are you afraid that you speak a lie? Listen to me, my lords, ye five hundred Yonakas, and ye eighty thousand priests! Milinda the king here says thus: 'I came in a chariot;' and being requested, 'Your majesty, if you came in a chariot, declare to me the chariot,' he fails to produce any chariot. Is it possible, pray, for me to assent to what he says?"

When he had thus spoken, the five hundred Yonakas applauded the venerable Nāgasena and spoke to Milinda the king as follows:

"Now, your majesty, answer, if you can."

Then Milinda the king spoke to the venerable Nāgasena as follows:

"Bhante Nāgasena, I speak no lie: the word 'chariot' is but a way of counting, term, appellation, convenient designation, and name for pole, axle, wheels, chariot-body, and banner-staff."

"Thoroughly well, your majesty, do you understand a chariot. In exactly the same way, your majesty, in respect of me, Nāgasena is but a way of counting, term, appellation, convenient designation, mere name for the hair of my head, hair of my body . . . brain of the head, form, sensation, perception, the predispositions, and consciousness. But in the absolute sense there is no Ego here to be found."[24]

THE REASON FOR THE CONTINUITY OF CHANGE: NO ATMAN

The king said: "He who is born, Nāgasena, does he remain the same or become another?"

"Neither the same nor another."

"Give me an illustration."

"Now what do you think, O king? You were once a baby, a tender thing, and small in size, lying flat on your back. Was that the same as you who are now grown up?"

"No. That child was one, I am another."

"If you are not the child, it will follow that you have had neither mother nor father, no! nor teacher. You cannot have been taught either learning, or behaviour, or wisdom. What, great king! is the mother of the embryo in the first stage different from the mother of the embryo in the second stage, or the third, or the fourth? Is the mother of the baby a different person from the mother of the grown-up man? Is the person who goes to school one, and the same when he has finished his schooling another? Is it one who commits a crime, another who is punished by having his hands or feet cut off?"

"Certainly not. But what would you, Sir, say to that?"

The Elder replied: "I should say that I am the same person, now I am grown up, as I was when I was a tender tiny baby, flat on my back. For all these states are included in one by means of this body."

"Give me an illustration."

"Suppose a man, O king, were to light a lamp, would it burn the night through?"

"Yes, it might do so."

"Now, is it the same flame that burns in the first watch of the night, Sir, and in the second?"

"No."

"Or the same that burns in the second watch and in the third?"

"No."

"Then is there one lamp in the first watch, and another in the second, and another in the third?"

"No. The light comes from the same lamp all the night through."

"Just so, O king, is the continuity of a person or thing maintained. One comes into being, another passes away; and the rebirth is, as it were, simultaneous. Thus neither as the same nor as another does a man go on to the last phase of his self-consciousness."

"Give me a further illustration."

"It is like milk, which when once taken from the cow, turns, after a lapse of time, first to curds, and then from curds to butter, and then from butter to ghee. Now would it be right to say that the milk was the same thing as the curds, or the butter, or the ghee?"

"Certainly not; but they are produced out of it."

"Just so, O king, is the continuity of a person or thing maintained. One comes into being, another passes away; and the rebirth is, as it were, simultaneous. Thus neither as the same nor as another does a man go on to the last phase of his self-consciousness."

"Well put, Nāgasena!"[25]

NO SUBJECT OF TRANSMIGRATION

The king said: "Where there is no transmigration, Nāgasena, can there be rebirth?"

"Yes, there can."

"But how can that be? Give me an illustration."

"Suppose a man, O king, were to light a lamp from another lamp, can it be said that the one transmigrates from, or to, the other?"

"Certainly not."

"Just so, great king, is rebirth without transmigration."

"Give me a further illustration."

"Do you recollect, great king, having learnt, when you were a boy, some verse or other from your teacher?"

"Yes, I recollect that."

"Well then, did that verse transmigrate from your teacher?"

"Certainly not."

"Just so, great king, is rebirth without transmigration."

"Very good, Nāgasena!"[26]

ALL IS TRANSITORY

There is change, movement, growth, death, and so on. This is a central point in so many texts. What does not exist, the same texts say, is an unchanging subject of change. In the first place, there is no experience of such a subject. Such an experience would be impossible. It would contradict our fluid, mutable experience of the things around us. Besides, this subject would be "beyond existence" — for if it did exist, we could not experience it. Secondly, its existence as an immovable subject cannot be logically defended. If we say that this subject is unchangeable, change will not affect it and so it becomes superfluous as a hypothesis for explaining change. And of course if the subject is regarded as changeable, in order to be able to be the substrate of change, then it will no longer be our immutable subject of motion.

This is the gist of many of the texts that I could cite. I do not, however, wish to overload my study with long extracts.[27]

5

Nirvana

The purpose of Buddhism is the attainment of nirvana.[1] Without nirvana there would be no Buddhism. But nirvana is beyond definition and description alike. Hence even in the schools of Buddhism the stance with regard to nirvana runs the whole gamut of possibilities.[2] Small wonder, then, that Western interpretations are discordant.[3]

As is well known, the word "nirvana" is absent from the Vedic and Brahmanic literature until the appearance of the Bhagavadgītā[4] and the Mahābhārata.[5] It is not that the Buddha is inventing the word, however. He is only conferring a new meaning on it.[6] Further, there are discussions in the Pali canon on non-Buddhist notions of nirvana.[7] The origin of these notions is not yet sufficiently clear for a theoretical explanation.[8] The word "nirvana" is often used in the ancient texts to refer to the death of Gautama.

The very etymology of the word is suggestive.[9] The Sanskrit verb *nirvā* means "to be extinguished," or "to be consumed"—never in a transitive mode, but as a fire "goes out" or a flame is exhausted for lack of fuel.[10] The root is reminiscent of the wind (as with the Latin *spiritus* or the Greek *pneuma*.).[11] Yet wind not only extinguishes fire, but tempers heat, so that, etymologically, nirvana means also "refreshing"[12] or "pleasant."[13]

Some scholars of the Pali language, however, reject the derivation of the Pali word *Nibbāna* from the Sanskrit *nirvāṇa*. For them *nibbāna* signifies extinction not in the sense of annihiliation, but as a being-covered-over, from a root meaning "to cover," "to wrap," indeed "to suffocate."[14] Only the five aggregates (*khanda*)[15] that compose the being of the individual achieving nirvana would be extinguished.[16]

But we must at once add a qualification, lest etymological speculation carry us too far afield. Etymology can furnish only a metaphorical approximation of the sense of the word "nirvana." Despite the impression we might gather from the various etymological studies of the word, the meaning of nirvana is not derived from any concept of extinction at all. Nirvana is not the effect of a lack of fuel, nor indeed is it the cause or effect of anything else, either. To conceptualize nirvana either as cause or as effect would be to destroy its actual denotation. Nirvana is neither condition nor conditioned. Its transcendence is pure, to the point where even transcendence becomes a misnomer. It would be altogether false to the Buddhist intent and intuition to regard nirvana as the goal and end of life.[17] Nirvana cannot be the human being's end psychologically, because this would destroy the purity of both the intention to reach it and of nirvana itself. Nor can nirvana be the human being's end ontologically. First of all, nothing that is really "beyond being"—to use a figure of speech—can be the object of an appetite of any sort. Secondly, there is no ontological bridge to the other shore. Nirvana is bottomless. There is no foundation on which such a bridge might rest.

At all events, we can be sure that nirvana means the extinction of existence considered as negative and contingent. It will be the "going out" of temporality, death, and all that is mortal—of all that can (still) be born. After all, where does all human experience, sensory or intellectual, end? In pain. But pain is the earmark and stigma of existence. Then the human being's end must be the pure negation of negativity itself—the *a-no-nada-miento,* the "to-nothing-ment" of Spanish mysticism, the destruction of that nothing, that *nonada,* that one "is." Obviously everything depends on the meaning one attributes to the verb "to be." For the Buddha, what one *is* "is" certainly not what one believes, thinks, or feels oneself to be, or ever could believe, think, or feel oneself to be. Nirvana is the cessation of all *saṃskāras.*[18] It is the dissolution of all bonds.[19] It is the extinction of thirst.[20] It is the annihiliation of the three cardinal vices.[21] Nirvana belongs to the "other shore,"[22] or *pāra,* the opposite bank from even what the Upanishadic tradition has sought to mean and communicate.[23] In a word, nirvana can be summed up as holiness (*arhatva*):

> Whatever, your reverence, is the extinction of passion, of aversion, of confusion, that is called nirvana.[24]

Perhaps the least inaccurate statement we could make about nirvana is that it is akṛta (*akata*)[25]—not made, not built, different from the elaborated (the *saṃskṛta*), the constructed, even the created.[26] If what is, is existence, then nirvana is nonexistence. If, on the one hand, there are the made, the confected, the manufactured, the created, the conditioned, then nirvana is the not-made, the not-confected, the uncreated, the unconditioned. We human beings, then, need not be concerned with this. We shall not salvage nirvana by defining it. Nor indeed could we ever hope to manipulate it in any way, however reverently and respectfully. For the Buddha, true faith is in the transcendent, in the unconditional, in that which in no way "is." Either we admit of a bridge between the absolute and the relative—after a manner of speaking—and then the very bridge contaminates absolute transcendence, for the absolute and the relative would now have something in common, some *quid analogatum*—or else the abyss is real and unbridgeable, and then there is no way to reach it but through the destruction of all ways, all paths.

There is no argument against the Buddha. No element of the "created" order, by definition, can touch him. He is the Enlightened One, the Present One. He knows the not-made, the uncreated.[27] And he does not communicate the incommunicable. Those who have ears to hear, let them hear.[28] He is silent.

The basic presupposition of this conception is that all things are made.[29] Accordingly, in order for them to return to their own origin, in order for them to achieve their own real end, there is no other way than for them to be un-made—destroyed.[30] The acquiescence of all *samskaras*—this is felicity.[31] This is nirvana, the return to the original Source, whence being itself has come, for from that Source it has been made (*samskrta*).[32] Only nirvana is *asamskrta*.[33]

According to the Upanishadic view, on the other hand, creation is conceived as a divine sacrifice, consisting in the dismemberment of the body of Prajapati. Here things are not so much a conglomerate of the "made" and "manufactured," but rather "residue" (*ucchista*), potency, possibility, even "imperfection," "fall," "sin," and the like.[34] For these to reach their proper end, their fullness, for them to arrive at the original Source and recover their own primitive integrity, they too must in a certain sense be un-made after having been "made," they must have their multiplicity eliminated in a reunification in the primordial, single all, Prajapati.[35] The notions are different, as are the words used to express them, but from a viewpoint of orthopraxy, of the work of salvation, the process is basically homogeneous. Surely the multiple must be undone in order to reach the original Source (as a Christian interpretation would have it), in order to reconstruct the primordial unity (in Brahmanic terms), or simply in order to be undone, *asamskrta* (according to the Buddhist intuition here reported). Indeed the efforts of any asceticism are bent on renunciation, on "undoing" the present state in order to rediscover the original state, whatever that is or has been.[36]

To return to Buddhism, the destruction of creatureliness will mean nothing but the annihilation of all limitation and the recovery of the primal origin. The image is no longer image when the prototype is attained. And the prototype "is" not, adds the Tathagata.

Here we encounter a basic ontological problem. In all religions, human-kind seeks a point of contact with a certain transcendent. But it immediately experiences the abyss that separates it from such a transcendent. In Brahmanism, as in so many other religions, the ontological abyss is bridged through (cosmic) sacrifice. In Christianity it is filled with the figure of Christ as ontological mediator. In both cases there is a bridge to carry creation across, for creation to "transcend," and reach divinity. Sacrifice, whether that of Prajapati or of the Son of Man, becomes the point of encounter between the relative and the absolute, between the contingent and the transcendent.[37]

At bottom Christianity does not say anything so very different from Brahmanism—only that, whereas the latter absolutizes the dynamic, cosmic sacrificial action, without referring it to a particular figure, Christianity personifies it, through the Son of Man. Incarnation takes the place of sacrifice—without being able to prescind from it, however,[38] and the Son must submit to it. Thus in Christianity it is the incarnation that becomes the bridge by which traditional Christian language can say that God became human so that humankind might become God.[39] Brahmanism speaks of participation in sacrifice as the means of the human being's divinization.[40] But the Buddha is so conscious of the transcendence of the transcendent— if I may be allowed to express myself in this way—that he will not admit the possibility of any bridges. For him the cosmos has a destiny utterly beyond it. *Saṃsāra* must altogether disappear in nirvana. Then how is the chasm filled, how is the distance covered? According to Buddhism, if distance, leap, passage, or anything of the kind be admitted, transcendence is canceled, and salvation becomes impossible. It is as if the force of attraction exerted on creatureliness were so powerful that the moment the latter touched the farther shore it is absorbed by the "beyond." Nirvana is therefore incommensurable, heterogeneous, and ineffable in every way, even ontologically.

There may be a third possibility, however. And indeed not only the Buddhist via media, but part of the advaita Vedanta, as well as more than one Western, Christian conception, could be adduced as examples of the attempt to overcome and sublimate the inescapable dichotomy between transcendent and immanent, God and the world, the absolute and the relative. This third way will attempt to convey that nirvana and *saṃsāra*, to use a classic terminology, are neither one thing nor two, nor equal, nor distinct. The difference is in something "accidental," something not "essential" (which a philosophical reflection will then attempt to clarify) that must be "broken," "disclosed," "created," or however one wishes to designate this act by which the human being "leaps to" or "reaches being," "arrives," "discovers" the "end," "the truth," "salvation," one's own "destiny," "God," and so forth. A Buddhist will never admit that the distinction in question is between two "aspects" of one "thing." For a Buddhist, this would be to fall into the trap of a monistic interpretation. A Buddhist seeks neither an absolutization of the relative (pantheism) nor a relativization of the absolute (nihilism, atheism). Precisely because nirvana and *saṃsāra* are incommensurable, they are not two "things," nor therefore "two" things.[41] The passage from one to another—if there is such a passage—is precisely a passage: praxis, then, and not theory. But let us not encroach on considerations reserved for the third part of this investigation.

It is not my task to subject to a critical review the various positions that are taken with respect to the concept of nirvana.[42] I shall, however, permit myself one observation along these lines — one that, it seems to me, may provide a kind of anthropological key to an understanding of at least the reason for such diversity of opinion. To those for whom thinking is not only criterion or judgment but also assertion of reality — that is, those for whom thinking tells us what being is, those for whom thinking "thinks being" — to posit a "something" that is in no way "thinkable" represents a contradiction, which it is possible to avoid only by asserting that this "something" — here, nirvana — is a chimera. By contrast, those who admit the possibility of a transcendence of thinking (not only in its concrete exercise, of course, but in its very formality) — that is, that there could be something that would not necessarily be "thinkable" at all — these will be inclined to interpret nirvana precisely as maximum positivity.[43]

In other words, a mystical temperament will have no difficulty in admitting the thesis of the positivity of nirvana, whereas a nonmystical one will be able to accept only the nihilistic thesis.[44]

Now let us consider some basic texts.

NIRVANA: WHAT UNIQUELY IS

Only suffering (*duhkha*) exists, not the person who suffers; there is no one who acts, only the acts exist. Nirvana exists, but not the person who seeks after it; the way (*magga*) exists, but not the follower of the way.[45]

NIRVANA: THE EXTINCTION OF THE PHENOMENAL

The king said: "Is there such a person as the Buddha, Nāgasena?"
"Yes."
"Can he then, Nāgasena, be pointed out as being here or there?"
"The Blessed One, O king, has passed away by that kind of passing away (*nirvāṇa*) in which nothing remains which could tend to the formation of another individual.[46] It is not possible to point out the Blessed One as being here or there."
"Give me an illustration."
"Now what do you think, O king? When there is a great body of fire blazing, is it possible to point out any one flame that has gone out, that it is here or there?"
"No, Sir. That flame has ceased, it has vanished."
"Just so, great king, has the Blessed One passed away by that kind of passing away in which no root remains for the formation of another individual. The Blessed One has come to an end, and it cannot

be pointed out of him, that he is here or there. But in the body of his doctrine he can, O king, be pointed out. For the doctrine (*dharma*) was preached by the Blessed One?"[47]

NIRVANA: THE BEGINNING

This verily was said by the Blessed One, said by the Sanctified One, so I have heard.

"There is, O monks, something not born, non-existent, not made, not compounded. If there were not this something not born, non-existent, not made, not compounded, there would not be known here deliverance from what is born, existent, made, and compounded. Since, indeed, O monks, there is something not born, non-existent, not made, and not compounded, therefore there is known deliverance from what is born, existent, made, and compounded."

To this effect spake the Blessed One, and hereupon said the following:

> It is not possible to delight in That which is born,
> Which has existence, is produced, is made, is compounded, unstable,
> Subject to Old Age and Death,
> A nest of diseases, fragile,
> And owing its operative cause
> To the current of subsistence.
> The destruction of This is a state that is tranquil,
> That hath passed beyond conjecture,
> That is not born and not produced,
> That is griefless and passionless—
> The annihilation of the conditions of Misery,
> A happy cessation of Doubt.

Exactly to that effect was it spoken by the Blessed One, so I have heard.[48]

NIRVANA: THE END

There exists, O monks, such a state in which there is neither earth nor sea nor air; where there exists neither infinite space nor infinite consciousness and not even emptiness, neither sensation nor non-sensation; where there is neither this world nor another nor both together, neither sun nor moon. O monks, there is neither going or coming or standing still; neither is there duration or decline or growth; nothing is fixed and still, nothing moves nor has foundation. This is the end of suffering (*dukkha*).[49]

THERE ARE TWO NIRVANAS

This verily was said by the Blessed One, said by the Sanctified One, so I have heard.

"What, O monks, is the Nirvāna Element which doth not have the Substrata remaining? A monk becometh sanctified here (in this world), if, while living, he hath done that which ought to be done, if he hath laid aside his burdens, if he hath attained good welfare, if he hath destroyed the Fetters of Existence, if he is emancipated by Perfect Knowledge. All his feelings, O monks, if not rejoiced in here (in this world) will become cold—This, O monks, is called the Nirvāna Element of not having the Substrata remaining. These, O monks, are the two Nirvāna Elements.

"There are, O monks, these two Elements of Nirvāna." "What two?" "The Nirvāna element of having the Substrata (*upādi-*) still remaining, and the Nirvāna element of having the Substrata no longer remaining.

"What, O monks, is the Nirvāna Element which hath not the Substrata remaining? A monk becometh sanctified here (in this world), if he, while living, hath destroyed his Taints—if he hath done that which ought to be done, if he hath laid aside his burdens, if he hath attained good welfare, if he hath destroyed the Fetters of Existence, if he is emancipated by Perfect Knowledge. He hath five moral qualities, *viz.,* his mind is unimpeded, he experienceth what is pleasant and unpleasant, and he cometh to know happiness and misery. His destruction of Passion, of Anger, of Ignorance, is called the Nirvāna Element of having the Substrata remaining."[50]

NIRVANA: BEYOND ANY DIALECTIC[51]

Verse 1 (The opponent contends)
If all is void (*śūnya*) and there is neither production nor destruction, then from whose abandonment (of defilements) or from whose extinction (of suffering) can *nirvāna* be attributed?

Verse 2 (Nāgārjuna asserts)
If all is *aśūnya* and there is neither production nor destruction,[52] then from whose abandonment (of defilements) or from whose extinction (of suffering) can *nirvāna* be attributed?

Verse 3
What is never cast off, seized, interrupted, constant, extinguished, and produced . . . this is called *nirvāna*.[53]

Verse 4
Indeed, *nirvāṇa* is not strictly in the nature of ordinary existence for, if it were, there would wrongly follow the characteristics of old age-death. For, such an existence cannot be without those characteristics.[54]

Verse 5
If *nirvāṇa* is strictly in the nature of ordinary existence, it will be of the created realm. For, no ordinary existence of the uncreated realm ever exists anywhere at all.

Verse 6
If *nirvāṇa* is strictly in the nature of ordinary existence, why is it non-appropriating? For, no ordinary existence that is non-appropriating ever exists.

Verse 7
If *nirvāṇa* is not strictly in the nature of ordinary existence, how could what is in the nature of non-existence be *nirvāṇa*? Where there is no existence, equally so, there can be no non-existence.

Verse 8
If *nirvāṇa* is in the nature of non-existence, why is it non-appropriating? For, indeed, a non-appropriating non-existence does not prevail.

Verse 9 . . . .

Verse 10
The teacher (Buddha) has taught the abandonment of the concepts of being and non-being. Therefore, *nirvāṇa* is properly neither (in the realm of) existence nor non-existence.

Verse 11
If *nirvāṇa* is (in the realm of) both existence and non-existence, then *mokṣa* (liberation) will also be both. But that is not proper.

Verse 12
If *nirvāṇa* is (in the realm of) both existence and non-existence, it will not be non-appropriating. For, both realms are (always in the process of) appropriating.

Verse 13
How could *nirvāṇa* be (in the realm of) both existence and non-

existence? *Nirvāṇa* is of the uncreated realm while existence and non-existence are of the created realm.

Verse 14 . . . .

Verse 15
The proposition that *nirvāṇa* is neither existence nor non-existence could only be valid if and when the realms of existence and non-existence are established.

Verse 16
If indeed *nirvāṇa* is asserted to be neither existence nor non-existence, then by what means are assertions to be known?

Verse 17
It cannot be said that the Blessed One exists after *nirodha* (i.e., release from worldly desires). Nor can it be said that He does not exist after *nirodha,* or both, or neither.

Verse 18 . . . .

Verse 19
Saṃsāra (i.e., the empirical life-death cycle) is nothing essentially different from *nirvāṇa. Nirvāṇa* is nothing essentially different from *saṃsāra.*[55]

Verse 20
The limits (i.e., realm) of *nirvāṇa* are the limits of *saṃsāra.* Between the two, also, there is not the slightest difference whatsoever. . . .

Verse 24
All acquisitions (i.e., grasping) as well as play of concepts (i.e., symbolic representation) are basically in the nature of cessation and quiescence. Any factor of experience with regards to anyone at any place was never taught by the Buddha.[56]

FOUR KINDS OF NIRVANA[57]

Then said Mahamati to the Blessed One: Pray tell us about Nirvana?

The Blessed One replied: The term, Nirvana, is used with many different meanings, by different people, but these people may be divided into four groups: There are people who are suffering, or who are afraid of suffering, and who think of Nirvana; there are the philosophers who try to discriminate Nirvana; there are the class of disciples who think of Nirvana in relation to themselves; and, finally there is the Nirvana of the Buddhas.

Those who are suffering or who fear suffering, think of Nirvana as an escape and a recompense. They imagine that Nirvana consists in the future annihilation of the senses and the sense-minds; they are not aware that Universal Mind and Nirvana are One, and that this life-and-death world and Nirvana are not to be separated. These ignorant ones, instead of meditating on the imagelessness of Nirvana, talk of different ways of emancipation. Being ignorant of, or not understanding, the teachings of the Tathagatas, they cling to the notion of Nirvana that is outside what is seen of the mind and, thus, go on rolling themselves along with the wheel of life and death.

As to the Nirvanas discriminated by the philosophers: there really are none.[58] Some philosophers conceive Nirvana to be found where the mind-system no more operates owing to the cessation of the elements that make up personality and its world; or is found where there is utter indifference to the objective world and its impermanency. Some conceive Nirvana to be a state where there is no recollection of the past or present, just as when a lamp is extinguished, or when a seed is burnt, or when a fire goes out; because then there is the cessation of all the substrata, which is explained by the philosophers as the non-rising of discrimination. But this is not Nirvana, because Nirvana does not consist in simple annihilation and vacuity.

Again, some philosophers explain deliverance as though it was the mere stopping of discrimination, as when the wind stops blowing, or as when one by self-effort gets rid of the dualistic view of knower and known, or gets rid of the notions of permanency and impermanency; or gets rid of the notions of good and evil; or overcomes passion by means of knowledge—to them Nirvana is deliverance. Some, seeing in "form" the bearer of pain, are alarmed by the notion of "form" and look for happiness in a world of "no-form." Some conceive that in consideration of individuality and generality recognisable in all things inner and outer, that there is no destruction and that all beings maintain their being for ever and, in this eternality, see Nirvana. Others see the eternality of things in the conception of Nirvana as the absorption of the finite-soul in Supreme Atman; or who see all things as a manifestation of the vital-force of some Supreme Spirit to which all return; and some, who are especially silly, declare that there are two primary things, a primary substance and a primary soul, that react differently upon each other and thus produce all things from the transformations of qualities; some think that the world is born of action and interaction and that no other cause is necessary; others think that Ishvara is the free creator of all things; clinging to these foolish notions, there is no awakening, and they consider Nirvana to consist in the fact that there is no awakening.

Some imagine that Nirvana is where self-nature exists in its own right, unhampered by other self-natures, as the variegated feathers of a peacock, or various precious crystals, or the pointedness of a thorn. Some conceive being to be Nirvana, some non-being, while others conceive that all things and Nirvana are not to be distinguished from one another. Some, thinking that time is the creator and that as the rise of the world depends on time, they conceive that Nirvana consists in the recognition of time as Nirvana. Some think that there will be Nirvana when the "twenty-five" truths are generally accepted, or when the king observes the six virtues, and some religionists think that Nirvana is the attainment of paradise.

These views severally advanced by the philosophers with their various reasonings are not in accord with logic nor are they acceptable to the wise. They all conceive Nirvana dualistically and in some causal connection; by these discriminations philosophers imagine Nirvana, but where there is no rising and no disappearing, how can there be discrimination? Each philosopher relying on his own textbook from which he draws his understanding, sins against the truth, because truth is not where he imagines it to be. The only result is that it sets his mind to wandering about and becoming more confused as Nirvana is not to be found by mental searching, and the more his mind becomes confused the more he confuses other people.

As to the notion of Nirvana as held by disciples and masters who still cling to the notion of an ego-self, and who try to find it by going off by themselves into solitude: their notion of Nirvana is an eternity of bliss like the bliss of the Samadhis — for themselves. They recognise that the world is only a manifestation of mind and that all discriminations are of the mind, and so they forsake social relations and practise various spiritual disciplines and in solitude seek self-realisation of Noble Wisdom by self-effort. They follow the stages to the sixth and attain the bliss of the Samadhis, but as they are still clinging to egoism they do not attain the "turning-about" at the deepest seat of consciousness and, therefore, they are not free from the thinking-mind and the accumulation of its habit-energy. Clinging to the bliss of the Samadhis, they pass to their Nirvana, but it is not the Nirvana of the Tathagatas. They are of those who have "entered the stream"; they must return to this world of life and death.

Then said Mahamati to the Blessed One: When the Bodhisattvas yield up their stock of merit for the emancipation of all beings, they become spiritually one with all animate life; they themselves may be purified, but in others there yet remain unexhausted evil and unmatured karma. Pray tell us, Blessed One, how the Bodhisattvas are given assurance of Nirvana? and what is the Nirvana of the Bodhisattvas?

The Blessed One replied: Mahamati, this assurance is not an assurance of numbers nor logic; it is not the mind that is to be assured but the heart. The Bodhisattva's assurance comes with the unfolding insight that follows passion hindrances cleared away, knowledge hindrance purified, and egolessness clearly perceived and patiently accepted. As the mortal-mind ceases to discriminate, there is no more thirst for life, no more sex-lust, no more thirst for learning, no more thirst for eternal life; with the disappearance of these fourfold thirsts, there is no more accumulation of habit-energy; with no more accumulation of habit-energy the defilements on the face of Universal Mind clear away, and the Bodhisattva attains self-realisation of Noble Wisdom that is the heart's assurance of Nirvana.

There are Bodhisattvas here and in other Buddha-lands, who are sincerely devoted to the Bodhisattva's mission and yet who cannot wholly forget the bliss of the Samadhis and the peace of Nirvana — for themselves. The teaching of Nirvana in which there is no substrate left behind, is revealed according to a hidden meaning for the sake of these disciples who still cling to thoughts of Nirvana for themselves, that they may be inspired to exert themselves in the Bodhisattva's mission of emancipation for all beings. The Transformation-Buddhas teach a doctrine of Nirvana to meet conditions as they find them, and to give encouragement to the timid and selfish. In order to turn their thoughts away from themselves and to encourage them to a deeper compassion and more earnest zeal for others, they are given assurance as to the future by the sustaining power of the Buddhas of Transformation, but not by the Dharmata-Buddha.

The Dharma which establishes the Truth of Noble Wisdom belongs to the realm of the Dharmata-Buddha. To the Bodhisattvas of the seventh and eighth stages, Transcendental Intelligence is revealed by the Dharmata-Buddha and the Path is pointed out to them which they are to follow. In the perfect self-realisation of Noble Wisdom that follows the inconceivable transformation death of the Bodhisattva's individualised will-control, he no longer lives unto himself, but the life that he lives thereafter is the Tathagata's universalised life as manifested in its transformations. In this perfect self-realisation of Noble Wisdom the Bodhisattva realises that for Buddhas there is no Nirvana.

The death of a Buddha, the great Parinirvana, is neither destruction nor death, else would it be birth and continuation. If it were destruction, it would be an effect-producing deed, which it is not. Neither is it a vanishing nor an abandonment, neither is it attainment, nor is it of no attainment; neither is it of one significance nor of no significance, for there is no Nirvana for the Buddhas.

The Tathagata's Nirvana is where it is recognised that there is nothing but what is seen of the mind itself; is where, recognising the nature of the self-mind, one no longer cherishes the dualisms of discrimination; is where there is no more thirst nor grasping; is where there is no more attachment to external things. Nirvana is where the thinking-mind with all its discriminations, attachments, aversions and egoism is forever put away; is where logical measures, as they are seen to be inert, are no longer seized upon; is where even the notion of truth is treated with indifference because of its causing bewilderment; is where, getting rid of the four propositions, there is insight into the abode of Reality. Nirvana is where the twofold passions have subsided and the twofold hindrances are cleared away and the twofold egolessness is patiently accepted; is where, by the attainment of the "turning-about" in the deepest seat of consciousness, self-realisation of Noble Wisdom is fully entered into, — that is the Nirvana of the Tathagatas.

Nirvana is where the Bodhisattva stages are passed one after another; is where the sustaining power of the Buddhas upholds the Bodhisattvas in the bliss of the Samadhis; is where compassion for others transcends all thoughts of self; is where the Tathagata stage is finally realised.

Nirvana is the realm of Dharmata-Buddha; it is where the manifestation of Noble Wisdom that is Buddhahood expresses itself in Perfect Love for all; it is where the manifestation of Perfect Love that is Tathagatahood expresses itself in Noble Wisdom for the enlightenment of all — there, indeed, is Nirvana!

There are two classes of those who may not enter the Nirvana of the Tathagatas: there are those who have abandoned the Bodhisattva ideals, saying, they are not in conformity with the sutras, the codes of morality, nor with emancipation. Then there are the true Bodhisattvas who, on account of their original vows made for the sake of all beings, saying, "So long as they do not attain Nirvana, I will not attain it myself," voluntarily keep themselves out of Nirvana. But no beings are left outside by the will of the Tathagatas; some day each and every one will be influenced by the wisdom and love of the Tathagatas of Transformation to lay up a stock of merit and ascend the stages. But, if they only realised it, they are already in the Tathagata's Nirvana for, in Noble Wisdom, all things are in Nirvana from the beginning.[59]

NIRVANA HAS NEITHER SUBJECT NOR OBJECT[60]

The monk, Chi-tao, a native of Nam-hoi of Kwong-tung, came to the Patriarch for instruction, saying, "Since I joined the order, I have read the Maha Parinirvana Sutra for more than ten years, but I have not yet grasped its teaching. Will you please teach me?"

"What part of it do you not understand?" enquired the Patriarch.

"It is this part, Sir: 'All things are impermanent and so they belong to the Dharma of Becoming and Cessation. When both Becoming and Cessation cease to operate, Cessation of Change with its bliss of Perfect Rest (Nirvana) arises.' "

"What obscurity is there in that?" enquired the Patriarch.

Chi-tao replied, "All beings have two bodies: the physical body and an essence body. The former is impermanent — it exists and it deceases. The latter is permanent, but it knows not and feels not. Now the Sutra says, 'When both Becoming and Cessation cease to operate, the bliss of Perfect Rest and Cessation of Change arises.' I can not understand which body ceases to exist, and which body enjoys the bliss. It cannot be the physical body that enjoys, because when it dies, the material elements disintegrate and disintegration is suffering, the very opposite of bliss. If it is the essence body that ceases to exist, it would be in the same 'unfeeling' state as inanimate objects, such as the grass, trees and stones. Who, then, will be the enjoyer?

"Moreover, essence-nature is the quintessence of 'Becoming and Cessation' whose manifestation is the union of the five 'aggregates' (body, sensation, perception, consciousness and intellection). That is to say, from one essence, five functions arise. This process of Becoming and Cessation is everlasting. When function and operation 'arise' from the quintessence, it becomes; when operation and function are 'absorbed' back into the quintessence, it ceases to exist. If reincarnation is admitted, there will be no Cessation of Changes, as in the case of sentient beings. If reincarnation is out of the question, then things will remain forever in a state of lifeless quintessence, like the case of inanimate objects. When this is the case, under the limitations and restrictions of Nirvana, even existence would be impossible to all things, much less enjoyment."

"You are a Bhikkhu," said the Patriarch, "how can you adopt the fallacious views of Eternalism and Annihilationism that are held by heretics, and venture to criticise the teaching of the Supreme Vehicle? Your argument implies that apart from the physical body, there is an essence body; and that Perfect Rest and Cessation of Change may be sought apart from 'Becoming and Cessation.' Further, from the statement, 'Nirvana is everlasting rest,' you infer that there must be somebody to play the part of enjoyer.

"It is exactly these fallacious views that makes people crave for sentiate existence and worldly pleasure. These people are the victims of ignorance; they identify the union of the five aggregates as the 'self' and regard all other things as 'not-self'; they crave for individual existence and have an aversion to death; they are drifting about from one momentary sensation to another in the whirlpool of life and death without realising the emptiness of mundane existence which is only a dream and an illusion; they commit themselves to unnecessary suffering by binding themselves to rebirth; they mistake the state of everlasting joy of Nirvana to be a mode of suffering; they are always seeking after sensual pleasures. It was for these people, victims of ignorance, that the compassionate Buddha preached the real bliss of Nirvana.

"Never for a moment was Nirvana either the phenomena of Becoming and Cessation, or the ceasing of Becoming and Cessation. It is the perfect manifestation of Rest and Cessation of Change, and at the 'time' of manifestation, there is no such thing as manifestation. It is called 'everlasting' Joy because it has neither enjoyer nor non-enjoyer.

"There is no such thing as 'one quintessence and five manifestations.' You are slandering Buddha and blaspheming the Dharma, when you go so far as to state that under the limitation and restriction of Nirvana, living is impossible to all beings. Listen to this stanza:

"The Supreme Maha Parinirvana
Is perfect, permanent, calm, radiantly illuminative.
Common and ignorant people miscall it death,
While heretics arbitrarily declare it to be annihilation.
Those who belong to the Small Vehicle and to the Middle
  Vehicle
Regard Nirvana as 'non-action.'
All these are merely intellectual speculations,
And they form the basis of the sixty-two fallacious views.
Since they are merely names, invented for the occasion,
They have nothing to do with Absolute Truth.
Only those of super-eminent mind
Can understand thoroughly what Nirvana is,
And take an attitude toward it of neither attachment nor
  indifference.
They know that the five aggregates,
And the so-called 'self' arising from the aggregates,
Together with all external forms and objects,
And the various phenomena of words and voice,
Are all equally unreal, like a dream or an illusion.
They make no discrimination between a sage and an
  ordinary man,
Nor do they have any arbitrary concept of Nirvana,
They are above 'affirmation' and 'negation';
They break the barriers between the past, the present
  and the future.
They use their sense organs when occasion requires,
But the concept of 'using' does not arise.
They may particularise on all sorts of things,
But the concept of 'particularisation' arises not.
Even during the cataclysmic fire at the end of a kalpa,

When ocean beds are burnt dry;
Or during the blowing of catastrophic winds,
    when mountains topple;
The everlasting bliss of Perfect Rest and Cessation
    of Change that is Nirvana
Remains the same and changes not."

The Patriarch then said to Chi-tao, "I am trying to describe to you something that intrinsically is ineffable, in order to help you to get rid of fallacious views. If you do not interpret my words too literally you may perhaps know a wee bit of Nirvana."

Chi-tao became highly enlightened and, in a rapturous mood he made obeisance and departed.[61]

6

Pratītyasamutpāda

Tradition[1] tells of that memorable night in 531 B.C. when, with evening drawing nigh, the Buddha seated himself beneath the now celebrated *ficus religiosa* in Bodh-gāya and underwent the illumination by which he acquired a triple knowledge: of the past, coming to a knowledge of his previous existences; of the present, deciphering the mystery of human death and birth; and of the future, for he realized that he had destroyed within himself all thirst, the cause of successive existences.[2] This triple knowledge, and the *rasa* (the gist, the essence) of all illumination generally, can be synthesized in the intuition that Śākyamuni had of *pratītyasamutpāda*. *Pratītyasamutpāda* is the central focus of all Buddhism. "Who understands this, understands dharma, and who understands dharma, understands this."[3] Or, according to another text, "who sees *pratītyasamutpāda* sees the Buddha, and who sees the Buddha sees dharma."[4] The figure is echoed in numerous other passages as well.[5] Indeed, *pratītyasamutpāda* is the key to a correct interpretation of the fundamental Buddhist intuition.[6] The Bodhisattvas are the instructors par excellence in *pratītyasamutpāda*.[7]

Understandably, simply in virtue of its importance, this "law" has been subjected to the widest variety of interpretations, depending on which Buddhist school of thought is the interpreter.[8] The whole *mādhyamika* is but a reinterpretation of *pratītyasamutpāda*.[9] There is no less diversity of opinion among modern scholars, as we see from their very translations of the formula.[10] These range from a reflection of a substantialistic causal law, to a more dilute kind of causality, to a simple mutual dependency without causality.[11]

Even the history of the noun is instructive. We are confronted both with a hesitancy as to its translation, and a variety of positions taken toward *pratītyasamutpāda* itself. Part of this uncertainty derives from the fact that the two Sanskrit words *hetu*, "cause," and *pratyaya* (in Pali, *paccaya*), "condition," were translated into Chinese by a single term.[12] Indeed, often enough "cause" and "condition" are used synonymously, which scarcely helps in a grasp of the problem.

Etymologically, the Sanskrit *pratītyasamutpāda* seems to indicate a reciprocally conditioned "origin," in virtue of a (cosmic) functionalism.[13] Furthermore, the word connotes more than a substantialistic[14] or ontological[15] causality. It indicates first and foremost a single network of connections among various elements. That is, we have a universal concatenation of some kind.

The basic notion of *pratītyasamutpāda* can be capsulized as follows:

All the human conditions—the constituting energies, the terrestrial situations[16]—are impermanent;[17] all that is impermanent *(anitya)* is filled with suffering *(dukkha);* all that is suffering does not have consistency *(atman);* and all that does not have consistency is empty *(sūnya).*[18]

Or again, we may cite the simple words that tradition places on the lips of the Buddha's first disciple, who had reached nirvana:

All that is subject to birth is destined to disappear.[19]

I may safely assert that this single sentence contains, as in a capsule, the Enlightened One's whole intuition. Birth is the origin of the chain of ek-sistence.[20]

What the Buddha sees is not so much the celebrated Buddhistic impermanence, as the radical, constitutive relativity of everything—the universal concatenation of all things, and accordingly their mutual essential relationship, given that they perdure only in virtue of being found in the flux of becoming, of *samsāra*. What the Buddha *sees* is not impermanence. To use language like this is to speak, as it were, from without. What the Buddha intuits is the permanence of impermanence, so to speak. That is, he intuits the entire cosmos in its becoming and in the interrelationship of all its parts, he sees the dependence of one thing on another, he discovers the absence of any independence whatever.

Further: the Buddha observes that if there were to be anything really independent, it would be altogether beyond the grasp of hand and mind, beyond any sort of apprehension, possession, or relationship. It would be impossible to speak of it. The intuition of *pratītyasamutpāda* is the intuition of *pure* contingency—but of contingency in its positivity, let us say—that is, in its mutual dependency and radical finitude. Contingency has no outside support. The Blessed One exempts not even himself, any more than any other human being. He simply does not exclude the human subject from this radical, constitutive nothingness. He speaks of the "nothing" that things are, and makes no exception for the ego of substantialistic thinking, that impartial spectator of the perishability of all. In the mind of the Buddha there are no exceptions. He reserves no special dignity to the human being.[21] Even the *ātman* is flung into the flux of relative existence, and the

Buddha acknowledges that he, too, is immersed in the universal concatenation. There is no room for a response adequate to overcome the transiency and relativity of the question. Therefore the Tathagata kept silent.

The contingency of a particular being can be discerned only in relationship to its bolster and support—in other words, only if I discover that something else sustains and supports it. Now, if the ultimate support and foundation of all things is found at the end of all, in some Being beyond all contingency, then, the Buddha asks us, on what basis do we arrive at this hypothesis? Our conclusion must be either the consequence of theoretical reasoning or the fruit of direct experience. If it is the consequence of theoretical reasoning, then the transcendence of our hypothetical Being is compromised, for our reason has attained to it. If our hypothesis is the fruit of direct experience, then how have we managed to communicate this experience, given that direct experience is incommunicable, incapable of translation and objectivization?

Hence the Buddha is mistrustful of all "pious" reflection on the transitoriness of human things against a background of the consistency and permanence of a God, a Being, or something of the kind. First of all, if this foundation of all things is *seen,* things are no longer seen as contingent, but as eternal and permanent, as they are seen in their eternal, immutable foundation. Secondly, if what we see are things, but not their foundation, then we may not say that we experience their consistency directly: rather it is deduced, in virtue of a mental hypothesis furnishing us with a plausible explanation within the limits of our thought, without any guarantee in direct experience. The Buddha's great intuition consists in "seeing" contingency in itself, divorced from any fundament. Hence his total vision of the cosmos and his intuition of the universal connection—the concatenation of all beings, forming a single ensemble by their mutual attraction. This is the intuition of the universal connection. But not even this intuition is absolutized. Hence the connection with the void. *śūnyata.*

However, this intuition is beyond the grasp of any reasoning. It is also beyond any possibility of communicable experience. To whom might such an experience be communicated? Accordingly, this intuition can be had only in an ineffable, mystical experience. And indeed the Buddha never pretended his enlightenment was anything else. It was a vision of the entire cosmos in a unitary intuition revealing the concatenation of all with all, the mutual responsibility of all beings, the transiency of all things, and the nothingness of the cosmos.[22] The Buddha did not see the "beyond." He saw the totality and interdependency of the "right here."

Thus the origin of one thing from another is the key to the intuition of the impression of substantiality that things can give when seen in isolation.[23] We discover that one thing is but the result, the modification, the consequence, the effect, the condition—call it what you will—of another, and the latter in its turn of yet another, without there being any need of a basis to support the motion of this reaction. We discover the circularity of all that exists. It has neither beginning nor end, either in time or in space, either through immanence, or through some impossible transcendence. And with this discovery we have the intuition of the radical contingency of all, not even excluding the subject of the discovery.[24]

The Buddha's intuition has a genuinely religious aspect. It has a cathartic effect. The discovery of pure contingency is a devastating experience, for it leaves no escape in the form of some "projected" transcendence. It is the acceptance of ontological death. It is the affirmation of the negative. It is an experience that arises after having crossed the threshold of utter desperation like that of Gautama at Bodh-gāya. But the very fact of having discovered the irremediable contingency, finitude, mortality, and final nothingness of human beings and the world around them, and to have accepted the inexorability of it all, is salvation — the discovery that leads to the most complete emptiness. And the name for this is nirvana.[25]

It is to be hoped that my discussion has rendered the notion of nirvana more comprehensible. All schools of Buddhism, logically enough, will defend the thesis that nirvana is to be found "outside" the universal concatention. Of course, the expression as such is inexact. Nirvana is surely not "outside" universal contingency in any substantialistic sense. It is neither beside nor above nor underneath nor beyond universal contingency, and still less does it sustain this contingency. Nor am I saying that there is a Being, called nirvana, that is independent of and untouched by the "dependent origination" to which contingency returns after being, as it were, delivered from its own finitude. Any attempt to situate nirvana in a like relationship with the world would be to deprive it of its unconditionality.[26] Hence, altogether logically, some schools (especially Mādhyamika) have stressed that there is no difference between *samsāra* and *nirvāṇa,* that both are the same thing — only, the latter is "seen" with a genuine knowledge that tears away the veils of ignorance.[27]

By way of summarizing the unitary, intuitive vision of the Enlightened One, it may be said: reality is one, but can be seen in three ways, each enjoying a higher degree of truth than the preceding:[28]

1. Reality can be seen as a complex of separate substances with an internal hierarchy that may extend all the way to an acceptance of a Supreme Being or God. This the Buddha would unhesitatingly qualify as a primitive conceptualization. After all, at bottom it is a dualistic one: any *thing,* by the mere fact of being a substance, would have to be a little god, thereupon to be appropriately ranged in the hierarchy and finally subjected to a Supreme Being. In the terminology of the Buddha's time this would be the conception of the eternalists, the *sāśvatavāda.*

2. Next in order will be the view of those who, discovering the contingent, changeable, and transitory nature of beings, and frustrated by their incapacity to attain what they unconsciously seek — a substrate, a

substance — find themselves constrained to renounce their quest and declare themselves nihilists. Now they are the defenders of pure phenomenalism, and the unreality of all. These are the followers of *ucchedavāda*. Their bootless pursuit of an ideal monism necessarily issues in agnosticism, if not in an out-and-out nihilism of pure negation.

Let us note that the Buddha repeated ad nauseam that he did not adhere to either of these doctrines.

3. For the Buddha, *pratītyasamutpāda* represents a middle way, the midway teaching *(majihema dhammo)* that avoids both extremes, being and nonbeing. "All is unicity; all is multiplicity" are the two extremes to be avoided.[29] As we know, the problem of the one and the many has occupied the human mind since the dawn of philosophical awareness. All philosophy, especially in India, has sought a way out of the basic dilemma between being and nonbeing. Siddhartha, too, is in the line of philosophical tradition, and his enlightenment consists precisely in an intuition of the ultimate structure of all things: their constitutive interdependency, a relationship so basic as to proceed from their very being. Things "are" only to the extent that they are produced and conditioned by other things, and no more.[30] There is no residue that might escape contingency, no concealed, no permanent nucleus, no "divine" element immune from the universal flux. There are no exceptions to the rule. There are no privileges, for anything or anyone. All the world is only this. Neither monism nor dualism corresponds to the truth.

But nirvana is not another reality. It could not be. That would destroy the very foundation of Buddhism. Therefore nirvana is scarcely "true reality" (as if there could be a false reality, and a certain Vedanta is pretty well constrained to admit that there could not be). Phenomenal reality is perfectly true — only, it is transitory and mortal. Strictly speaking, nirvana "is" not. There "is" no nirvana.[31] And so when one asks what nirvana "is," the only answer is silence. And the only possible intelligible translation of this silence is that nirvana is *saṃsāra* itself, simply the existential flux (and not a hypothetical, problematic substrate), the only difference being that now nirvana is "seen," actually "experienced." From here it is only a short step to the philosophical interpretation of Buddhistic and Vedantic absolutism alike.[32]

Let us examine some of the key texts.

GENERAL FORMULATION

I shall teach you the dharma: if one thing exists, another thing comes into existence; from the appearance of one thing there follows the appearance of another; if a certain thing does not exist, another thing cannot come to be; from the cessation of one thing there derives the cessation of another.[33]

A PRIMORDIAL LAW

Pratītyasamutpāda is deep, O Ānanda, and at the same time it bears the aspect of profundity (*gambhīrāvabhāsa*). For not having penetrated this dharma and for not having understood it (*an-anubodha*), this generation has remained imprisoned.[34]

ALL THINGS ARE MUTUALLY CONDITIONED

Once a certain monk named Sāti, the son of a fisherman,[35] conceived the pernicious heresy that, as he understood the Lord's teaching, consciousness continued throughout transmigration. When they heard this several monks went and reasoned with him . . . but he would not give in, but held firm to his heresy. . . . So they went to the Lord and put the matter to him, and he sent a monk to fetch Sāti. When Sāti had come the Lord asked him if it was true that he held this heresy . . . and Sāti replied that he did hold it.

"What, then," asked the Lord, "is the nature of consciousness?"

"Sir, it is that which speaks and feels, and experiences the consequences of good and evil deeds."

"Whom do you tell, you foolish fellow, that I have taught such a doctrine? Haven't I said, with many similes, that consciouness is not independent, but comes about through the Chain of Causation, and can never arise without a cause? You misunderstand and misrepresent me, and so you undermine your own position and produce much demerit. You bring upon yourself lasting harm and sorrow!" . . .

Then the Lord addressed the assembled monks:

"Whatever form of consciousness arises from a condition is known by the name of that condition; thus if it arises from the eye and from forms it is known as visual consciousness . . . and so with the senses of hearing, smell, taste, touch, and mind, and their objects. It's just like a fire, which you call by the name of the fuel — a wood fire, a fire of sticks, a grass fire, and cowdung fire, a fire of husks, a rubbish fire, and so on."

"Do you agree, monks, that any given organism is a living being?" "Yes, sir."

"Do you agree that it is produced by food?" "Yes, sir."

"And that when the food is cut off the living being is cut off and dies?" "Yes, sir."

"And that doubt on any of these points will lead to perplexity?" "Yes, sir."

"And that Right Recognition is knowledge of the true facts as they really are?" "Yes, sir."

"Now if you cling to this pure and unvitiated view, if you cherish it, treasure it, and make it your own, will you be able to develop a state of consciousness with which you can cross the stream of transmigration as on a raft, which you use but do not keep?" "No, sir."

"But only if you maintain this pure view, but don't cling to it or cherish it . . . only if you use it but are ready to give it up?" "Yes, sir."

"Or would you support the rituals, shows, or festivals of other ascetics or brāhmans?" "No, sir."

"Do you only declare what you have known and seen?" "Yes, sir."

"Well done, brethren! I have taught you the doctrine which is immediately beneficial, eternal, open to all, leading them onwards, to be mastered for himself by every intelligent man."[36]

ORTHODOX VIEWPOINT

Inasmuch as it is dependently on each other and in unison and simultaneously that the factors which constitute dependence originate the elements of being, therefore did The Sage call these factors Dependent Origination.

By the first word: The word "Dependent" (*pratītya*), as exhibiting a full complement of dependence and inasmuch as the elements of being are subject to that full complement of dependence, shows an avoidance of such heresies as that of the persistence of existences, the heresies, namely, of the persistence of existences, of uncaused existences, of existences due to an overruling power, of self-determining existences. For what have persistent existences, uncaused existences, etc., to do with a full complement of dependence?

By the second word: The word "Origination" (*samutpāda*), as exhibiting an origination of the elements of being and inasmuch as the elements of being originate by means of a full complement of dependence, shows a rejection of such heresies as that of the annihilation of existences, the heresies, namely, of the annihilation of existences, of nihilism, of the inefficacy of karma. For if the elements of being are continually originating by means of an antecedent dependence, whence can we have annihilation of existence, nihilism, and an inefficacy of karma?

By both together: By the complete phrase "Dependent Origination" (*pratītyasamutpāda*), inasmuch as such and such elements of being come into existence by means of an unbroken series of their full complement of dependence, the truth, or middle course, is shown. This rejects the heresy that he who experiences the fruit of the deed is the same as the one who performed the deed, and also rejects the converse one that he who experiences the fruit of a deed is different from the one who performed the deed, and leaning not to either of these popular hypotheses, holds fast by nominalism.[37]

THE TWELVE BONDS[38]

The twelve bonds may be enumerated as follows:

1. *Avidyā:* ignorance. Not to know the Four Noble Truths and the other pillars of the Buddhistic conception.[39]
2. *Saṃskāra:* karmic formations. Psychic constructions of phenomenal origin.[40]
3. *Vijñāna:* consciousness. The ensemble of the cognitive acts that have their origin in the activity of the senses.
4. *Nāmarūpa:* name and form. Corporeality—or better, perhaps, concrete individuality.
5. *Ṣaḍ-āyatana:* the six senses. The six bases of cognition, which has its origin in the eye, the ear, the nose, the tongue, the body, and the spirit.[41]
6. *Sparśa:* contact. The connection (of the senses) with the external world, inasmuch as nothing would be set in motion without a stimulus from without.[42]
7. *Vedanā:* sensation. The individual's reaction to stimulus from the outside world.
8. *Tṛṣṇa:* thirst. Desire to possess, to be satisfied (to be filled up). Thirst for gratification, with special reference to the sexual appetite.
9. *Upādāna:* attachment. Desire of possession. The tendency to appropriation—especially, attachment to one's own life.
10. *Bhāva:* existence. The state of arrival at being, the being of the world. Or: what we might call the current of successive "re-existence,"[43] reincarnations.
11. *Jāti:* birth. The act of coming into the world and living in space and time.
12. *Jarānamaraṇa:* old age and death. The result, the aftermath, of birth and existence, in the form of pain and suffering.[44]

IT IS IMPOSSIBLE TO PREVENT THINGS FROM DYING

There are five things that no being in this world can accomplish, neither monk nor brahman, nor God nor demon—not even Brahman. They are: that being subject to aging, one avoids becoming older; that being subject to infirmity, one prevents sickness; that being subject to death, one avoids dying; that being subject to decline, one prevents deterioration; that being subject to disappearing, one prevents disappearance.[45]

Other texts are equally clear, but broader in scope. For example, we have the *pratītyasamutpādasūtra,*[46] with Vasabandhu's classic commentary, the *pratītyasamutpāda vyākhyā,*[47] and the long commentary known as the *śālistamba-sūtra.*[48] They all of them only confirm what I have been saying in these pages.

7

Avyākṛtavastuni

According to unanimous Buddhistic tradition, there are fourteen propositions to which the Buddha refused to give any answer. They have to do with formulations of four basic problems: the eternity of the world, its finitude, existence after death, and the identity of soul and body.[1]

Interestingly, the problem of God is not explicitly mentioned. Yet surely we may not say that the Buddhistic writers had never heard of gods. On the contrary, they mention them continually. The gods do not, however, correspond to what "God" means in the Abrahamic tradition. And here the Buddha's silence is total, to the point of not even permitting the question to be asked.

Two observations seem to be in order at this point if we hope to be in a position to respond to the question of the Buddha's supposed atheism. Both emerge from the cultural ambient in which Siddhartha moves. The first is in reference to a special characteristic of Indian religious speculation. Here the problem of the world takes precedence over the problem of God. Or better, the question of the world is posed according to the form and method reserved by other religions for the question of God. What seems problematic to classic Indic speculation is not the Absolute as such, but the existence of the relative and its justification vis-à-vis the Absolute itself.[2] Thus we discover the reason why our four basic questions regard not God, but the world and the human soul. Obviously we are dealing with four religious questions. They could scarcely be described as purely mundane. But all four have connections with the world. The Indian wonders not about God or the beyond, but about the religious dimension—a dimension at once transcendent and immanent—of cosmic existence, human existence included. The Indian wonders about the invisible dimension of this visible world—a question of pure faith, then. In short, for India the problem of God is an anthropological problem.[3]

The second observation is complementary to the first, and issues from the peculiar familiarity of the Indic mentality with the realm of the divine.

There is an infinitude of gods, *deva*s.[4] For the general mentality of the Buddha's time, they constitute a reality more palpable than that of the trees that offer men and women shade, and the gods and goddesses hospitality. In short, for India the anthropological problem is a theological problem.

Now, if by "God" we mean the mightiest and highest of the *deva*s, then the identity of God will merely vary from sect to sect as we follow their disputations. But if by "God" we mean the Absolute, or Being, the Creator of all things, then the Buddha refuses an answer, rejecting even the formulation of such a question, wherever and whenever in so doing we abandon the terrain of the strictly religious to indulge in the meanderings of philosophico-theological interpretations.

The Buddha—as indeed his disciples, ancient and modern—admits the reality of the *deva*s.[5] He recognizes both their existence and their power. To the explicit question posed to him by the Brahmin Sangarava, "Do the *deva*s exist?" the Enlightened One categorically replies: "The *deva*s exist! This is a fact that I have acknowledged, and the whole world is in agreement about it."[6] The religious world of Buddhism, no less than that of other religions, is populated with beings superior to humans and standing in relationship with them: angels, asuras, *apsara*s, *devatā*s, and the like.[7] However, the Enlightened One considers this spirituality, based on a personification of the divine, suitable only for persons of the world, for secular persons. Those proficient in the way of the spirit no longer depend on the gods.[8] The Tathagata has "seen" and revealed that the world's fate depends on causes and conditions, so that the wise no longer have any need of turning to the *deva*s or to any other divine power.[9]

On these premises, the designation of Buddhism as atheistic would have been incomprehensible in bygone times. Is it not possible, then, that the epithet is applied in view of a particular conception of the divinity—that of the Abrahamic religions or the philosophies of being?

Clearly the Buddha does not reject the God of the lowly, the God of the little ones, the gods with which Buddhism itself will shortly be replete. No, what Siddhartha categorically rejects is the God of the philosophers and theologians. He simply refuses to let himself be drawn into dialectical discussions (which cannot but be of this world) of the genuinely transcendent. He is opposed to the notion that God can be manipulated in any way, even for the purpose of reaching God as a conclusion. Who can "package" God?[10]

All of the texts in question are explicit on this point. The Buddha utters neither negation nor affirmation. If he denied one proposition, he would be implicitly affirming its contradictory and vice versa. The Buddha simply refuses to allow himself to be drawn into the game of mere dialectics, and therefore unambiguously rejects the affirmation of a doctrine, its negation, and finally the affirmation and negation of both.[11] Hence his silence. The gentle, smiling Buddha does not refuse to speak, but, as we see from our texts, he surely refuses to answer.[12]

The better to understand our texts, it will be helpful to formulate the fourteen propositions to which I have referred above:

1. The world *is* temporally finite.
2. The world *is not* temporally finite.
3. The world *is* and *is not* temporally finite.
4. The world neither *is* nor *is not* temporally finite.
5. The world *is* spatially finite.
6. The world *is not* spatially finite.
7. The world *is* and *is not* spatially finite.
8. The world neither *is* nor *is not* spatially finite.
9. The Tathagata *exists* after death.
10. The Tathagata *does not exist* after death.
11. The Tathagata *exists* and *does not exist* after death.
12. The Tathagata neither *exists* nor *does not exist* after death.
13. The soul *is* identical with the body.
14. The soul *is not* identical with the body.

Above all else it is necessary to grasp the intelligibility of the propositions.

The purely affirmative propositions, 1, 5, 9, 13, are straightforward, like the purely negative ones, 2, 6, 10, 14. They are in the form "A is B," "A is not B," respectively.

The propositions that are simultaneously affirmative and negative, 3, 7, 11, do not signify simple internal contradiction; they cannot, for internal contradiction is of its very nature nonsignifying. Let us replace, for instance, proposition 3 with: "The world is partially (or "in one respect") finite and partially (or "in another respect") not finite temporally." Now the proposition becomes intelligible. Its intelligibility will be still clearer if we keep in mind that the Buddha's response will not consist in admitting such a proposition, but in denying that such a proposition represents his opinion – or, equivalently, that such and such a proposition does not contain the truth as the Buddha sees it (without implying, as the *Mādhyamika* will repeat ad nauseam,[13] that truth lies with either the contrary or the contradictory.)[14]

There are greater difficulties with the propositions that deny both the affirmation and the negation, 4, 8, 12. Not surprisingly, these immediately became the object of lengthy discussions in the schools of Buddhism.[15] These propositions have been interpreted both conjunctively and disjunctively: that is, (1) as negation conjoined with the affirmation of the proposition immediately preceding, or (2) as the separate negation of each of the two parts of the proposition. In other words, proposition 4 has been seen as signifying either (1) "The world is not finite-and-not-finite," or (2) "The world is neither finite nor not-finite."

On my own view, the second interpretation, the disjunctive, would be reducible to a simple repetition of the first and second propositions taken together, and thus would not constitute a new proposition.[16] For this reason, then, as well as out of considerations of parallelism with the third kind of proposition vis-à-vis the two immediately preceding, I am inclined to share the first interpretation, the conjunctive. Among other things, this interpretation admits of a more obvious meaning, for it will yield the affirmation that neither finitude nor nonfinitude adequately expresses the temporal state of the world. It is in this inadequacy of being and nonbeing vis-à-vis the self-identity of the real that, it seems to me, we have the hermeneutic key to the problem.

We have before us four types of propositions, then. They would seem to exhaust the logical possibilities in respect of any affirmation:

I. A *is* B.

II. A *is not* B.

III. A *is and is not* B.

IV. A *is not (is-and-is-not)* B.

The problem is therefore quadruple:

1. To demonstrate that a rejection of a proposition of type I does not necessarily imply a proposition of type II.

2. To demonstrate that types I and II taken together do not cover the same ground as types III and IV taken together, and thus leave place for the pair III-IV.

3. Finally, to demonstrate that we have covered all the ground—that is, that all possibilities of affirmation and negation are exhausted in these four propositions.

4. Only then will the Buddha's attitude be intelligible. His rejection of all four propositions, implying a transcendence of ontology, will signify neither the negation nor the destruction of that ontology, but only our liberation from ontolatry.

Let us address each of these four points in order.

1. In virtue of the principle of noncontradiction—a condition considered indispensable for our intellection—it would seem at first blush that if we reject a proposition of type I, we automatically accept one of type II, at least implicitly. Nevertheless, despite what may seem, and despite common sense, the Buddha does not admit this dilemma. The profound reason for this seems to me to reside not in some misapprehension of the laws of logic on the part of Buddhism, but in the denial of a one-to-one correspondence between thinking and being. Let us not forget that the first formulation of the so-called principle of noncontradiction was not that of Aristotle,[17] but of Parmenides[18]—and that with the Eleatic the principle is indisputably ontological, in immediate consequence of his identification of thinking and being.[19] The principle of noncontradiction, on which the discipline of logic is constructed, especially in the West, is valid precisely in this sense, and only in this sense: that the negation of one of two contradictory propositions necessarily implies the affirmation of the other.

But the Buddha's intuition takes its leave of this schema, and, availing itself of the elasticity of the word "being," uses it as a transitive verb instead of as a substantive—thus resolving the dilemma without either falling into a contradiction or surrendering intelligibility.

For, in virtue of the ductility of the verb "to be," proposition II, "A is not B," can mean either:

A is non-B

or

A is-not B.

In the first case we have a negation of B; in the second, a negation of "is." Now, in virtue of the principle of noncontradiction, only the former of these two propositions contradicts a proposition of type I. The contradictory proposition of "A is B" is "A is non-B," not "A is-not B."

What we must do in a contradictory proposition of type II is predicate of A the attribute contradictory to that predicated of it in the affirmative proposition of type I. But we must not change the predicating formula, by changing the active verb joining subject to predicate. "A is" must remain intact in both propositions, for, after all, it is under the same aspect that the predicate B is attributed to A in the proposition of type I, and negated (non-B) in the proposition of type II.

The Buddha's subtle response, " 'A is B' is not my opinion," however, is by no means tantamount to an assertion that A is non-B. This would be contradiction. Very simply, he is saying, "A is-not B." But this is not the contradictory of the first proposition. Hence he has not fallen into a contradiction,[20] but is simply communicating his thought: If someone wishes to know, "Is A B?" he will reply, "A is-not B." And if the other pursues the question "Then is A not B?" he will reply, "A *is-not* B."

To put it another way:

"A *is* B" is logically incompatible with:

"A is non-B," but not with:

"A *is-not* B."

Indeed, if the first proposition is true—if A actually is B—then I may substitute A for B, and easily see which of the propositions containing a negative holds and which does not. "A is non-A" is a contradiction; "A is-not A" merely indicates that A is not absolutely identical with itself—which, after all, must be the case, for otherwise it could not have equaled B in any respect whatever,[21] and the proposition "A is B" would have been a sterile tautology. This second interpretation is the one that leaves the door open for the Buddha's response.

Let me exemplify this with the first of our fourteen propositions. If the Buddha is not of the opinion that:

The world *is* (temporally) finite,

then, in virtue of the principle of noncontradiction, it must follow that:

The world is nonfinite,

but not that:

The world *is not* finite.

To deny the proposition, "the world is nonfinite" is tantamount to the proposition that the world *is* not nonfinite"—that is, that the nonfinitude of the world does not tell us what the world *is*. And this is altogether consonant with the Buddha's attitude. Surely nothing can tell us what the world is, for neither question, that of being or that of nonbeing, can be asked with regard to the world. Ontology is not false, it is just that it is caught in an endless circle. Ontology insists that *to on* corresponds to *ho logos*. The Enlightened One has seen beyond this. What has he seen? Nothing! *Śūnyatā, nirvāṇa*.

2. From a rejection of a proposition of type I, it follows that "A is non-B." Meanwhile, "A is-not B" remains untouched. But this proposition too is rejected by the Buddha. It does not take much reasoning to see perfectly well that if both "A is B" and "A is-not B" are rejected, there must be a fissure between the "is" and the "is-not" that must be filled in by affirming and denying the two previous propositions—that the world is finite and that the world is nonfinite. Hence the dilemma of propositions 3 and 4.

And indeed these are the questions next addressed to the Enlightened One: if he is not of the opinion of either proposition I or proposition II, then it would seem that he must necessarily accept either the affirmation or the negation of propositions I and II together. Surely the rejection of proposition I and proposition II will necessarily entail the acceptance of either the affirmation of propositions I and II together, or their denial—or else from the denial of propositions I and II there will necessarily follow proposition III or proposition IV.

But the Buddha's reply is still in the negative. For greater clarity, we may consider Figure 1. The circle is A, the square is B.

The area common to circle A and square B legitimates the affirmation "A *is* B" (proposition type I).

At the same time the area lying within the circle alone legitimates the negation "A *is not* B."

But Figure 1 also shows that propositions I and II fail to exhaust all possible relationships between A and B. Thus if we consider the *whole* circle, we can truthfully formulate proposition III: "A *is and is not* B."

Next, taking account of that portion of the square lying outside the circle, we can truthfully formulate proposition IV: "A *neither is nor is not* B"—or alternatively, "A *is not (is-and-is-not)* B."

For the sake of greater clarity, I have gone through the four propositions individually. I could also have demonstrated them on the basis of their rejection by one another:

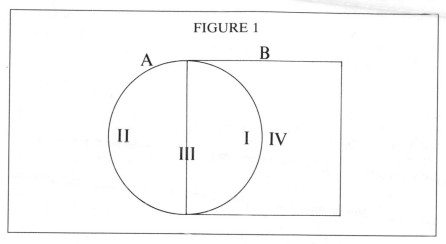

FIGURE 1

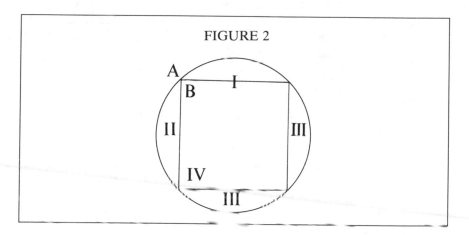

FIGURE 2

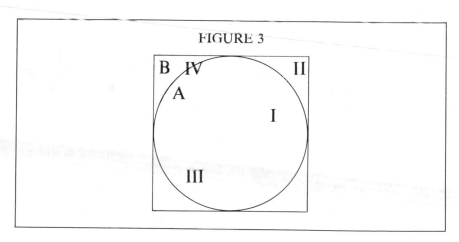

FIGURE 3

The areas of the diagram labeled II and IV exclude the truth of the first proposition, "A is B."

Area I excludes the truth of the second proposition, "A is not B."

The square B inscribed within the circle A would be the expression of the second proposition:[22]

Finally, the circle A inscribed within the square B would be the expression of the third proposition.[23]

Thus we have room for a second pair of alternatives: and just as with the first pair, we shall see that the negation of the former alternative, in this case proposition III, will not necessarily entail the acceptance of the latter, proposition IV: for if a proposition of type III is proposed to the Buddha as the truth—for example, that the world is finite and nonfinite—its acceptance would imply the opinion that the world transcends and comprehends the categories of finitude and nonfinitude.

Indeed, in virtue of the considerations we have entertained above, a proposition of type III cannot mean "A is B and non-B." In order to be intelligible, proposition III must mean: "A *is* and *is not* B." In other words there is no contradiction between "is" and "is-not," because the predicate B is affirmed and denied of subject A from two viewpoints. Now, if this proposition is rejected, it does not necessarily follow that proposition IV is accepted. In denying proposition III we of course deny that a predicate B is attributable and is not attributable to a subject, but this does not imply that this predicate is absolutely unattributable to subject A. The rejection of proposition IV implies that the subject is not exhaustively defined in terms of the contradictory alternatives of a given predicate B: subject A may simply transcend predicate B ontologically, so to speak. On these premises, the Buddha, rejecting proposition IV as well as III, denies that such a transcendence can be considered an ontological transcendence: it is not correct that the world is finite and nonfinite, inasmuch as neither finitude nor nonfinitude exhausts or adequately expresses the being of the world.

The Buddha's position, then, is unequivocal. None of the four alternatives is adequate to express his opinion.

Are we dealing with absolute agnosticism?

I think not. The Buddha, and all later tradition along with him, held that only the negation of the four alternatives under consideration opens the way to the real answer—although that answer will not allow itself to be imprisoned in words or propositions. And this is my third point.

3. But then have we not initiated a process *ad infinitum?* May we not now go on to posit hypothetical propositions V and VI as the negations of propositions III and IV? I think not, for these propositions would be identical with propositions III and IV. Surely the propositions

    V. "A *is* (is-and-is-not) B"

and

    VI. "A *is not* (is-and-is-not) B"

would add nothing to the content of propositions III and IV. Whether in virtue of the law of the excluded middle, or in virtue of the very principle of noncontradiction, propositions V and VI add nothing new to propositions III and IV.[24] Indeed, the middle ground that the analogy of being might have provided between propositions I and II has now been sealed off by III and IV, and no avenue of escape remains. After all, propositions III and IV have their meaning not in themselves but as correctives of I and II. It would be meaningless to ask whether the world is simultaneously finite and nonfinite without first establishing that neither finitude nor nonfinitude expresses its actual condition.[25]

What I am saying is confirmed by the fact that the list of propositions does not go on to add propositions 15 and 16. Some scholars have been puzzled that propositions 13 and 14 are not complemented by two more propositions (15 and 16), by analogy with the first three series of propositions. On the contrary, it seems to me that their traditional omission is highly significant.[26] Let it be observed that the propositions

15. "The soul is and is not identical with the body"

and

16. "The soul neither is nor is not identical with the body" are mutually contradictory—which is not the case with their analogues, propositions 3 and 4, and 7 and 8. The latter pairs predicate not identity, but merely a determinate property. In other words, propositions 13 and 14 suffice, between them, to exclude all other possibilities; whereas the previous pairs require a double negation in order to exclude middle ground onto which some other response could be interjected in the conceptual order. If soul is identical with body, the proposition that the soul "is and is not identical" with the body will be meaningless; similarly, if the soul is not identical with the body, the proposition that the soul "is and is not" (or "neither is nor is not") identical with the body is likewise devoid of signification. Hypothetical propositions 15 and 16 would be out of place, then. The fact that tradition omits them, far from presenting a problem, actually helps shed light on the question. What the Buddha is doing, then, is not denying the principles of identity and noncontradiction, but transcending any affirmation or negation that would rely on them exclusively.

We are dealing with *avyākṛtavastūni*—things (literally) inseparable, ineffable, inexpressible—things "inexplicable,"[27] in the etymological sense of being so tightly intertwined as to thwart all unraveling.[28] The principles of identity and noncontradiction, properly speaking, or *primario et per se,* are logical principles—principles of thought, raised to the status of ontological principles in virtue of the "dogma" of identity, or at least of the adequation, of being and thinking. The Buddha has "seen further."

4. Let us observe that *avyākṛtavastūni* are not unknowable truths, but things *(vastūni)* that cannot be separated or untangled. Why not? Because, we are tempted to say, they are simple, they are primordial, they are

transcendent, they are beyond all analysis. However, it may be that we are unfaithful to the Buddha by saying anything at all, for he himself was silent.[29]

If my interpretation is correct, then it seems to me that the intentionality of the *avyākṛta* does not regard the logic of thought — does not bear upon a softening of the principle of noncontradiction or of the excluded third, but rather points to the imperfection, the limitation, the inability to express the real, intrinsic first of all to the verb "to be" and then to the very concept of being, inasmuch as, ultimately, being itself is not deprived of membership in the kingdom of the impermanent, the changeable, the contingent. There are actually propositions that are inexpressible, owing to the limited grasp of the ontological comprehension available to us. Accordingly, although there is no third alternative between A and not-A, there is between "is" and "is not." Here, it seems to me, is the root of more than one misunderstanding in this area — not excluding that of Buddhistic "atheism." One falls victim to a reifying logic in which the schema is nothing other than the "object" A, whether identical with itself or not. On the contrary, what we are dealing with here is not the object. It is not as if the Buddha were concerned to defend a tripartite logic, and so managed to find middle ground where logic finds none. Our propositions tell us merely that A *is* B. But this does not exhaust the identity of A. Therefore there is room for "A *is-not* B," precisely because it is on account of an "A is-not B" that "A is not-B" likewise fails to exhaust the identity of A. This is why propositions 3 and 4 are invoked — to convert "to be" itself into an object of affirmation and negation, so that Śākyamuni — and his disciples after him — will see themselves constrained to deny that even one of *these* two propositions contains the truth. Only by transcending *ho logos* can one transcend *being*. The weakness, the inadequacy, lies not with B, or not-B, but with A itself, the subject itself, which neither is nor is not, and can therefore scarcely be self-identical. At bottom the Buddhistic intuition is single. Everything falls together: *anātma-vāda,* impermanence, momentaneity, universal concatenation and dependency, inexpressibility, nirvana, and silence.

Let us examine some particularly pregnant texts.

THE ONE THING NEEDFUL

Mālúnkyāputra, a disciple of the Buddha, once asked the Master the celebrated questions on the nature of the world and of existence, at the same time begging him, if he had no answer, to tell him so simply and honestly, and not evade the issue. And the Buddha replied:

> "Pray, Māluṅkyāputra, did I ever say to you, 'Come, Māluṅkyāputra, lead the religious life under me, and I will elucidate to you either that the world is eternal, or that the world is not eternal, . . . or that the saint neither exists nor does not exist after death'?"

"Nay, verily, Reverend Sir."

"Or did you ever say to me, 'Reverend Sir, I will lead the religious life under The Blessed One, on condition that The Blessed One elucidate to me either that the world is eternal, or that the world is not eternal, . . . or that the saint neither exists nor does not exist after death'?"

"Nay, verily, Reverend Sir."

"So you acknowledge, Māluṅkyāputra, that I have not said to you, 'Come, Māluṅkyāputra, lead the religious life under me and I will elucidate to you either that the world is eternal, or that the world is not eternal, . . . or that the saint neither exists nor does not exist after death;' and again that you have not said to me, 'Reverend Sir, I will lead the religious life under The Blessed One, on condition that The Blessed One elucidate to me either that the world is eternal, or that the world is not eternal, . . . or that the saint neither exists nor does not exist after death.' That being the case, vain man, whom are you so angrily denouncing?"

It was on this point that the Buddha spoke the parable about the man wounded by an arrow.

"Accordingly, Māluṅkyāputra, bear always in mind what it is that I have not elucidated, and what it is that I have elucidated. And what, Māluṅkyāputra, have I not elucidated? I have not elucidated, Māluṅkyāputra, that the world is eternal; I have not elucidated that the world is not eternal; I have not elucidated that the world is finite; I have not elucidated that the world is infinite; I have not elucidated that the soul and the body are identical; I have not elucidated that the soul is one thing and the body another; I have not elucidated that the saint exists after death; I have not elucidated that the saint does not exist after death; I have not elucidated that the saint both exists and does not exist after death; I have not elucidated that the saint neither exists nor does not exist after death. And why, Māluṅkyāputra, have I not elucidated this? Because, Māluṅkyāputra, this profits not, nor has to do with the fundamentals of religion, nor tends to aversion, absence of passion, cessation, quiescence, the supernatural faculties, supreme wisdom, and Nirvana; therefore have I not elucidated it.

"And what, Māluṅkyāputra, have I elucidated? Misery, Māluṅkyāputra, have I elucidated; the origin of misery have I elucidated; the cessation of misery have I elucidated; and the path leading to the cessation of misery have I elucidated. And why, Māluṅkyāputra, have I elucidated this? Because, Māluṅkyāputra, this does profit, has to do with the fundamentals of religion, and tends to aversion, absence of passion, cessation, quiescence, knowledge, supreme wisdom, and Nirvana; therefore have I elucidated it. Accordingly, Māluṅkyāputra, bear always in mind what it is that I have not elucidated, and what it is that I have elucidated."

Thus spake The Blessed One; and, delighted, the venerable Māluṅkyāputra applauded the speech of The Blessed One.[30]

TRUE FREEDOM IS INEFFABLE

Thus have I heard.

On a certain occasion The Blessed One was dwelling at Sāvatthi in Jetavana monastery in Anāthapindika's Park. Then drew near Vaccha, the wandering ascetic, to where The Blessed One was; and having drawn near, he greeted The Blessed One; and having passed the compliments of friendship and civility, he sat down respectfully at one side. And seated respectfully at one side, Vaccha, the wandering ascetic, spoke to The Blessed One as follows:

"How is it, Gotama? Does Gotama hold that the world is eternal, and that this view alone is true, and every other false?"

"Nay, Vaccha. I do not hold that the world is eternal, and that this view alone is true, and every other false."

"But how is it, Gotama? Does Gotama hold that the world is not eternal, and that this view alone is true, and every other false?"

"Nay, Vaccha. I do not hold that the world is not eternal, and that this view alone is true, and every other false."

"How is it, Gotama? Does Gotama hold that the world is finite, . . ."[31]

"How is it, Gotama? Does Gotama hold that the soul and the body are identical, . . ."

"How is it, Gotama? Does Gotama hold that the saint exists after death, . . ."

"How is it, Gotama? Does Gotama hold that the saint both exists and does not exist after death, and that this view alone is true, and every other false?"

"Nay, Vaccha. I do not hold that the saint both exists and does not exist after death, and that this view alone is true, and every other false."

"But how is it, Gotama? Does Gotama hold that the saint neither exists nor does not exist after death, and that this view alone is true, and every other false?"

"Nay, Vaccha. I do not hold that the saint neither exists nor does not exist after death, and that this view alone is true, and every other false."

"How is it, Gotama, that when you are asked, 'Does the monk Gotama hold that the world is eternal, and that this view alone is true, and every other false?' you reply, 'Nay, Vaccha. I do not hold that the world is eternal, and that this view alone is true, and every other false'?

"But how is it, Gotama, that when you are asked, 'Does the monk Gotama hold that the world is not eternal, and that this view alone is true, and every other false?' you reply, 'Nay, Vaccha. I do not hold that the world is not eternal, and that this view alone is true, and every other false'?

"How is it, Gotama, that when you are asked, 'Does Gotama hold that the world is finite, . . .'?

"How is it, Gotama, that when you are asked, 'Does Gotama hold that the soul and the body are identical, . . .'?

"How is it, Gotama, that when you are asked, 'Does Gotama hold that the saint exists after death, . . .'?

"How is it, Gotama, that when you are asked, 'Does the monk Gotama hold that the saint both exists and does not exist after death, and that this view alone is true, and every other false?' you reply, 'Nay, Vaccha. I do not hold that the saint both exists and does not exist after death, and that this view alone is true, and every other false'?

"But how is it, Gotama, that when you are asked, 'Does the monk Gotama hold that the saint neither exists nor does not exist after death, and that this view alone is true, and every other false?' you reply, 'Nay, Vaccha. I do not hold that the saint neither exists nor does not exist after death, and that this view alone is true, and every other false'? What objection does Gotama perceive to these theories that he has not adopted any one of them?"

"Vaccha, the theory that the world is eternal, is a jungle, a wilderness, a puppet-show, a writhing, and a fetter, and is coupled with misery, ruin, despair, and agony, and does not tend to aversion, absence of passion, cessation, quiescence, knowledge, supreme wisdom, and Nirvana.

"Vaccha, the theory that the saint neither exists nor does not exist after death, is a jungle, a wilderness, a puppet-show, a writhing, and a fetter, and is coupled with misery, ruin, despair, and agony, and does not tend to aversion, absence of passion, cessation, quiescence, knowledge, supreme wisdom, and Nirvana.

"This is the objection I perceive to these theories, so that I have not adopted any one of them."

"But has Gotama any theory of his own?"

"The Tathāgata, O Vaccha, is free from all theories; but this, Vaccha, does The Tathāgata know, — the nature of form, and how form arises, and how form perishes; the nature of sensation, and how sensation arises, and how sensation perishes; the nature of perception, and how perception arises, and how perception perishes; the nature of the predispositions, and how the predispositions arise, and how the predispositions perish; the nature of consciousness, and how consciousness arises, and how consciousness perishes. Therefore say I that The Tathāgata has attained deliverance and is free from attachment, inasmuch as all imaginings, or agitations, or proud thoughts concerning an Ego or anything pertaining to an Ego, have perished, have faded away, have ceased, have been given up and relinquished."

"But, Gotama, where is the priest reborn who has attained to this deliverance for his mind?"

"Vaccha, to say that he is reborn would not fit the case."

"Then, Gotama, he is not reborn."

"Vaccha, to say that he is not reborn would not fit the case."

"Then, Gotama, he is both reborn and is not reborn."

"Vaccha, to say that he is both reborn and not reborn would not fit the case."

"Then, Gotama, he is neither reborn nor not reborn."

"Vaccha, to say that he is neither reborn nor not reborn would not fit the case."

"When I say to you, 'But, Gotama, where is the priest reborn who has attained to this deliverance for his mind?' you reply, 'Vaccha, to say that he is reborn would not fit the case.' And when I say to you, 'Then, Gotama, he is not reborn,' you reply, 'Vaccha, to say that he is not reborn would not fit the case.' And when I say to you, 'Then, Gotama, he is both reborn and not reborn,' you reply, 'Vaccha, to say that he is both reborn and not reborn would not fit the case.' And when I say to you, 'Then, Gotama, he is neither reborn nor not reborn,' you reply, 'Vaccha, to say that he is neither reborn nor not reborn would not fit the case.' Gotama, I am at a loss what to think in this matter, and I have become greatly confused, and the faith in Gotama inspired by a former conversation has now disappeared."

"Enough, O Vaccha! Be not at a loss what to think in this matter, and be not greatly confused. Profound, O Vaccha, is this doctrine, recondite, and difficult of comprehension, good, excellent, and not to be reached by mere reasoning, subtle, and intelligible only to the wise; and it is a hard doctrine for you to learn, who belong to another sect, to another faith, to another persuasion, to another discipline, and sit at the feet of another teacher. Therefore, Vaccha, I will now question you, and do you make answer as may seem to you good. What think you, Vaccha? Suppose a fire were to burn in front of you, would you be aware that the fire was burning in front of you?"

"Gotama, if a fire were to burn in front of me, I should be aware that a fire was burning in front of me."

"But suppose, Vaccha, some one were to ask you, 'On what does this fire that is burning in front of you depend?' what would you answer, Vaccha?"

"Gotama, if some one were to ask me, 'On what does this fire that is burning in front of you depend?' I would answer, Gotama, 'It is on fuel of grass and wood that this fire that is burning in front of me depends.' "

"But, Vaccha, if the fire in front of you were to become extinct, would you be aware that the fire in front of you had become extinct?"

"Gotama, if the fire in front of me were to become extinct, I should be aware that the fire in front of me had become extinct."

"But, Vaccha, if some one were to ask you, 'In which direction has that fire gone — east, or west, or north, or south?' what would you say, O Vaccha?"

"The question would not fit the case, Gotama. For the fire which depended on fuel of grass and wood, when that fuel has all gone, and it can get no other, being thus without nutriment, is said to be extinct."

"In exactly the same way, Vaccha, all form by which one could predicate the existence of the saint, all that form has been abandoned, uprooted, pulled out of the ground like a palmyra-tree, and become non-existent and not liable to spring up again in the future. The saint, O Vaccha, who has been released from what is styled form, is deep, immeasurable, unfathomable, like the mighty ocean. To say that he is reborn would not fit the case. To say that he is not reborn would not fit the case. To say that he is both reborn and not reborn would not fit the case. To say that he is neither reborn nor not reborn would not fit the case.

"All sensation . . .

"All perception . . .

"All the predispositions . .

"All consciousness by which one could predicate the existence of the saint, all the consciousness has been abandoned, uprooted, pulled out of the ground like a palmyra-tree, and become non-existent and not liable to spring up again in the future. The saint, O Vaccha, who has been released from what is styled consciousness, is deep, immeasurable, unfathomable, like the mighty ocean. To say that he is reborn would not fit the case. To say that he is not reborn would not fit the case. To say that he is both reborn and not reborn would not fit the case. To say that he is neither reborn nor not reborn would not fit the case."

When The Blessed One had thus spoken, Vaccha, the wandering ascetic, spoke to him as follows:

"It is as if, O Gotama, there were a mighty sal-tree[32] near to some village or town, and it were to lose its dead branches and twigs, and its loose shreds of bark, and its unsound wood, so that afterwards, free from those branches and twigs, and the loose shreds of bark, and the unsound wood, it were to stand neat and clean in its strength. In exactly the same way doth the word Gotama, free from branches and twigs, and from loose shreds of bark, and from unsound wood, stand neat and clean in its strength. O wonderful is it, Gotama! O wonderful is it, Gotama![33]

NO ADEQUATE RESPONSE

Then Vacchagotta the Wanderer went to visit the Exalted One . . . and said:

"Now, master Gotama, is there a self?"

At these words the Exalted One was silent.

"How, then, master Gotama, is there not a self?"

For a second time also the Exalted One was silent.

Then Vacchagotta the Wanderer rose from his seat and went away.

Now not long after the departure of the Wanderer, the venerable Ānanda said to the Exalted One:

"How is it, lord, that the Exalted One gave no answer to the question of the Wanderer Vacchagotta?"

"If, Ānanda, when asked by the Wanderer: 'Is there a self?' I had replied to him: 'There is a self,' then, Ānanda, that would be siding with the recluses and brahmins who are eternalists.

"But, if Ānanda, when asked: Is there not a self?' I had replied that it does not exist, that Ānanda, would be siding with those recluses and brahmins who are annihilationists.

"Again, Ānanda, when asked by the Wanderer: 'Is there a self?' had I replied that there is, would my reply be in accordance with the knowledge that all things are impermanent?'

"Surely not, lord."

"Again, Ānanda, when asked by Vacchagotta the Wanderer: 'Is there not a self?' had I replied that there is not, it would have been more bewilderment for the bewildered Vacchagotta. For he would have said: 'Formerly indeed I had a self, but now I have not one any more.' "[34]

THE TYPICAL BUDDHISTIC CALM[35]

At that time, not seeing any chair on which he could sit in the dwelling of sick Vimalakīrti], Śariputra thought to himself, "Where will the assembly of the bodhisattvas and their disciples be able to sit?" Vimalakīrti said to him, "Why have you come, to listen to the *dharma* or to look for a chair?" . . . Vimalakīrti said, "O, Śariputra, "the one who looks for *dharma* attaches no value to life or to the body; much less should you concern yourself about a chair. . . ." The one who looks for *dharma* has no attachment to the Buddha, or to *dharma*, oɪ the *saṅgha*. The one who looks for *dharma* does not at all look for the contemplation of sorrow, nor does he look for the cessation of sorrow, nor does he look to walk the path that leads to the extinction of sorrow. And why? Because *dharma* stands apart from whatsoever discourse. . . .

Dharma knows of no attachment; if there were attachment to *dharma, nirvāṇa* would be a bonding. . . . There is no refuge in *dharma*. If there were refuge in *dharma,* there would be attachment to the refuge, and not the pure search for *dharma.* . . . The one who searches for *dharma* should not search for anything [else] in *dharma.*[36]

She said, "When did you attain liberation?" Śariputra, remaining in silence, did not answer. The divine maiden asked him again, "Why do you remain so silent although you are so venerable and intelligent?" Śariputra answered, "Liberation stands apart from all discourse. Hence I do not know what to say." The celestial nymph said to him, "Every word and every letter are aspects of liberation. Why? Because liberation does not take up a position inside or in the middle. And so, Śariputra, it is impossible to speak of liberation apart from letters. Why? All things are aspects of liberation." Śariputra asked, "Perhaps liberation is to be freed of passion, anger, and ignorance." The heavenly girl replied, "The Buddha calls liberation being freed of all passion, anger, and ignorance only for those who are egocentric. For those who are not egocentric the Buddha will say that the nature of passion, anger, and ignorance is liberation itself." Śariputra said, "O maiden, very well said, very well said. Who made you so eloquent?" She answered, "I have not obtained anything, I have not acquired anything. That is why I am so eloquent. And why? If someone thinks he has obtained or acquired something, that person, according to the *dharma* of the Buddha, is called an egocentric. The Vimalakīrti, turning to all the bodhisattvas, said, "O venerable ones, how can a bodhisattva penetrate the doctrine of nonduality? I ask you, please, to explain it with the light of your intelligence." There was in the assembly a bodhisattva named Dharmeśvara, who spoke as follows. . . .[37]

Then Mañjuśri turned to Vimalakīrti and said, "Until now each one of us has been explaining his own opinion. Lord, I wish now that you would explain your opinion of what it means for a bodhisattva to penetrate the doctrine of nonduality."

Vimalakīrti remained silent; he did not say a word.

Mañjuśri praised him, saying, "Very good, very good. There certainly are no better words. This is exactly what it means to penetrate perfectly the doctrine of nonduality."[38]

Part III

Interpretation

8

Change of Human Awareness, Then and Now

Avert thy glance, that I may compose myself
before I go and no longer am.[1]

ATHEISTIC RELIGION

To be sure, one could attempt to "justify the Buddha's atheism" with an appeal to the history of his time. One could point to the religious inflation of the Brahmanism of his day, and insist that the attitude of the Enlightened One is altogether comprehensible simply in terms of a healthy reaction to baroque religion.[2] A bit of sobriety, a call to return to the essential — which turns out to be the existential — would more than account for the phenomenon of the Buddha.[3]

For my part, I have no doubt that this is indeed true. But it is precisely on this account that I am loath to content myself with an explanation of the Buddha's attitude based on a reference to superficialities. Let us plumb the reasons in their anthropological depth.

Human consciousness is faced with three great problems — problems that have troubled humanity ever since it began to make use of its faculty for thought. They are: the world, the godhead, and humankind.

The World

The first reality that human beings discover is not themselves, but the things around them, the things that threaten them or protect them. The first philosophical position (or prephilosophical, if one prefers) is an ecstatic attitude toward things. We wonder what things are. Astrology, music, and medicine are the first sciences; in parallel fashion, agriculture, hunting, and architecture become the first technologies. Nature is full of "things," some of them hostile, some of them benign, and human beings must ascertain their behavior and adapt to them. Humans are fully aware of the world around them, and religion as a way of salvation—however it be interpreted—follows a path of pure objectivity: what counts is right action, in due respect for human constants and the rhythm of the universe alike. The principal human form of worship is the offering of firstfruits, with a view to the propitiation of natural forces.[4] What we are today accustomed to call the supernatural, the superhuman, even the divine, still had the aspect of a metacosmic "numinous," standing in intimate relationship with the "things," physical or psychical, that filled the human world.

Human beings seemed not to know themselves, or even to be aware of their peculiar position in the cosmos. A human being was just one more thing among so many others. This is how all men and women considered themselves to be, and they behaved accordingly. Consciousness was full, but self-consciousness had not yet been awakened. In mythological terminology we might call this period that of paradisiac innocence, where original sin had not yet been committed on a cultural level. The human mind had not yet folded back upon itself.[5]

The Deity

Things, by their beauty or their wickedness, by their power or their weakness, seemed to point to something different from and superior to themselves, some invisible force or supreme power—immanent or transcendent, but always unattainable and hidden. Human beings noticed that they were not alone in the universe—that they were in the company of a great many other beings, superior beings, protecting them or thwarting them just as the things around them had always done.

Humans studied the world of the gods and the place of God, interpreted in the most varied forms. They discovered their own dependence on this or that force, this or that god, and could not but try to stabilize a relationship with the numinous world. Religion was what regulated relationships with the suprahuman sphere and permitted humankind to determine to what extent it could approach the divine.

Sacrifice was a primary category, a sacred act that stabilized the bond between the human and the suprahuman. Sacrifice differs from the offering of firstfruits because of the awareness that the human being had something to offer of itself ("fruit of its own labor"), and not only to return what had been received from divinity.[6]

Sacrifice is the religious moment par excellence: the presence of the numinous seems to absorb every human faculty. There is scarcely place for anything else: created things are considered unimportant, and the human being is overlooked. Human activity no longer turns to things, but to the sacred. Temples are more important than are houses. The best that society has to offer—whether persons or things—is dedicated to the divinity, from virgins to fields. The sciences cultivated are those that come to be called sacred sciences. The principal human interest is not about the earth but about the heavens. The king and the savant are subordinated to the priest, if these roles are not already united in a single person.

This does not mean that every stage of history derives from the preceding stage as its inevitable development. I wish only to point out these two attitudes of the human mind, influenced also by a different lifestyle: being ecstatic vis-à-vis things, and letting oneself be absorbed by divinity. There is no doubt that one stage has preceded another "kairologically," but we cannot say, with the evolutionistic thesis, that the one is the "development" of the other, and therefore, implicitly, give a value judgment, "preferring" the successive stage as the better. Between the two stages there is a revolutionary leap in the social, economic, religious, and philosophical field, whose scope escapes us, inasmuch as our history, like our protohistory, generally originates only at the moment of the disengagement of the cosmic from the divine.

The Human Race

If in this world things point to God, God points to humankind, as it were. God's interest seems to be concentrated on human beings. They seem to be the object of the divine preoccupation. The gods, without the world of mortals, seem somehow to lose their raison d'être. Thus it comes about that, discovering God's attention to be focused on themselves, human beings as it were follow this divine glance and in turn discover themselves. After a certain period of reflection on themselves, they finally conclude that they themselves are at the very center of reality.[7]

Things now shift into a constitutive relationship with humankind. God is interiorized, to the point that a divinity that existed for itself alone would be all but meaningless. Human beings discover themselves, and within themselves find (or lose) both God and things. This is the moment of the awakening of self-consciousness, or reflexive consciousness, a moment quite like that of the great religious reforms. For a certain period of time, anthropocentrism will evaporate. It will be dissimulated, manifesting itself rather as a purification and interiorization of the notion of deity.

Then it will return with a vengeance. Once human beings have come to consider themselves unambiguously the "measure of all things,"[8] once humankind is mediator between heaven and earth, the human being becomes the center of a self-reference. The word of humankind becomes ultimate reality[9] and is transformed into a primordial word (*vāc*).[10] It is divinized.[11] Now the *logos*, identified with the cosmic Christ,[12] has thrust all else aside. Even God, certain Christian theologians will come to say, is devoid of all existential meaning except through Christ, who humanizes God and thereby transforms divinity into something real.[13]

THE CRISIS OF HUMAN CONSCIOUSNESS

These three phases, here sketched in bare outline, are not, let me repeat, three dialectical moments of an automatic process. The sequence of occurrences—historical and individual—may at times look like an evolutionary process at work in human history, as indeed there can at times be in the development of the given individual. In point of fact, however, these historical changes are but seldom the products of an internal process. More often they are due to the vigorous intervention of some one or several persons whose dynamic intuitions unleash a revolutionary change. This is surely what occurred in the change undergone by civilization at the beginning of the second and first millenniums B.C., with the birth of the great Middle Eastern, then the Greek and Roman, civilizations, shortly after the Vedic, although the rise of these civilizations is lost in the origins of our protohistory. This is also what occurs around the turn of the seventh and sixth centuries, in the era of the Buddha, which represents as it were the third moment in the history of humanity in the schema I have proposed.

Almost certainly, in 563 B.C.,[14] at Kapilavastu (Kapilavatthu), the principal city of the Śākyas, was born Siddharta, the son of Śuddhodana and Māyādevī, probably of the family (*gotra, genos*) of the Gautamas.[15] This sixth century before Christ saw a series of events so new that they have inclined historians to posit the existence of a particular *Zeitgeist*, which they dub a "historical axis."[16] Indeed the change wrought in the human race at this moment is profound.[17] This is the century in which astrology, humanity's first science, takes a new direction.[18] This is the century of the beginning of the great trek from *mythos* to *logos*, a process perhaps coming to something like a conclusion only in our own age of "demythization." Fissures now appear in humanity's ecstatic consciousness, permitting the infiltration of a self-reflection that will grow and expand to our very day.

Let us now consider some very basic data that will aid us in acquiring the outlook we shall need for a comprehension of the scope of the Buddhist religious revolution. Of course we must not forget that, in order to set in relief the main lines of our story, we must perforce simplify a number of extremely complex religio-cultural processes.

Were we to attempt to sketch these main lines in broad strokes, we should speak of a tissue of *mythos, logos*, and *spirit*. Humankind cannot live without myth. But neither are human beings fully human until they have developed their logical potential and spiritual capacities as well.[19] Just as the essence of the "primitivism" of an archaic culture lies in its mystical characteristics, so the essence of the "barbarian character" of contemporary Western culture lies not in the material component of a given civilization, but in the supreme power that it confers on the *logos*. If there is a single concept in which we might capsulize the contribution that the Buddha could make to our times, it is the conviction that the *logos* cannot be divinized in any of its forms, either ontological or epistemological or cosmic. *Mythos* and *logos* can exist only in *spirit*. But spirit cannot be "manipulated," either by *mythos* or by *logos*.

The spirit is freedom, and freedom may not be converted into either *mythos* or *logos,* or indeed into both at once. And if the sixth century largely represents the awakening of the *logos* in the word of its great reformers, the Buddha's share in this great religious upheaval is all but unique, for it is the Buddha who directly stresses the importance of the silence of the spirit.

Israel

In 587 B.C. Jerusalem fell to Babylonian invaders. The turning point in history represented by the fall of Jerusalem is a qualitative change less in history itself, however, than in the very consciousness of the Semitic peoples.[20] Even Christianity, through its ties to the Old Testament, registers the change of scenario effected by the Babylonian captivity, and this event will forever stand as the symbol of an axiological change for European peoples.[21]

But the fall of the temple of Jerusalem represents the triumph of the religion of Israel rather than its collapse. Generally when national religions, bound up with a single people, lose their places of worship, they collapse. The opposite happened with Israel. How is this to be explained?

A transformation of the religious awareness of this people had already taken place. This was precisely the accomplishment of the great prophets of the century just past—those colossal, solitary figures, so often in conflict with the "official" prophets, who rose up against the representatives of tradition and convention, and not only preached the purification of worship from all its syncretistic influences,[22] but introduced radical innovations in that worship.[23] The great prophets of Israel shattered the cosmic notion of sacrifice that had so often become a matter of mere magic, and substituted the interior sacrifice of moral comportment.[24] "Mercy, not sacrifice" now constituted the leitmotiv of the prophetic preaching.[25] Humankind began to be more important than the act of worship, and mercy and social justice became a form of worship more agreeable to the divinity than sheer ritual could ever be.

The effects of this change of attitude toward worship were not limited to the area of liturgy, where it indeed provoked a radical renewal. Now the very concept of God was called into question, and with it human relationship to that God.[26] By the time the enemy was within striking distance of Jerusalem, and about to destroy the places of worship, especially the principal one, the temple, the localization of worship in a fixed, exclusive place had already lost most of its deeper significance. Thus Yahweh had relatively little difficulty surviving the catastrophe.[27] Yahweh survived the destruction of the temple because Yahweh had been delivered from nationalistic particularism, and had been transformed into a single, personal God with the care of all nations.[28] Paradoxically, it was precisely

Israel's surrender of its own God, a God of one people alone, that placed the nation in a position to be entrusted with a special charge and mission in the economy of salvation. Now this salvation was the work of Yahweh who was concerned with other peoples as well.[29]

In a word, Israel's religiousness became reflexive. Now it was human beings and their individual requirements that were the center of the prophets' concerns. Worship, for its part, now interiorized so as to allow commitment to a superior social justice, had also been universalized, simultaneously universalizing the deity to whom it was addressed.[30]

In a word, humankind now emerged as a social entity.

Iran

During the same period, just before 600 B.C., in Iran, at the hands of a solitary prophet of the first magnitude, an analogous transformation occurs.[31] Reacting to a religiousness resting primarily on a ritual relationship between humanity and the divinity, a religiousness erected chiefly on the sacrifice of oxen,[32] Zarathustra rose up as a reformer whose religion was centered on humankind, and his message was one no longer simply of collective salvation, but of personal salvation as well. Humanity is at the center of the great cosmic struggle between the principles of good and evil. Human beings bear the burden not only of their own destiny, but of the transformation of the whole world.[33] Humankind is no longer a simple spectator in this great cosmic struggle between the principles of good and evil, at the mercy of superior forces, as had so often been the case with the religions of the first two stages described here. Now humankind is at the very center of the struggle, called to effectuate the final, eschatological victory of good over evil.

This responsibility implies freedom, and freedom demands that moral behavior step front and center. Personal conscience is elevated to the status of the ultimate norm of morality.[34] Complicated ritual mechanisms are eliminated. So are bloody sacrifices. Both are replaced with the consecration of one's own life and actions.[35] Not only does the human position become central; the concept of divinity itself is transformed. Ahura Mazda, the "thinking Lord," or "wise Lord,"[36] is not only one, but in his very universality is absolute spirit, creator ex nihilo through the mediation of his own intellective activity,[37] and, at least in the beginning, altogether beyond the notorious dualism of good and evil traditionally attributed to the Iranian conception.[38] God is the Holy par excellence.[39]

Summing up: with Zarathustra, humankind emerges as personal conscience.

China

During this same period, the great civilization of China passed through a similar politico-social and religious crisis, experiencing, in Confucius and

Lao-tzu, the same reaction (if in different modalities) to a fossilized cosmic-imperial order and a resultant thrust toward a more personal sense of justice and morality. The reaction is typical, we see. One rejects ritualism and answers the call of personal conscience, thereby discovering the nature of one's own salvation and that of the whole world.

To be sure, Confucius will repeatedly assert the salvific import of the act of worship. But he will insist no less energetically that that particular action is salvific only when performed with a reflexive awareness of the rites, and only if the individuals performing them are conscious of their place in the cosmos. Behavior is what counts. For the rest: silence.[40]

Once more the human element is at the center of all religious concern. Wisdom holds first place among values.[41] As for the divinity, Confucius's reform refuses to allow itself to be drawn into metaphysical speculations. Confucius's message is eminently practical.

For Lao-tzu, on the other hand, humankind is saved only through mystical union with the Tao, on a level superior to all ritual apparatus.[42]

Even here the process is ultimately the same: *personalization*.[43]

Greece

This same passage from the cosmological to the anthropological is to be observed, in striking, profound fashion, in the Greece of this period. The spirit of the Greek movement is markedly religious, and this explains the almost religious fervor of the great figures of the time, however it may be that their formulations and speculative thrust belong to the order that has subsequently come to be called philosophical. The absence of a central prophetic personage is counterbalanced by the speculative character of the reform.

Humankind ceases to be just one thing among many. The human being is transformed into a spectator, and later, into a judge, and with a critical attitude goes in quest of the unity that lies hidden in multiplicity. Let us observe that, for an ingenuous mentality, plurality is the datum and unity the problem; whereas, by contrast, a critical mentality perceives multiplicity as unintelligible, provisional, and struggling for oneness at any price. Setting aside traditional mythology, and taking their point of departure in an autonomous critical reflection, the first philosophers did not convert Zeus, Ananke, and so on, into a First Principle, but sought the unity of apparent multiplicity elsewhere. Thales of Miletus, for example, sees water as the primordial element in which all things subsist.[44] Anaximander[45] and Anaximenes[46] spiritualize and intellectualize this principle into something less palpable, such as *to apeiron* ("the limitless"), or air as indivisible.[47] These thinkers do not yet advert to the deep conflict between the new intellectual exigencies and traditional religion. Only with Xenophanes will we finally have a global condemnation of mythology, in virtue of a moral exigency.[48] Not without reason was Xenophanes dubbed "the theologian."[49]

The pioneers who would reconcile the demands of intellectual research with a deep, and markedly personal, religiousness, will be, especially, a Heraclitus, an Empedocles, a Pythagoras. The last will found a school whose purpose will be personal salvation.[50] Empedocles—later worshiped as a god—teaches, besides a cosmology and a scientific metaphysics, a method of escape from the cycle of reincarnations.[51] Heraclitus discovers, as it were, the *logos*,[52] the cornerstone of the whole subsequent Western edifice.[53]

At about the same time, we see a resurgence of interest in the Mysteries, especially the Orphic and the Eleusinian. The latter will soon attain the peak of their splendor.[54] And this is of significance, inasmuch as the center of the salvation that the Mysteries preach and secure is precisely the individual.

The movement is the same in other places and other cultures. Still, it cannot be denied that the Greek miracle of this period—irreversible and everlasting, inasmuch as the clock of history cannot be turned back—is the discovery of humankind in its secularity.[55]

India

India knew no period of crisis like Israel's, where the people knew it was on the verge of catastrophe, or Iran's, where religious reform had an economic and social aspect, or the one in Greece, where tremendous political upheavals occurred, or China's, where the imperial order was contested. In India the principal movement was interior, and began with the priestly class, with individuals who had perceived the necessity of a simplification of their sacrificial worship. To be sure, the spiritual history of Dravidian India has yet to be written.

In India the phenomenon seems universal. Besides Buddhism, we have Vardhamāna Mahāvīra, practically the founder of the Jain religion, preaching his message of renunciation and total nonviolence by virtue of this same attention to interiority, by virtue of a human meditation on the human subject of that meditation.[56]

But it is not only in the so-called heterodox systems of reaction against Brahmanism that this movement is manifested. At the heart of orthodoxy itself we witness a whole movement of interiorization, antiritualism, and antitraditionalism. We have personages like Uddalaka Āruni, we have his son Śvetaketu, we have King Janaka. We have the celebrated genius Yājnāvalkya, especially, and of course we have Śandilya. All of these are eager to see traditional religion preserve its continuity, and not break with the Vedic *śruti*. And yet, they profoundly alter and transform Hinduism.[57] Their reaction—these vessels of a new awareness whose repercussions will be felt not only in a different conceptualization of humankind, but also in a new idea of the deity itself—is a matter of historical record. Even the relationship between the divine and the human is no longer lived according to the Vedic schema, with its great emphasis on a *karma-mārga*. Now that relationship takes the form of an intellective, cognitive process, replacing the karmic structure of the old ritual without destroying it — claiming indeed to exalt it.[58] In short: *Aham brahman*: The I in *brahman*.

Thus the meditating human becomes the center of the salvific, and sacrificial, process. At the same time the very divinity is unified and universalized. We find this even in the later hymns of the *Rg Veda*, with their search for unity in multiplicity.[59] The single principle underlying all and present in all is the *brahman*,[60] which is compared with salt dissolved in water, lending its savor to the whole loaf.[61] The *brahman* is thereupon identified with the *ātman*, and the discovery of this equation is the foundation of the Upanishadic way of salvation.[62] The efficacy of rite consists not in the external action, but in the intention, and ultimately in consciousness.[63] Meditation on the sacrifice is equivalent to the sacrificial action itself.[64] The offering of self,[65] including the oblation of the word in and from the breath residing in the word,[66] conducts its subjects to the sublimation of all cultic worship in the realization of the self: *tat tvam asi*.[67] If Greece, in this period, has discovered the human principle of all things, India notes the divine principle in humankind: *aham brahmāsmi*.[68]

In this context, the revolution of Gautama the Buddha seems more intelligible, if scarcely less extraordinary. Indeed, the context in which the Buddha's message appears is not, it seems to me, susceptible of circumscription by the particular ambient of his immediate environment, but belongs rather to that decisive, peculiar moment in the history of humanity at which, sociologically at least, the human consciousness of subjectivity appears. In all the cases I have cited from that remarkable sixth century, there is a common denominator: on the one hand, a reaction against pure objectivity, whether that objectivity goes by the name of ritualism, transcendence, God, tradition, custom, or what have you, and on the other hand, the ascent of humankind. The great prophets of Israel, the sages of the Upanishads, the great Chinese reformers, the Greek philosophers, and so on, only turn the searching regard of humankind inward, to discover that the intention is essential in any activity, and that a critical attitude is indispensable for any genuinely human act. Never again will it be possible blindly to follow the opinion of the ancients or to have a magical faith in traditional rites. What matters is human beings, and consequently their intention. Mere speculative disquisitions, which the Buddha labels useless and pernicious, represent dead objectivity here. What matters is the concrete person and his or her existential liberation. All ideas, not excluding the idea of God, are a sort of refuge where human beings have fled because they were afraid of themselves. The Buddha seeks to deliver human beings from all these fears, making them aware of a decisive, universal fact that is surely a testimony of unanimous human experience: the fact of suffering, and of our innate tendency to deliver ourselves from it.

What counts are not things, but humankind, Greece will say. The essential is not external sacrifice and ritual worship, but the human intention, and interiorization, the Upanishads will preach. The essential is consciousness of the harmony of humankind with the all, China will teach. The fundamental thing is conscious personal salvation, Zarathustra will preach. Yahweh does not save or hear unless our heart is pure, the prophets of Israel will cry. Human beings and their consciousness are transformed into the heart of the religious and human reforms of the time.

Humanism, with its peaks and troughs, begins its course through human history.

THE BUDDHA'S REVOLUTION

The phenomenon just summarized is by and large common to the universal reform of the sixth century B.C. But in the Buddha we discover a new tonality. All the other reform movements are centered on humankind. The Buddhist preaching simply transcends it. The Buddha directly addresses Origen's fourth principle: *revelation*.[69] Revelation for the Buddha is the unveiling of the way of salvation, without ontological frills of any kind—neither the world, nor divinity, nor humanity.[70] Just as each of the first three principles has had a tendency to swallow the other two, as it were, this fourth principle, analogously, leaves the other three in the shadows, if indeed it does not prescind from them.

To what avail is it to demythicize God, the Buddha would surely ask us, could he use the language of our time, if we thereupon mythicize the human? What advantage is there in discovering how easy it is to transform God into an idol, if we thereupon set humankind in God's place?

The three basic questions are cut off at the root by the Buddha. What are the *things* of the world? Who is the *God* who sustains them? Who are the *human beings* who enjoy and know them? In order to transcend any response, he dissolves the questions with his silence. He cancels the very locus of human query, and asks trust in his salvific enlightenment—for he believes that all others can attain it as well. He states that the only thing that matters is right *action* for the purpose of achieving the extinction of all limitation, contingency, and therefore existence itself. If we look carefully, we see that the trust the Buddha asks is not a new acceptance of someone else's experience, but a reliance on our own experience once it has been enlightened. It is not a matter, then, of the renunciation of knowing, on the implicit presupposition that there is something real to know and some real subject to do the knowing. It is a question of recognizing that creatureliness cannot transcend itself, and that consequently nothing in the order of being, nothing that develops in space and time, can be included in the realization of what ultimately matters. And what ultimately matters is the orthopraxis that eliminates contingency—that is, suffering.

Humanity at the time of the Buddha was discovering self-awareness. The Buddha goes further. He discovers the fallacy of this self. That is, he shows us how, despite all, this *autos*, the self of consciousness, is regarded as a *heteros*, a more or less objectified other. When the subject directs its regard to itself, when the subject becomes self-consciousness, it reifies itself, objectivizes itself—it ceases, at bottom, to be subject. It splits itself in two, and one part of itself (at least the part that is known) is converted into an object. The deepest awareness cannot be self-awareness. In other words, the identity A *is* A is impossible. It is a deception. Either A *is* A', and then the identity is not complete, or else the identity is absolute—A *is* A—and then the identity is superfluous, for absolutely everything that the first A *is* is what the second A *is*, so that it becomes simply meaningless to speak of a first or second A. The only nontautological formulation, then, would be the simple proposition, A *is*. But at this point the Buddha would say: the A that *is* in "A *is*" is the A that would be not the subject of the formula of identity, but its predicate. That is, the first A *is* not; the only thing that is, is the second A: *is* A. There is no identity, because there is no subject. Whatever *is*, is predicate; therefore we exist. Surely we are the predicates of a subject that is not a subject at all—for in expressing the world, or rather in expressing being, the subject has died, has emptied itself altogether, has totally immolated itself, has given all that it has and that it was, all that is its own authentic, total expression, to its *logos*, its manifestation, its epiphany, its person, its cosmos, its world, its *saṃsāra*.[71]

It is the failure to understand the Buddha's genial intuition in conceiving reality that has led more than one scholar to say that Buddhism is not a religion.[72] And indeed, what is specifically sacred and traditionally religious belongs to the second phase of human consciousness, the theocentric. Thus, for example, religious, sacral Christianity, as it has commonly been interpreted until now, belongs to this second kairological moment. Christianity—and, strictly speaking, the intuitions of the sixth century B.C.—had to pierce the thick crust of twenty-five centuries to come to a general awareness of humanity. This is what is commonly called "secularization" today (divorcing it from its overnarrow historical origins): the secularization of both culture and religion. Its result can be called "secularity."[73] To be sure, more than one attempt has been made, down the archway of the centuries, to express that other dimension of humankind and of reality. But perhaps humanity as a whole was not yet mature enough for that. Perhaps the other two dimensions would have risked being eliminated altogether. Sociologically, Christianity's role in the West has consisted in maintaining a link with the first two dimensions, and in resisting with might and main any premature victory of the third. But the fate of the human race largely depends on its capacity to harmonize all three dimensions. It is here that the role of the Enlightened One seems to me to be of an exceptional importance.

I realize, of course, that the initiative, like the acute awareness of the problematic, lies with Christianity this time, or better, with the West. But perhaps the solution is to be found in a symbiosis between the traditional and the contemporary religions of East and West.

Strictly speaking, can there be an atheistic religion? The Buddha's answer is trenchant. Only an atheist religion can actually be a religion. All the rest is idolatry, the worship of a God who is the work of our hands or our mind.[74]

The Buddha will not say that God is a "creation" of the human mind. After all, neither is a fetish a total creation of the idolatrous artist. There is the material, just as there is God. There is the adorability of the material, just as there is the divine demand that we adore God. But just as the theist will object to the fetishist that the latter is forgetting that God infinitely transcends the idol, so, analogously, the Buddha will reproach the theist for having forgotten that "God" is still infinitely distant from what the theist claims to worship, or at least to name.[75] The word "supratheism" would be as unsatisfactory as "theism," for strictly speaking no word can express that which declares itself inexpressible.[76]

The Buddha does not elaborate on the transcendent character of the divinity. Just because he believes that the divine mystery is transcendent, he prescinds from it altogether—he is not God's keeper and defender—and addresses himself to the ultimate end of religion: human salvation, showing others the way. Buddhism is religion not because it "re-links," as the Latin etymology suggests, but because it disconnects, because it liberates.

The Buddha's century is a religious century par excellence. All of its reforms, even the most advanced and daring, even those that sounded scandalous at the time, were religious reforms. The novelty of Śākyamuni's revolution consists in the elimination of what so many of his day and ours think to be the basic religious category: God. It cannot be denied, then, that the concept of a godless religion, or better, of atheistic religion, if correctly understood, corresponds to the religion of the Buddha. This, in my view, is at once the point of contact and the difference between Buddhism and the attitude of our own times. Religious atheism, a religion without God (to use language that would have sounded strange indeed to his ears), was what the Buddha preached. And a denial of God as the basis of life (that is, of the human religious attitude), epitomizes and synthesizes the phenomenon of contemporary atheism.

RELIGIOUS ATHEISM

We lack the vantage point, obviously, that would enable us to characterize our time definitively, the outlook from which we might authoritatively recognize the "signs of the times."[77] Still, it does not seem to me that I would be very far from the mark if I acknowledge in so-called contemporary atheism a new, urgent phenomenon of the first magnitude, one of the great moments of humanity, deserving to be placed side by side with the sixth century before the Christian era. To be sure, certain external aspects of our epoch are of an astounding novelty. I need only mention the discovery of the sciences, and the technological achievements that have created conditions and human situations that would have been simply inconceivable a hundred years ago. Nevertheless, this is all only superficial modification—whether by way of cause or effect is of no concern here—in comparison with the more basic questions, regarding not what humankind can and should do, but what its very being is. The new situation alters not just our doing, but our being. Science and technology can be cultivated— and actually are, in the case of the majority of persons who reap their fruits—with a traditional mentality, more or less corrected and adapted. But something new is happening to human beings. A change is occurring in their very structures. The change suggests a biological mutation.[78] Technology is penetrating the very being of humankind, like an intravenous injection. Not that humanity is necessarily dominated by the machine, not that the machine has conquered humanity—but it seems as if a hybrid, a new type of humankind, is in the process of painful, and problematic, gestation. Great perceptive, prophetic figures and thinkers have appeared, yes, but scarcely any of the stature of a Śākyamuni, a Zarathustra, or a Confucius, any of the stature of a representative of the whole course of the age, any in a position to guide, "sublimate," cause to "precipitate" (in the chemical sense of the word), or at least to assist at the birth of, the "new humankind" still in gestation.[79] So far the chief attempt has been to furnish a basis for social, sociological, and even economic comportment. The problem has not yet been addressed from a deeply religious standpoint, a theological and anthropological standpoint, in the awareness that a structural human mutation is transpiring. That is, a *gauging force* is still wanting, one that could intuit the direction this change might or ought to take. What is needed today is a force that, in the old, traditional schema, could be defined as "prophetic "—in order to search out, with the authority of fully lived personal experience, a path to the altogether human assimilation and vanquishing of the new, dehumanizing positions imposed by contemporary civilization.

Further, such a force would need to operate in partnership with another that could be defined as a *unifying* force (having the function that traditionally developed from the ancient "royal" power), and having the capability of authoritatively channeling the various currents of humanity's atheistic change in a harmonious coordination. Without this coordinating power, there is the risk either of seeing the message of "modernity" dispersed in rivulets of neither form nor consistency, or else of attributing a value to aspects that are actually sterile or too unilateral.

But if such an individual figure, or movement, endowed with this manner of unifying force could finally be produced, we would still require a *mediating force*, between the human situation and a transcendence that, precisely as such, escapes human experience. The human situation may appear self-sufficient in its reciprocal solidarity, but the fact remains that, shut up within its own limits, it will suffocate. Its very sacrality projects it toward the infinite, toward eternity, and unless it is willing to remain irremediably closed off within the spatio-temporal coordinates that delimit it, it will have to be able to find a mediation with an extrahuman order of salvation. This is the traditional function known by the name of "priesthood."

These three conjoined forces would be indispensable, first, in order to embody the spirit of the present time—to channel the spirit of our time toward a physiognomy that would not be too scattering or dehumanizing—and secondly, to supply an orientation to the new generations that can no longer breathe the air of the prairies of an "agricultural civilization," but who are as yet without the capacity to live a fully human life again in the world of *techniculture*. In the new framework, already taking shape in outline, it is not, after all, the objectivity of science and technology, or relationships with the social environment, that have produced what is really important, but their subjectivity—which is penetrating human beings and transforming them right down to their essence.

Now, it is precisely here, and in this new and profound sense, that the phenomenon of atheism appears, which I am endeavoring to grasp in its contemporary dimension. Atheism represents precisely one of the most tangible signs of the anthropological change that I have been sketching—understanding the word in its merited depth and seriousness, of which its polemical use by critics and apologists sometimes deprives it. The atheism to which I refer is not that of the "moderns" who have pronounced God dead. Nor does it reside in the fact—although this, as well, is new in the history of humanity—that an ever-increasing number of persons live a practical atheism. This is surely an important phenomenon, but, precisely in virtue of its importance, it has already been adequately investigated, and I surely need not dwell on it here.[80] Rather, the new phenomenon in the contemporary movement of the West is that those who declare themselves believers define themselves as unbelievers by living with scarcely any vital reference to a transcendence that would condition them in any way.[81] On other occasions, from time to time, humanity has seen God supplanted, and traditionalists have cried scandal and atheism. But in those instances a new series of absolutes, in objective form, to a certain extent replaced God, however rarefied their consistency, or however they might displace the center of reference to earth and humankind.

Without the idea of an objective mainstay in some absolute, however the latter be conceived, human beings themselves, it was said, would be reduced to nothing. This has always been the strong point of the opponents of atheism: human beings need an external ideal to sustain them, and give them a reason for living. It matters little—we hear today, with regard to certain concrete attitudes—that this ideal no longer rests on a foundation beyond the visible world. The transcendence in question can just as well be posited on the human level, and transferred to abstract ideas of reason, humanity, society, and the like—concepts that, after all, in one way or another also transcend the individual as such and give a person an objectified motive for living, offer the individual something to believe in. And surely there is no denying that the overwhelming majority of persons still live lives supported by "something" that, in its various sociological forms, to genuine atheists looks like a desperate attempt to make up for or alleviate human limitation and contingency. But this does not seem to me to be the main focus toward which atheism in the new style gravitates. That human beings rely on an ideal that fills and supports their finitude is rather evident. Without an objective something outside themselves for which to strive, human beings may fall victim not only to the self-centeredness that issues in dishonesty with their neighbor, but to the ennui that flows from the meaninglessness of a contingent life that comes to constitute its own stifling limitations. Human beings must lift their eyes to a horizon that is higher than simply themselves and their own story. What I consider the earmark of the new atheism is rather the emergence in contemporary humankind of a tendency to adopt an ideal that is personal in nature. That is, each individual consciously adopts some particular ideal in order to maintain the very need to believe.[82]

Another reason for this phenomenon is that many of the functions traditionally discharged by God are now realized by humans, with the aid of science and efficiency of technology. Everything having to do with the material aspect of existence is today in the hands of modern humanity, not only where the health of the body is concerned, as we continue to struggle against death, as we defeat various infectious diseases, and so on, but even in the area of ecology. Droughts and floods can be brought under human control. It is increasingly difficult to find someone who will turn to God rather than the doctor for healing,[83] or who does not bother to have an emergency water supply in case the seasons fail. The coming of modern technology has put humankind in a position consciously to assume the role formerly attributed to a god more or less ex machina. Religion, consequently, as well as some kind of ideal, even God, can very well be maintained. Indeed they are still in some sort largely necessary. But their internal meaning is changing profoundly. Religion, and the worship of something like a personal God, is becoming a private affair.[84] No longer is it the driving force of a whole civilization, a whole society; nor is it the factor responsible for the preservation and enhancement of existence and subsistence.[85]

From a practical point of view, it might be said that what is happening to humankind is the implementation of a sort of concentration of the world/humanity/God triad into a single "thing" clearly more akin to humanity than to the other two dimensions of the real. Thus we are not dealing precisely with the "death of God," but with something much more like an assimilation, a swallowing, of God by humankind. God is not dead. Humankind has eaten God. The analogy is felicitous, for the phenomenon is partly the consequence of a secularized development of the principal Christian rite. Humankind has received its God in communion, gulping God down for good and all. Not that God has been transformed into something immanent — rather I would be tempted to represent this "atheistic" process as a "sublimation" of God, in the chemical connotation of the concept. In other words, God understood as Other, as abiding Substance, as Establisher of all, or again as the unyielding one, as Being, is sublimated, volatilizes, passes into the gaseous state of function, horizon, ideal, dimension — of oneself and one's neighbors.[86] The corrosive force of human consciousness, and especially of thought, destroys the objectification and hence the substantialization of any transcendence, to the point of corroding the entrails of subjectivity itself.

To the atheistic religion of Buddhism corresponds the religious atheism of our own day. I call it religious — in full cognizance of the imprecision of the word — because I wish to underscore the fact that I am dealing with an ultimate, radical attitude. This is a question not of a simple philosophy or even ideology, but precisely of the phenomenon that, from the advent of Christianity onward, and in virtue of a preponderance of the Mediterranean spirit, convention has called "religion" — thus universalizing this Western word and extrapolating it beyond its deserts.[87] It ought to be clear, then, from one point of view, that when I call this kind of atheism "religious," I have no intention of ranging it with the theistic religions in the schema generally employed in speaking of "religion."[88] I mean only that this atheism "saves" human beings from the clutches of transcendency as from the quicksands of immanence, delivers them from the oppression of superstition as from the credulity of the sciences. And the privilege of securing "salvation," whatever we may mean by "salvation," of course belongs to what is called religion. This is an atheism that, vanquishing the mirages of past and future, finds itself once more before the present, and sees itself obliged, in one fashion or another, to endow that present with all the consistency that "eternalists" would bestow upon it, but without substantializing it, without converting it into eternity, into an "other," an idol.[89] Again, then, I am confronted with the acceptance of pure contingency, although this time I approach such a "truth" along a different route from that traversed by the Buddhist intuition, and hence I discover different elements.[90] This is another aspect in which the encounter with Buddhism can be fertile.

My hypothesis, which I advance only as a humble hermeneutic of the present time, comes to this: the heart and essence of what until now has been called atheism — which of course were better called by another name, seeing that the connotation of a simple negative reaction does not attach to it — is not, as until now the "believer" has granted, a kind of reaction against a series of tenuous propositions upon the existence of a Supreme Being. It is not a kind of corrective for theism. It represents, rather, a new stage along the journey of humanity, a new degree of awareness comparable to the one that occurred at the moment of the great reform of the interiorization of the religious spirit of humankind, as we have seen: there "is" no God, but ultimately only because neither "is there" humankind. Atheism seems to be arousing in human awareness a sort of new alteration, one that need not necessarily be interpreted in the framework of a social biology, or of a return of the old myth of the "superman."[91] This new modification, not yet concluded, but manifesting itself sporadically, and striving to express itself correctly but failing, means neither that the creature is nothing and God is all,[92] nor that the creature is all and God is nothing,[93] nor that there is a little cavity for the created in the bosom of the divinity.[94] In other words, neither monism nor dualism — neither pantheism, nor atheism, nor theism — corresponds to the profound experience that persons of our time seek to express. The world, humankind, and God are as it were incompatible as three separate, independent entities.[95] They are intertwined. A world without human beings is without meaning; a God without creatures would cease to be God; humankind without a world would be unable to subsist and without God would not be truly human. God is sublimated, as I have said, but the sublimation must now be condensed somewhere, and it is the human interior that will supply the walls on which God will crystalize in humanity — not, however, as a distinct being, come to take refuge in our interior, but as something that is ours by right, and that had only been momentarily removed. But all metaphor is dangerous here, especially if it be interpreted in a substantialistic key. Perhaps God did die; but in that case what is happening now is that God is risen, albeit not as "God" but as humankind. But something similar should be said about humankind. Human beings are not God, not the center either. There is no center.

It is not just that in praxis we ought to live *as if* God did not exist,[96] as Buddhist monks had already acknowledged of old and Zen has subsequently popularized.[97] It is not just that in the ethical order the believer cannot have recourse to the privilege of a detailed law of God, or feel bound by such a law.[98] The new atheism is not limited to this. Strictly speaking, the new atheism rises up neither to combat nor to deny God unequivocally. All that the modern mentality really demands is that God not be absolutized, either in the traditional theistic sense,[99] or in a radical position of the death of God.[100]

At this point, however, not only the old substantialistic mentality but the new mentality as well will be on its guard with respect to a basic fact: a God who can be manipulated,[101] who can be bracketed,[102] is not the true God. Indeed the Buddha would say that the true God is precisely the one who "is not."[103] If it is possible to live on the terms of a hypothesis of the denial of God, this is because there really is no such "God." As a mere hypothesis, either the hypothesis is necessary, and then it cannot be prescinded from —

that is, it ceases to be a hypothesis; or it is not necessary, and then God ceases to be God, because God, by definition, is the one who cannot be prescinded from.[104] It may be that God is not a *hypostasis*; but in no case is God a mere hypothesis.

Is there any escape from this impasse? Perhaps there could be some fusion — without confusion — with humankind, at the deepest level, in a discourse upon God in a secular mode,[105] a discourse that would despoil God of the halo of absolutization, and transform God, in personalistic fashion, into a meaningful factor only for those who recognize God?[106] Perhaps then a creator God, ruler of all things and responsible for our existence as well, will vanish from the human horizon, to reappear in the person of an Icon, an *iṣṭadevatā*, a Redeemer, or a Love of whom there would be need for support along the highway of life. And here we are again with Buddhism, which does not deny the presence and succor of the gods, the *deva*s, the God of the lowly, but surely denies the God of the philosophers and theologians.[107] It is probably here, then, that what certain recent Western theologians were seeking to express through the concept of the "death of God"[108] could find a more adequate formulation, if one could manage to maintain an attitude like that of Buddhism, however differently Buddhism intuited the measure of experience, however different the mentality according to whose parameters Buddhism lived.

It is significant, for that matter, that precisely the key personages of this modern theology spontaneously turned to an exploration of the spirituality of Buddhism, and of the East in general.[109] But it is enough for my purposes to have broached the problem.[110]

Let me now move on to another characteristic of our time. At once the cause and the effect of the great development of science and technology, it is what I have elsewhere called "functional thinking," in contradistinction to predicative, substantial thinking.[111] Science does not tell us, nor does it pretend to tell us, what things *are*. It tells us only how they *function*.[112] And in the wake of science even philosophy has permitted itself to be encouraged to move in this direction. A goodly part of modern Western philosophy is functionalistic, and from this new direction of investigative thought have emerged those new key concepts of human speculation — the historical dimension and evolutionary process of humankind. They both point in an antisubstantialistic direction. If human beings are not yet that toward which their evolution tends, it will surely be meaningless to speculate on their hypothetical being, inasmuch as they are still in process of evolution (strictly speaking, humankind "is not") — as indeed to speculate on their future state, seeing that they have not as yet acquired their shape, and one cannot foretell, but only conjecture, what form humankind will take at the end of evolution (if indeed it makes any sense to speak of an "end" of evolution).

Now, if functionalistic thinking will have the effect of supplanting substantialistic thinking with regard to the world and humankind, there is no reason why we should not attack the third point of the triad as well: God.[113] Indeed, as we shall see below, for many centuries now the mighty fortress of God has been Substance, and consequently Being.[114] Thus the advent of functionalism—which, less wisely than the Buddha, did not rest content with keeping silence with regard to matters that escape human comprehension, whether for positive solutions or negative ones,[115] but undertook directly to deny the substantiality of God—ultimately denied this third dimension altogether, thereby perhaps outdistancing its original intentions. Being and substance, even the being of God, had been identified to the point that a denial of God's substantiality was regarded as tantamount to a denial of God's being, hence of God's reality in any form. And reality was equated with truth.[116]

We have a counterexample in the celebrated *Atheismusstreit* of the close of the eighteenth century, in Europe, particularly in Germany. This dispute was based in the main on the discussion occasioned by the proposition of an idealistic philosophy, especially that of Fichte, that God is not a substance.[117] And to deny God any substantiality was *ipso facto* to deny God altogether.

The second, more successful, step taken by the functionalistic mentality was that of simply ignoring the problem, and instead of posing the question of what God "is," which seemed a useless question, concentrating its particular interest on seeking to know God's works and functions. As once upon a time the world, and then humankind, had found a proper space only or mainly for whatever *function* they might still have—room for their use only[118]—so now with God: in order to be accepted, the divinity must justify its own presence no longer through what it *is*[119] but through what it is *good for*. The traditional proofs for the *being* of God were now deprived of all relevancy, so that, in order to justify a continuing need for God, some apologists, failing to find an appropriate language for the new situation, were constrained to employ the classic "proofs" no longer to demonstrate the existence of the divine Being, but to justify its acts and thus open some space for it in the contemporary mentality.

The attempt does not seem to have been very successful. The old "proofs" were distorted, and nothing was proved. After all, God cannot "justify" God's own presence by demonstrating a practical need for God.[120] The very fact that God can be subjected to discussion, or that apologists must justify God, means that this God has now ceased to exist, even for defenders. The two principal justifications for the "proofs" of the existence of God are devoid of convincing power today: divine providence has been unable to protect the human race from evil and its own sin; and the "hypothesis" of God as the cause of phenomena as yet unknown has long since vanished.[121]

Christian apologetics has understood the stakes. It does its best to "save" God both from the bankruptcy of all values and from all possible progress on the part of science.[122] The lesson of the Galileo affair has not been lost on the champions of God, and adequate care has been taken to avoid its recurrence.[123] The result is that we find ourselves spectators at a downright "demythicization race" — a rush to relieve the field of God of anything not strictly religious, that the Divinity may forthwith throne on heights so inaccessible that no future science will be able to reach up and pull it down. Thus God, the Supreme Being, is constrained to withdraw once more into a pure transcendence, and leave the world for human beings to wrangle about.[124] In a word, God's apologists would reserve God one last refuge: the furthest summit of the pyramid of being, where the human being comes only through faith or death.

And yet the modern mentality seeks to dislodge God from this last bulwark as well — with contradictory intentions, some of the launchers of this final assault seeking to deal the "myth" the coup de grace and thus "liberate" the human being from it for good and all, others striving to "purify" God in depth.[125]

And some modern human beings finally burned God at the stake. They took over God's functions wherever simple earthly existence was concerned. But soon enough these same persons adverted to the fact that their existence, perhaps indeed their very "being," was not exhausted in the sphere of the merely mundane. The enhancement of a quality of life, the attainment of the visible and the concrete, often appears to humankind as intrinsically insufficient for life in its fullness. Human beings have need of another "salvation" as well, one that will sink its very roots deep into invisible dimension of their nature.

But Buddhism has eliminated God from the way of salvation, radically transforming the conception of the ultimate. Could modern atheism perhaps take its cue here?[126] And this brings me to my next consideration.

9

Ontological Apophaticism

THE BUDDHA'S POSITION

*"Whilst I meditate, am I to avoid dwelling on
any idea?" the disciple asked his Zen master.
"Get rid of that idea," the master replied.
"What idea?" asked the disciple, perplexed.
"You may keep your idea about not having
ideas," answered the master.*[1]

*It is related of Chao-chou, another Zen mas-
ter, that when a monk once asked him, "What is
the last word on truth?" he simply replied
"Yes"—whereupon the disciple, thinking that the
master had not understood, repeated the question. And Chao-chou, feigning anger, boomed
back at him: "What do you think I am, deaf?"*[2]

Something rather similar is occurring in modern civilization. Though
born into that civilization, and conditioned by technology, human beings
still feel impelled to ask themselves about life's ultimate problems. But the
answers given by their traditional teachers seem as meaningless, not to say
annoying, as the questions the disciples asked their Zen masters in the
epigraphs just above. We have lost confidence in "that which" has
customarily been called "God," and so find it annoying and meaningless to
have to listen to ourselves continuing to repeat that the final answer regards
precisely that God. After all, if, as we have seen in the preceding section,
God no longer has the "power" to be the mainstay of a goodly part of a

humanity defined as "modern," then God can no longer be foisted upon us as the one and only remedy for every need. "God is a private, subjective affair," we have learned to say. No longer, then, can God claim to legislate an "objectively" ethical behavior.

And yet does it really seem wise to break with a tradition, a religious one as it happens, that for centuries, for better or for worse, has furnished a large part of humanity with an effective support? Indeed, have we not begun to see that the drastic solution, tested several times now in the course of history, of discarding religion, does not seem to have yielded very satisfactory results? On the contrary, it seems almost as if the "place" vacated by God has been filled by . . . nothing at all — and that this "nothing" has loomed up before an unprepared modern humanity with a force that terrorizes it, threatens to swallow it whole. Only silence has filled the void left by divinity. God is gone now, and the silence seems even more disappointing and incomprehensible than the God who has been wished away.

I shall return to this point.[3] Meanwhile, it would seem advisable, if not urgent, to renew tradition rather than abandon it — to respect it, to continue it. After all, even a superficial glance at history shows that no great, enduring spiritual revolution ever simply broke with the past, not even that great upheaval of the sixth century B.C. A mature, balanced solution for the problems of life has most often been the product of a wise compounding of the *nova et vetera*[4] with which every culture is endowed.

Thus if we now return to the message the Buddha preached twenty-five centuries ago, it is not out of some inordinate attachment to anachronism, or any propagandistic *parti pris*; it is because we see that message as containing an indispensable element for the spirituality of modern human-kind. Both cultures, the modern, of Western stamp, and the Buddhist, are atheistic. Their attitude toward the ultimate questions upon reality is apophatic. It is only that Western apophaticism may be of a more epistemological character than its Buddhist counterpart, while the latter, as we have seen, acquires its full meaning only on the ontological level. But then their juxtaposition and composition could be a great boon in the search for a new identity of contemporary humanity.

Indeed, the position that I have advanced in the foregoing chapters as being the basic position taken by the Buddha with respect to ultimate problems could be defined as an ontological apophaticism. If the Buddha's message were to be reduced to a simple epistemological apophaticism, then of course we should have nothing "new" to contribute to a resolution of the current problematic. We do not need the Buddha to tell us that Ultimate Reality is ineffable. Human beings can only approach it, not penetrate it, not attain to its "essence." The human being is incapable of an adequate expression of what reality is, and why, accordingly, "nescience" must be regarded as the supreme cognition. In a word, the notion that apophaticism is the ultimate human possibility on the epistemological level is scarcely the exclusive property of Buddhism. Nearly all of humanity's religious and philosophical traditions contain this same emphasis, albeit in varying degrees.[5] No, what appears to me to be revealing in Buddhism is its effectuation of this reduction on the ontological level, and indeed with respect not only to the object of philosophical reflection, but with respect to philosophizing subjects.[6]

Let me present this problem in the classic terminology of the Indic philosophies. Human philosophical tendencies can be divided into two great currents, the orthodox systems or *astika*s, and the heterodox systems or *nāstika*s, in accordance with their respective attitudes toward Being and hence the different directions taken by their philosophizing. The *astika*s journey in quest of a reality conceived as transcendent. That is, they address reality as the *object* of reflection. As their investigation proceeds, however, it ultimately fails to find a formula that would satisfy this being, comprehend it, express it. Ultimately the object dissolves in the very light of the cognition to which the *astika*s subject it. Along the way of the *astika*s' journey, being reveals itself to be ineffable, transcendent, unknowable, beyond all determination; and so the orthodox systems become convinced that the object of their investigation has been lost along the way, which opens the door to the reform movement proposed by their opponents.[7]

The *nāstika*s, in particular the Buddhist *nāstika*s, take just the opposite direction. They address the immanent. Inasmuch as Being is not found in the transcendent, which does not admit of any expression, the *nāstika*s turn their consideration to the immanent—the concrete reality (because it is available to the senses) of the thinking *subject*. But the *nāstika*s come to the opposite, analogous conclusion: the very *subject* of cognition has been lost along the way. That is to say, even immanent being, and hence the human being itself as being, does not exist, has no basis, offers no substrate for the impermanence that is seen as moving across its static foundation. It too, just as that transcendent being posited as the foundation of contingency, "is not"; the subject, too, is found to be beyond any claim to define it under any aspect. In its attempt to overleap the barrier of limitation to which the impermanent is heir, the subject has "fallen" . . . into nowhere, into nothingness, as it were. Strictly speaking, therefore, it cannot actually be said to have fallen. How could it have fallen? To do so, the thinking subject would have had to emerge from itself and overleap its own shadow. But this is absolutely impossible. The human being—mortal, impermanent "being"—belongs to the sphere of the contingent, and consequently whatever the human being is capable of doing, thinking, reaching, and even being, belongs irremediably to this sphere, one that can be overcome, if at all, only without any external point of reference, and without leaving any traces. The leap will be a leap into Nothingness.

To put it another way: to the *essential*, or essentialistic, incursion of the *astika* philosophies, which investigates what things *are*, centering the whole philosophical problematic on the quest for Being (which of course alone can offer a response to such an inquiry), corresponds to the *existential*, or existentialistic, *nāstika* incursion, which limits itself to seeking *how* one reaches the goal, *how* one reaches the end.

Naturally the essentialists, engaged as they are upon an investigation of Being, will find it difficult to accept the existentialist position, indeed will not even succeed in understanding how it would be possible to indicate *how* the end is to be attained without first knowing *what* the end to be attained *is*. It is at this point that Buddhism can enter the picture, with its reply that the need for this antecedent knowing, even were such a need to be valid within the narrow purview of intramundane speculation, certainly has no relevancy for the spiritual life.

Strictly speaking, neither of these two ways, that of the *astika*s, and that of the *nāstikas,* is immediately evident. Each remains "without proof," so to speak. Indeed, the claim to be able to move toward a goal only when that goal is known in advance is just as gratuitous as the Buddha's invitation to follow a road without knowing where it may lead. But at least the Buddhist position has in its favor not only common sense — as may be seen in, for instance, the parable of the arrow[8] — but the simple fact that the vast majority of individuals normally live in the sphere of the existential, not that of the essential. Furthermore, the Buddha will say that action need not depend on or proceed from contemplation, not only because in practice this would entail the exclusion of the majority of humanity from the attainment of the goal (and they would still have to be content with knowing the *how* in the shape indicated by "those who know"), but also, and principally, because knowing and saying anything of the "goal" would be tantamount to reducing it to the limited parameters of the intramundane, and hence converting it into something finite, limited, and imperfect. If the target can be known when we are still short of it, when we remain in contingency, this would mean for the Buddha that the target enters into this contingency, so that even if one succeeded in reaching it, one would not emerge from limitation. But if the goal is really "beyond," how can one know what it is? After all, one has never reached it to identify it. But when it is reached, nothing else is any longer of any importance. The interest of the Enlightened One, as we have seen, is concentrated on the fact that the *ultimate* end, by definition, cannot be known before being reached.

But there is more. Buddhism actually goes further than the functionalists. First of all, the distinction between the recognition of an existence and the cognition of its essence is the fruit of a determinate metaphysics, which itself can be either accepted or rejected, and in any case is invalid for our case. To the objection that it will be sufficient to know that a goal *exists*, without thereby necessarily knowing what it *is*,[9] Buddhism responds, quite convincingly, that either essence is categorically separated from existence — and then to admit that a goal *exists* does not mean that this goal *is* (indeed it may well be nothing, as in the Buddhist position, which of course the adversary will not accept); or else, if essence and existence cannot be separated, to maintain that it will be sufficient to know that a goal exists without necessarily knowing what that goal is, is to bring essence in by the back door — that is, now the assertion implies that the goal not only exists, but that it is something that cannot be known before it is reached.

But, it will be objected, it is one thing to reach an object through cognition, and something else again to arrive at it in reality. Once more essence and existence are separated. To this, Buddhism, rending its garments at the epistemological blasphemy, will reply that a cognition that were not to be real could not be called true knowledge, and that the only guarantee derives from experience — in this case, from the experience of having arrived at the goal. But the problem lies not so much with the dialectical discussion as with the original religious intuition of reality on the part of each of the two respective approaches.

For Buddhism, "to be" is a verb, not a substantive. Things *are*, by being, but there is no *esse* (Being) that would sustain them, make them be. To speak of "being" as a substantive is to murder it, inasmuch as a being that were not to be (by being), a being that did not abide in being (by being), a being that would not be — the verb — transitory, is no longer a being; it is not, it has petrified, it has died; it "was," it "has been," but it *is* no longer; it is a simple *been*. To be is to be transient, is to be fleeting. To be is really *to be*: to continue to be, to become, to arrive at being in this instant only to cease at once to be what the "thing" has been, for it must give way to the continuation of being. To be is to *exist*. There is no such thing as "being" in the sense of a something like any other something. Things *are*, but they are not "being." Being is not a predicate. Nor is it even a subject.

Returning to the classic formula "A is B," the Buddhist intuition will retain the simple copula. If A is B, B determines A to the extent (in order to be really B) that A loses its own identity, to be petrified in B — that is, A will have to cease to be what it "is" (what it was, actually), cease to be A to be transformed into B. But neither can it be said that A "is," simply, for then it will be A itself that will stem the fluidity, the truth of "is" as a verb. And we might add, paradoxically, that there is "no such thing," so to speak, as an A that would be "is." After all, the "is" has neither subject nor predicate. Things *are* insofar as they pass, decline, and end, insofar as they proceed-and-cease to "be" in order to continue to be. To be is to pass through existence.[10]

So far, these lucubrations are on the level of philosophical formulation.

As such they may be more or less comprehensible, perhaps even acceptable. The scandal begins when we touch on what more than one tradition regards as being par excellence: God.[11] This is the problem to which I devote the following section of this chapter.

THE CURRENT PROBLEMATIC

The identification between God and Being cannot be regarded as a universally recognized axiom. Not only will a certain contemporary atheism deny God — because it will not acknowledge God's monopoly on Being — without thereby denying Being; but there are, and have been, a goodly number of religions, besides, that, although accepting God, do not identify God with Being. Hence we must confront the problem from two angles:

1. *Divinization of Being* (the God of Being)
2. *Deontologization of God* (the "being" of God)

Nor may the problem be treated lightly. After all, on the answer hangs the fate not only of a broad area of philosophical thought, but also, and especially, of a great number of religions — particularly a Christianity so profoundly committed to this equation for which it would seem to be largely responsible.[12]

One thing seems beyond doubt: in the West the problem arose with the appearance of the first Greek philosophical activity in the sixth century B.C. Once the first philosophers turned their attention to discovering the foundation, initial or ultimate, of reality, and began to search out a possible unity beyond concrete, transitory multiplicity, the adventure of Being began — and almost at once came into conflict with divinities already existing.[13] The history of human thought seems to me to lead to an exclusive choice between divinizing Being or ontologizing the Divinity. It does not appear that God and Being can be supreme each in its own sphere. There seems to be no third alternative, and the struggle is to the death. Either God and Being are identified, with the divinization of Being or the ontologization of the Divinity, or else one slays the other, so that only Being without God, or only God without being, remains. But both solutions presuppose God and Being as the twin fulcrums of our understanding of Reality. Will Buddhism perhaps tell us that both must be destroyed — that there is no Being precisely because there is no God and no God because there is simply no Being?

Let us now take up the analysis of the problematic just outlined.

If we proceed from *logos to myth*, — that is, if we begin "philosophically," with Being — sooner or later we shall inescapably collide with what religion worships as God. There will have to be a place in metaphysics for God. But God brooks no reduction to a secondary place on the ladder of beings, so that, in one way or another, God will have to be provided with a bridge to Being.

Analogously, if we proceed instead from *myth to logos* — that is, if we begin mythically, with God — the problem of Being will appear at the moment when this God is seen concurrently with the World. Now there will have to be an elucidation of God's relationship with the World. Here an identification of the two will not be so immediately and dialectically necessary as it was in the first alternative. But in one way or another God by nature will tend to dominate over beings, resisting subjection to anything that would not itself be divine. A particular God may escape identification with Being. But once a divine hierarchy and a ladder of being are erected, the twin pinnacles will inevitably strike a relationship too intimate not to eventuate in identity.[14]

This has always been the position of Western thought. Ontology and theology, indefinitely protracted, will inevitably coincide. But our present age has suddenly cast doubt upon the very identification that has cost the West so many centuries of speculation and "progress." Mistrust of the glorious triumph proceeds from the West itself, indeed from the de facto legacy of the very Christianity whose proudest boast has been this unequivocal consolidation of the union of the twin cusps.[15]

It was not ever thus, not even in Greek speculation. Even as elaborately developed a philosophy as that of Plato was without such an identification — and without being labeled atheistic, or Plato being regarded as an atheist, for all that. And so it will scarcely be out of place to inquire whether it might not be possible today to concede some space to a God who would have no affinity with that *organon* of Being, thought; or whether indeed there is nothing for it but to abandon a God who has usurped the throne of Being for centuries.[16] Here our speculation will have to adopt a culturally and religiously pluralistic outlook if it is to have any hope of finding paths to a solution of the problem before it. The challenge of the present age will be to examine whether it is possible to "de-divinize" Being, and de-ontologize God, without either one suffering any detriment, so to speak. Apart from such a possibility, only one alternative remains: identification or nihilism.

THE GOD OF BEING (*DIVINIZATION OF BEING*)

An equation of God with Being can scarcely be essential where a religious God is concerned. After all, not only do the so-called ethnic or national religions never so much as dream that Being might be God, but even in the vast majority of the so-called higher religions, such an identification is certainly not an indispensable, essential characteristic of the divinity worshiped there.

It would be fascinating to retrace the meanderings of the road to the divinization of Being, seeing when and how it occurred.[17] But it is not my purpose to embark on a point-by-point reconstruction of this phenomenon.[18] I shall be content, then, to capsulize the broad stages of this evolution, after the fashion of a drama in three acts.

I visualize these "acts" neither as a historical sequence, nor again as successive periods in an ideal time, nor indeed even as three necessary moments in a dialectical process. They are rather the expression of a threefold problem inherent in human relationship with God. The solution of the problem, it seems to me, may reside in the union and fusion of all three components of the drama—provided we can raise all three directions of human thought to their respective melting points and thus permit their harmonious combination, without contradictions and without artificial syncretisms. Finally, let me observe that unlike the schema set forth above, the present approach will be philosophical rather than exclusively historico-religious.[19] My concern is to set in relief what seem to me to be the most important aspects of human philosophical and religious experiences. Because they are aspects rather than concrete entities, the content of these three "acts" will often be contemporaneous, and will often subsist within one and the same religion and in the character of a single Divinity.

Let us now turn to our drama.

Anthropomorphism

In the first act, humano-divine relationships are founded on reciprocal similarity. God is regarded as having created humankind in the divine image and likeness.[20] Philosophically, of course, it will be said instead that humankind, from time immemorial, has represented God in human image. One of the basic traits of the God of the religions is personality.[21] First and foremost, God is always a *someone*. God may be the personification of a natural force or phenomenon, God may be the projection of a human attribute, or of one of the eminent virtues possessed by humankind, but always and everywhere God is *someone*—someone loved or feared, someone who metes out reward or punishment, someone who can create (or abstain from creating), someone who can be subject to other Gods or a higher law (or God may be seen as the Lord of all cosmic law), and so on. However the case may be with any of this series of characteristics, the Divinity is unfailingly a "someone." Now the series of personal relationships proper to religious life is in order: sacrifice, prayer (in its various forms—adoration, praise, petition, invocation, and so on), consecration, and love.

Let me repeat that I am not using the term "anthropomorphism" in the sense introduced by a certain approach to the history of religions in order to characterize what it considers to be the prime type of all religions, the so-called ethnic and national religions. I am using the word and the concept in their anthropological rigor; I am not referring, then, only to a merely "physical" anthropomorphism, as for example that attributed to the Gods of the Greeks, or only to a "psychic" anthropomorphism, as for example that of the God of Israel—although on the other hand neither do I exclude these two aspects. I use the term "anthropomorphism" to underscore the constitutive character—"like unto humankind"—that is necessarily possessed not only by any human conception relative to the Divinity, but also by any God who means to be a God of human beings. Without entering into a detailed recital of cases, let it merely be recalled that to this category belong not only all the divinities that, from prehistoric times until today, have been represented in images,[22] but also the divinities of a more profound, more developed "degree" of revelation, as for example Yahweh of prophetic reform,[23] or the highly idealized Prajapati of the Vedas.[24] These are eminently personal Gods. They are persons.[25] And indeed a God to whom one could not pray, a God to whom one could not turn either directly or indirectly, a God who would not in some fashion intervene in human affairs, would not be God. God—the religious God—is always God of human beings and for human beings.[26] Let God's prestige increase as it may, let the divine perfections and attributes be elevated to the infinite, God must always maintain a bond with human beings that will permit the exercise of God's function as God. In a word, God is always the Lord.

The main path to the attainment of this God is the path of ritual and sacrifice, which with time and the consolidation of the importance of humankind and its world, becomes the path of deed and action. This is the *karma-mārga* of the Indic tradition—the existential, concrete, human, historical, personal path.

The personal Divinity plays in this act of our drama even when it assumes more highly developed theological and philosophical characteristics. That is to say, it belongs in this act even after assuming the divine morphological characteristic that appears relatively late in history, transcendence vis-à-vis human beings and human nature—a transcendence that, in this degree, is intrinsic to God's very personhood, and that has no need of defense or theological demonstration.

Finally, there is another characteristic pertaining to this first moment. To be sure, it appears later in history, and only as the fruit of theological reflection. I am referring to the divine otherness. God is essentially the Other, the "outside," the "above," the "beyond." God is independent, the one never confounded with others, the sacred, separated, "holy" one, abiding in transcendence, in lordship, and in sublimity in the realms of the numinous. God alone is good;[27] the Gods are always pure.[28] God is God to the extent that we are human beings: our relationship with God (through sacrifice and deeds, including moral activity and deeds of mercy), represents the most profound nexus that could ever be: it is the complementary relationship par excellence, for God has all that we lack.

To put it another way: the concept, or the experience, of God or the Gods, in this first act of our drama, is that of purified, sublimated (in varying degrees according to the culture) personalization of what human beings are, of what they have, of what they desire, indeed of what they lack.

I shall not enter into a discussion here of the origin of the several characteristics of God, nor on their gradual manifestation to human consciousness down through the course of history. What is of interest to me here is that, in one form or other, the personal character is present in each and every divine characteristic.[29] In every case, God is Lord of humankind, God is the Other—the Creator, the Protector, the Remunerator of humanity.

The traits described here will of course be refined and purified according to the degree of philosophical nicety inhering in a given culture. But at bottom God remains humankind divinized. Let it be very clear that I am saying more than just that human beings cannot help representing God anthropomorphically. I am also saying that the Divinity itself has no way of revealing itself other than the anthropomorphic, regardless of the degree of perfection a given spirituality may attain. Anthropomorphism is a radical necessity of any human experience, even an experience of the Divinity. If the point of reference is lost—if the subject of the experience disappears—God, too, vanishes.[30] This is precisely what occurs in Buddhism. But let us not get ahead of our story.

We must not forget that, wherever and howsoever human beings have need of a concept, an idea, an experience, or anything of the kind bearing upon God, this concept, experience, and so on, can only be the fruit of a human act. Even if the very Divinity reveals itself, it has to accommodate to the human receptacle. And therefore it cannot but present, to one degree or another, an anthropomorphic character.

The personal character of God is further accentuated by the fact that each individual divinity is worshiped and invoked under a proper name. In classical Greek only the proper names of the divinities—Zeus, Apollo, Heracles, and so on—have a vocative case form. On the other hand these nouns do not have, nor can they have, a plural form. Proper names are in the singular: each denotes a given personality, and a personality is unique. *Theos*[31] in classical Greek is a common noun, properly denoting an event, a divine fact.[32] Only with appearance and the spread of Christianity was the generic term *theos, deus*—originating in "polytheism"—pressed into service in order to designate, in Greek and Latin translation, the Father of Jesus of Nazareth. This is highly significant. In the Hebrew redaction, God is still given the proper name—Yahweh, a designation carrying a personalistic connotation. And yet the word that Christianity adopts to designate the Father of Jesus Christ is none other than the generic word "God," thereby accentuating universality at the expense of personality (and unicity?). In other words, the name utilized by Christianity to designate God in no way underscores the entitative, personalistic aspect of the Divinity. Rather it sets in relief the dynamism of a divine event. Eventually this divine event came to be considered so unique and special[33] as to entail the elevation of the common noun "God" to the status of a proper name designating God by *antonomasia*. This elevation constitutes a part of the peculiar, and today the problematic, character of Christianity as such. The God of Christianity has become, on the one hand, the religious God who has been personalized and thus has acquired a vocative designation; but the accepted indeterminacy opened the door to the philosophical influences that would slowly but surely substantialize God. In this way Christianity starts down the road toward a greater ontological consistency, as well as perhaps toward more frailty in conceptualization, from a religious point of view, so that Christ will come to be needed as a personal mediator between God and humanity.

Ontomorphism

The curtain rises on our second act. We find several human traditions here. This moment in our drama opens roughly in that same remarkable sixth century B.C., and reaches its climax and most complete formulation at approximately the turn of the first millennium of our era.

Act two owes its origin to the assiduous effort of the human intellect to purify the concept of God — to de-anthropomorphize God. The result of the process will be God's gradual metaphysical condensation, ultimately issuing in a God who is Being. In this new, intellectual perspective, in order really to be able to exercise functions in divine fashion, God can no longer act from without, as "other," as if God were but one more human being, albeit a superior one to whom obedience is owed. For God to be able truly to be God, this new antianthropomorphic mentality will say, God will have to cease to be "other," will have to be interiorized, so that God's every action will correspond to the intimate interior of each thing.

This process of immanentization is the passage through which God will be transformed into Being. We see the process in a highly developed form in the Upanishads, which finally lead traditional, anthropomorphic Vedic religion to the highest degree of rarefaction and sublimation of the Divine. But here the process has not influenced the formation of a specific equation of God with Being, the equation that has led, by way of reaction, to Western secularization. Because my own interest in the development of this equation is in reference to this typical modern atheism, I shall leave the Indic component out of account and concentrate on the Western phenomenon.[34]

We have a fascinating example in the Aristotelian sequel to Plato's purification of metaphysics and elaboration of the idea of the Good (which is not considered "God" or "Being").[35] Aristotle declares his prime substances to be divinities;[36] thus the door is open for an identification of God and Being.[37] As we know, this is the route later taken by the philosophers of the new Western religions, who brought the process to its culmination in a Christian scholasticism refashioned to the mind of the Stagirite.

A verification of the depth to which this union of the religious God with the philosophical God or First Principle penetrated the consciousness and systems of Christian theologians is at hand in their metaphysical hermeneutics of the name Yahweh. Initially the name revealed to Moses[38] had no per se connection with the Being of the philosophers.[39] It is significant, then, that the rapprochement, indeed the identification, of the twin cusps, God and Being, eventually came to be seen in the very name God, as a proper name: "Yahweh" came to denote precisely Being.[40] Notwithstanding the fact that other considerations in the interpretation of the divine name in the Exodus text far from confirm an identification of Yahweh with the Being of the philosophers, no Western Christian or post-Christian metaphysics has been able to overlook this identification, and must forthrightly accept, deny, or transcend it. Today Christian theology is conscious of this.[41] The whole problem of so-called Christian philosophy is bound up with this equation.[42]

Thus it becomes equally significant that Christian exegesis in our own times looks for other ways to interpret the God of Moses. One modern hermeneutic sees the Exodus passage as containing a revelation of God as future, as the absolute Future: "I am he who shall be." God *is*-not because humankind is-not-yet. God is presented as the human complement, infinitely transcending, and yet neither heterogeneous nor extraneous to human nature.[43] Another interpretation, not without better claims to exegetical precision, would have it that a correct translation of the divine name should emphasize not the *being*, but the *acting*, of Yahweh. Here the name would constitute not the revelation of God's being, but of God's (salvific) action.[44]

As we see, each interpretation drinks at its own well, seeking to decipher elements in the revealed name that will lend support to its own theory. When the prevailing philosophy aggrandized Being, God's name of course reflected God's being. Today the reigning philosophy is a philosophy of the future, and of activity, and so it is God's temporality and activity that emerge from the sacred text. But the discovery of the dynamism inherent in the divine name is still too recent to have overcome the inveterate habit of substantialization, and the common tendency continues to be to interpret the future as the locus of the epiphany of precisely the divine being, and to understand action as presupposing substance.[45] Voices from Buddhist milieus, in turn, are raised to remind us that the genuine sense of the Hebrew verb *hāyāh* is not "being," but "becoming," "toiling," and even "occurring."[46] Neither do we lack for interpreters who, under the influence of the apophatic attitude of a certain current philosophy, translate the Exodus expression as: "And what concern is that of yours?"[47] Still others, from various viewpoints, assert that Yahweh means "he who causes being," and God becomes essentially cause of what exists.[48]

But let us return from our digression on the fate of the divine name at the hands of its Christian interpreters, to our examination of the equation, Being = God. With all due respect to the reaction of which it has been made the object in our day, surely we must say that the achievement of this identification has been a genuine intellectual feat, and not a betrayal of the intellect as some today would have us believe. Indeed, the demands of human reflection are crystal clear in this regard. If God is to live up to the demands of the human mind and heart, God cannot continue to be a kind of master or landlord, decreeing, imposing from without, all that God would deem conducive to the proper destiny of humans and other things. Rather God will have to be the one who supports and sustains these beings, charging them with a force from within them, from their deepest interior. And when the reflective, speculative mind has discovered the universal and perfect concept of Being, it accepts the consequence: only as Being can its God effectively and honorably discharge the divine functions that the speculative mind must needs attribute to God. The God of the intellect, then, will be the font, the origin, the creator, the basis, the foundation of all things. In a word, God will be Being par excellence. The rest of things, not excluding the human being, will "be" in the measure that they proceed from God, participate in God, grow in God, and so on. Here God is not so much the Other as the One, from whom and in whom all things are.

The advantages of this conception are numerous. It sets the stage for the transcendence of so many antinomies. A God "outside," however compassionate, can always become either a capricious tyrant, or a superhuman force simply unconcerned with human needs. Now this danger is averted. God is transformed into our support. After all, we come from, are in, and return to God. Thus is the will of God "tamed," as it were, without detriment to a reverence for God, and without limiting God in any way, because God is conceived as being the ultimate law of things. God cannot "go against God."[49]

Another intellectual difficulty, as well, goes by the board in the presence of the identification of God and Being: the radical dualism between God and humankind, between the One and the many. The totality of things is but the body, the creation, the manifestation, the work, the expression, and so on, of the Divinity. There is nothing outside God (and indeed it is from nothing that God will create).

Further: only such a conception will permit any real collaboration between religion, theology, and philosophy. Only an identification between God and Being seems to make it possible for the mind not to flee the religious field. Now the intellectual can continue to have religious faith.[50]

The point of this synthesis, evidently, is to demonstrate that the God of reason is none other than the God of religion. But the God of the thinking mind can be nothing other than Being, and we are off on the road to the philosophization of theology. Now Aristotle's Prime Mover will be transformed into the God of the Christians, now Plato's supreme Good will be only a new name for the Divine Providence of the religious God, now Indra, Varuna, and Śiva will be only a series of names for, different manifestations of, the one *brahman*,[51] and so forth. There cannot be two "Gods," one for faith and one for reason. God is absolute Being.[52]

The road to the divinization of Being is a process of extraordinary scope and import. Besides providing a solution for the antinomies that torment the human mind, it bestows the reconciliation and harmonization of human existential tensions. If God is Being, then Good is Being, as well, and no longer the cold discharge of duty. If God is Being, then Truth acquires its whole religious sanction, and the scandal of the medieval Christian philosophers—that individual Divinities can lie, or behave immorally, as the Gods of the Greeks, or can be capricious, as the God of the Old Testament—falls by the wayside. Nay more, not only will the truth make us free, and the good make us happy, but the conflict of the classic Greek tragedy will never more recur. Never again can there be an irreconcilable conflict between God and the law of destiny. Now Being is God most high, Reality is one, and the world is a *kosmos*—an ordered, regulated whole— in which the human being is part and partner. The will of God is the very expression of the intimate law of Being.

If God is Being, religion holds the key to all problems, human and cosmic alike. Mortals may not always know the solution, but there always is one. There is no such thing as a World spinning on its own while its sovereign must rule over it to "keep it in line." Now the relationship between God and the World is strict, because it is intrinsic: beings are beings only because in one way or another they participate in, proceed from, are, and so on, Being. The Christian dogma of "creation" seeks to express nothing else: the total dependence of beings on Being, in a new union of philosophy and religion.[53] God as absolute Being is the God of Paradise, and in Paradise there is no room for nonbeing: no place for evil, ugliness, suffering, or anything of the kind.

Slowly theology has been converted into philosophy. Slowly God has been absorbed by ontology. The true theologian is the philosopher and the contemplative. Contemplation of the world of being not only brings the greatest felicity, it is the very end of human life.

This same process, which we have now seen to have occurred in the Greek, then in the Christian, world, was realized in India as well, where the authentic religious person came to be seen in the human being who knows, in the sage; and the way that the sage follows is precisely the path of awareness (*jñāna-mārga*). If the identification occurs differently, indubitably the discovery of *Brahman* as Absolute, as that beyond the kingdoms of being (*sat*) and nonbeing (*a-sat*) alike, derives from the universal call of the spirit for a unification of the discoveries of the mind with the exigencies of religion.[54] The whole of a certain Christian, Hindu, and Muslim spirituality is founded on this premise: knowledge of the truth means religious fulfillment. *Gnosis, jñāna, al-hikmat* saves.

We have suggestive examples of the ontomorphic position in both the Christian discussions of a natural law considered divine because it pertains to "nature," and in the Vedantic lucubrations on the salvific role of cognition, which, in the very discovery of truth, attains reality.

Personalism

But there are thorns, too, on the ontomorphic bed of roses. If God is Being, then many disquieting questions of the human mind are resolved.

But if Being is God, a new series of problems arises, with which the denizens of the anthropomorphic moment had no need to deal.

First, the personal character of the divinity is now somewhat obscured by its ontological weight. It is not easy to see how one might strike a personal relationship with Being. And indeed one of the characteristics of the ontomorphic moment is the purification of worship and the all but total elimination of sacrifice.

But another problem looms on the horizon when God is ontological. This time it is in the moral field. God must now accept, so to speak, a complex of ethical exigencies that seem necessary to Being, despite the great disadvantages they represent for Divinity. Along with Being, God is found automatically to have the attributes of Power, Perfection, Goodness, Beauty, Omniscience, and so on—all attributes that satisfy the intellectual demand for perfection, but encounter difficulties when it comes to harmonization. The classic example is the problem of evil and suffering. As long as God and Being walked their separate ways, the presence of suffering and evil constituted no problem. God was absolute, all-powerful Lord, enjoying the unchallenged right of life and death with regard to creatures. They had no recourse but to supplicate God, seek to appease God, turn away the divine wrath, change God's mind.[55] God was not necessarily good, although perhaps merciful.[56]

As for the obvious imperfection of the World, often enough some other agent was made responsible for that, and God was none the worse for it. God was under no obligation to answer for evil, as God will be when identified with Being—either on grounds of omnipotence, or omniscience, or goodness, or perfection.[57] Where God is not Being, evil is a human, not a divine, problem. God can even be responsible for evil, and not be in the least diminished thereby. Indeed, such responsibility can actually be a sign of divine power.[58] But in becoming Being, in becoming the Absolute, God acquires all other perfections as well, and the presence of evil poses a dilemma that has never been resolved: either God is not almighty (if so, God would have been able to eliminate evil and suffering), or else God is not good (if God were good and able to eliminate evil and suffering, God surely would have done so, and the failure to do so now becomes "immoral" rather than a token of divine power).[59] As for the attempt to exempt God from responsibility for evil on the grounds that evil is due to human malice, and not to God, this piece of theodicy fails to do justice to the premise that God is absolute Being: even human malice ought not to be beyond God's "universal dominion"—almighty, perfect control.

Neither is the problem resolved by attacking it from a strictly philosophical perspective. Saint Augustine's ingenious response solves it only partially and provisionally. Evil, Augustine explained, is a privation of being, is nonbeing, and God cannot be responsible for what "is-not." But this compromise fails to come to grips with moral evil: the human being can maintain a negative will even beyond and against the almighty will of an infinitely good God. Besides, such a conceptualization stirs up a whole new problematic of nonbeing and nothing. A God-Being who in one fashion or another is limited by non-Being, a God who can be in some fashion diminished by nothingness, is no longer the absolute Being that the philosophy of Being had postulated. Of course, it is instructive to observe that the problem of evil arises with a determinate conception of Being— namely, that stemming from Aristotle. Where the *Brahman* and its ontologization is concerned, the problem of the World is presented in much the same way, it is true, but here it is not the existence of evil that is the stumbling block, but rather the existence of plurality, of the corporeal, and of ignorance (*avidyā*).

As we continue to examine the philosophical process, we begin to see that the only logical response that might in some way safeguard the "rights" or "attributes" of God in their entirety will consist in an assertion that evil and suffering are illusory. They are not actually evil and suffering, but only appear to be. After all, if God permits them, basically they *are* good.[60] And let us be clear about what we are saying here. For this "solution" to be plausible, the thesis we are formulating must not be interpreted, in the spirit of a certain spirituality, to the effect that God permits evil in order that good may come of it. This too, would be immoral, in the hypothesis of God's omnipotence. No, the thesis here is that, strictly speaking, evil and suffering are not actually laden with the negativity that appears to attach to them. Our vision of reality is based on an error. Evil is not evil. Evil is not real.

Here the difficulty is that if evil is not evil, then neither are human beings human beings. The logic is the same, for evil is an inextricable ingredient of human clay. The divinization of Being leads to the annihilation of humankind. If God is Being, humankind is (as yet) nonbeing, is not (as yet) made, is in becoming, is in gestation, is appearance, is simple transitus: *māyā*, Vedānta will say.

Nor is this the only difficulty of such an identification. Another resides in the implied coercion of the divine liberty. It is not at all evident how a God who were to be "pure Being" could act after the fashion of the God of the religions. A perfect God must be "good," impartial, and just. God cannot permit favoritisms, or acts of wrath. In strict logic, then, God cannot answer the prayers of the faithful, for these often consist of requests for personal favors and protection. But then the God of Being cannot *love*. Furthermore, the perfection of such a God seems to call for immobility and immutability—seeing that, in this same philosophy of being, any change presupposes the absence of that which not-yet-was and hence imperfection in either the point of departure or the term. God cannot "stoop" to creatures, condescend to them, "draw near" them. And indeed Aristotle's Prime Mover, that supreme Being of such a great part of Christian and Vedantic scholasticism, is deprived of any real relationship with the world.[61] How, then, will this God, identical with Being, be able to love creation?

Scholasticism never solved this problem, for all its crucial meaning for

Christian faith. Strictly speaking, perfect Being cannot love beings, does not approach them, is not concerned that they attain It in order to be saved and divinized. These expressions, deriving from the metaphysical premises of Being, no longer have any meaning. It is devoid of sense to say that Immovable Perfection "is moved" toward beings, and even more devoid of sense to say that these beings attain Immovable Perfection.[62] A mediator will be needed (Christ, or Īśvara, or at any rate the *iṣṭadevatā*) in order to have a religion. But this will breach the divine self-sufficiency.

When all is said and done: if God assumes the character of Being, there is no longer room for beings. Pantheism or atheism is at the gate. The alternative is exclusive: either Being or beings. After all, Being admits of no plural—if Being could be multiple, it would abdicate its prerogative of being Being. Beings, in turn, have no singular—if there were only one being, that one being would be Being. The two are incompatible.[63] Theories of analogy and participation will be able to rescue some of the aporias that we have seen, but their doughty struggle both to save God and to preserve Being will be in vain.[64]

But philosophy has moved in another direction, as well, and from the very beginning (without, of course, in any way shelving either the demands of reason or the claims of Being): God is neither the Other, the distinct, the extraneous—nor the One, the identical, the undivided. God is "neither of the above." God is neither altogether transcendent nor perfectly immanent. Neither dualism nor monism do justice to the divine mystery. The demands of reason would have God as Being; but those of the heart, of love, would still—or once more—have God as Person.[65] Hence the concept of personal being, and the effort to characterize Being not by its ontological weight, so to speak, but by its personalistic content. The divine Being would be a Person, then, a personal Being; an intelligence, yes, but also a will; a consciousness, but a love, as well.

This would seem to be a happy synthesis. Many centuries old, it is still alive in traditional religious circles. Now we have neither the pure anthropomorphism that leaves the God of the philosophers and the demands of reason altogether out of account, nor the simple ontomorphism that ignores the rights of the heart and the need for loving dialogue. Now we have personalism—that is, the conceptualization of Being itself as personal. Now the effort of personalization derives not only from natural or cosmic forces, as in the previous solution,[66] but also, and principally, in the concept of Being itself. The Gods are not anthropomorphized; Being is personalized. The *sat* is the *puruṣa*.[67] Being is human, which in the case before us can only mean that complete, absolute being is none other than absolute Person. Religion will then be neither pure voluntaristic submission (symbolized by sacrifice), nor mere intellectual contemplation (in which worship is expressed in meditation), but personal dialogue, loving interchange, reciprocal cognition (taking the ritual form of adoration, prayer, hymnology). This is *bhakti*, this is loving dedication to the divine mystery.

But neither is the conception of Being without its difficulties. In the first place, as we have just seen, if full account is taken of the exigencies of Being, this Being has no plural and is unique. Person, however, cannot be alone. It is difficult to admit, especially for substantialistic thinking, that there could be cognition and love without there being an object of this cognition and love. After all, person is fundamentally relationship. This being the case, it must be admitted that Being is simply relationship, without any subject as its substrate. But can this still be called Being?

Person cannot be alone. Person, at bottom, is neither singular nor plural. The trinitarian explanation is an attempt to respond to this difficulty, but the explanation functions only when it is interpreted precisely apart from substantialistic schemata.[68] Relational dualism seems to be the result, and the inevitable result, of the conception of God as Person. This is not a serious problem for anthropomorphism. But it becomes a problem for personalism, the moment that personalism seeks to retain the exigencies of Being. Is there any possible metaphysical reconciliation between Person and Being?

If God is person, other difficulties arise when we seek to maintain an identification between God and Being. Indeed, we are told that there is something called a "theological difference," as contradistinguished from an "ontological difference" in both the transcendent and the transcendental sense.[69] The "theological difference," we are given to understand, is the difference between God as Supreme being and Being itself — that is, it is the difference between quiddity and being, which in the case before us becomes the difference between the religious God and philosophical being.[70] Thus God is no longer Being *tout court*, but only the Supreme being: God is no longer *Esse*, but *primum Ens*.[71]

But, then, will God as person not seem to abdicate universality of Being?[72] The refutation of our objection is very simple, we are told. If the addition of a personal character to the Divinity leads to a new separation, there is nothing to militate against the acceptance of this separation. After all, God and Being were distinct in our preceding schema as well — *quoad nos*. That is to say: let us maintain God as Person, but let us deliver God from Being.

Even so, difficulties arise. If God is Person — that is, relationship — but not substance, it will be difficult to explain the bond between this God and nonpersonal beings. Besides, in order not to have to return to our twin cusps — which, as we have seen, cannot coexist — there will be a tendency to eliminate the metaphysical category of substance, with all the disadvantages attaching to such an elimination (unless one completely changes the ontological schema). But there is more: eventually a God who is purely Person will be unable to preserve the traditional transcendence over the human persons with whom God enters into a personal relationship. After all, one cannot play a double game: over here, "subsistent relations" are posited to avoid the obvious difficulty we have cited; over there, we have "relations of reason" between creator and creatures, which will therefore no longer be personal relationships.

Today there is an attempt to escape between the horns of the dilemma by forcing the process of the personification of Being to its ultimate limits. In the guise of a critique of Western philosophy's traditional definitions (Boethius, Thomas Aquinas, Richard of Saint Victor, Alexander of Hales, Bonaventure, and so on) as resting on a reified conception of being and ultimately positing personal being as a species of the genus "being," modern theology seeks to get beyond the *dingliches Seinsverständnis* (the reified "thinged" understanding of being) via a genuinely personalistic conception of being itself.[73] Now many of the aporias tormenting the contemporary mind vanish, or at least are explained with greater verisimilitude and more in depth.[74] At the same time the door is open for a religious personalism that would seek to protect the believer from the erosion to which atheism submits both the concept of God and the proofs for the existence of God. If God is no longer "cause," there is no longer any need to seek to "prove" God. Only a "cause" can be searched for, only a "cause" has need of "proofs" and "demonstrations." God as person eludes any attempt at demonstration. God cannot be demonstrated, because persons cannot be "demonstrated," but only *encountered*. If God is person par excellence, God will be found only at the term of an experience of encounter. God will vanish from the horizon of those who have not had this direct relationship.

But even this solution does not appear to be altogether satisfactory. Unless we are to fall into a total solipsism and desperate individual subjectivism, the external world, that which is impermeable to consciousness and love, the existence of matter, will continue to be a problem. In order to save human beings and their exigencies of love, and perhaps seeking to rescue God as well, personalists have had to sacrifice God's creation.

Thus the problem goes deeper than would at first appear. Of course we must purify the concept of being. Surely we must not reify God and humankind. But today not even the most highly refined of the personalistic conceptions seem altogether satisfactory.[75] Could the reason be that the difficulties we encounter in applying a certain concept of being to the human being—to the person—are encountered as well, indeed perhaps to a greater degree, when we attempt to apply the concept of person both to the human being and to God?[76]

At all events something does not "fit" when we seek to identify God and Being. Personalism seems to offer a via media, but it is still far from furnishing a solution. The Person known as God is still problematic. God stands at the crossroads of a new anthropology, ontology, and cosmology.

The path we have been following has been a spiral. True, we have not returned to our starting point, but the point that we have reached is only "up a notch" from the starting point. If all that I have said is true, the God of religion is once and for all distinguished from the Being of philosophy, but after those long centuries of God's being identified with beings, the chances that God will fall back into an anthropomorphic condition have been forever canceled. What becomes of God if we avoid anthropomorphism and separate God from Being? This is our new problem.

DEONTOLOGIZATION OF GOD (*THE "BEING" OF GOD*)

Ever since Aristotle, being in the fullest sense in the West has been substance—that which subsists, that which is self-sustaining. Invisible and hidden—precisely because it is the basis and fundament of all else—it is no less real on that account. On the contrary, as foundation of all it is "more real," if I may be permitted the expression, than the things that rest upon it. Being is subject, *ousía*. In the East, as well, beginning with the Upanishads especially, the subject is real. The subject is the foundation, the *ātman*, to be contradistinguished from the world of impermanence.

If Being is substantial, a God considered "real" must inevitably be identified with Being. Thus God emerges as the ultimate subject by antonomasia—Substance, the foundation of all. Philosophically then, God will be First Cause, Unmoved Mover, ultimate Creator, infinite Good, perfect Idea, Reason in fullness—in a word, supreme Being.

But today this identification is flawed by reason of the difficulties we have considered, either from the side of Being or from the side of God.

From the side of being, chinks in the armor are owing to the well-founded reasons for which substantialistic thought is no longer as dominant and determinative in philosophy today as once upon a time. Substance has lost its privileged ontic position.[77] Numerous thought systems today no longer regard substance as an indispensable concept in their speculations, either for purposes of defending it or denying it.[78] Even problems that would seem of their very nature to bear on substance—as for example the so-called ontological difference, or even the classic distinction between essence and existence—are addressed from other premises than the primacy of substance.[79]

From the side of God, the difficulties are those that we have considered above.

A first line of approach—promptly abandoned, however, for all practical purposes, and for compelling reasons—is the once celebrated, if only for a brief span, philosophy of values.[80] God is not being; God is value. God is-not; God is-worth.[81] Of course, value philosophy at once ran up against a philosophical difficulty. The plane of value was now independent of the sphere of being. But being was by definition universal. Then again, we must not forget that the metaphysical axiology of the West arose precisely as a last desperate attempt to salvage an ontology that had momentarily lost the notion of Being. But the attempt failed—not for any lack of frantic attempts on the part of the intellect to reduce God to a value, to the supreme value, and to the source of all value, but principally because the upshot of all this effort was either a simple terminological transposition, with the content in question still that of the concept of being, or else a helplessness to render an account of the very function that the concept of God is intended to discharge.[82] God would have had to be content with being a simple value-as-such, a raw axiological model calculated to bestow value on things, without being their foundation, principle, end, and ultimate cause.[83] But this was tantamount to depriving the supreme Value of the very functions of the traditional God. Thus God's place was left vacant. The merits of the philosophy of value are undeniable, especially with respect to its enrichment of regional ontologies.[84] But it cannot claim to have constituted a valid substitute for ontology.

Let us now attempt to formulate our problem in two distinct ways, first negatively, then positively.

The *negative* formulation might be: How does God escape ontology? How can God be rescued from the confines of ontology in such a way as to safeguard the rights of both? A peaceful symbiosis between Being and God prevails no longer. And yet all through the history of Western thought, even when the pair seemed to be demanding to be sundered, they have always reached a mutual accord, in order to salvage some situation that seemed in danger of being compromised by their divorce. When ontology found itself in a blind alley, it appealed to God. The case of Descartes, with his need for the divine veracity in order to maintain his system, is not unique here. And when God was hard pressed, theology more than once had recourse to ontology, via a concept of Being whose purpose was the rescue of an apologetics with its back to the wall.[85]

The problem of "divine justice," and in Christian circles the current theory of the redemption, stand as counterexamples to the protection offered the God of religion by the concept of Being.[86]

Can Being and God be disentangled in such a way as to leave a place for God beside, or over, or under, the Being of ontology? The problem here is not so much one of Being as one of God, who ought to be independent of the tutelage and refuge received from the hand of metaphysics. How is God to escape the category of Being?

A *positive* formulation of our problem, on the other hand, will simply ask the nature of God's relationship with Being. One can scarcely ask to what class of being God belongs, or what place falls to God within the universality of Being. The aim of the question is religious: How are we to arrive at God without colliding with Being? The believer seeks to enter into a relationship with the Divinity, to recognize God, without having to accept all manner of philosophical connections. In other words, how can the believer reach God without clashing with the palace guard, Being? How can the believer pierce the network of Being with which philosophers, theologians, and the whole of Western culture have surrounded God? In a word, is it possible for the religious attitude to elude the nets stretched for it by thinking? After all, the organ of Being is surely thought. From Parmenides onward, it has always been regarded as valid to inquire into the exact nature of the relationship lying at the basis of the linkages between being and thinking. But one thing has always been exempt from question: if being is, thought reveals it. This is the least that can be said of their relationship, although it may be far more intimate still.[87] Will it be possible to adopt a postcritical attitude — that is, one that is not simply nonreflexive or merely instinctive, vital, preconscious — and make room for a genuine relationship with God, and yet not be obliged to enter upon the terrain of thought, indeed not contact the sphere of Being straightway? We know very well that there can be thinking that makes no reference to God.[88] Can there be a God who makes no reference to our thinking, without thereby returning to anthropomorphism? Or, if there can be a God who bestows self-manifestation on us apart from our thinking faculty, can this situation obtain without concomitant limits on human thinking?[89] After all, if such limits were not to be real, or were to be imposed from without, there would be nothing to prevent thought from contravening the prohibition and continuing to impose Being on any awareness of ultimate reality.

It is difficult to give a satisfactory response to the questions that arise. The history of God's being has largely been written. That of God's "nonbeing," the source of these questions, not only has not yet been written, but has yet to be traversed by the modern Western world. It seems to me that it is here, in respect to this journey yet to be accomplished, that the *kairos* of the present world inheres. Any new journey along unknown paths is an arduous task. It is here that the message of Buddha — one not far away from the problematic with which we are beset — may be of great help to us.

Contemporary criticism has generally occupied itself with the attempt to deontologize God. The reaction is understandable, but not always very felicitous, as in the overhasty denial of God without first proceeding to the reformation of the concept of God.

Once again, the drama, or perhaps I should say the tragedy, seems to lend itself to a presentation in three acts. Let me attempt to describe, synthetically and constructively, the positive process now in gestation.

Negation of Being: Atheism

First comes the phase that, since Hegel[90] and Nietzsche,[91] has been popularized in the expression "God is dead."[92] God's death followed hard on the demise of the Being with which God had been identified. This being of ontology had at least become problematic, if it had not outright expired. The first meaning of the death of God is that of the rejection of any *meta*physics — the denial of any reality beyond what is certified by our senses.[93] Here the true atheism would be *materialism*, or the most radical empiricism, "sensism." God does not exist, because nothing exists beyond what is available to our senses. There is no God, because there is no transcendence of any sort.

Furthermore, there is no transcendence, because there is nothing to transcend: and now we have *nihilism*. Nihilism tells us that there is neither being nor nothing.[94] There is a radical difference between "*seeking* nothing" — that is, considering reality to be nothing, nonbeing, with the subject, the will, the desire (so violent that it fails to find an object adequate to its own search, and therefore characterizes it as "nothing") preserved intact — and nonseeking, "seeking *nothing*" not because the object does not exist or is nothing, but because the subject cannot pretend to be a solid enough launching pad to catapult us all the way to Being. In the latter alternative, it is the subject that fails. Humankind fails to qualify as subject. This would be the Buddhist position, as contradistinguished from an active, violent nihilism. Unlike Western nihilism, which rejects the object because it fails to find it, Buddhist nihilism rejects the subject, as falling short of what a subject is required to be.

Perhaps Nietzsche's poetic and grandiose expression, that human beings have "slain God," is not the way to put it. Perhaps it would be more precise simply to say that God "has died," as if from an inner exhaustion, or because of the deprivation of the foundation on which God had been resting. That foundation, after all, was Being, and Being has vanished in a puff of smoke.[95] The process of its vaporization has been too abundantly investigated for us to tarry on it here.[96]

Neither is this the place for an overview of the question of atheism in the modern world. The spectrum of positions held by both atheists and their critics is a very broad one. Some scholars see a positive value in atheism without espousing it, and exhort believers to adopt a more open mind in its regard.[97] Others study it in its philosophical evolution.[98] There are even those who see it as latent in all postmedieval, modern philosophy.[99] This last thesis does not seem to me to be altogether erroneous — although I would extend its history back to the origins of Western thought, and broaden it to include all of that thought, not excluding the various "believing" philosophies. It is not by chance that atheism is a modern Western phenomenon.[100] Not only is there a theism implicit in modern atheism, there is an atheism implicit in every theism as well.[101] The moment God is transformed into an object of philosophical reflection, no list of cautions will be adequate to prevent the reification, or at least the objectification, of this subject, with the attendant evacuation of its character as the living God of the religions. The God of philosophy will be at most the God of philosophy, and identifiable with the living God of the religions, if at all, only in virtue of an extraphilosophical postulate.

What I propose to do instead is to describe the atheistic dimension of existence — in other words, to lay out the dimension of unbelief inherent in faith.[102] I see atheism as one of the moments that seek to clarify the ultimate problem of the human being — seeing that one treats precisely of this problem when one speaks of the "Being" of God, or of the structure of Reality, or of Humankind.

From a historico-religious standpoint — that is, from an empirical one — much the same could be said with respect to the problem under examination.

The "Gods," in the general sense of the word, are the first realities to come under human awareness — not in the sense of polytheism, as it was understood in the past century, however, but in the realistic sense of the living religions: as personal beings severally concretized in determinate symbols that exercise a determinate function in human life. This does not militate against the recognition, once the question of the unicity or plurality of divine beings is posed, of these several Gods as but different names for the one God. But a name is something more than a *flatus vocis*. (Is not a person's true "name" perhaps the very person?) With the awakening of human self-awareness, this process deepens. That is: ecstatic innocence, which in any case recognizes only the concrete determinate theophany that is, as it were, exhausted in the very act of worship (and this is what makes it a theophany), becomes reflexive, strikes a rapprochement with thought, and thereupon recognizes that all theophanies are but epiphanies of the one "*theos.*"

In other words, faith in the Gods is gradually eroded by a twin reality. From the one side, the growth of reflection leads to the discovery of God behind every "God." From the other side, this same growth in reflection sets in motion the curiosity, or perhaps the need, to have an explanation, on the level of thought, for things and the World, in terms of rationally plausible hypotheses. Universalization and the desire for unity destroy the concretion of "God," and philosophy and science destroy God's creative and transcendent aspect. The very process of the unification of the Gods represents a loss of ecstatic innocence, registers a certain disappointment: the worship of "God" does not totally exhaust the devotion of the believer, but leaves the mind free to "think" a *Deus semper maior* not reached by worship alone.[103] Those who genuinely affirm that God is unseizable no longer *believe* in God, but only *think* God, and discover that their thought cannot embrace, cannot surround, cannot *apprehend* God. They think they have purified their own faith through the concept of a much "higher" God than the God of the believer who still turns to many Gods. But in reality the one who has intuited that "besides" the God of worship there is "more," an "other" God with whom the actual God (of the "monotheist") is identified but not confounded, is the one who has sundered the intrinsic unity of the Gods, to create two distinct "levels" in the godhead: the one attained in worship, and the one that eludes understanding. The person who clings to the God of worship, seeing no left-over portion that would be "more pure" — that one, despite appearances, has a notion (if I may use such a word, for in actuality the attitude of this worshiper is beyond the concepts governed by the intellect) of the Divine much more genuine and unitary than the other. In other words, the practical "polytheist" has an attitude that is precisely "monotheistic," rather than vice versa.

On the other hand, as I have already had occasion to observe, once thought is under way it is difficult to halt. In virtue of the inclination of the human mind to reduce its objects to unity,[104] reflection converts the Gods into diverse manifestations of a single God. And reflection, again, impelled by its other tendency, the drive to search for an explanation of things, also discovers in God, now become one, the plausible cause of the origin, the essence, and the character of the things and phenomena that surround humankind and form the human universe. But then, precisely in virtue of this, religion, now clad in the raiment of a spirituality purer and more profound, begins to vacillate. When the Gods, in addition to being personal beings that intervene in the life and destiny of human beings, are converted into a kind of philosophical factotum as well, fissures appear in the edifice of religion, and the outcome may be crisis. By way of example: suppose we accept the existence of a toothache demon who can be routed by Saint Anthony the Abbot, but who also reacts to aspirin! From here to denying either the existence of the demon or the power of the saint is a short step.

By withdrawing God from the struggle with science, for which God is no match, we can sublimate God to Supreme Being. Now we have "monotheism": God is the only God, the Supreme Being. From "polytheism" we have moved to "monotheism." But then something terrible occurs. Humankind cannot but struggle with the Gods — not out of hatred or jealousy, but because this is apparently part of the dynamism in the subatomic world, in the molecular, in the living, and in the spiritual world. Antagonism, tension, and struggle are part and parcel of life. The struggle can be with the Gods, and the necessary tension, the cosmic dynamism, can go on. Greek and Hindu religion alike offer us grandiose examples of this fundamental human attitude. Even in the Bible Abraham must grapple with God,[105] Jacob struggle with a mysterious theophany,[106] and Moses all but play the role of Yahweh's blackmailer.[107] But one cannot struggle with the one God and absolute Being. This would not only be blasphemy, it would be suicide, besides being meaningless.

If human beings have no recourse against God — if there is no avenue of escape from the closed, finite world of human beings, because above it there is only the celestial dome of a perfect, and hence immutable, God — then the full responsibility and weight of existence, of evil, and of unsolved and insoluble problems falls back on these wretched human beings. With a single God, the supreme Being — with neither Gods nor angels, nor demons — human beings find themselves alone, cut off, alienated, weighed down by the whole burden of their existence in the presence of a Being against whom they have no recourse. The Supreme Being is perfect. It brooks no contradiction. It is infinitely wise, it is infallible, and all that it has done is good and done well. Popular piety — that whipping-boy of the "pure" — knows perfectly well that there are "saints," "intercessors," and "miracles," because there is movement in the world, there are exceptions, there are privileges, there are favors: in a word, there is liberty. Alone before a perfect God, humankind chokes, suffocates, in the presence of the divine perfection. The only recourse is to "kill God" in order to find oneself. Of course, the theistic philosophers and theologians will tell us that this conception of God is incorrect. And theoretically they will always be right. But what counts for ordinary persons is not the idea that specialists have formed of God, but the living God of their invocation, the popular God, the God within arm's reach and daily dealing. Besides, the apologetical, philosophical, and theological defenses that develop an ever more perfect concept of God[108] obtain only the opposite effect: now all that human beings had sought to bear "on their own" falls back into the lap of God.

I want to emphasize this last point. If God is absolute Being, then all of the conundrums, essential and existential, of human life will ultimately finish in God. When all is said and done, it is God who must offer a solution to the problem of evil, of suffering, of death, of broken lives and failed existences. It is God who must take on the burden of all that occurs in the world. But this represents a contradiction, as we see from the examples we have cited. God is happy, at peace, and in joy everlasting. It is human beings who struggle to survive, who suffer, who fail. What repercussions can anything human have on an impassible, immutable, and yet good and omnipotent God?[109] It is not to be wondered at, then, that human beings should wish to do without God. Atheism, as also Christianity, is at the gates.

Now, with the elimination of a God who is Substance and Supreme Being — the theme of our investigation — and with atheism on the scene, the situation is scarcely improved. Quite the contrary. God may be or appear to be no more than a handy, bourgeois solution for so many of the problems of modern human life; but at least God represented a hypothesis that, once accepted, really did solve problems. Left to themselves, without their Gods and without God, human beings simply "don't make it." They must forge themselves every manner of idol in order to survive. Atheism is powerful when it comes to destroying a determinate conception of God; but it betrays its impotence the moment it pretends to transform itself into a worldview that would replace what it has destroyed. Now the cure is worse than the disease.

Let us stop a moment on this last point. What is it that atheism actually denies?

Let us move from our historico-religious vantage now, to enter into the heart of atheism itself. If we keep in view not the conception of "God" that atheism makes the object of its assaults, but rather the "something" that is consistently "intended" under the name of "God," we can safely assert that authentic atheism can scarely deny "that" of which the theist professes the existence. How could one deny that which constitutes by definition the very possibility of thinking, that which is the very foundation of both the principle of noncontradiction and of the human being who makes use of the principle? What the atheist certainly will deny is that "that" is precisely God; and what the theist affirms is that "that" is indeed God. If we prescind for a moment from any "material" concept of God that we may have, and attend only to the "formal" concept of God (to use the terminology of Christian scholasticism), we shall have to agree that the formal concept of the divinity is not being—is not a substance, or the supreme Being—but consists in something more general, more subtle, something with less content. Indeed, we shall see that it will be possible to formulate a kind of *theological argument*, not to prove the actual "existence" of God, but merely to define God's "essence," God's space in the human mind.

The point of departure of our theological argument will not be the Anselmian definition of God: "something greater than which cannot be thought," but will simply develop a formal description of what is intended by the raw concept of God as concept, prescinding from the content with which a given "thinker" may wish to endow it. Now, when we say "God" we think of many things—but we refer to "something" (which naturally need not be necessarily reified as a substantial *quid*, nor as a "real" being), without which one can neither be nor think. This "God" is the term of desire for one who desires, the basis of thought for one who thinks, Being for that which is, Person for the person, Love for the lover, the One for the multiple, Nothing for the contingent something, Matter for materialists, Spirit for spiritualists, the State, Humankind, the Absolute, the Absurd, Nonexistence, Evil, or what have you. For fish this "God" would be simply the Great Fish, for plants Life, and so on.

Let us be very clear: by no means am I saying that such notions are all equivalent. I am merely asserting that they all refer to "something" unique—the "something" that is undeniable because it underlies and founds negation itself, the theist will say—the "something" that cannot be affirmed because it overcomes and destroys all affirmation, which is necessarily limitation, the atheist will say. But theist and atheist alike will have to acknowledge that they are speaking of one and the same "thing," unless we are to be bogged down in mere word-juggling. What the theist affirms is a determinate "notion" of this something: that it exists, or that it is good, or that it is creator and directs the destinies of the world, or the like. What the atheist denies are only these assertions. Neither does the theist *affirm* something presupposed before the very affirmation, nor does the atheist *deny* that which is the very condition of the denial. Because we have no terms available to express the nakedness of this formal "something," it may seem to us that the theist and the atheist are at opposite ends of an ontic plane, whereas in reality their dispute is only on an ontological plane. In other words, what is under discussion is not the subject of the discussion—for then there could be neither dialogue nor communication, nor for that matter even contradiction—but the predicate of the sentence, "God exists."

"God exists," says the theist; "God does not exist," responds the atheist. But as for the subject — God — both interlocutors agree that this is what they are speaking of. And here we have what I would call our theological argument.

This argument does not prove that God exists; it only demonstrates that both parties to the dispute are speaking of the same "thing," and that what is crucial is this "same thing," even if the disputants thereupon attribute to it altogether different characteristics — characteristics so different that our interlocutors cannot even be said to be treating of the "same" thing. And indeed, this "thing" is-not.

The force of the theological argument consists in showing that the subject (God) is beyond the attribution of existence or nonexistence — that "there is such a thing" as what the theist calls God, however questionable its existence may be. The subject — God — of the theological argument is that for which both the proposition "God exists" and the proposition "God does not exist" have a meaning.

Reducing our theological argument to its core: God is "that" whose reality theists affirm and atheists deny. Their discussion is not concerned with the character of its being there. As concept, or historical force, or psychological factor, God evidently exists. The discussion turns on the affirmation or negation of God's independent reality. The atheist is ever the "realist." Herein lies atheism's strength. The shift of the center of gravity of thought and life alike from the transcendent to the immediately given is the ultimate, sound characteristic of the atheistic position. Hence the atheist's negation of both the transcendence and the immanence of any "something" whose existence would seem to supplant that of the concrete, immediate human being. The theist, by contrast, is ever the transcendentalist, in reason, sentiment, faith, and so on. In the last analysis the theist will assert the existence of something "higher" than, and hence transcending, what the immediate data of awareness will certify. Theism's strength lies in the acknowledgment of the anthropological openness to the infinite.

The theological argument does not pretend, nor can it pretend, to reconcile the two parties to the debate. It can, however, show us not only that the propositions of the discussion signify something (because both interlocutors are "talking about the same thing"), but also that, by definition, the real "thing" under discussion (God) is impermeable, so to speak, to theistic affirmation and atheistic negation alike. If "there is" a God, in virtue of the very characteristics that distinguish God morphologically from all of the other objects of our experience, this God is independent of epistemological acknowledgment, positive or negative, on the part of humankind. Neither affirmation nor negation in any way regards God.[110] Nor must we forget that, even from a sheer methodological viewpoint, the question of God is not open to the same manner of approach as are intramundane problems.

But it is not our task here to examine the problem of atheism in all its complex variety. There are a great many types of atheism, of course, and more or less complete classifications of it abound. I shall restrict my own considerations to the central notion that atheism denies the affirmation of God made by theism or by any other system asserting God's existence.

In the second place—without for the moment entering upon a disquisition concerning the possible significations of the concept of existence—let us also note as a basic characteristic of atheism its denial of the character of Being to God. God "is"-not for the simple reason that God is neither Being, for there is "no such thing" (for some), nor supreme Being (for others). God is toppled from the throne of Being: thereby, for some, God is eliminated; for others, on the contrary, the dethroning comports a purification of the very notion of God.

The theological argument identifies God's particular "space": God is that which cannot be denied; God is that special subject beyond all predicates, even those of existence and nonexistence. Discussion of God belongs to the plane of human disputes, not to God's plane. One may discuss whether God is a simple idea of our mind, a postulate of our reason, a projection of our desires; but in each case one is speaking of the same thing, or of something (which indeed can be regarded as unreal) that, strictly speaking, is not attained by human predication, for its function consists in the conceptual clarification of content. That "that" is God, the theist will say. That "that" is not God, the atheist will say. The discussion of God then becomes a discussion of God's attributes.

Finally, we may add that atheism is an attitude characterized by the negation of a particular Presence. There is no pre-essence—that is, there is no preexistent essence—the atheist will say. Human beings are alone. Nowhere have they any superiors, for human beings "are" in the measure that they make themselves what they are. The Presence is alienation: it leans upon another. The Presence is interference by another. Because there is no God as superior instance to replace it, human beings find themselves alone, solitary, without company. The Presence is cowardice, the projection of one's fears, a negation of the human condition. God, for the atheist, is the great Absent One: God is nowhere, God is not. We are not far from mysticism.[111]

Negation of Nonbeing: Apophaticism

Long before atheism introduced a series of basic correctives in the idea of God, a whole orientation of thought, with ties to what we might call mystical apophaticism, consistently maintained that the best knowledge to be had of the Incomprehensible is to know that we neither know, nor can know, that Incomprehensible.[112] It even defended the dimension of absence as God's most fundamental characteristic.[113] God is the one who is absent, and always absent, to the point that were God ever indeed to appear, the divine presence would not be of the divine essence, but only a manifestation, a veil, the mere shadow and outline of God's being, a pre-essence.[114]

Besides, the true essence of God *is* not, in that Being itself is God's first veil—the first epiphany of God, but not God in person.[115]

God "is" not only Being, but also Nonbeing, declares more than one tradition. Strictly speaking, God is beyond Being and Nonbeing, however self-contradictory this formulation.[116] Silence, then, is the vehicle par excellence of this mystique. Only that one contemplates God who contemplates God not, the adept of this approach will go so far as to say.[117] The ultimate reality is absolutely transcendent—that is, so transcendent as to transcend being itself: the ultimate reality not-even-*is*, more than one mystical school will repeat. It is not a matter of the transcendence of limited forms of human thinking and being: we are dealing with absolute transcendence, to the point that, transcending transcendence itself, the ultimate reality ceases to *be* transcendent: it ceases to *be* altogether. "Blessed the one who has arrived at infinite ignorance."[118]

The "ontological argument," as we know, asserts that God is that than which nothing greater can be thought.[119] I have formulated a theological argument, as well, to the effect that God is "that" which cannot be denied.[120] But there is also an *apophatic argument*, whose cataphatic translation would say that God is so great that the greatness precludes existence, and precludes our conceiving the divine essence, transcending all our thoughts and all our forms of *thinking* being or even of *being*.[121]

This human attitude, which can have a mystical form as well as an agnostic, or again a merely secular form, is reducible to the position that the absolute is incapable of predication—"you can't talk about it"—and that any attempt to do so is a transmittal and "handing over" not only in the sense of a "translation" and interpretation, but in the sense of a betrayal, as well, of the reality that transcends even being. God is denied both to be and not to be, inasmuch as any human affirmation, we are told, implies an attribution of nonbeing: after all, any affirmation is always a limitation, inasmuch as it succeeds in affirming only by virtue of a contraposition to a presumed horizon against which it is possible to make such an affirmation. If, then, all of our affirmations are constitutively imbued with nonbeing, the only way to approach God is by way of the negation of all our radical negativity.

A modern formulation—with ancient, and Christian, roots—approaches the problem of the Being and Nonbeing of God within the notion of God as Love.[122] Through the subtle exegesis of a second Christian text, it is concluded that "Being is Love."[123] We must proceed in this direction, we hear, not with a simple assertion that "being is love" in virtue of a facile syllogism (God is "Being"[124] and God is "Love," so Being is Love), but in full cognizance of the fact that God is Love precisely because God is not being: God is love, and love is neither being nor is being love. Being is self-assertion; love is self-immolation. In this formulation, God is pure love, but not a love hypostatized in a substance, which is the basis of all of the antinomies lodged against *bhakti* (between two beings who love each other, there can never be total oneness, hence love necessarily presupposes this dualism), but a love without support, without substance, without "beings" loving each other, a pure love, a movement of approach and union, a simple *habitus amorosus,* the loving dimension of all things, thereupon discovered to be not a mere dimension among so many others, but the very constitutive element of things. Things "are" insofar as they love.

The difficulty with this vision lies in the danger of a facile sentimentalism that would entail the risk of reducing the Divine to a simple effusion rarefied in things. God could be converted into a mere psychological motion, and instead of having a radical apophaticism, one would fall into a kind of amorphous pantheism.

Whatever its merits or demerits, what we have here is another of the various attempts to deontologize the Being of God, without wanting to lose God altogether.[125]

Apophaticism, however, will not content itself with a simple transposition from Being to Love. The characteristic of every apophaticism, as regards our problem, consists in the negation of any affirmation about God, seeing that any affirmation originating with us finite, limited beings is at bottom never a real affirmation, but a simple delimitation against a broader horizon. Hence the use of the category of absence, which I have already cited, in an attempt to give expression to this most elusive of contentual material.[126] According to this conception, in which no words can be adequate to their "object," God is always absent. Any presence of God is a presence precisely, and a presence only, a veil, a manifestation, and thereby a disfiguring, or at best a figuring. A God who is not absent will be a simple idol. *Resurrexit, non est hic!*[127] God is always the one risen from the dead and absent among the living. God is not everywhere; how could God be everywhere? Strictly speaking, God is no-where, in no place. God is pure absence, nonexistence. The presence of God is only for making God's absence, God's *ab-esse,* noticed. God is not an *esse-ad*—a being present and facing things—but an *esse-ab,* a "being" from which beings draw their origin. Strictly speaking, God neither has nor is *esse,* but "is" *esse-ab,* an absence, a nonbeing from which beings take their origin.[128] Hence *ecstasy,* emergence from oneself, loss of being, genuine *ek-stasis,* is the only path to the attainment of the Absent One and the achievement of oneness with the Absent One. Unless you lose your own life, . . .[129]

It should be clear that we are not dealing with a strategic absence, a divine self-hiding, for the purpose of attracting and purifying us. It is a matter not simply of a God hidden from the furtive glances of human beings, a spatial absence, but of an absence of being, of essence: a true *ab-esse,* an *Ab-wesenheit* (and not precisely a *Nichtgegenwärtigkeit*). But neither should this absence, precisely, be confused with the "nothing" of the atheist or nihilist. It is precisely absence that permits presence. It is absence that renders possible quest, change, and infinitude. Absence is-not; but it is what permits to-be; it is what makes it possible for presence to appear and indeed to be. Evidently an attempt to interpret such an attitude by seizing it by the lapels, so to speak — that is, dialectically — would dissolve God into a mere possibility of thinking and being: a possibility that, deprived of all ontological density, would be forced to appeal to an epistemological justification, or to a right to logical existence. But this is not what I imply by underscoring the preontological aspect of the absence of God. Could I so speak without excessive abuse of paradox, I should be tempted to say in this regard that God is at once ever-present absence and ever-absent presence. God "is" never what is thought, or what "is"; and in turn God is always what is thought, as indeed underlying all that in any way "is."[130]

Another category, if I may so term it, that could be of some help to us in grasping our problem is that of *pardon*. God is not Being, nor indeed being, for any being, by the mere fact of being, is pardon — donation or condonation of being. Being is the gift (of being) that is pardoned (that it be). To be — that is, to exist — is *to-be-pardoned*. Being is not the ultimate. Or better, being is the ultimate only for us beings, inasmuch as beyond the frontier of being there is no being. Being, then, is originated, bestowed, pardoned. The pardoner, who is-not, but who pardons (that something be), is God. Creation means pardoning — condoning being, pardoning being for being.

Let me put it another way. It is written, "Little is forgiven the one whose love is small."[131] Conversely, the one whom more has been forgiven loves more: the one who has received more pardon *is* more. That is, the one to whom is given *more* to be, is pardoned (forgiven) more; or, the more pardon, the more being. Existence, being, is pardon, condonation on the part of nonbeing (God). When God "gives us" being, that which God "gives" us is not nothing; God simply pardons us for not not-being, pardons us for not being God. God cannot *give* being; God can only give divine self to divine self (in the Trinity), or God can forgive not having given divinity *ad extra* (in creation). This forgiveness is what we call being. Creation, the making of something that is not God, is God's "sin," God's sacrifice.[132] Non-God is sin, and we ourselves are to the extent that we are not God. And this is sin. The *simul justus et peccator* of Christian tradition that has given rise to such controversies acquires a meta-theological profundity here.

God's forgiveness goes hand in hand with God's gift. God gives me "being": God forgives my not being God. For human beings, to love is not necessarily to restore what has been given them. No, the more the pardon, the more the love. The response to forgiveness, to pardon, is love. I am to the degree that I love, for I love to the extent that I am forgiven and it is this divine forgiveness that is my being. I am a divine pardon. Spirit is the plenary gift: creation is pardon, the gift that God gives to God and that the creature plunders, so to speak, when it closes itself off, when it refuses to restore, when it forges an "I" for itself and thereby loses its being a "thou." Creation is that simple pardon that, being pardoned, loves. Sin is shutting oneself off. Sin is twisted love, "unlove." The creature leaves off being ec-static and turns in upon itself. To pardon sin is to pardon existence: left to itself, without recourse, without a hand to draw it from its nothingness, the creature is lost, wanders, fails to return, sins.[133]

Now, to be pardoned, I must repent. But I cannot repent if I believe in the positivity of my own being.[134] I can repent only if I repent not-being, not being God, possessing still an "I" that prevents me from ceasing to be, that does not allow me to free myself from the limits of my being.[135] It is then that the sacrifice of Christ, in taking away the "sin of the world," becomes the pathway of expiation for the "sin" of creation.[136]

This conception is paralleled by the Vedic notion of human existence as the debt that constitutes precisely what the human being is on this earth.[137] Accordingly, the primordial duty of humankind is that of paying or canceling these debts to the ancestors, to the devas, and to other human beings.

This interpretation will also shed more meaning on the parable of the Pharisee and the tax collector.[138] The message is unmistakable. Inescapably, those who acknowledge themselves to be just, by that very fact cease to be so; in like manner, those who recognize themselves as sinners, by this very acknowledgment attain to justification. Therefore, the just cannot acknowledge themselves as such. Only when we acknowledge or become conscious of our own being and at the same time realize that being itself is debt, through the gift of the one who alone can grant it, only then do we leap the barrier and reach justification. And vice versa: the fact that the sinner is justified does not mean that sinners' acknowledgment of themselves as such is not true. Being is sin, and in its recognition as such, in its negation, in the quest for its extinguishing (the extinguishing of thirst, Śākyamuni would say), the goal of the pilgrimage is reached: precisely the eviction of being. To have consciousness of being is to discover ourselves debtors. Sin occurs when being comes to a standstill, when it is substantialized—when it attributes to itself a density or self-sufficiency, an *autos*, an *ātman* of its own: in other words, when being ceases to be a transitive verb gliding directly to its terminus and is instead converted into *esse*, into substance. Sin is the *sistence* of being that has grown weary of the tension of its constitutive *ek* and thus has transformed itself into a (false) *con*sistency.[139]

This being the case, if the world of being is the world of our experience, then the God of religion is found to be beyond our experience. Not that God is-not and is nonbeing, but simply that God stands at the origin of being. This assertion, however, is valid only if by being we mean a mere privation, a *thirst*, a simple not-yet, a pardon.[140] If being were something positive, the cause or origin or giver of being would have to be being as well, for one does not give what one does not have. God can be beyond being only if the experience of being is not that of a positivity but simply that of a lack. And we are once more very near Buddhism.

Without entering here into further disquisitions on apophaticism, or analyzing its manifestations down through the centuries,[141] together with the reactions it has provoked, or lingering on the universality of the phenomenon,[142] we can nevertheless surely say this: in various degrees, and out of various philosophical and cultural matrices, apophaticism has always sought in one way or another to deny of God any attribution, even that of being, in order not to contaminate God with our own creatureliness.[143]

The morphological difference between apophaticism and atheism consists in this, that atheism proclaims its incompatibility with any theistic, deistic, or pantheistic assertion, but apophaticism allows room for the most diverse affirmations concerning divinity. It will only beg that these affirmations not be absolutized and converted into idols. In other words: atheism takes its position on the cataphatic level and from there develops a destructive critique of all affirmations concerning God; apophaticism takes an antecedent stand, from which any affirmation or negation of God loses all absolute, definitive signification — hence its recourse to nothingness,[144] the void,[145] and nonbeing.[146]

Radical Relativity

A third approach to or attempt at the deontologization of God might be characterized as *radical relativity*, or *total reciprocity*. The key notion here is that of the constitutive relationship of everything with everything else. This approach must by no means be confused with a pure and simple *relativism*, which would be tantamount to a mere agnosticism, a premature renunciation of any attempt to make valid assertions. Relativism is pessimistic. It surrenders all possibility of arriving at any criteria of truth. Relativity, on the other hand, refusing to absolutize such criteria, recognizes them as legitimate.

Further, I prefer to use the term "relativity" rather than "relation" in order to emphasize that the notion I am about to consider is not that of a simple relational entity, but one of a constitutive relativity of the divinity, applicable both to the *ad intra* and the *ad extra* reality of divinity.

Finally, because we are dealing with a relativity of the whole of the real, I term it "radical."[147] Alternatively, I could have used "reciprocity" rather than "relativity"; indeed the former expression might have been a more effective label for conveying precisely what I intend. But "relativity" is a more familiar word, hence easier to use and understand.

I do not intend the appellation "relativity" to merely designate the fact, now accepted as evident, that the *notion* of God is relative to the various degrees of human awareness, or to the diverse existential situations in which human beings find themselves. What I am proposing is that relativity as applicable to God means that God is not considered as Being, as Substance, as the more or less transcendent Absolute, but as "genitival" Relationship. Radical relativity regards God as the Genitive of reality, the Reality *of* reality, the Truth *of* truth. God is a reality so "real" as not even to be capable of being thought as existing externally or independently of the things for which God is precisely God. God then genuinely appears as the most intimate part of things themselves. In a word, God would be the constitutive, truly "generating," genitive *of* each thing: so that, whereas things *are* insofar as they are *of* God, God in turn *is* nothing else but the God *of* things.

Taking its point of departure in a certain sense in the apophatic position, radical relativity or reciprocity further specifies that the reason why God is not "being" is that ultimately God is not a "thing," not even the sublimest of things. God neither is nor has substance. God is pure relationship. As such, God does not even consist of and in divinity itself. In the final analysis, God has no "selfness" to defend or to support. God is not the "other"; but neither is God the "same": hence God cannot be in any way the object of human thinking or willing. No reifying thought, no intellectual activity, will ever succeed in deciphering the mystery of this *Of* of all other relationships. This *of* is ineffable: the relationship of relationships cannot be explained apart from the relationships themselves, and yet this *Of* abides precisely apart from them all. Once again the intuition begins to dawn that silence will be the least inadequate expression of this reality.

Let us note, however, that there are two categories of silence. The first might be styled a silence of departure; the other would be that of arrival. Silence as point of departure is religious. Through, and in, this silence human beings find and live God. Silence as point of arrival, on the other hand, is the ripened fruit of a whole process of approach to the essential, is the final goal to be attained in the effort on the part of the *logos* to strip itself of all that is superfluous. The silence of arrival is a silence reached after a long discourse: one knows that the moment has come "to enter *once more* into silence." Therefore, unlike its counterpart, the silence of arrival makes use of the word, a word that must needs draw its points of reference from life and daily experience in order to be intelligible. Hence the impasse in which philosophy — and theology — have confined religion. Their need for analogy, for approximation, for symbol, has clad in a "coat of many colors" the invisible "body" of God.

Reason's difficulty in this area is reason's substantive thinking. When we think "relation," it is difficult not to think this "relation" substantively: that is, either we think of a *something* that unites, separates, conditions — in a word, sets in relationship — two or more things with one another; or else the entire thinking capacity is drawn precisely to the substantiality of the things that enter into the relationship. But this is to fail to think "relationality" itself. Even if by some manner of mental gymnastics we were to manage to prescind from the terms of relationship, so that "pure" "relationality" would remain — seeing that all we have left is a simple constitutive reference *between* two things — still *things* continue to be regarded as the foundation of the relationship. Instead, then, let us think what would happen to our relationship if its two terms were not only bracketed, but really did not exist outside this determinate relationship—that is, if they were not to be independent entities at all. Our relationship would then appear to be converted into a mere formal concept, without consistency of any kind, seeing that now the "shoe is on the other foot" and the relationship now no longer depends on the "things" but the "things" depend on the relationship.[148]

Let us consider, for instance, the relationship of parenthood. Let us ask what would remain of such a relationship were its terms to be not simply bracketed, but totally eliminated. Would the very idea of parenthood thereby lose its signification? And we must reply: "Of course not. It would acquire it." A relationship is not "something" that sets antecedently given or existent "other" things in relationship; it is the very constitution of the things as "such." Neither is the Radical Relativity, God, "Something" obtaining between antecedently given "other" things. It is the very constitution of these "things" as things at all. Let us recall the Buddhist intuition that things themselves are but simple relationships, nothing more.

Let us now recast our line of reasoning from another viewpoint, with a view to greater clarity. Relationship is commonly regarded as founded in substance. Relationship is thought of as a relationship between things. In the case under consideration, however, the situation is reversed: rather than seeing things as foundations of relationships, we discover that things *are* relationships. In the example used above, that of the relationship of parenthood, it would no longer be the parent that would found the relationship; it would be parenthood that would provide that "there be" a parent, and filiation that "there be" an offspring. Furthermore, "there is" neither parent nor offspring independently of parenthood and filiation. And this can be asserted of everything: there are not substances first, which thereupon enter into relationship with one another; rather what we call "things" are only simple relationships.[149] The so-called substance of Aristotelian terminology would thus be nothing but a crystalized relationship, a relationship whose umbilical cord had been cut to make it seem independent. In reality such a "substance" would be dead. One cannot strictly say that relationship is the foundation of things. This would mean that we were still back in the substantialistic schema. Rather from our perspective there are not "things" that "rest" on relationship so that they may subsist; this would be to convert relationship into substance, and our viewpoint would have contributed nothing but a switch in terminology. No, things, as we have said, are but simple relationships.[150] The parent in our example *is* insofar as this individual is-parent. But a word of caution: no biunivocal relationship exhausts relational "being"; relationship is always polyvalent, always polyhedral. The parent in our example is at the same time offspring, friend, spouse, colleague, citizen, and so on. But this individual *is* nothing other than radical relativity: *in se* this individual is nothing. Not only is that person a citizen with respect to a *civitas*, a creature with respect to the

Creator, and so on, but the very character, complexion, intelligence, will, and so on—all accidents that would seem to belong to this individual as "substance"—are actually nothing but relationships distinguishing this person from other similar groupings of attributes. None of these attributes possesses a sense "in itself": persons are intelligent in relation to the things they understand, they are of a particular coloring only vis-à-vis that of others, they act by reason of what they desire. The body itself is only a complex of relationships.

This "relational" polyvalency is important for an understanding of what I am proposing as this third aspect of the divine deontologization. If relationship were solely biunivocal, it would always be instantaneous, and of immediate dependency.[151] The mother, in our example, were her reality to be exhausted in the parental relationship, could not have existed antecedent to this function. Her being would consist precisely in her parenthood. The same would hold true for God. If God were to be set in biunivocal relationship with creation, this would be tantamount to denying God any distinction from things themselves; God would be converted into the mere ensemble of existing things under the aspect precisely of their reciprocal relativity. But this would be a distortion of what we have called *radical* relativity. After all, things can be constitutively mutual relationships only in the presence of a more profound relationship that would permit transcendence of the duality of these constitutive relationships (and here it will be in order to recall what we have said apropos of the Buddhistic intuition of *pratītyasamutpāda*).[152] The relativity is radical, precisely. No biunivocal relationship is sufficient to exhaust it, no biunivocal relationship is sufficient to explain any being. A simple glance at the world reveals that the relationship among beings is not only polyhedral, but radical. No "being" is totally explained by a limited number of relationships. There is always an "open space" underlying any duality. Radical relativity is the constitutive openness of the whole universe in all its relationships.

Radical relativity explains how there can be an atheism that denies God as a separate substance, as a supreme Being, as the projection of unsatisfied human desires. Radical relativity likewise understands and shares the claims of apophaticism: the total ineffability of the absolute and hence the negation of all nonbeing, in view of the fact that any human affirmation is a negation and a limitation, and not a positive positing of anything.[153]

In this third conception, God *is not* (as things are, and we have no other criterion at our disposition), and yet God neither *is nothing* nor *is-not nothing* (seeing that the negation of being is vulnerable to the same criticism as its affirmation: any nonbeing that we could affirm or deny of God belongs necessarily to the sphere of our experience, and as such can touch God neither positively nor negatively). Radical relativity is therefore incompatible neither with atheism nor with apophaticism.

Analogously, the attitude of radical relativity will accept the three positive positions that we have described relative to God as Being: it will understand anthropomorphism, ontomorphism, and personalism as so many other basic human attitudes adopted in order to express the mystery of the "ultimate," or whatever this latter be termed. On the other hand, it will admit neither a substantialization of God that would totally separate God from the world, nor an absolutization of the divinity that would likewise render that divinity extraneous to the things of which it pretends precisely to be God.

The fundamental intuition of radical relativity begins with the positive and actual experience of the divine radicality in its quality as the most profound human experience that it is possible to have. As we have already seen in the central part of this study, this experience and intuition was the origin and culmination of the Buddha's enlightenment. Let us now attempt to describe this experience from another point of departure: one that has been the object of a great deal of study, and that is traditionally regarded in the West as the beginning of every spiritual journey. We are accustomed to hear that the experience of human contingency—that is, the lived experience of human "self-insufficiency," of one's own self-inconsistency, and of the consequent need to lean on something else to subsist—is the beginning of wisdom, humility, and philosophy.

In considering, in these paragraphs, human introspection or mystical experience, two important observations will come to mind. *First*, this experience is not positive, but merely negative. Nothing is experienced but the void, the absence of what ultimately is the most coveted thing of all: being, the foundation, the subject. The experience of contingency appears as the experience of a great disappointment. What one—secretly?—"hoped there was," is not. Genuine being slips through our fingers. We do not contain the *ratio* of our existence, we do not of ourselves maintain ourselves, and so on.

The *second* observation is that we realize how groundless it has been to presuppose a psychological or individual ego (we need not go into further distinctions) that we considered strong enough and well enough equipped to undergo the ultimate human experience. Thus when it is observed that this kind of ego does not possess the solidity that we have always attributed to it, the experience of contingency takes the form of a negative, pessimistic, alienating experience, and becomes the jumping-off point for a leap into the arms of the "Other."

The very etymology of the word "contingency" can shed light on the concept. It is derived from the Latin *cum-tang-ere*—to have contact, to touch mutually, to depend, to lean on one another. The contingent, then, is that which leans not on itself but on . . . on what? On the Other, someone will say, in an effort to give verticality and transcendence their due. On Itself, another conception will declare, underscoring the profound nucleus of divine immanence. On its own individuality, in a deep mistrust of any sort of imaginary projection, will be a third position. On the others in their totality, the Buddha has suggested, proclaiming the total solidarity of all beings with one another.

I am describing the experience of radical relativity from a point of departure precisely in the contingent because, despite its negative axiological colors and its metaphysico-substantialistic hue, at bottom if the experience is genuine, it is an actual experience of radical relativity, regardless of how this might be expressed. When the human being succeeds in having the experience of its own contingency in positive form, what it experiences is not a mere privation, the lack within itself of its own raison d'être, but the ultimate basis and footing of (its own) being, which transcends its ordinary awareness so completely as to leave its psychological ego completely behind. For this reason, I prefer to refer to this experience as an intuition of the *radical relativity* of human being, for it discloses the *relativity*, or *divine radicality*, of being.

In other words, when the human being "listens to itself," in depth, it readily discovers what I have called "negative contingency"—that is, it discovers that the "I" to which we attribute all our acts does not possess sufficient consistency to be the ultimate foundation of these acts, inasmuch as now that same "I" is seen to be as fleeting, as transient, and as fragile as everything that rests upon it.[154] Nor is this all. Now the human being discovers that this very I rests in turn on an I that is the true I—that it rests on the I for whom one's own "ego" is nothing but that other I's thou.[155] This intuition could be expressed in the Spanish formula, *Yo soy tuyo* ("I'm yours"), but understanding *tu-yo* in the sense of "your I"—"I am your I."[156] However, I have no wish to indulge in any metaphysical meanderings here. I seek only to describe what appears to me to be relevant to the matter at hand.

To express myself in the simplest way possible, then: persons discover that, in their deepest heart, there is a "bottomless bottom," that "is" what they largely are, and at the same time is identical to what each "other" human can likewise experience—the bottom that constitutes what is deepest in every human being, as anyone who has had this experience can attest— that same depth, moreover, that is lived, perceived, intuited as the unique source of all things, and yet never exhausted in any of them, so to speak.

I have called this experience an intuition of the divine radicality. It is equivalent to the discovery of an ultimate root in the remotest depths of our being as that most genuine and profound part of what we ourselves are. This radicality transcends individuality, and even human personality, to reach a common root, a single bottom, an ultimate foundation. This experience can be clad in a great variety of forms, and can be expressed in even a greater number of ways; but this does not militate against its being basically the experience of the ultimate, constitutive relativity of each being: "there is" an ultimate "something," at once immanent and transcendent, that is what we really "are." This "something" is not distinct from me: it is my deepest I. And nevertheless I cannot truly say that it "is" what I "am." This "something" does not exist separately from me; nor yet is it a sort of common denominator in which all beings participate. Perhaps it is the "part" of each being that is most that being's "own," so that the more "I am," or rather "am not," the nearer I stand to this ultimate root of all. But this too, is inexact—but we have no other words to express it.[157]

If I have used the adjective "divine" in speaking of this radicality, I have done so for two reasons. In the first place, we are dealing with something that transcends the mere individual, something that is not confounded with the individual and that can be applied to any individual. Thus it would seem that, phenomenologically, the appellation "divine" will be suitable for it. Secondly, this "something" is what the most heterogeneous traditions of humanity have regarded as ultimate and definitive, and is what in the common terminology of Western tongues is customarily called God.

Translating this fundamental intuition into still different expressions, we might venture to describe the divinity as that unique radicality inhering in all beings that brings it about that every being be what it is. And what is it that every being is? Precisely relationship among beings—of which, nevertheless, considered in itself, we cannot say either that it *is* (for, after all, it is beings that are)—nor again that it is not, for it lies precisely at the very root of each being. This radicality is the only dimension of the divinity of which one can speak, and it consists in a pure relativity. We are not dealing with a Being that "dwells," as a more or less welcome guest or stranger, in the furthest depths of each being. This would be begging the question: it would be saying that each being is an individual, and that God is the "other" who sustains it. No, the discovery in question is that every being is what it is precisely because it is itself an ensemble of relationships and enters into intimate, constitutive relationship with other beings. And this relationship is such that it forms a radical unity that does not render things uniform, but, on the contrary, permits them to be diverse. Unity, then, and not the contrary, is the fundamental fact. This radical unity of relativity is intimate to each thing, and yet at the same time it is transcendent, inasmuch as no thing really exhausts it, nor indeed all things together. The relativity of things is not merely their sum.

Perhaps it will be of some help, in order to grasp what is being said here, to visualize the indispensable reversal of the typically rational outlook that is culturally characteristic of the West. By the Western outlook I mean the dynamic perspective, in contradistinction to what might be called not simply static, but "unitary." Dynamism begins with multiplicity, and feels itself propelled toward an end, a goal, that can easily be supposed to be more perfect than the point of departure. The dynamic vision represents the ascending path of things toward their goal: God is the goal reached by the world asymptotically in the infinite (be this "God" seen as Being, Power, Person, Future, Social Perfection, or what have you). The path is conquest, and the means is progress.

The other mentality, the unitary view, is precisely the opposite. Here the path is reconquest — redemption, if you will — and the means, return. Unity is primary, and multiplicity is derived. God is origin rather than end, and things emerge from the divinity rather than move toward it. The path of return is genuinely return; hence perfection consists not in being filled with being, in managing to become that which one is-not (yet), but in being emptied of being, in ceasing to be what one (still) is.

We could put it still another way. The first vision of the world can be considered from the point of view of multiplicity and then we have a multitude of "things" that will perforce be considered substances — that is, centers of operations, with laws regulating them, and centrifugal and centripetal tendencies constituting them (seeing that the real is the individual, the concrete). Or else one adopts the opposite view, according to which the real is constituted by the universal, by totality (to use the terminology of the first outlook), and it is the world in its entirety that shows true consistency. Individuals are then seen simply as parts, in and of themselves truncated, being nothing but mere relationships of a whole. If addition and multiplication represent the mental operations of the first position, subtraction and division characterize the intellective form of the second.[158]

Were I to undertake to express in Christian vocabulary what I have sought to describe in a more or less phenomenological manner, it would come down to this: the authentic Christic concept of the Divinity, without ignoring its enormous, and positive, debt both to the Judaic conception of Yahweh and to Greek speculation upon being, contains intrinsic possibilities that have not yet been suitably exploited.

Christianity's key idea is surely the dogma of the Trinity, which for our present purposes I shall distinguish from the various theological interpretations of which it has been made the object.[159] The very notion of the Trinity ought to suffice to banish any substantialistic interpretation of the divinity, for such an interpretation would be tantamount to tritheism (Islam's very accusation where Christianity is concerned). If the Father is Being, the Son Being, and the Holy Spirit Being, then either there are three Beings and so three Gods — tritheism — or else the one God is a single, absolute Being, of which Father, Son, and Spirit are but different manifestations — and this would be the contrary error of modalism. And indeed the most traditional trinitarian theology will tell us that the "divine persons" are only subsistent relations: each consists entirely in a relativity with respect to the others, in such wise that each reciprocally implies and embraces the other two without thereby being those others. The two key concepts elaborated by Christian orthodoxy, so patiently and tenaciously, over the course of the first Christian centuries — "nature" and "person" — were developed precisely to avoid sliding into either of the two extremes cited above, tritheism and modalism. This being the case, let us observe that, in the perspective of my interpretation of the divinity in these paragraphs, I shall be able to assert that the Trinity is radical relativity par excellence.

A second point, equally traditional in Christian theology, is a corollary of the divine simplicity—that the act by which the Father "generates" the Son must be the same act as that by which the Father both "creates" all creatures[160] and knows himself.[161] Now, in light of what I have been saying in these paragraphs, I can assert that God's radical relativity *ad extra* is a mirror image of the same radicality *ad intra*:[162] that is to say, the whole universe, as image or "vestige" of the Trinity, is endowed with the trinitarian character of radical relativity. Things "are" in the measure that they cease to be in order to give themselves to other things. Things are but reciprocal constitutive relationships. There are no windowless monads. Radical relativity is not only vertical, but also horizontal. To borrow yet another expression from the purest of Christian terminology: to the intratrinitarian *circumincessio* corresponds an extratrinitarian *perichoresis*.[163]

The New Testament contains a hapax legomenon expressing, in verb form, the tension that typifies Christians in that they hurl themselves with almost a physical force, as in an athletic contest, at something lying ahead, lying beyond them. I refer to Saint Paul's autobiographical "I give no thought to what lies behind but push on (*epekteinomenos*) to what is ahead."[164] I let fall everything that in any way weighs me down: all substantiality, every possession, every spiritual, or even ontological, acquisition—in a word, all that I am—and I strive, I stretch, I tend toward something ever before me, ever beyond, something ever unreachable and unseizable not only in this world but in the definitive life as well, for, you see, the ultimate nature of reality is neither static nor dynamic, but *epecstatic*: pure tension, simple transcendence, superation, not in the sense of rectilinear change, nor again of a circular process, but in a kind of spiral progression, continually begun again, yet always new and original—after all, we find the very universe of being to be in a process of expansion. The vision of God, then, consists in "seeing" God precisely as invisible,[165] seeing God as one whose existence rests upon having none.[166] Just as we ourselves are not yet being, as a certain metaphysical conception would have it, and approach being asymptotically, just so, God is on the other side of the frontier of Being, and withdraws from it indefinitely. Being is but a limit concept, for the creature as for the Creator, albeit under contrary signs: the former takes its stand short of that limit, but the latter lies beyond. Being is a mental catalyst that enables us to place the incommensurable in relation, or indeed to speak of the ineffable at all. Once used as a category of thought, as the axis of the cylinder of the intellectual piston, it must be discarded, lest, excluded from the vital process of intellection, it congeal, and thereby become the greatest hindrance of all to what it was intended precisely to expedite.

The foregoing explanation, in which I have sought to express the Buddhist position in another context, draws its inspiration from Gregory of Nyssa, author of the concept of *epextasis*.[167] Although very parsimonious with the substantive[168] (something the Buddhist will readily comprehend), the Cappadocian bishop uses this suggestive term[169] in verbal form to frame one of the central motifs of his mystical conception.[170] Most significantly, however, it has scarcely ever been used outside scholarly circles,[171] as witness the silence into which it has fallen even in the more familiar theological or biblical dictionaries.[172]

The importance of the concept of *epextasis*—not the same as that of "ecstasy," which is not yet a technical term in Gregory of Nyssa[173]—seems to me to reside in its implicit synthesis between a static, substantialistic vision of reality and a dynamic, temporal conception of it. The way of *epextasis* would seem to be the via media between the substantialistic vise and the dynamic piston, the path that Gregory would call paradoxical par excellence (*to paradoxoteron*).[174] *Epextasis* signifies progress, and thus is more than simple change or movement;[175] yet at the same time it not only expresses a characteristic of our manner of knowing,[176] but, it seems to me, proceeds far beyond, to the point of bearing upon the nature of ultimate reality itself. Here an encounter with Buddhism will be unstrained and fecund. But let us see some examples.

"True cognition . . . and true vision consist in seeing that [God] is invisible."[177] After all, strictly speaking, there is nothing to see.[178]

"That which it is necessary to know of God consists in knowing that to know [God] is nothing other than to discover that nothing of what the human mind can know is knowledge of God."[179] Therefore "the divine voice grants what is asked of it through that which precisely it does not grant."[180] *Epextasis* is not only precisely the human condition,[181] but the symbol of the very structure of ultimate reality, as well. We do not have to emerge from ourselves into a transcendent ecstasy in order to reach ultimate reality. It will suffice to adopt this attitude of continuous tension without arrival, ever transcending ourselves—not, however, in virtue of a simple dynamics bearing upon some distant target, existent but unreachable, but in a constitutive tension bearing ever upon the beyond, and "advancing by virtue of one's very immobility."[182] For the end, God, the ultimate, is precisely the abyss that never ceases its motion, proceeding "from beginning to beginning, or still better, from principle to principle (*arche e ex archēs*)— through principles (beginnings) without end."[183]

The principle, the foundation, the *arche*,[184] the *agra*,[185] consists in beginning ever anew, in being continuous beginning,[186] in leaving nothing behind—for one is always beginning anew—in being incessant point of departure unattached to oneself, never turning back,[187] not amassing riches of any kind[188] (absolute ontic poverty, then—it is the spirit itself that has been enjoined to the poor),[189] and "being" only in the measure that one advances, continues, lives, "flees nowhere from nowhere," in a "stationary flight."[190] The divine transcendence is a divine transcendence of Being. "If one fancies one knows—one does not yet know,"[191] Christian scripture says, echoing a wisdom not only Socratic, but Eastern as well.[192] And

Gregory comments[193] with an explanation of why "finding God consists in endlessly seeking God":[194]

> Contemplation of God's face consists in journeying toward God ceaselessly, in moving forward constantly in the endless following of the Word.[195]

Only on the journey, only in the search, is God to be found. Indeed, the expression "finding God" is terminology calculated to disorientate. It leads us to entertain the idea that God can be "found" so as to be seized and possessed, like any other object—whereas God is nothing other than the abyss that is beyond being, and hence beyond any possibility, even theoretical, of grasp;[196] and the journey is simply allowing your own bulk and dross to fall away.[197] Hence Gregory does not scruple to call any representation of the divine an "idol" of God and nothing more.[198]

My purpose in interjecting this brief digression has been to demonstrate the likelihood that there are certain important points of contact between Christianity and Buddhism with a potential for cross-fertilization. All that we must do is to set these points in profound relationship with each other.

GOD AND BEINGS

Not by way of concluding our question, to be sure, for the question is still a very open one—indeed, it has scarcely been posed at this point—but simply by way of an appendix and synopsis, I should like to attach certain considerations here, and express certain convictions, that will bring us to the last stage of this investigation, whose design has been to present to the contemporary world a central aspect of the Buddha's message.

A *first consideration*, which in a way frames all that I have said up to this point, bears on the fact that the contemporary mentality—not by way of rebellion or recalcitrance, but out of a deeper experience and awareness of "human being"—is anything but inclined to countenance a volatilization of the concrete beings of the empirical world in favor of an eschatology, a religion, a God, or whatever else belonging to an extrahuman world. The divine reality is not there to "swallow up" beings. It is there to "potentiate" them from within, as it were. What has brought the traditional conception of divinity to its present crisis are not so much theological or philosophical arguments, but deeds, and a lived experience of antagonism between God and beings. It has seemed that the traditional concept of God—a concept that, when all is said and done, sought only to protect, to console, to ground, humankind—now curbed human freedom, or at least the aspirations of that freedom to manage intramundane affairs, and the tendency of that freedom to assert itself.[199] The traditional concept of religion has seemed (I repeat) to promise humankind another world in exchange for a renunciation of this one, has seemed to wish to slake the human thirst for happiness with the promise of a future paradise in which all the frustrations of the present would be finally vanquished and overcome.

There are many forces at work today toward the self-affirmation of humankind. If no God capable of guaranteeing this self-affirmation can be found, humankind will declare itself favorable to atheism. The modern mentality continues to tend to see an incompatibility between God and beings. In the past, however, the problem was how to save the "ontonomy" of things vis-à-vis God, how to "save appearances." Today the question is turned around, and the problem is that of finding room for God in such a way as not to damage beings — how to "save God." Stripped to the bone, the question comes down to what God is good *for*, or how God is of any use to *us*.[200] And so more than one traditional religionist violently reacts to the very state of the problem. If God exists, tradition reminds us, God must have absolute priority. To which the new believers respond that, apart from the perhaps somewhat crude way in which the problem is sometimes presented, we must not forget that the problem of God is not only methodologically, but even ontologically, an anthropological problem. In fact, no revelation, no aspect of the divine, can disregard human self-consciousness, which is keenly aware that the question of God is a question of something that, however sublime and transcendent, must not only pass through human structures, but must ultimately resolve the anthropological problem itself. After all, it is in view of the latter that the problem of God is posed at all.[201] It is the ultimate human question.

When all is said and done, undeniably the state of the problem of God in the contemporary mentality can no longer be crystalized in the biblical cry, "Speak, Lord, for your servant is listening" (1 Sam. 3:9),[202] but now takes the form of the demand, "Tell me your name" (Gen. 32:29).[203]

A *second consideration* would be, again, the problem of the insufficiency of the six responses corresponding to the various positions taken on the problem of God.[204] None of these "answers" seems convincing. But neither can any of them be said to be altogether false. Each of the six "solutions" considered can very readily be reinterpreted as six valid aspects of divinity, or of our conception of divinity — only, none of the six, notwithstanding their extreme diversity on the theoretical plane, can altogether eliminate the validity of any of the others. Contemporary reflection on the problem of God cannot be legitimately regarded either as a premeditated assault on the living God, or as an outrageously a priori defense of the God of religion. Rather, such reflection is a humble, sincere effort to find room for what has always been called God, prescinding from the various functions that, in varying degrees of legitimacy, have been attributed to it. Nor again can it be said that God is a sort of synthesis of the various conceptions we have considered: first of all because God is simple and not a combination of attributes, and then because our conception of God should be possessed of the same simplicity if it has to approach the truth.[205]

By way of a *third consideration*, I should like to underscore the antagonistic character of identity and of difference presented by the reality of God. On the one side, God is that which is most identical with, most interior to, every single thing. God is that which ultimately anything at all "is." On the other side, God is that which is most different, most distinct, and most removed from any being, to the point that if beings are really beings, God cannot be Being; if beings are real, God cannot be real; if things exist, God has no existence, and so on. Thinking that addresses God, then, transcends all categories that help the human being to maneuver in this world. Discourse about God has no terms of comparison. It is by definition unique, and consequently it is incomparable.[206] Once again, silence beckons.

Some *convictions*, in spite of all, do seem to derive from an analysis of the contemporary situation. *First* of all, the problem of God is simply everywhere in some form or another. Theism and atheism are not the only presentations of the problem: any ideology and any cosmology are nothing but attempts to resolve, in a way peculiar to each, the question of what is ultimate and definitive. Indeed in one way or another, any philosophical system eventually runs up against the limits of philosophizing itself, and so must "have it out" with what traditionally would be called the problem of God.

A *second* conviction seems to me equally indisputable: that traditional responses are inadequate. The first confirmation of this comes from the very efforts of those who consider the responses still valid enough to reinterpret them, translate them, and adapt them to the mentality of today. This only demonstrates that the traditional answers, though responding to a real problematic, and doubtless containing a sizable morsel of truth, are unavailing in their present form for convincing today's humankind.

A *third* conviction—one that seems to me to be of nearly universal validity—is that of the need for a purification and "reform" of the notion of God. Perhaps even the word itself should be replaced. The reason why I use it here is to avoid having to produce an endless series of synonyms and equivalents. Now, a reinterpretation of the idea of God will have to comport not only a kind of modernization and adaptation, but a radical revolution, which we can only describe as still another change of awareness in humanity itself, such as has perhaps but rarely been seen in human history. Might it not be that humankind has once more spied the tree of life, and is now braving the angel guardian's flaming sword in order to eat of it and live eternally?[207] The God of the religions, as these religions represent God to us, is not enough. The Absolute of the philosophers is not enough. Neither the infinite limit of the scientists nor the indescribable horizon of the poets is enough. Neither matter nor spirit, neither humanity nor the cosmos, satisfies. The present malaise, and the current so-called lack of faith in the sacred and the transcendent are an ongoing, and positive, sign of this new quest for the ever unknown God.

Let us attempt to present a topography of the terrain in which contemporary mortals move in this quest.

In the first place, God is neither transcendent nor immanent. God is neither ourselves, abiding in immanent identity with us, nor an "other" being, "out there" somewhere in Olympian aloofness. God is neither the same as the world nor different from it. God cannot be identified with the human being, but neither can God be separated from the human species. In a word, dropping all circumlocutions: God neither exists nor does not exist. To say this does not mean abdicating rationality, or attempting to escape from this world by placing God beyond human disputes. On the contrary, to say this is tantamount to positing God at the very heart of all that is human. To be sure, our age does not yet have its hand on the intellective tools of which it will have need in order to be able to express this, its deepest intuition. And yet every individual coming into this world participates in this light.

Nec cum te, nec sine te, as the Latin poet says. God's presence is annoying; God's absence is agonizing. Traditional language fails to convince us; modern formulations, for their part, are obviously inadequate. Perhaps we may say that one of the convictions of today's humanity comes down to a glimmer of what, discerned in its totality, would be the mystical intuition that God cannot be the noun-subject of a sentence — because God is not a subject — but that neither can God be the object of any predication — because this would represent the reification and destruction of precisely what God means to be.[208] This is what the Western and Christian mentality is rediscovering[209] — so very slowly[210] — today.

10

Silence of the Buddha

TO DARE TO BE SILENT

Sculptures of the Buddha, which, as we know, are found only after the fecundation of the Indic mind by the spirit of Hellenism (might Buddhism have remained iconographically mute without this hybridization?), are placid, smiling, as if they saw without looking, seeming to dissipate into nothingness the anxious inquiring of the human beings who gaze up aloft at them. They make no reply. They only aid in deciding that the very question is devoid of sense—not only because it is ill posed, but because it lacks any basis in reality. Buddhist iconography seems to wrap all things in an atmosphere of irrelevance[1] and thereby simply to eliminate the anguish of any problematic at all. It is not only that the Buddha himself is silent. He silences all anxiety, all perplexity, besides—by revealing its nothingness.[2] We make our deferential approach to Gautama, the Buddha . . . and then suddenly it is as if we were not there to pose at all those awful problems that torture us.

As I have already observed, not only is the Buddha silent, but his response is silence as well. Now I must add something else. It is not simply that his is a silent answer, whereas the responses of so many others are lively and verbose. It is a matter of something else altogether. The Buddha makes no reply because he eliminates the question. It is not that he does not respond to what is asked. Rather, strictly speaking, nothing is actually asked. The Buddha silences our anxieties—the human thirst to know, to go, to "get there," to possess, to be capable, to . . . be. The Buddha would have us humble.[3]

More than a few readers might have experienced some surprise in the face of that flinty reaction on the part of the Illuminated One when one of his disciples sought to know human destiny—sought to decipher the mystery of life. The Buddha's attitude seems to contradict the anthropological norm, the axiomatic inquiry that, in Europe as in pre- or extra-Buddhist India, was

148

regarded not only as inescapable, but as positive, as something necessary for authentic human life.[4] From Plato to Kant—as well as before and after[5]—it has always been the peculiar trait of Western humanity to assume that asking the ultimate questions regarding the meaning of existence is a sign of culture, of a "humane" degree of civilization. Religion was regarded as the source of the responses to such questions, so as to render one's life fully human.[6] How would we ever bestow meaning on our daily actions unless we knew the ultimate scope of these actions? How could we commit ourselves to an enterprise that really transcended us if we did not even know whence we come, whither we go, and what we have come on this earth to do? At bottom, the entire discussion, not only of the proofs of the existence of God, but of anything concerning God at all, is based on this presupposition, regarded as basic and unshakable: what gives meaning to existence, personal or historical and cosmic, to the human being, society, and the world, is God. Without providence, without a foundation, without an end, without a creator or lord, human beings, we are told, collapse, society destroys itself, and the cosmos crumbles.

One of the things we see in the texts to which I have referred is the attitude of "holy indifference" on the part of the Buddha, not for things of little account, but for the thing that human beings—in the excess of their zeal?—have always regarded as the most important, most transcendent thing in their lives. The Buddha's first lesson in this regard is simply a matter of common sense: if the question of God's existence, or of an extraterrestrial life, or the like, which are said to be of such vital importance, were actually so, they would not present uncertainties of any kind. Their answers would be evident to all human beings, and absolutely uncomplicated. Air is necessary for human life, and obviously either we have access to air, and we breathe, or else we die of asphyxiation. Analogously, if these inquiries were as vital as we are led to believe they are, it would be impossible to live without the answers to them. But history and everyday experience alike teach us that very few individuals have a claim on anything like precise answers to such problems. And behold, the rest do not die a slow death from asphyxiation.

In the first place, the ones with the "answers" pay their own tribute to death. In the second place, we have no objective criterion by which to diagnose the death of the others as one by asphyxiation. Not only should the sheer multiplicity of opinions be a scandal that would demolish the very basis of what we seek to prove—How can God permit such enormous chaos in a matter we regard as so vital?—but should indicate to us, as well, that, after all, it can scarcely be such a crucial problem when it is open to so many different answers.[7]

And so the Buddha seems to wish to prescind from these "fundamental" questions altogether. And he steadfastly resists even being drawn into them.

Then comes modern atheism with its wish to demonstrate that it is both theoretically and practically possible to have a meaningful and even morally positive life without recourse to the hypothesis of a "God" to furnish the whole cosmic and human edifice with an ultimate, definitive support. But although, on the one hand, this new proposal on the part of contemporary atheism is surely fascinating, as witness its welcome by such a great portion of humanity—on the other hand, its application in the philosophical or political field has often produced effects that would seem to corroborate the pessimism of those who remain attached to the "theistic" tradition: without an external, "transcendent" bolster, humanity fails to cope, and falls into chaos, or dejection, or existential despair, and engages in the totalitarian exploitation of humankind by itself.[8] Contingency, after all, even regarded in its positive aspect and constitutive radicality, is ever fleeting, wandering, without a foundation—contingency is "contingent," precisely. To wish to build upon it, to seek to consolidate it, can lead only to its collapse. The Buddha's proposal, indeed, emerging from the radicality of his discovery, is precisely to eliminate this contingency without having it "reabsorbed" into any manner of God.

The Buddha delves to the root of the problem—not via a direct, violent denial of God, nor again through some harmonization of the various paths, but with a demonstration of the *superfluity* of the very question of God or of any ultraterrestrial world. In the Buddha we see the *vacuity* of any possible response, because of the *nullity* of the entire question. Yet we are not obliged to renounce the possibility of an outcome in terms of salvation and liberation. The Buddha's argument—if we may call it this—unfolds along the following lines.

As for the *superfluity* of the question: the message of the Enlightened One appeals to the fact of daily experience that preoccupation with these problems very often fails to lead either to their solution or to a better life. Indeed, anxiety about such questions is one of the causes of evil on earth. Human dissatisfaction immerses humankind in a constant state of discontent. Human beings spend all their forces inquiring into the beyond, and thus perpetuate their very malaise. Battered, ill at ease, nervous, they go ever in quest of the "answer" that cannot quite be found. Then they think they have found it; but their tranquility is short-lived, for they presently come across someone claiming to have found it too, but whose solution is altogether incompatible with their own. And so once more into the breach, filled with new doubt.

As for the *vacuity* of any response: the Buddha teaches that the reason why any "answer" can be anything but vacuous and empty is not so much because the number of answers is roughly equal to that of the population of the earth, but essentially because the response is inevitably conditioned by the question. Because the question necessarily arises within the contingent space inhabited by human beings—and their intellects—the answer can only be as contingent as the question. And then it will scarcely be the ultimate answer that is asked for and expected. What is being sought is precisely a response that will withdraw us from all contingency; whereas, the

Tathagata will point out, no answer to a contingent question will ever rise above contingency. Supposing, even merely out of a fondness for discussion, entirely apart from any desire to delve into the ultimate meaning of life, one were to obtain a response of a transcendent order, such a response would no longer be relevant to the question—besides being unintelligible because of being of a transcendent order.

Of course, the logical objection to this line of reasoning would be that it is based on a particular sort of metaphysics, one far from being universally accepted. Such an objection will scarcely ruffle a Buddhist. For the Buddhist all schools of metaphysics are peas in a pod. Of course, the answer that we have formulated would not be the Buddha's answer. It can only be that of a disciple of his. The Buddha's answer is silence—and silence not as a different kind of answer, but as transcending any answer at all. What else could we possibly conclude from his discreet invitation to eliminate the very question? After all, he calls upon us to acknowledge the radical incommensurability between the root of our question—that is to say, dissatisfaction and contingency—and the only possible adequate answer, which could scarcely be an answer to the question asked, given that the answer must necessarily be precisely of that order to which the question itself can never belong.

And this at once betrays the nullity of any question bearing on what of its very nature transcends the relative. But we must be careful here. I have already recalled that the Buddha is not an agnostic.[9] For him it is not a matter of foregoing knowledge of the answer, by way of some negative ascesis resting in turn on a fideism that would incline us to leave out of account what we consider to be precisely the most important thing in life. It is a matter of discovering that any statement of the problem in space and time will inevitably be caught in the trammels of these limited coordinates. Human beings are of an itinerant, contingent condition. They cannot leap over their own shadows. Their question, then, can receive no satisfactory answer. After all, were that answer to be found, the last state would be worse than the first: the answer would represent the absolutization of contingency, the capture of the Absolute in the nets of creatureliness.

Will it not be a matter, then, of accepting the utter transcendence of God, or of any absolute, where intellectualism or voluntarism are concerned? The idea of God is not God.[10] To make demands on God, when God, even supposing God were to exist, would be by definition that which renders the very question possible, would be to plunge into a vicious circle. At the same time, it would be fatuous to pretend to deduce God's nonexistence from God's silence. That I obtain no response to my demand upon God will by no means prove that God does not exist. Let God's existence be affirmed or denied as it may: neither "answer" will be of any importance, for both are equally invalid.

What the Buddha would have us understand, then, when all is said and done, is that the so-called ultimate question is unfounded and irrelevant.

He wishes to lead us to the discovery that our very inquiry proceeds from an erroneous presupposition, deriving as it does from the illusion that the creature must be able to overleap its own shadow. This is the import of the Buddha's tireless refusal to make any reply. In his own words, as tradition would have them, when a certain monk asked him the purpose of nirvana, Gautama responded: "O Rādha, this question cannot set its own boundaries."[11]

Thereby he sought to indicate that the question is unintelligible in itself. One does not know what one is asking. How then could one understand the reply? The text continues: "*Nirvāṇa* is it own purpose; *nirvāṇa* is its own goal."[12] And that is all there is to say.

However, Buddhism cannot be accused of preaching a methodological nihilism. Few religions in the world have been more scrupulous in developing the infinitude of anthropological traits necessary for human beings to reach their proper end. Doubtless the Buddha was more sober than his disciples, but he was no less clear. His via media is a genuine and real *via* — precisely because it is and is intended to be precisely a way, a path — an effectuation, and not mere lucubration. It is not only a midpoint between two extremes lying in the horizontal; it is found not only "between" the opposite poles of two contrasting opinions, it is "midmost" because, in all sobriety, it stops "halfway there." It does not pretend to take us "all the way up." It is "midmost," then, vertically as well, for it has the wisdom to call a halt before the road could ever "exist" — which would represent an internal contradiction. There is a road, as long as it leads somewhere, as long as one is moving toward the goal. But let that road step beyond the vestibule of the "pure earth" (*Amida*) and, like any other path or journey, it will lead you straight out of paradise:

> There exists a nirvana and a path that leads to nirvana; and I am here as one who shows [that path]. O Brahmin Moggalana, among the disciples, whom I exhort and teach, there are some who will attain the supreme goal, nirvana; and there are others who will not attain it. The Tathagata, O Brahmin, limits himself to showing the way.[13]

The Buddhist "middle way," then, consists in refusing to carry anything to an extreme, pursuing nothing to the very end. All idolatry, even that of thought, is erroneous.[14] To claim to exhaust the truth, to pretend to deduce every consequence, is not only a piece of prideful pretension; for Śākyamuni it is impious rationalism as well. It would capsize reason. Like an octopus grappling with itself, it would lose what life it has.[15] Of course, it would be equally mistaken to depreciate thought, and embrace contradiction in disregard of the demands of reason. Time after time the Buddha preached:

> The world attaches itself successively to existence and to nonexistence: everything exists (one extreme), nothing exists (the other extreme). But

those who have the right vision of things, as they truly are, do not affirm that things do not exist, given that they are produced, or that they exist, given that they change. It was thus that the Tathagata, avoiding extremes, taught the middle way. . . . Those who have the right vision are not prisoners of their own thoughts, like worldly persons. They who are not attached to systems or merely speculative research do not say, "This is my *ātman*," but say to themselves, "Everything that appears is nothing but sorrow." Such ones are free from doubt and disquietude.[16]

The old refrain returns: to strive for substance and destiny (Pascal would perhaps call it "playing the human role"),[17] to wish to absolutize anything whatsoever in this world, is to commit the great religious sin.[18] The pedagogy of the Buddha consists not in inculcating solutions, but in inviting us to dissolve the very state of the problem by acknowledging its inadequacy—not because I am not able to pose it correctly, but because I myself, who pose it, am the actual reason why any posing of it at all will be incorrect.

Gautama Siddhartha is perfectly well aware of what he is preaching. And he knows its consequences will be revolution. He fully realizes that he is setting in motion, for the first time, the wheel of the Law (*dharmacakra*) and of knowledge of that Law, when he pronounces the Sermon of Sarnath (*Vārāṇasī*):[19]

I have penetrated this doctrine which is profound, difficult to perceive and to understand, which brings quietude of heart, which is exalted, which is unattainable by reasoning, abstruse, intelligible [only] to the wise. This people, on the other hand, is given to desire, intent upon desire, delighting in desire. To this people, therefore, who are given to desire, intent upon desire, delighting in desire, the law of causality and the chain of causation will be a matter difficult to understand; most difficult for them to understand will be also the extinction of all samkhâras, the getting rid of all the substrata [of existence], the destruction of desire, the absence of passion, quietude of heart, Nirvâna![20]

Independent of the belief, common to nearly all religions (including those that honor the Bhagavadgītā[21] and the gospel[22]), that very few persons are capable of understanding the way of salvation and still fewer of following it, the position of the Buddha is surprisingly modern. It does not pretend that religions give us solutions. It seeks to withdraw human beings from their wish to play the little God—to read a part not written for them. The Buddha asks that human beings simply understand the impermanence of all that exists, not excluding themselves—that they not rely on an "answer." That is, he demands the perfect act of faith, the total, unconditional leap: we cannot even be sure that the subject will make that leap, for it altogether transcends the subject.[23] What the Buddha is communicating, wordlessly, to the one with ears to hear and interpret, is that we must have the daring to enter into silence, that we must be prepared to lose our own life completely, that we must be willing to prescind from any object whatsoever and even to slough off the subject. Siddhartha is not inviting us to set an object before our faith—thereby objectifying, reifying, and so destroying that object.

Faith, though of course comporting an intellective dimension, is not fundamentally an act of the intellect. It is an act of the whole person.[24] The perfect and universal formula of faith is not "I believe in God," but "I believe," as an expression of total self-bestowal, as an utterance of the abandon with which the answer given in the gospel by the person blind from birth is charged: "I do believe, Lord."[25] Faith is an act of sheer openness. Any closure upon an object wrings it dry. The very presence of God is detrimental to the constitutive openness of faith. Neither the Buddha, nor the Prophet, nor the Christ can remain at the believer's side without representing a dangerous obstacle to that believer's leap of faith:

> Kill everything that stands in your way. If you should meet the Buddha, kill the Buddha. If you should meet the Patriarchs, kill the Patriarchs. If you should meet the arhats on your way, kill them too.[26]

Buddha announces his definitive entry into *nirvāṇa*, lest, by his remaining with us, we become slothful. Everyone has to strive to find and follow the way to *nirvāṇa*:

> From the moment the Tathagata announces his own entrance into nirvana, the people will be alert to follow the way; if the Blessed One remained, the people would become lazy.[27]

To help and guide followers, he will leave them the dharma and the sangha. A similar comportment is asked of the Christian: if you meet Christ on the way, consume him! Indeed, the teacher of Nazareth himself proclaims that it is best for him to take his departure—otherwise the Comforter, the Spirit who acts from within, cannot come.[28] For the rest, he too will leave behind, along with the eucharist, the church community, as the depository of his own message.[29]

I note that, according to the Buddhist tradition, as in so many other mystical traditions, there are three types of silence on the level of practice: that of the body, that of the voice, and that of thought.[30] All three are important and necessary for ascesis. But clearly one counts most, and the others are subordinate to it: the preeminent silence is silence of thought. It is also the most difficult of the three to attain. In order to be able to enter it, we must dare to plumb the depths of the silence of our very mind, stilling all the internal sounds of our thinking faculty.[31]

This holds for the present instance as well. The only way to understand what I am saying, and shall be saying in the remainder of this book, will be to enter into the authentic silence of the mind. The whole effort of the Buddha is directed to the attainment of such silence; and like the whole of Buddhism after him, he has placed as the condition of entry into this silence, first and foremost, not speculation, or doctrine, but meditation, contemplation, the quiet of the mind, and interior silence:

> Cultivate concentration, O bikkhus, for the bikkhu with a concentrated mind knows things as they really are.[32]

In a certain sense we might say that Buddhism is purely and simply a school of prayer—understanding prayer not in the sense of vocal prayer, however, but as interior contemplation. All that the Buddha has said gains its significance and beauty when we understand it from the viewpoint of contemplation. If we leave out, or attempt to prescind from, the life of prayer and meditation, we slip into mere dialectic and subtle lucubrations and all that the Enlightened One has said will not only not be fully grasped, it will be altogether beyond our surmise. Unless we have attained interior contemplative silence, we shall allow the message of the Buddha to "go in one ear and out the other," and understand nothing of what he wished to teach:

> Therefore, Ananda, a man who tries to practice *dhyana* [meditation] without first attaining control of his mind is like a man trying to bake bread out of a dough made of sand.[33]

Buddhism cannot be really and truly "spoken of." It must be "prayed."[34] This allusion to prayer, and to ritual generally, seems to me to have an importance of its own; but it can also help us discover the function of Buddhistic silence from the viewpoint of religious phenomenology. It is common knowledge that silence occupies a relevant place in all ritual. Alongside action stands contemplation; alongside words, the silences.[35] Rarely, however, has an overt, explicit development of the meaning of silence received more minute attention than in Vedic worship. And inasmuch as it is in the Vedic horizon that Buddhism has taken its point of departure, it will not be without interest to devote a brief excursus to it here.[36]

In Vedic worship, formulas to be recited or sung aloud by the priests and celebrant are distinguished from the barely audible murmurs to be uttered by a priest. These in turn are distinguished from formulas to be "thought" silently with the mind alone (*manasā*) by the celebrant. Finally, there are the silences proper, as when certain actions are to be performed "in silence" (*tūṣṇīm*).

We note that in many cases the action performed in silence is addressed to Prajapati.[37] Silence is Prajapati's hallmark,[38] and it is by silence that he is rendered propitious.[39] But Prajapati is the sacrifice par excellence.[40] He personifies the act of worship.[41] Indeed, there is a point at which silence and Prajapati become so "fused" that the silent action of the individual executing the sacrifice, such as the spreading of the antelope pelt — another typical ritual action — comes to be regarded as simply constituting the sacrifice as such. After all, "the sacrifice is Prajapati, and Prajapati is the ineffable."[42]

On the other hand, it seems that silence became part of ritual in a later development. Vedic literature feels a need to justify its introduction with a myth. The reason why word is absent from one of the actions culminating the rite of the oblation to Prajapati, who is the very personification of sacrifice as such, we are told, is that word (*vāc*) is "retaliating." Prajapati, of old, settled the dispute between word and spirit (*manas*) by assigning preeminence to spirit.[43] It would not be impossible, then, that the introduction of silence into the ritual of sacrifice might owe its origin to a quasi-official acceptance, at the heart of Brahmanic worship,[44] of a mystical element. After all, it is precisely the withholding of word as an act of worship that becomes the fulcrum by which the sacrificial ritual is shifted from the physical performance of sacrifice to sublimation in an interior ascesis.[45] By holding word in check, sacrifice and its power are transferred to the interiority of the individual. It is the individual who, in silence, undergoes the mortification[46] that eventually leads to awareness that the act of immolation is perfectly present in silence. "When one is silent, breath devours word."[47]

The value of ritual silence is enormous. It unites us to divinity for good and all. It possesses a force all its own. It is the eye and root of sacrifice.[48] It renders sacrifice visible.[49]

The offering of a mute oblation comports the transcendence of distinctions. It wins the divine glory — to the point where it actually confers that glory on divinity.[50] The silent offering vanquishes totality,[51] conquers the unlimited[52] and the inexpressible[53] — "for what is not obtained with the word is obtained through silence,"[54] and we have seen the essential bond between thought and silence. There are instances when silence has the power to effectuate the sacrificial act.[55] Perhaps it is for this reason that silence is regarded as particularly appropriate in funeral rites[56] and rituals of expiation,[57] for it is here that certain obscure forces enter into play.[58]

Ultimately, then, liturgical silence is more than a rite. It is more than a means. It is also the very end attained through silence.[59] This is why no religion can dispense with silence. Even in a tradition like the Judeo-Christian, in which praise is so often the dominant element in ritual, the observance of silence cannot be dispensed with when one comes face to face with God.[60] And of course the tool par excellence of the contemplative life is the silence that not only hushes word, but also, and especially, thought.[61] Silence regards mystery.[62]

THE FOUR NOBLE TRUTHS

It is not simply by way of a personal statement that I now propose the following text and commentary. Rather, I think that this approach might be just the way to address the religious spirit of our time. Most of humanity's religious traditions bear on a "liberation" of the world and its inhabitants, although from widely varying points of vantage. Buddhism is no different in this respect. The "liberation" on which Buddhism concentrates is the elimination of suffering—a negative outlook in its basic statement, as we see, but an outlook charged with a hidden positivity. It is this positivity that I shall now attempt to express in the following reformulation for our times of the message of the Enlightened One.

Text

There are two extremes to be avoided by the human beings of today in order to attain to a life that is truly human, in order to achieve the peace and joy to which they aspire. What are these extremes? One is the quest of ourselves—selfishness, the pursuit of pleasure, comfort, and self-satisfaction, in contemptuous disregard for the rest of humankind. The other extreme to be avoided is alienation from ourselves—to conquer the world or God, to conquer others, to gain exteriority and effectiveness, to win power, prestige, and fame, whether in this world or the other. Each of the two extremes leads to suffering, failure, disappointment, war, despair, and the destruction of humanity.

By contrast, the via media of the Blessed One eludes these two extremes. His is a luminous, serene, personal, concrete way that can be traversed by any pilgrim at all, and it leads to peace, joy, fulfillment, and plenitude. And which, O people of today, is the way that leads to peace, joy, human fulfillment, and plenitude?

That way is the via media, O people of today, and it contains within itself the very peace and fullness that it proclaims.

This is *the noble truth of joy*. Every person desires to be happy. What the human being seeks, covets, is happiness. We know, we see, that everything around us is conditioned by the pursuit of happiness. When human beings initiate any work, perform any action, or desire anything whatsoever, they wish nothing but to move toward happiness. All of their reasons for acting are guided by the star of happiness.

This, O people of today, is *the noble truth of the origin of joy*: to *believe* that joy exists and is possible. Human beings come from happiness, are sensitive only to happiness, move only in order to be happy, and are happy only when they have attained genuine life. Their deep desire, existential weight, and center of gravity, all proceed from a center comprised of pure joy, unadulterated happiness, perfect glory. Human beings would not move toward happiness in this way were happiness not the very center of their life.

This, O people of today, is *the noble truth of the acquisition of joy*: the *hope* of reaching it, the true hope of happiness, which prevents us from forgetting that the path is only a path, and that, provided we do not stop along the way and convert the path into an end—even by thought—the path is joyous simply as path. With the actualization of Good, Truth, and Beauty as well, human beings drink at the fountain of living water that slakes their thirst at every moment along the way.

This, O people of today, is *the way that leads to joy*: the simple, noble route of *love* of all things—without being caught in their net. The noble way of love, then, is the total bestowal of oneself. And this bestowal can have no end, for it is inexhaustible.

Until such time as the triple intuition of *faith, hope*, and *love* are purified by the *four noble truths*—until then, human beings with their passions, resentments, arrangements, machinations, societies, ideas, and accomplishments will not reach the illumination that brings them peace, joy, and true freedom.

Corollaries

The Question of Happiness

The first immediate difference between my text and the traditional Buddhist position is that the latter has focused primarily on suffering, as the characteristic of contingency that one seeks to eliminate. For my part, I put the accent on joy, the characteristic of reality that one seeks to attain. The common element is the concrete reality about which we question ourselves, and our confidence of finding an adequate answer. The difference is that one approach is negative (the elimination of the suffering inherent in contingency), and the other positive (the attainment of joyous reality, after the expurgation of the imperfections of contingency). This difference is reflected in the very statement of the question, and this calls our attention to the capital importance of how the question is posed. The way in which the question is posed determines the manner of answer it will receive. The question is the cornice into which the answer will be chiseled. So completely does each of the questions ontically contain its response, that its respective answer is in turn but the ontological manifestation of the question.[63]

In the traditional Buddhist perspective, the question of God or the Being of God is a futile one at best. It can receive only three types of answers: affirmative, negative, and agnostic. But the Buddha calls our attention to the fact that it is at most only the question, and not God, that can be exhausted by these three responses. There is simply no question of being or nonbeing on God's part, nor of ignorance on our part—it is a matter of a "something" here that does not lend itself to inscription within the scheme of this or any other question we might pose. Hence the message of the Buddha to "distract" us from the question of God — and to attract the focus of our attention instead to the immediate problem of suffering and its elimination. This message of his implies neither theism, nor atheism, nor finally agnosticism on his part. This is not the question. It cannot be, and Gautama repeatedly refuses to allow himself to be entangled in this game. The Buddha's problematic is a problematic not of rational explanation, but of the intuition of human existence as the anthropological task. In this task, God is the object neither of thought nor of will, and still less that of preaching or proclamation.

And so Siddhartha always drastically refused to allow himself to be "enmeshed" in the dialectic of his own time, bonding himself directly to the practical plane of existence and its elimination. He prefers to rely on a *prise de conscience* of suffering and the need for its elimination, rather than to concentrate on the more human, more immediate, quest for joy. Māra (the Tempter) says:

> The joy of a father is in his children, as are herds the joy of their owner. Though a person rests in joy, he does not have any joy whose life depends on nothing.

And the Enlightened One responds:

> Upon his children is based a father's woe, as on his herds their owner's woe. But woes assail not him whose life depends on Naught.[64]

And yet, provided we are aware that true joy does not consist in the ephemeral attainment of temporal pleasures, the quest for felicity is fully as "Buddhist" a characteristic as that of the elimination of suffering.[65] Indeed few religions present a more smiling, optimistic, serene face than Buddhism, at any rate in the majority of its forms.

If, then, in my reformulation of the Discourse of the Four Noble Truths I have allowed myself to "change the sign" (mathematical) of the human quest for realization, I shall scarcely have deviated by much from the spirit of one Buddhist approach. At the same time, I shall have entered upon a terrain in which the contemporary spirit is much more comfortable. To boot, both suffering and joy are universal factors, and both enjoy the character of ultimacy. To be sure, each has its own concrete ideas about how joy is to be conceived and the practical way to attain it.[66]

Primordial Joy

It is typical of religious tradition to regard the human condition as rooted essentially in an original purity whose primordial characteristic is not suffering, but joy.[67] Suffering then presents itself as a kind of superstructure, which is adventitious to the human race and from which the latter must be liberated. The groundwork is joy.[68] And so when the Buddha says that human liberation is obtainable through the elimination of the super-structure of suffering with which contingency is impregnated, though he hesitates to call it "joy,"[69] this is what he basically means. Later tradition has corroborated this, and *nirvāṇa* itself is called "supreme felicity" (*paraman sukham*):

> Health is the greatest possession. Contentment is the greatest treasure. Confidence is the greatest friend. Nirvana is the greatest joy.[70]

When joy is seen as the initial state, and not as the final state, not as a goal to reach, then the method of obtaining it cannot but be the negative way of stripping, of spoliation. When joy is regarded as the primordial, natural, human state, there is no need either to know what it is, or to move toward it, or to add anything whatever to our condition. All that need be "done" is to strip ourselves of the superstructure of suffering—eliminate all that life has layered on in the course of existence. In a word, all that need be "done" is to destroy contingency, so that joy and pristine glory may blaze forth unimpeded. To this end, we need no antecedent knowledge that would enable us to start down the right road, or that would indicate to us the direction or goal toward which we ought to move. The practical way proposed by the Buddha is the one available in all of our experiences, for it falls within our limits: the elimination of suffering and the destruction of the contingency that we "are," that thus the initial glory may shine.[71]

Indeed the Enlightened One himself has said:

> So spoke once the beloved disciple Ānanda to the Master: "The goal of the holy way, O Lord, consists in friendship with the lovely, in communion with the lovely." The Master answered: "No, it is not so, not so, O Ānanda. This is not the goal but the totality of the holy way."[72]

The Thirst for Happiness

Our existence is impregnated with "thirst": the concrete, objectified, ever-unquenched desire for any limited good, along with the thirst for eternal life.[73] The former thirst remains ever unslaked. Each quenching of it ultimately eventuates in our not having quenched it at all, and this becomes the prime cause of the sense of ennui and frustration of which our age has such deep experience.

The second thirst is the holy desire whose stimulation we cannot forego if we are to move in the direction of its slaking.[74] This thirst too, however, remains unsatisfied for such time as we find ourselves still in this life. After all, salvation is infinite, whereas we ourselves are finite. This second thirst is so much a part of the message of salvation that, were it to become dulled in the course of our quest to assuage it, that message could no longer be acknowledged as authentic.[75] This thirst is the prime condition for the blossoming of hope. This is the thirst that can be defined as the infinite yearning for the infinite.[76]

If we observe carefully, this thirst has a positive aspect. It is a desire for liberation, a yearning for completeness. It is a spur in the direction of our proper perfection, whatever that be, without necessarily a "God" or any other object as its point of reference.[77] It is a desire, a thirst, for perfection, simply. It is the window of human finitude upon the infinite.[78] It is a desire that launches us out beyond our contingency. It relentlessly obliges us to overcome ourselves and thus to attain to our plenitude. The reason why the thirst for justice renders us blessed is that this justice is unattainable in this world.[79]

And yet we entertain a lingering doubt. Is this what the Buddha means with his repeated enjoinder to search out our salvation with diligence?[80] Is it not rather the case that any thirst, even that which we might regard as the most perfect of thirsts—the desire of one's own salvation—is to be stigmatized as impure and not conducive to the goal?[81] Does not the Buddha seek to temper desire itself, be it desire for the spring or desire for any kind of living water?[82] After all, he has shown that all thirst produces a malaise, because it continually deceives through the object in which it clothes itself. Even to thirst for living water is but to preserve that inquietude, except that now it is interiorized. This thirst too, then, would seem to constitute an obstacle to the unconditional satisfaction of all thirst.[83] The teacher of Nazareth himself adverted to the anomaly of an inextinguishable thirst, and spoke of the extinction of such thirst.[84] Tradition would have the spring of living water none other than humankind itself.[85]

The Loss of Contingency

The adventure of joy is an adventure of life and death. All our life is at stake. Here the one who triumphs loses life. The Buddha is altogether clear on this point. He speaks explicitly of the elimination of suffering as the elimination of all that is most intimately bound up with human creatureliness. For the Buddha, salvation is attained (to use an imprecise word, inasmuch as the progress in question is actually one not of "attainment," but of a "stripping") through the total loss of one's life, as we leap beyond space and time, bursting the cosmological bonds, transcending *saṃsāra* in every way, shape, and form—that is, as we transcend creatureliness and contingency. For the Buddha, nothing, absolutely nothing, of what belongs to this world, by very definition, can pretend to stand on the further shore, in the region of the Absolute, the intemporal— *nirvāṇa*. Of no one can it be truly said, "Such a one has attained *nirvāṇa*." After all, "who" might such a one be, for anyone finally arriving beyond existence has ceased to exist?[86] One cannot husband one's contingency (and who succeeds in doing so?) and then assert that the last end of the creature is the Absolute.

Equally explicit on this point is the Christ, the Lord's Anointed, with his reiterated admonitions to give up life.[87] The adventure of joy is an adventure of life and death, and if it is true that the steps toward death are all of them, or almost all, accompanied by the proclamation of resurrection, it is no less true that when we come to the actual practice of life, resurrection is no longer our affair, nor can we know how it will be bestowed or what form it will take. The message of the Buddha causes us to reflect that the accent of the evangelical exhortations falls on the first member, the loss of one's life, and not on the second, the reward of resurrection. The latter is something beyond our will.

One must have the courage, then, to renounce contingency—to renounce, in the last analysis, being, in any of its possible acceptations. There is no room for a non-God in God.[88] Notwithstanding some discordant voices, even in the *bhakti* spirituality, the final embrace has no room for a real two. Separation is no longer possible. In love, in joy, in embrace, in union, consummation, there is no room for two. The two *were* two—but in order that they might come to be one, or rather nontwo. The moment the kingdom of dissimilitude, *regio dissimilitudinis* (to use the beautiful European medieval expression),[89] is at an end, any idea of dissimilarity must obviously disappear, must simply be over and done with.[90] But without dissimilarity there is evidently neither contingency nor creation. Creation "has been," creation "was." But when the end has been attained, the scab of temporality has healed over for good and all.[91]

This means too that the world of today, strive as it may to continue to acknowledge joy as the ultimate end of the human adventure, notes that, when all is said and done, there can be no perfect felicity as long as any remnants of contingency remain. These must be burned. Creaturely residues must be consumed. Indeed, the human individual can be likened to a drop of water, side by side with so many other drops—to use a comparison dear to the Upanishadic tradition[92]—which, at the close of its particular temporal existence, enters the sea of Divinity.[93] And yet the fear of losing one's "own" individuality has often drawn Christian philosophy and theology into a defense of individual survival—which is not the same as personal survival.

But everything depends on where we think true value lies: in the finite, or in the infinite.[94] If true value lies in what constitutes human individuality—in the surface of the drop, that both delimits the drop and permits it to be a drop—then obviously this value is lost the moment we plunge into the immense ocean of Divinity (however one might choose to construe this appellation). If, on the other hand, the true value resides in what constitutes the very essence of personhood—that is, in that personhood, being an image, a spark, of the All, a participation in the All (in the divine, some will say; in the human, the social, others will say; in the collective Unconscious, still others will say; in the Naught, the Buddha will say)—if, in a word, the essence is the water and not its delimitation in the form of a drop, then, when this drop returns to the sea, how can it be said to have abdicated its nature as water? It has scarcely lost the essential. Are we the *drop* of the water or the *water* of the drop? Indeed, any mysticism will speak of the emptying of oneself, the disappearance of one's *ego*, as an essential condition for the attainment of the Absolute, God, the further shore— *nirvāṇa*.[95]

The Social, or Collective Human, Aspect

Although the conclusion drawn above is viable from a certain "spiritual" standpoint, it leaves many with a certain malaise. Today's new prophets of humanity see the most noble and ultimate end of that humanity in the service of neighbor. Now, it is objected, if the spiritual end of humankind is the loss of self, should we not perhaps think, or desire, that all other human beings become likewise "nothingness"? But if human beings and the world are of themselves nothingness, what need is there to concern ourselves with them? In other words, if the human ideal is to be "saintly" (in the etymological sense of the word: "separated"), *arhat* (one who retires from the struggle of the world), *sannyāsin* ("renouncers"), and so on, would those apostles of a suffering humanity not be correct in considering this attainment "selfish," precisely, and thus false the philosophy supporting it?

On the other hand, can the most authentic representatives of so many traditions really be accused of selfishness? Obviously not. This ought to be clear enough in the case of Christianity. A good part of the gospel of the teacher of Nazareth is devoted to the service of one's neighbor.[96] The parable of the good Samaritan[97] is taken to represent the most genuine Christian spirit. But the teacher engages in no philosophical speculations here, either on the character of God or on that of humankind. He only proposes a concrete paradigm for his followers' behavior in behalf of a humanity seen to be in need.[98] Indeed the whole of Christian tradition, from its very inception, has done nothing but reinforce and underscore the oft-repeated instructions of the Apostles in scripture[99] regarding activity in behalf of one's neighbor. That tradition has never tired of reiterating the evangelical proclamation that the two loves—God and neighbor—are at bottom but one, for the object upon which they bear is one.[100]

Hinduism is no different in this regard, nor is Buddhism.[101] One of the primary qualities of one who has reached enlightenment, and even more of the *bodhisattva*, is *mahākaruṇā*—"great compassion," or love of neighbor. Indeed, in Mahayana Buddhism it is frankly preferable to nirvana itself.[102] Further, mercy and compassion are regarded as important aspects of asceticism. The four spiritual exercises (*brahmavihāras*) recommended by tradition are formed of mercy (*maitrī*), compassion (*karuṇā*), joy (*muditā*), and equanimity (*upekṣā*).[103] Nor did the Tathagata himself disdain to offer his own, concrete service in behalf of a sufferer. Tradition recounts that one day the Enlightened One stopped at one of the monasteries in which his monks were dwelling and found there a *bhikkhu* lying in his own excrement, the victim of a fatal intestinal affliction. It was a terminal illness and nothing could be done about that. Yet, Śākyamuni washed the poor wretch with his own hands, had his cot removed, and laid him in his own bed. Then he turned to the other *bhikkhu*s and said:

> O mendicant monks, you have neither father nor mother to look after you; if you do not look after each other, who will do it? Those who wish to be concerned about me, should be concerned about the sick.[104]

The Buddha's action is totally disinterested, not only with respect to himself, but even with regard to the suffering monk, who is cared for not in view of a cure, but only that he might have death with decency. The sense of the Buddha's *karuṇā*, then, resides in the superabundance of his state of "grace." When one has reached the state of "buddhahood" — when one is in perfect calm, with every desire, even that of salvation, removed, and is stranger to any kind of emotion — then *karuṇā*, or love of neighbor, comes as a corollary of the new Buddha's liberation, becoming part of the nature of this newly "realized" person.

Couched in these terms, the Buddha's *karuṇā* can be likened to what one hears as a description of the divine motive for creation: the "externalization," in the concrete, of the superabundance of an interior love. The same will apply to the attitude of the spiritual person toward the neighbor: a superabundant love overflows upon one's fellow human beings, without any other intent than the well-being of these persons and the alleviation of the burden of their earthly pilgrimage.[105] There is not the faintest suggestion of selfishness here, or even of "paternalism" — those inevitable defects of any reflexively conscious "good deed."[106]

THE SILENCE OF GOD

As we have seen, the questions continually assaulting human beings from the moment they attain reflexive consciousness are principally three: the problem of God, the problem of the world, and the problem of humankind, especially the question of one's own lot after death. Everyone has sought to have an answer, within the matrix of each one's own cultural coordinates. In the interest of brevity and clarity, let me group the various responses in three general categories: (1) the attitude of cosmic trust, more typical of the East; (2) the critical attitude, more typical of the West; and finally, (3) the anthropocentric position, which seems to prevail today.

In the *first* position, the most widespread attitude is: any meaning that God and the world might have is independent of any knowledge of mine. This frame of mind certainly does not involve the abandonment of the use of the intellect or the renunciation of philosophizing. Still, the spiritual attitude deriving from it tends to locate genuine knowledge of ultimate reality beyond the grasp of conscious awareness. This position can be aptly expressed in the aphorism, "One who speaks, knows not; one who knows, speaks not."[107] Trust is placed in reality.

The *second* case is the reverse of the first. If God and the world had meaning, I should surely know that meaning. If I do not, then either I am inexcusable,[108] or such meaning simply does not exist: then God, or else the world (depending on where one prefers to place the emphasis), is not real. Here, as in the former case, the correlation between thinking and being is all but perfect. If by thinking I fail to arrive at Being, then either my thinking is culpably inadequate, or else such Being does not exist. Gnosis is salvation.

In the *third* case, if the world and God have any meaning it is that conferred on them by humankind. Nothing exists independently of humankind. God is actually efficacious only for those who believe in God. For those who do not acknowledge God, God is completely dead.[109] This position — which is not necessarily equivalent to subjectivism — is an attempt to resituate one's own center of gravity, and is typical of contemporary humanity. Humankind is at the center of the universe.

It has become rather the fashion today to repeat that "God is silent." But this statement carries very different connotations from those traditionally implied by the religions when they have spoken of the silence of God. Traditionally, God is silent because, by definition, God is hidden.[110] God seeks darkness.[111] Thus understood, silence is the hallmark of God's most important characteristic: mystery. A God who would not be "mysterious" would *eo ipso* cease to be God. Such a God would be a philosophical statement, a target of thought, at most a First Cause — but not God in the meaning ordinarily given to this word. Those who have "understood" God have acknowledged that silence alone describes[112] and expresses God.[113] Silence alone is God's finest praise.[114] In any case the intellect must be still before the divine Mystery, and honor it with silence. Any testimony that the human mind could excogitate would be inadequate to express or define God.[115] Even theology, especially in India, has no more adequate conceptualization available for presenting the divine than to present it as Silence — Silence distinct, though not separate, from all that appears as its manifestation. Thus we have texts like the following:

> In the beginning (*agre*) there was only Prajapati; his Word (*vāc*) was with him; the Word was his second. I put myself to contemplation: I wanted to speak that Word, and it would perdure through all [this world]. So I spoke the Word and it produced all this [the world].[116]

Eventually the Upanishadic philosophy came to distinguish a Brahman that is "sound," or "word" (*śabda-brahman*) from another, altogether superior *Brahman* (*parambrahman*), *Brahman* the supreme, *Brahman* not manifest, *brahman* the "silent," the noiseless, the unsounding[117] — Brahman the "empty of being."[118]

Christian theology has expressions of its own, but arrives at analogous conclusions. The very concept of the Trinity is, in a way, an attempt to express the same intuition — namely, that what is, what one can contact, what can be uttered as it were, is the Logos, and not the Father.[119] Christ is the Logos who issues from Silence.[120] Even his birth *ex Maria Virgine* has been interpreted as representing the emergence of the Son from the womb of Silence.[121] The father is Silence par excellence. No one has seen the Father.[122] His Word is no longer himself, but his Logos, the *Verbum,* the Second Person — or indeed his very Son,[123] come to lend force and visible form to the "silent Mystery from eternity."[124]

The silence experienced by modern persons is altogether different. A God silent because mysterious "says" nothing to the modern mind. With the advent of the "scientific mentality," persons began to accept as true only what they can rationally verify, and whose functions are understandable to them. From that moment on, they have virtually canceled the word "mystery" from their very world. In reality, however, they are still terrified by Mystery, and this is why they seek to eliminate it by explaining it as best they can. Graphically put, they would like to convert everything into audible, communicable Word. The fact that God does not speak to them on their wave length perplexes them. They become skeptical. Then terrified.[125] And so they explain the silence of God rationally — the only way they can put God in a box. This way, they reassure themselves, there is nothing to frighten them with some unexpected, unfamiliar Word.[126] Religion, then, is seen as a convenient means of keeping the masses in their illusion. It keeps them at a distance from the one thing important for their well-being — namely, their human awareness, basically in a political sense.

Notwithstanding all explanations and justifications calculated to eliminate the terror with which they are stricken by the silence of the hidden God,[127] our contemporaries have not succeeded in distancing themselves from the negative psychological effect of the Silence. It wraps them all around. It terrifies them still more than before. Now they have expelled from within themselves the figure of the mysterious God who had so dismayed them with an unfathomable silence. But now they find themselves wrapped in an absolute Silence beyond all possibility of redemption, rupture, or manifestation. Now it is the silence of absence, and this is all the more terrible and terrifying a silence.[128] Our contemporaries can no longer exorcise it by striking a harmony with the Silent. And so they stand oppressed by the silence of the world, tortured by their own silence, which they can no longer bear, and disoriented by the silence of society.[129] The infinity of astral space frightens and dismays them.[130] The malady of contemporary humankind is "sigephobia," fear of silence. No longer does silence strike them with the fear of a God who might punish them. The silence is their proof that there is no God. And now, without a God anymore—a God to be feared, yes, but a God who could be consulted, as well, and to whom one might recommend oneself and entrust one's destiny (even giving it a meaning)—without this inconvenient but useful foothold of a God, persons feel helplessly alone. They discover the terrifying meaning of . . . freedom![131] Hence the anguish of modern humanity, but hence also its ennui. This type of solitude offers nothing by way of an alternative to the giddy terror of the Nothing, other than the tedium from a lack of a companionship forever lost.[132] This, it may be, is the reason why moderns can no longer bear to be alone—can no longer "stand the silence." A frenetic life, progress, even contemporary architecture,[133] confine modern humanity in an immense solitude. Agitated, individuals run after the crowd. They hope they can drown their terror by embracing din, blare, uproar.[134]

The Buddha counsels silence. Tradition recounts that on a certain occasion the Blessed One chanced to pass a group of monks who were distracting themselves by chattering about this, that, and the other thing. He paused, and said to them:

> When the mendicant monks (*bhikku*) come together, they should do one of two things: either talk about the Dharma or maintain a noble silence.[135]

Physical silence is the first step toward an understanding of cosmic silence. It was not for nothing that Candrakīrti, as a good disciple of the Enlightened One, was able to say: "The most noble of the truths is silence."[136] Silence is the ground of the Buddha's entire message, from the silence of meditation to the silence of *nirvāṇa*. This does not mean silence is easy to bear, or that human nature does not seek to fill with words the awful void produced by Silence. On the same subject, it is once more Candrakīrti who refers us to a passage of the *Āryatathāgataguhya*:

> On the night, O Santamati, when the Buddha attained the supreme enlightenment, the night when he was about to pass into the final nirvāṇa, on that occasion the Buddha did not utter a single syllable; he did not speak, he does not speak, he shall not speak. But because there are living beings who, given the intensity of their fervor, appear with different characters, with different ends, they imagine that the Buddha preferred a great variety of discourses on a variety of occasions.[137]

Another kind of silence is the silence that has inspired the present work: the philosophical silence that reigns where the grand questions that plague us are concerned, especially philosophy's silence about God. As for God, the Buddha holds his tongue. As I have already observed, by his silence the Enlightened One has shared with us a glimmer of his insight that ultimately there is "nothing" to be said about God because God "is" precisely this "nothing." In other words the divine silence simply corresponds to the divine absence of being. Perhaps the specter that affrights the minds of these moderns—who, through their wish to be free of God's paternalism, have denied God the right to Existence and so have plunged headlong into the void—is precisely this "nothing."[138] But the Buddha assures us that there is Nothing to fear! The giddy leap into the metaphysical Void strikes terror into the heart. But it is a leap that can be exalting. We must approach it slowly, however, prepared for a leap into the dark, and reach silence simply by keeping still, simply by not making an effort to speak.[139]

Of course, where silence is concerned, as the Buddha has shown us, one cannot speak. If I have allowed myself to do so here, it is only in order to communicate what I can, and I do it in full awareness that translation means treason. All that we seek to transmit can really only be a matter of experience, deep within us, through a meditation capable of stilling the tumult of our thoughts. But after all, Gautama Siddhartha renounced his own *mahāparanirvāṇa*—his own silence, that he might save others.[140] Thereby he used words to set the wheel of wisdom spinning.[141] Perhaps the best approach, then, will be to use the word, knowing that that word takes its point of departure in, and acquires all of its meaning and intelligibility from, silence.[142]

Now let me attempt to unfold this meditation on the silence of God. This silence takes three distinct directions. It is addressed (1) to humankind, (2) to God, and (3) to both.

The Silence of God in Humankind

It has become something of a commonplace today to say that God does not make the divine voice heard, that God does not speak to humankind, that God has vanished.[143] The disappointment is enormous. But why such expectations?[144] What do we expect of God? Perhaps that God would redress social wrongs, remedy injustices? But then what would this be, this so ardently desired God? We should once more be hauling God into our human anguish. Only, this time, God would not be responsible for our evil behavior;[145] God would be the defender of our individual and collective selfishness.[146] This would be a good deal more serious.[147] At bottom, the lament of modern humankind is dictated by the increase of its own selfishness. In order to justify their refusal to listen, moderns prefer to convince themselves that God does not speak, or that there simply is no God at all. When all is said and done, the assertion of the disappearance of God reveals a still (or once more) Ptolemaico-anthropocentric dimension of the problem: humans speak of the eclipse of God when they become opaque to themselves.

Let us be straightforward. The Silence of God indicates first of all that any pretense to a total intellection must be abandoned. Secondly, it might well be said that, since God's breach of silence at the beginning of the ages, the only thing that God has "uttered" exhaustively has been the Logos.[148] But we cannot comprehend it until we, in our turn, are (have become) totally the Logos. For we are but a single tonality of this total Word. Perhaps indeed, in a certain sense, we are precisely the disappearance of God.

It is now evident, then, that the moment has arrived to pose the problem anew. The time has come to abandon anthropocentrism and effectuate a conversion — one as necessary as it will be vital. The moment has arrived to acknowledge that ultimately God and humankind cannot be separated this drastically. As long as there is separation between them, the second member of the dichotomy will eventually begin to look for a way to overcome that separation, and historical experience teaches us that the shortest way to this end is via the disappearance of one of the two poles. A certain mystique would have it that the one who disappears ought to be humankind. But it is obvious that, inasmuch as humankind is its own most immediate reality, it will be easier in the long run to have God disappear instead. But as we have seen, the disappearance of God entails, as if by sorcery, the subsequent disappearance of humanity as well.

The efforts of all "religions" (whether or not we accept the derivation of the word from *religare*) have always been exerted toward overcoming the discrepancy obtaining between God and the world — and humankind particularly — without losing the reality of either.

In Christianity the presence of the Logos in the Trinity and its divinization constitute an attempt to resolve this dilemma by maintaining, in the intimate reality of God, total identity and total distinction between the Father and the Son. At the same time, the Son is the head of the Mystical Body, head of the cosmic Christ.[149] The Son, as Logos, is the Father's breach of Silence, the Father's expression. He is one with the Father and identical with him, and yet infinitely distant from him, with all of the distance between originator and originated. In a framework of this scope, the individual human person can only be a tonality of this total Word, an incomplete sound, a projection of God in time and space, God's apprentice. Human individuals become their own downfall, an internal contradiction, when they wish to ignore their own character as itinerants on the journey toward the completeness of the Word. That is to say, the individual participates in God precisely through participation in the Logos. Reversing the manner in which one normally turns to God — directly, as to a Thou — the human individual becomes simply the *thou* of God. My *that* can only be the thou of God's *I*. In this theological description God is the only I, and the creature is but thou. Thus one who prays will say, "I am 'thine' ('thy I')."[150] The philosopher who thinks propositions will think, "I am 'his' ('his I')."[151]

It is not so much that God is manifested to me today in contradiction.[152] It is rather that I myself am this contradiction of God. But the philanthropist (in the etymological sense of the word) can only object to this conclusion. The human being is neither willing nor able to accept its own annihilation—or at least abasement—in favor of God's I. This is why atheism is so uncompromising. In the contest between a transcendent God and an immanent humanity, atheists grasp the danger of their own annihilation. And so they deny God before religion can deny God. After all, when religion comes to the conclusion that humankind is the "contradiction of God," the "non-God on the way to becoming God," human annihilation is all but a fait accompli.

There is simply no escape. If God is canceled, then humankind too, is automatically canceled. The silence of God's absence brings with it the silence of humankind's absence. Here the messages of the Buddha and of modern philosophies converge to a degree. Once you start down the street of the denial of God, sooner or later you must admit the denial of humanity as well. The elimination of God as the support, entails the elimination of humankind as the supported. Indeed, Buddhists pay with their own life for their serenity before the Naught. Without God, neither does humanity exist. As we have seen in the foregoing pages, the message of which the Buddha wished to convince humanity was precisely that it, too, has no basis, no footing, no support of any kind on which to lean, no Ultimate sub-ject that could bestow value upon all things.[153] There is only one provisional support: the three gems—Buddha, sangha, dharma. And these are but, respectively, a symbol, a community of provisional, itinerant beings, and a behavior. All is "penultimate" on this earth. No utterance can be made regarding the ultimate without rendering it ipso facto "penultimate" in its own turn. At bottom the very concept of "ultimate," as applied to an object, is contradictory. Such "ultimacy" is in itself not so much a limit concept, as the limit of a concept.[154]

But even the proposition "all is penultimate" cannot be affirmed without involving a contradiction. Hence, silence—the very silence within God.

The Silence of God in God

All that I have said, it will be well to recall, is but part of the effort of the human intellect to decipher the mystery of God. Have we perhaps betrayed the message of the Buddha by seeking to render it intelligible through words and concepts? Ought we to have respected its silence, and made no attempt to interpret its meaning on a rational level? But the suspension of the intellect entails the risk of falling into the opposite excess, irrational pietism. The Buddha—to repeat—declares himself equally far from either extreme. The renunciation of philosophy as a vehicle incapable of carrying us to the goal because it is too weak, is an extreme as pernicious as the pretension to a wish to understand all. *Credo quia absurdum* is anything but rare as the expression of an attitude on the part of religions or believers. Often these find no other way to accept the "existence" of God.

The Tathagata's via media is equidistant from the pretenses of an intellect deemed mighty enough to be able to understand all things—God, the human race, the world, and their reciprocal relationships—and from the depreciation of an intellect accounted too weak to attain to an understanding of anything at all. This via media is not an abdication of reason. It is merely reason's way of understanding that it cannot discover adequate answers to life's most urgent questions, especially the question of God. Thus it is a penetration to the very heart of the target of the investigation, but in a hush, and the question is stilled at its root.[155] The silence that the Buddha wishes for his disciples is not a philosophical silence, but a mystical attitude, an interior experience. The Buddha's silence is not a defeat but a victory. He refuses to delve into the *ātman*, or to attempt to define *nirvāṇa*. He will not answer the fourteen basic questions that appear as so vital to the satisfaction of the intellect. The only philosophical argument into which he allows himself to be drawn is that of the impermanency of all that exists, not excluding humankind.

But God, too, is silence. Indeed it seems to me that it is precisely this that Buddha has wished to "tell" us. What falls within our form of thinking is being, and we have seen what difficulties derive from the identification of God with Being. God is the very absence of being. God is God for creatures alone: *in se* God is nothing at all, least of all God. As Christian theology phrases it, the name of God indicates a power, not a property.[156] Or, again in Christian language: the Father *is not*, because what the Father *is* is the Son, and what exist in the world are things. If God is both cause and being, God would be *causa sui*, and how could God be this? God would be a contradiction.[157] Thus perhaps God can be defined as that which gives, gives being, inasmuch as "for God, 'being' consists in the bestowal of being."[158] And at all events, the classic, traditional concept of "act" comes nearer the ultimate intuition of the divine reality than do those of being, substance, or existence.

What I wish to assert here, and what the Buddha has expressed in different language, is not that God "is" silence—that God's being is silence—but that God's silence is precisely a silence of being. Perhaps we should say simply that silence is the locus of God. This "place"—an empty place, to be sure—is, if you will, the psalmist's "abyss of the abyss" (Ps. 72:8), the midnight silence of the moment before creation (cf. Sap. 18:14), the silence that is beyond being,[159] the silence that reigns in the void that neither is nor is not,[160] the silence from which, by the might of its spirit and its internal creative warmth and fervor,[161] reality, in the more than one tradition, draws its origin.[162] I do not deny the distinction between Mystery and what Christian theology styles the "created order."[163] The creature initiates a temporal process, but time does not exhaust reality.[164] The relationship between the atemporal and the temporal remains the same withal. Everything is equidistant from eternity.

Further: the silence of the Buddha, as I have said, is not only a liturgical silence. Nor is it simply the implementation of a mystical way. These are in no wise to be excluded, and many are the religions and schools of spirituality that join the Buddha in telling us so.[165] In fact there are various forms of silence that we can adopt before the numinous.[166] It does not seem to me, however, that this is the specific, decisive point of the Enlightened One's intuition. For the Buddha it is evident that the absence of thought and the silence of the mind are necessary prerequisites for attaining "God" precisely because in God there is nothing to be thought.[167] The Buddha spins no theories of silence. He does not tell us, as Proclus does, that the Logos has need of a silence on which to rest, a silence that must be "before" him.[168] No, this silence cannot be a new hypostasis.[169] The Buddha simply "distracts" persons from their thinking activity by directing them exclusively toward their principal, their only, task—deliverance from sorrow. The Buddha does not permit anyone to reflect and speculate on the *anakkhātam*, the ineffable.[170] The only thing that matters to the Enlightened One is to help us reach our silence—the silence of the creature, the annihilation of creatureliness.[171] The rest is no task of ours.

At the heart of his "revelation," the Buddha directs followers to renounce not only the quest for God, in order to know "how God is made," but *God*, as well, as support along the human journey. In the seeking of God, whether intellectually or mystically, all human powers are directed without. Our forces are brought to bear on a task that distracts us from what we are really called to: the destruction of our own contingency. There is no God along the pathways of our journey. When the Mahayana tradition[172] (in the same spirit as so many later mysticisms, the world over,[173] not excluding the Jewish[174] and Christian[175]) has the Buddha say that he renounces *nirvāṇa* to save his fellows, it is in a mystical spirit that it does so.[176] Indeed, when we hear that we must renounce God for God's sake, this is only a manner of speaking, calculated to quiet the scruples of those not willing to renounce God, those who lean on God for salvation so that it will not require all too much effort on their own part. God cannot be a kind of catalyst that is found intact after the reaction. The renunciation of God is not a methodological operation or an intellectual exercise. To renounce God means to do without any manner of support at all, including the social, the human, the scientific, or the ideological. In a word, the renunciation of God is a leap to the further shore—that mortal leap in which everything goes topsy-turvy and one's individual life is lost.

Nor let it be said that this is too much. We see how many modern atheists have come to a similar conclusion. However, for many of them nihilism, and the loss of an "eternal" life or of the soul's survival, is the conclusion forced on them by their conscious elimination of God from their own horizon. For the Buddhist, the elimination precisely of human existence, suffering, and contingency is the aim and scope of the religious attitude itself.

And so we come to the third and last part of our meditation. I should like to begin with a typical text:

If the *prajñāpāramitā* [the epitome of sapiential liberation] cannot be acquired or practiced, why does the ascetic search for it?

This is the last question of the voluminous work attributed to Nāgārjuna, lost in the Sanskrit original and recovered in a Chinese manuscript tradition:[177]

Answer: the things that cannot be attained are of two types: first and especially, one cannot attain the pleasures of the world; though they can be sought after, they never correspond to one's expectations; second, one can never attain the true character of the dharmas whose characteristic qualities are beyond all perception. Granted that there is existence, merit is enriched, as well as wisdom, and the roots of good increase. People of the world who are involved with human affairs go about their earnings, etc; and the same is true of all the good qualities. But to speak of acquisitions is something typical of the spirit of the world. According to the spirit of the Buddha, nothing is to be acquired.[178]

Liberation

This has been our hermeneutics. Śākyamuni is more discrete, more consistent, more prudent. He has not expressed himself in my terms. He has not spoken of God at all, not even to say that God corresponds to Silence, or that God is the unfathomable abyss of Nothingness. Instead Śākyamuni has spoken of humankind. To speak *of* God, even for the purpose of denying God's existence, is to "transform" God into the order of creatures, and so is tantamount to destroying God. All that the Buddha has said, all his striving, regards humankind. If for my part I have sought to interpret his silence through an application to the problem of God and have taken up that problem directly, it has been because my position in history comes centuries and millennia later than his. It is no longer possible for us to preserve the innocence that the genius of a Siddhartha would have wished for us. After all, for centuries, the problem of God has consistently occupied a central place not only in the life, but also in the thought, of diverse peoples. A refusal to name God would be at least suspect on my part. And so I have spoken of silence, and I have undertaken to specify it as a silence of and in God.

The Tathagata would have spoken of a silence of humankind, a human silence. In his refusal to allow himself to be drawn into philosophical and theological disputes, what the Enlightened One is endeavoring to do is to lead us to silence. He would hush us, and thus guide us to a knowledge of the condition of human nature itself. That condition is one of an incessant referral to suffering as the experience most profoundly and most essentially human. The Buddha wishes to lead us little by little to an elimination of the suffering in which we are plunged at every step along the pathway of life. A compassion for persons surrounded by—indeed, we may surely say, kneaded with—suffering leads the Enlightened One to center his regard on the manner of extracting them from that suffering. In such wise, preoccupied with the practical, lost in the immediate task of delivering them from what causes them to suffer, they will forget themselves. They will forget their own *ātman*. They will even forget to pose the problem of God. Then, if in the process of this elimination of suffering—which in the concrete can actually take the positive form of a concentration on the bodily healing of some illness[179]—persons discover that to succeed they must finally eliminate their very contingency, and therefore their nature as such, the Buddha will only be able to rejoice. For it is precisely the idea and belief that one is a subject, an *ātman*, a concrete individual, immortal, and with an immortal destiny, that makes it possible for suffering to exist and perpetuate itself at all.

What matters, then, is not "God," in the classic sense. What matters is only a path, a way that leads in the direction of liberation. Ultimately our lot is in our own hands. We and we alone can deliver ourselves from the suffering that assaults us on every side. The only help available is a reliance on the experience of the Buddha himself and of the monastic community of his followers, in the observance of right conduct. This is what is traditionally known as refuge in the Triple Gem: the Buddha, the sangha, the dharma. Nothing else must concern us. Not even *nirvāṇa* must be the object of our cares or investigations. But then, the Enlightened One will be asked so often, is there no *nirvāṇa*? Is there nothing at all? No, no, the Buddha responds, this is not at all what I mean. Now the questioner is perplexed. How can these things fail to be the legitimate object of concern and research, and yet not not-be? And Gautama's response is: Because the practice of the dharma is not sterile.[180] When all is said and done, neither *orthodoxy* nor *orthopoiesis* matters. What saves is the refusal to entertain any ideology of philosophy that in some degree would center on God. What is of true value, what carries us beyond this nearer shore of ours is *orthopraxis*. Now we "arrive" indeed, but without vaulting into the arms of a transcendence that can be manipulated, one that is but the product of our unsatiated desires. The dharma is not infertile, and indeed per se. It suffices to follow it; there is no need to concern oneself with it by reflecting and willing. One need only rely on the Buddha, who has indicated the way, and on the community—that is, on solidarity.

The Buddha has not affirmed God, but neither has he denied God. On the contrary, as we have seen, he defended himself against the latter accusation even more earnestly than against the former.[181] But he is unconcerned whether or not we satisfy our speculative quest. His intent is to stave off our very desire to wonder about God. Not that we shall become drunk on things ephemeral, and no longer feel stimulated to turn to God, but that ultimately, in our effort to eliminate suffering, we shall have reduced our very being to silence, and have discovered its nothingness.

But the Buddha's hope to reduce his followers to silence is not a desire to destroy them. On the contrary, the Buddha intends to "liberate" them. He makes them realize their nothingness. He does this not via any philosophical dissertation, however, but through concrete experience. Thereby he delivers them from every external yoke and influence. The Buddha's reduction of them to silence is not only for the purpose of liberating them from the internal and external din within and without them, but to calm them as well, and to reconcile them with all the factors that displace their center of gravity.

The Buddha is silent on God. Thus he stills our impatience and our curiosity about the "thing" that really terrifies us. God can be no menace, no peril, for us. God is not our enemy. At bottom, God frightens us because, notwithstanding all possible efforts to attain God completely, all our striving to succeed in understanding God rationally, God remains obscure, unknown, imcomprehensible, mysterious. On his salvation journey, Śākyamuni prescinds from God. Thereby he opens the door to freedom — a freedom, first of all, from any fear. But at the same time a freedom from all limit. And this means freedom even from the limit that is ourselves.

How often our humanistic reaction to a certain divine *heteronomy* that had oppressed us with a false fear of God has caused us — in an attempt to deliver ourselves — to fall into the opposite extreme: that of a pretended *autonomy* of the human being, an "autonomy" that converts that human being into its own slave, rendering us the victim of the exalted concept that we have formed of ourselves. Instead, the Buddha proposes the via media, which I shall call *ontonomic*. The ontonomic third way seeks to deliver both from the apotheosis of an exterior God and from the divinization of the human element. The via media admits neither the relativization of the absolute, nor the absolutization of the relative. Hence the sense of liberty in the message of the Buddha.

> "And what, o woman, is the opposite of ignorance?"
> "Knowledge, o friend Visakha, is the opposite of ignorance."
> "And what, o woman, is the opposite of knowledge?"
> "Freedom, o friend Visakha, is the opposite of knowledge."
> "And what, o woman, is the opposite of freedom?"
> "Nirvana, o friend Visakha, is the opposite of freedom."[182]

The Enlightened One does not tell us, however, that we are "free *for*. . . ." He does not instrumentalize human freedom. He does not place it at the service of a higher ideal that would then immediately suppress human freedom. The preaching of the Buddha seeks to render us free *of* . . . everything: free of an objectified God, free of an idealized humanity, free of a programed society, free of a science of daydreams. The preaching of the Buddha points to a profound freedom, one by no manner of means connoting caprice or libertinism. The teaching of the Buddha is directed toward total liberation, a deliverance from both external coercion and interior will.

It seems to me that the consequences of this message — and not only the religious and mystical connotations, but the sociological, and for that matter those others of a practical order that can derive from it — are now within our grasp. And so I leave these conclusions open, lest I proceed to betray the silence, profound and wise, of the Enlightened One. Let us, then, fall back once more into silence.

Then The Blessed One addressed the monks:

"It may be, O monks, that some monk has a doubt or perplexity respecting either The Buddha or the Doctrine or the Order or the Path or the course of conduct. Ask any questions, O monks, and suffer not that afterwards ye feel remorse, saying, 'Our Teacher was present with us, but we failed to ask him all our questions.' "

When he had so spoken, the monks remained silent.

And a second time The Blessed One, and a third time The Blessed One addressed the monks:

"It may be, O monks, that some monk has a doubt or perplexity respecting either The Buddha or the Doctrine or the Order or the Path or the course of conduct. Ask any question, O monks, and suffer not that afterwards ye feel remorse, saying, 'Our Teacher was present with us, but we failed to ask him all our questions.' "

And a third time the monks remained silent.

Then The Blessed One addressed the monks:

"It may be, O monks, that it is out of respect to The Teacher that ye ask no questions. Then let each one speak to his friend."

And when he had thus spoken, the monks remained silent.[183]

NOTES

EPIGRAPH

1. "The *ātman* is not the *ātman*," or, in context, "one and the same person is not of himself/herself" (does not belong to himself/herself) — *Dhammapada,* V,3, the chapter dedicated to the fool (*bālavaggo*).

2. "Veneration to the Blessed, the Holy, the Perfect, the completely Enlightened One" — the traditional invocation to the Buddha in Pali writings.

3. Ten years after writing this introductory matter, I came upon a poem by the recently deceased Spanish poet Ricardo Molina, "Respuestas" (Answers) (English translation):

> What if
> in the very question the answer hid?
> What if
> in the divine silence were heavenly acquiescence?
> What if
> the inquiry itself were our salvation?
> > (quoted by Gerardo Diego, *ABC,* Madrid, Jan. 1968).

PREFACE TO THE ORIGINAL EDITION

1. "Avoid sin, practice good, purify the mind: this is the message of the Buddha" — the celebrated distich repeated in so many documents, e.g., *Dhammapada,* XIV, 5 (183); *Dīgha-nikāya,* II, 49; *Nettipakarana,* 43. Except as otherwise noted, translations of Pali texts are from the editions of the Pali Text Society, London.

2. *L'ateismo contemporaneo,* 4 vols., edited by the Faculty of Philosophy of the Salesian Pontifical University in Rome, and directed by Giulio Girardi (Turin: Società Editrice Internazionale, 1967–70).

3. Ibid., 4:449–76.

4. See Matt. 10:39; 16:25; Mark 8:35; Luke 9:24; 17:33; John 12:25. These passages are not to be understood in the sense of a kind of "preventive therapy" or "life insurance," but simply as an echo of Acts 20:24 and, especially, John 15:13.

5. The sole purpose of my notes and references is to foster communion with tradition and communication with readers. Virtually all of the text has been composed without notes and references.

1. A CRIME OF LÈSE HUMANITÉ

1. *Si vobis dixero non credetis;* "If I tell you, you will not believe me" (Luke 22:67; cf. John 3:12; Wisd. 9:16).

2. See Schrader, *Stand;* the monumental work of Paul Mus, *Barabuḍur;* Schayer, "Prehinayastic Buddhism"; idem, "New Contributions"; and more recently, the first part of the book by Edward Conze, *Buddhist Thought.*

3. See the critical study of the theories of Hermann Oldenberg, T. W. Rhys Davids, and others, together with an attempt at a stratification of the various texts of the classic collections themselves, by Govind Chandra Pande, *Studies.*

4. See W. C. Smith, *Meaning and End,* chap. 2, especially for his analysis of the arbitrary use of the word "religion."

5. Lamotte, *Histoire,* p. 57.

6. Bloch, *Inscriptions,* p. 154.

7. See the citations and references in Lamotte, *Histoire,* 1:58. Cf. exactly the same attitude, even the same words, apropos of Christ and Christians in Christian patristic literature, e.g., Justin, *Apology,* book 2, chap. 13 (PG, 6, col. 465: *hosa oun para pasi kalōs eirētai hēmōn tōn christanōn estin:* "Any truth, no matter who utters it, belongs to us Christians"). See also 1 Cor. 3:22. This proposition is the basis, past and present, of the capacity of Christian doctrine to assimilate other doctrines.

8. See Lamotte, *Lo spirito,* which underscores this unity.

9. That Buddhism could be called "without doubt the most important spiritual fact in all history" (Henri de Lubac, *Aspects,* p. 8) or that Romano Guardini could write, "Perhaps Buddha will be the last religious genius to be explained by Christianity," immediately adding that "as yet no one has really uncovered his Christian significance" (*Lord,* p. 305) — despite immense bibliography on the subject — is maddening, to say the least.

10. See de Lubac, *Rencontre,* for numerous examples of the quid pro quo to which I allude.

11. Charles Couturier, "Religions," p. 6, claims to be able to identify 1925 as the year of a dividing line between missiological labors of negative and positive orientation, respectively.

12. See my *Māyā,* pp. 99–130.

13. I do not deny the superficiality of many of the "Eastern" movements found in the West, but this scarcely justifies their equally superficial criticism by a theologian of the stature of Hans Urs von Balthasar, "Meditation als Verrat," *Geist und Leben* (1977) 260–68.

14. Cf. chap. 3, n. 40.

15. See a brief treatment of the subject in my *Religione,* pp. 13–24.

16. See my "Relation," pp. 303–48, esp. 324–25; reprinted in *Cross Currents,* 22 (1972) 281–308.

17. See Cuttat, "Fait," p. 19.

18. See, e.g., Winternitz, *History,* vol. 2, p. 415 (also New York: Russell & Russell, 1972), as well as many of the works listed in the Bibliography, e.g., von Garbe, "Contributions," pp. 509–63.

19. See Cuttat's incisive, profound conclusion in his commentary on the eminent work of Romano Guardini: "The authenticity and depth of the encounter of Christian interiority with that of Buddhism are determined by the degree of our own insertion into the existentiality of Christ" ("Innerlichkeit," p. 469).

2. A SURFEIT OF OPINIONS

1. Consider, e.g., the diversity of opinions on as important a point as that of dharma. While for some (e.g., Otton Ottonovich Rosenberg, T. Stcherbatsky) the

theory of dharma is central to Buddhism, for others (e.g., Arthur Derriedale Keith, S. Schayer) it is all but a foreign body. See von Glasenapp, "Geschichte," pp. 111–24.

2. For Suzuki's claim to the contrary, see his *Essence,* p. 64.

3. E.g., many of the forms of Mahayana Buddhism; cf. Bhattacharyya, "Pantheon," pp. 518–37.

4. Cf. Regamey, "Buddhismus," pp. 261–64.

5. This is the most widespread idea in certain circles. It corresponds to the traditional division of Indian wisdom into *astika* and *nāstika,* referring respectively to the acceptance or rejection of the Vedas, and almost immediately entailing faith in or rejection of transcendence. Cf. Murti, *Philosophy,* pp. 3–103.

6. "Buddhism is atheistic—there is no doubt about it," states Junjirō Takakusu, in his *Essentials,* p. 45. Haridas Bhattacharyya: "Original Buddhism is therefore atheistic in a double sense—in the Indian sense of denying the authority of the Vedas and in the Western sense of refusing to discuss the necessity and nature of God" (*Foundations,* p. 109). See further the important monograph by von Glasenapp, *Buddhismus und Gottesidee,* in which he defends the thesis of Buddhism as an atheistic religion.

7. Cf. Keith, *Philosophy,* p. 63. This position would also seem to be that of L. de la Vallée Poussin, which is criticized in Stcherbatsky, *Conception,* p. 21.

8. Caroline Augusta Foley Rhys Davids could be cited here as an exponent of this interpretation, with her numerous works and her translations of Buddhistic materials. See below, pp. 10f.

9. Cf. Fatone, *Nihilismo,* which delineates various aspects of the question; and E. J. Thomas, *History,* p. 128, who questions this interpretation, which he attributes to Oldenberg, among others. For his part, Henri de Lubac, denies that Buddhism is an "atheistic nihilism" (p. 161), or a "religion of nothingness" (p. 265).

10. Cf. Coomaraswamy, *Hindouisme,* pp. 79–80, who also notes (p. 154), that, for the same reason, the appellation "Tathagata" is applicable to the Buddha, the Dhamma, and the Sangha.

11. Cf. Coomaraswamy, *Elements.*

12. See Mus, *Barabaḍur* (chap. 1, n. 2, above). For tantric Buddhism, see Dasgupta, *Introduction.*

13. "There is no reference to God; but neither do the four Holy Truths contain any hint—and this should be noted—of 'atheism'" (Graham, *Zen,* p. 14).

14. "Religious atheism" is what Buddhism is called by G. van der Leeuw, *Phänomenologie,* p. 194. And more recently we have W. C. Smith, "Religious Atheism?" p. 7: "If this was atheism, it was a religious atheism."

15. See, e.g., W. Schmidt, *Ursprung,* p. 4, due to his interpretation of the essence of religion as a personal *religatio* or bond with a superhuman power.

16. As we know, Schopenhauer, like Kant, considered Buddhism as unambiguously atheistic, the former interpreting theism as a species of the genus "religion," in which atheism had its place as well. See the relative citations in von Glasenapp, *Buddhismus,* p. 8.

17. Utilizing the classification proposed by Jacques Maritain, *Signification,* one divides atheism into "practical," "absolute," and "pseudo-." Fernando ("Truths," pp. 83–84) puts Buddhism under the last category, as a pseudo atheism of a conceptual order. That is, Buddhism would acknowledge God practically, but would deny God conceptually.

18. "Although a hundred years have elapsed since the scientific study of Buddhism has been initiated in Europe, we are nevertheless still in the dark about the fundamental teachings of this religion and its philosophy," wrote Stcherbatsky in 1927 (*Conception,* p. 1). Murti's comment a generation later was that Stcherbatsky's observation "remains no less true today" (*Philosophy,* p. vii).

19. Cf. the Latin dictum, *Quae non sunt, simulo; quae sunt, dissimulo:* "What is not, I feign that it is; what is, I feign that it is not."

20. We know of a similar attitude on the part of the Rabbi of Nazareth, who never gave a direct answer to any "philosophical" or theoretical question. See n. 56, below.

21. Cf. Hopkins, *Religions,* pp. 321–22.

22. Cf. Welbon, "Understanding," p. 314, who explains the possible genesis of such an attitude.

23. *Ācāryamusti* or *ācariyamuṭṭhi* (cf. *Dīgha-nikāya,* II, in the edition of N. K. Bhagwat, p. 100) was an ancient usage, not yet altogether neglected, according to which, shortly before his death, the father would confide to his son, or the guru to his favorite disciple, the authentic, most important message.

24. Cf. *Mahāparinibbāna-sutta,* II, 25.

25. Christ manifests a similar attitude when he says that he has made known to his followers everything he has heard from his Father (John 15:15; cf. John 16:25, 18:20).

26. Cf., for example, Rosenberg, *Probleme,* pp. 155–56. Rosenberg makes reference to Vasubandhu's *Abhidharmakośa* and Chinese commentaries. It is difficult to understand the reference to the abhidharmic school, for it appears rather to favor the position of an epistemological realism. Cf. Murti, *Philosophy,* pp. 41–44.

27. Saint-Hilaire, *Nirvana,* pp. 321–24, seeking, of course, to safeguard his own interpretation, maintains that, for Buddhists, the ultimate end of Buddhism is total nihilism.

28. See the classic work by Burnouf, *Introduction,* and the synthesis of his position in Welbon, "Understanding," pp. 307ff.

29. See the various texts presented in the second part of this book.

30. This is the thesis popularized by the numerous works and translations of Caroline Augusta Foley Rhys Davids, especially after the death of her husband. See the texts in Welbon, "Understanding," p. 317, and a scathing critique in Murti, *Philosophy,* pp. 20ff.

31. See Kcith, *Philosophy,* p. 45 and passim; de la Vallée Poussin (n. 7, above); Monier-Williams, *Buddhism,* p. 119.

32. Among the defenders of this position will be Carl Jung. On the question of the nature of *karman,* he thought that the Buddha had left it open, and did not himself know with certainty what it was (Aniela Jaffé, ed., *Erinnerungen, Träume, Gedanken von C. G. Jung* [Olton: Walter, 1972], p. 320). English translation, *Memories, Dreams, Reflections* (London: Fontana, 1983).

33. He had just taught them the Four Noble Truths; cf. *Saṁyutta-nikāya,* V, p. 437 (*saccasaṁyutta,* 31). Note the parallelism with Christ (John 16:12) — although the motivation is quite different: the disciples "cannot bear it now," whereas for the Buddha nothing else is of utility for attaining the goal of life.

34. See n. 23, above.

35. See Hiriyanna, *Outlines,* pp. 137 and passim.

36. Compare the attitude of Christ, who "constructed no theory of the origins of

evil or furnished any explanation of the fact of original sin and the circumstances of its appearance, but became sin for us (2 Cor. 5:21)" (François Roustang, *Une initiation à la vie spirituelle* [Paris: Desclée, 1963], p. 52).

37. This would be the position of, for example, T. W. Rhys Davids: see Welbon, "Understanding," p. 312.

38. For example, by von Glasenapp.

39. Cf. *Majjhima-nikāya*, I, 426–27 (63), as well as *Aṅguttara-nikāya*, IV, 67–68. The matter under consideration is the *cūla-māluṅkya-sutta*.

40. Actually the Buddha rejected nihilism *(ucchedavāda)* more often than so-called eternalism *(śaśvadavāda)*.

41. *Mahihima-nikāya*, I, 139 (in V. Fatone, *Nihilismo buddhista*, p. 30).

42. "Vasubandhu (*Abhidharmakośa*, 5, 22) reports that it was a rule of dialectics at the time of the Buddha to answer by silence those questions which were wrongly formulated—e.g., all questions which were regarding the properties of a nonexisting thing. Professor Oldenberg rightly remarks on another occasion *(Lehre, p.* 133: 'Upanishaden'): "The most typical language of this mysticism, as of all mysticisms, is silence" (Stcherbatsky, *Conception,* p. 22, note). Pande (*Studies,* p. 506) maintains that a silence of pure etiquette is out of the question.

43. Cf. Organ, "Silence." If Organ's solution were to be correct, he would be saddling the Buddha with a very weak philosophical position indeed. Tathagata would be ignoring both the natural human tendency to philosophize, and the fact that any attitude at all, however pragmatic and anti-intellectual, presupposes at least an implicit philosophy.

44. See, e.g., the texts of pp. 72, 76.

45. It seems to me that I might cite, as examples of this interpretation, in past generations the position of Louis de la Vallée Poussin, and today that of Edward Conze.

46. *Saṃyutta-nikāya*, IV, 39B. See also the text cited on p. 10, above.

47. Cf. the well-known assertions of Wittgenstein, Heidegger, Gabriel Marcel, Simone Weil, and others.

48. *Saṃyutta nikāya*, III, 138.

49. This seems to be T. Watsuji's position. "That the metaphysical questions of this kind were not answered by the Buddha does not immediately mean that the Buddha denied the validity of philosophical or systematic thinking. On the contrary, there can easily be defended a case in which such an attitude [of silence] constitutes the essential characteristic of a philosophy" (*Practical Philosophy of Primitive Buddhism* pp. 133–34; quoted in English by Nagao, "Silence").

50. See Murti, *Philosophy,* pp. 47–48.

51. The work of two Japanese philosophers, T. Watsuji and H. Ut, has application here. A summary of their thought is to be found in Takeuchi, "Schweigen."

52. See, e.g., Radhakrishnan, *Indian Philosophy,* pp. 682–83.

53. See, e.g., a characteristic passage from the *Gītā* (VII, 28) on deliverance from the deceit of the polarity of contraries. A whole system could be constructed on the dialectic of (1) the acknowledgment of the reality of the negative (error, suffering, etc.), (2) the discovery of the unilateral character of the positive (truth, pleasure, etc.), (3) a synthesis of both viewpoints, and (4) a genuine unity of the two that would transcend both.

54. It is a commonplace that *Theravāda* is much further removed from this solution than is *Mahāyāna*.

55. See my *Māyā,* pp. 99–130, where this "pretension" of the *Mādhyamika* comes under scrutiny and criticism.

56. "It seems to us, however, that Buddha's *Madhyamā Pratipad* sought to resolve the opposition of being and non-being, not by synthesizing the two categories, but by transcending them both" (Pande, *Studies,* pp. 420–21).

57. An antonomastic title of the Buddha signifying, as is commonly known, one who has attained to truth, who has finally "realized" truth.

58. That the "letter killeth" (cf. 2 Cor. 3:6; Rom. 2:29; 7:6) is so much the case that divine providence has taken great care that the Christian scriptures be preserved only in translation.

59. See the interpretation suggested by Takeuchi, "Schweigen," p. 18, in reference to Beckh's *Buddha.* Nagao, too, in his article cited above, n. 49, seems to me to move in the same direction.

60. "One does not know the Buddha as long as one judges him by what he has uttered," asserts Beckh, *Buddha* p. 113, and continues to speak of the "power of silence," stating that "a correct understanding of the meaning of this silence is of the greatest importance for the whole understanding of Buddhism (ibid.). Nagao, also cites this observation of Beckh.

61. "Buddha's silence is an indication of his conviction in the inexpressibility of certain truths of spiritual life. It does not mean that he held negative views and had not the courage to express them" (Radhakrishnan, "Teaching," p. 352).

62. To put it in Buddhist language, let us recall an anecdote. A Confucian once went to the twenty-eighth Buddhist patriarch, Bodhidharma, for the sake of the "pacification of his soul." The patriarch addressed him thus: "Show it to me and I shall pacify it for you." The Confucian replied: "This is precisely my sorrow, that I fail to find it." Whereupon Bodhidharma told him: "Your wish has been granted." The Confucian understood and departed in peace. (As recounted by Suzuki, "Zen," p. 13.

63. We must also consider the difference between *Mahāyāna* Buddhism, which leans toward a metaphysical interpretation of the Buddha's silence, and *Theravāda* Buddhism, with its inclination to prescind from any reference to metaphysics.

64. Cf. below, p. 23.

65. See my "Bild."

66. This cannot be said, however, when he refuses to give information about, e.g., *karma.* See *Aṅguttara-nikāya,* II, 80; *Dīgha-nikāya,* III, 138; *Saṁyutta-nikāya,* III, 103.

67. Cf. *appasaddakamo,* in the *Dīgha-nikāya,* I, 208.

68. See the texts in Pande, *Studies,* pp. 391ff.; Caroline Augusta Foley Rhys Davids, *Sakya,* p. 185.

69. Cf., e.g., *Majjhima-nikāya, sutta* 77; *Dīgha-nikāya,* 1, 60; etc., in Pande, *Studies,* pp. 391ff.

70. Cf. *Majjhima-nikāya,* I, 161; *Saṁyutta-nikāya,* I, 60; etc., in Pande, *Studies,* pp. 391ff. and p. 285, n. 472.

71. Cf. the well-known biblical *sedere et tacere* of Lam. 3:28, the locus classicus of Christian monastic silence; as well as the following text, selected at random from among a thousand like it: *Juge quippe silentium et ab omni strepitu saecularium perpetua quies cogit caelestia meditare;* "Continuous silence, perpetual quiet, far from all bustle and noise, constrains one to meditate things of heaven" (Saint Bernard, *Letters,* 78, 4 [PL, 182, 193]).

72. *Sarvajna.* "A point on which the Buddhist tradition is unanimous" (Pande, *Studies,* p. 383).

73. Cf. *Lalita-vistara,* XXV, p. 287. Cf. also C.A.F. Rhys Davids, *Gospel.*

74. Cf. Dutt, *Aspects,* p. 100.

75. "Caecilius, in his *Octavius* (13, 1), praises Socrates' discretion. When questioned about celestial matters, he responded: 'How can we know what is above us?' *Quod supra nos, nihil ad nos*"—What is above us does not pertain to us (Festugière, *Idéal,* p. 34. See Gronovius's edition of 1709 edition (Lugduni Batavorum), p. 128, which cites Lactantius, book 3, chap. 19, and Girolamus, *In Apolog. adv. Rufinum,* chap. 8, and Xenophon, book 1, folio 710, and other ancient authors who have commented on Socrates' dictum, *quod supra nos, nihil ad nos.*

76. See, in another tradition, John 1:18; 1 John 4:12; and other New Testament passages.

77. See, in the Jewish tradition, Exod. 33:20 and similar Old Testament texts.

78. See, for example, *Yato vaco nivartante,* in *Taittiriya Upanishad,* II, 4, 1 (II, 9); and other, similar, passages.

79. By way of indication, let us recall here at least the names of scholars of the caliber of Walpole Rahula, André Bareau, Erich Frauwallner, Etienne Lamotte, Giuseppe Tucci, Jean Przyluski, Robert Caesar Childers, Christian Lassen, as well as many others, including those already mentioned or to be cited in the course of these pages.

3. BUDDHISM: ATHEISTIC RELIGION

1. "Atheism is a cruel, tireless enterprise": Jean-Paul Sartre *(Les Mots)*—cited by me in "Sartre," 109: "But to lead someone to an end, whatever it may be, is a profession of faith." Cf., "Atheism today has been raised to the rank of a substitute for religion with their Deities" (Nishtani, "Sartre," p. 68).

2. See below, pp. 92ff.

3. "Atheistic religion" seems to me to be a more precise description of Buddhism than is van der Leeuw's "religious atheism," which he applies to both Buddhism and Brahmanism is his *Phänomenologie,* p. 194.

4. "The essence of religion consists not in a particular representation of the divine to be grasped statically, but in a dynamic intercourse with the holy. Religion is not a simple act of thinking of or about transcendent objects, but a behavior. . . . Religion is not a theoretical affair, but an eminently practical one. . . . Religion is . . . worship of Mystery and surrender to the same" (Heiler, *Erscheinungsformen,* pp. 561–62).

5. *Majjhima-nikāya,* II, 263.

6. Cf. ibid., I, 426ff., as well as *Anguttara-niyāka,* IV, 67ff.: we are dealing with the *cula-malunkya-sutta.*

7. Cf. 1 Cor. 7:29 (and Rom. 13:11).

8. Cf. Eph. 5:16; Col. 4:5.

9. Col. 2:8.

10. Cf. 1 John 2:15.

11. Cf. 1 Cor. 7:31.

12. *Ariya-saccāni* (in Sanskrit, *ārya-satyāni*), whence the translation by some, "Aryan truths."

13. As we know, this same notion appears in non-Buddhist texts, as for example *Yogabhāsya,* II, 15; *Nyāyabhāsya,* 1, E, 1, etc., and serious doubts have arisen as to the primitive authenticity of the *ariya-saccāni.* See a resumé of the controversy in Pande, *Studies,* pp. 397ff. In sum we may say that, although the text of the first *Vārānasī* sermon seems to be a later reworking at the hands of monks, the spirit and the ideas correspond to the Buddha's actual message.

14. The parallel between the fourfold Buddhist division and the fourfold medical approach, as more than one scholar has pointed out, is significant. It represents one more connection between the Buddha and the scientific, secular spirit. See the commentary on *Yogasūtra,* II, 15, traditionally attributed to Vedavyāsa: "Just as the medical system has four divisions — disease, cause of disease, health, and remedy — this system, as well, presents four moments: the cycle of rebirths, the cause of the cycle of rebirths, liberation, and the path to liberation."

15. Here we have the celebrated *iti vattaka,* with which so many pronouncements attributed to the Buddha are introduced. See also the traditional Buddhist expression, *evam māyā śrutam ekasmin samaye* ("Once upon a time I heard . . .") and the monumental commentary on the first two chapters of the *Mahāprajñāpāramitāśastra,* attributed to Nāgārjuna in the meticulously documented translation of Lamotte, pp. 56–114.

16. See another text, one that takes full account of the fact that the first Varanasi sermon contains, in germ, the whole of the "revelation," and that it basically expresses the Buddha's entire mission, which not only sets in motion the "wheel of existence" (*Majjhima-nikāya,* I, 171), but has a strictly religious meaning as well, indeed one of an authentic personal theism: "It was in this deer park of Varanasi that the discoverer of the truth, the holy *(arhat)* and enlightened one, set in motion the sublime wheel of the *Dharma (Dhamma)* that no one will ever be able to reverse, neither a penitent, a Brahmin, God, Mara, *Brahmā* himself, nor anyone else in the universe: that is, the proclamation of the four noble truths, the teaching, declaration, and institution of these four noble truths, with their setting forth, exposition, and manifestation" (*Majjhima-nikāya,* III, 248).

17. The passage from the *Majjhima-nikāya* cited in the preceding note furnishes the classic resumé of the four truths: "suffering, the origin of suffering, the cessation of suffering, and the path leading to the cessation of suffering."

18. The eightfold path follows.

19. *Duhkha* in Sanskrit, and *dukkhā* in Pali. "All that exists is suffering *(sabbe sankhārā dukkhā)*" — "All created things are sorrowful," as S. Radhakrishnan translates it in the *Dhammapada.* "When I traverse wisdom, [this] is discovered, then one is not touched by suffering; this is the path to purity" (*Dhammapada,* XX, 6 [278]). The root *dus* means "to be wasted, to squander oneself," and hence to commit sin and impurity, to be at fault, to be harmed, to perish, etc. *Duhkha* would come from *dus* and from *stha,* originally meaning to be ill (or ill at ease, uncomfortable, etc.), to be unhappy, poor, miserable, etc.

20. The five *khandas* (groups, aggregates) that constitute the psychological ego and, according to Buddhism (cf. *Visuddhi-magga,* XVIII, in Warren, *Buddhism, Translations,* pp. 132ff.), must be discovered in order to bring to light the insubstantiality of the subject, are: the forms, the sensations (which may include the sentiments, the "feelings" in this sense as well), the perceptions (including the volitional dispositions), the psychic dispositions (and moreover the impressions), and (intellective) consciousness. Strictly speaking, we are dealing with groups of apprehension, *upādānaskandha* (in Pali, *upādānakkhandha*) or, as Lamotte trans-

lates in his *Histoire,* 1:28, following the translation of his mentor, Alfred Foucher: "In sum, the five sorts of objects of attachment are suffering." Lamotte, again (ibid., 1:30), based on the *Saṁyutta-nikāya* (III, 59–61; III, 47, 86–87), explains the five aggregates in the following way: (1) Corporeity *(rūpa)*—i.e., the four elements: earth, water, fire, wind, and the matter derived from them. (2) Sensations *(vedanā),*resulting from contact had by the ear, eye, nose, tongue, body, and spirit. (3) The notion *(saṁjñā)* of colors, sounds, odors, tastes, tangible things, and mental images. (4) Volition *(saṁskāra)* with reference to colors, sounds, odors, tastes, tangible things, and objects of thought. (5) Cognition (*vijñāna*) of the ear, eye, nose, tongue, body, and spirit.

21. Some authors translate "cause of suffering." But the original, *samudāya,* suggests rather a union, combination, or gathering. *Duḥkhusamudaya* would be the accumulation of suffering.

22. It is generally customary to translate "desire," or "appetite," but the literal, correct translation of *tṛṣṇa* (in Pali, *taṇhā*) is "thirst." For this important concept, see *Aṅguttara-nikāya,* III, 416; IV, 400; *Saṁyutta-nikāya,* I, 1; I, 8; *Majjhima-nikāya,* I, 6; II, 256; *Itivuttaka,* 30, 50, 58, 105, etc. See as well Pande, *Studies,* pp. 434, 400. Besides *tṛṣṇa,* see *icchā, kāma,* etc. It will surely be indispensable to have a philosophico-theological monograph on the series of concepts at play in the present anthropological dynamism, with an exposition of their connotation, both ethical and metaphysical, and a comparison with Western anthropology, especially scholastic anthropology.

23. Here too some scholars translate with a certain freedom. We are dealing with a triple anthropological thirst: a thirst for affirmation, a thirst to be affirmed, and a thirst for negation—that is, an appetite for pleasure (*kāma,* love, delight), for existence (*bhāva,* "to be"), and for nonexistence (*vibhava,* "not to be"). Let us not forget that neither existence nor nonexistence has an intramundane denotation, as we see from the classic Tibetan translations. J. Filliozat, apropos of this typical thirst, makes the following excellent observation: "The first kind is self-explanatory: desires are causes of suffering because they cannot be indefinitely satisfied, as well as because they are attached to painful existences. The second bears on the direct appetite of these existences. The third is an appetite for nothingness, which, contrary to what it is in its object, is no less an appetite, and as such an act that bears fruit in existence: suicide entails rebirth" (Renou and Filliozat, *Inde,* 2:247).

24. *Nirodha* is from the root *rudh,* "to obstruct." With the particle *ni* it acquires the meaning of imprisoning, shutting up, suppressing, destroying, controlling, restraining, halting, and so on. See YS I, 2: *yogaś cittavṛtti nirodha* ("Yoga is the suppression of mental functions").

25. It is practically impossible to translate the concepts of the Eight Ways in single words. Even the adjectives "right" or "straight" are not completely adequate to translate *sammā,* which also means "perfect, balanced, complete." I could also have translated: "perfect evaluation, perfect thought, perfect word, perfect action, perfect discipline, perfect lucidity, perfect spirituality." Cf. a Spanish translation: *correcta opinión, correcto pensamiento, correcta palabra, correcta acción, correcto género de vida, correcto esfuerzo, correcta autoconciencia, correcta concentración* ("correct opinion, correct thought, correct word, correct action, correct kind of life, correct effort, correct self-awareness, correct concentration") (*Dhammapada,* translated, edited, and annotated by G. Dragonetti [Lima: Universidad Nacional Mayor San Marcos, 1964], p. 61). Inasmuch as the text at hand is such a basic one, let us

examine still another translation, that of A. Foucher, used by Lamotte in his *Histoire,* p. 28: *C'est le chemin sacré, à huit branches, qui s'appellent foi pure, volonté pure, langage pure, action pure, moyens d'existence pure, application pure, mémoire pure, méditation pure* ("this is the sacred path, having eight branches: pure faith, pure will, pure language, pure action, means of pure existence, pure application, pure memory, pure meditation").

26. See *Saṁyutta-nikāya,* XXII, 90 (Warren, *Buddhism,* p. 165).

27. Cf. below, p. 62.

28. Māra may be likened to "prince of this world," the demon in Christianity. See Windisch, *Mara;* other bibliographical references are in von Glasenapp, *Buddhismus,* p. 19.

29. Brahmā, although the most important God of the Buddhist pantheon, bears no resemblance to the *brahman* of Upanishadic speculation. The God Brahmā is not omniscient *Dīgha-nikāya,* II, 81 [I, 221]. Although he is acknowledged as a kind of *Īśvara,* or "omnipotent creator and lord of the earth, father of all that has come and will come to be" (*Dīgha-nikāya,* I, 2, 5 [I, 18]), he nevertheless belongs to the *saṁsāra,* as well, to the Brahminic *brahmaloka,* and thus according to Buddhist teaching can in no wise be equated with *nirvāṇa.* There are even texts that present Brahmā as the Buddha's devoted worshiper.

30. *Saṁyutta-nikāya,* V, 420ff.

31. For a detailed scholarly commentary, see Lamotte, *Histoire,* 1:28–52.

32. "It would be presumptuous to remark upon the depth of the insight revealed in these statements. They have no parallel, that I know of, in the religious literature of the West" (Graham, *Zen,* p. 14).

33. As Eriugena justly remarks, "God does not know what he is, because he is not any what" (cf. the Buddhist *ākiṁcañña*). It is only God's possibilities of manifestation that become "whats," of which there can be science or omniscience (Coomaraswamy, *Recollection,* p. 13).

34. It would be an interesting study to set these Buddhist principles over against Freud's principles of psychoanalysis, inasmuch as Freud centers the human being on the desire for pleasure and the care to avoid suffering. See Brown, *Life,* although it contains no reference to Buddhism.

35. Cf. Luke 24:7, 26.

36. Cf. Rom. 8:32.

37. Cf. John 3:16; 1 John 4:9.

38. Cf. John 4:34, 5:30; Matt. 26:42; Luke 22:42; Heb. 5:7, 10:9; etc.

39. Cf. 1 Pet. 4:13; Rom. 8:17; Acts 5:41; etc. Consider too the attitude of saints like Francis of Assisi.

40. One mistake does not justify another. To categorize the devotion to the crucified Christ as a "sadistic impulse of a psychically affected brain," as does Daisetz Teitaro Suzuki (*Mysticism,* p. 136), would be an example of a mistake on the Buddhist side. The same author, in the same chapter, "Crucifixion and Enlightenment," seeking to contrast these two attitudes, describes them, but this time in their profundity: "What is needed in Buddhism is enlightenment, neither crucifixion nor resurrection. A resurrection is dramatic and human enough, but there is still the odor of the body in it. In enlightenment there are heavenliness and a genuine sense of transcendence. Things of earth go through renovation and refreshing transformation. A new sun rises above the horizon and the whole universe is revealed" (ibid., pp. 132–33).

41. Cf., e.g., the grandiose description of the "true gnostic" in Clement of

Alexandria—e.g., the entire book 7 of the *Stromata* (PG, 9:401ff.). Or, sample the preceding book (*Stromata*, VI, 9, PG, 9:205a): The gnostic "desires nothing *(oude zēloi)*, as he lacks nothing to be assimilated to Him who is good and beautiful. He loves no one with a common love *(oude ara philei tina tēn koinēn tautēn philian)*, but loves the creator through creatures *(alla agapa ton ktistēn dia ton ktismaton)*. He falls victim to no desire *(epithumia)*, or appetite *(orexei)*, for he lacks no good of the soul, united as he is by love to the friend to whom he belongs by free election. . . . If the gnostic has no desire, adversaries will say, how can he love? But such as these know not the divine character of love *(to theion tēs agapēs)*. After all, love is not a tendency *(orexis)* of the one loving: it is a loving intimacy *(sterktike de oikeiōsis—benevola conjunctio)* that establishes the gnostic in oneness of faith, without any more need of time and space." *(Non est enim utique charitas eius qui diligit appetitio, sed est benevola conjunction, in unitatem fidei restituens eum qui est gnosticus, locu et tempore minime indigentem,* as Migne's Latin version has it. Christ is the *gnōsis* of God, says Ignatius of Antioch *(Ad Ephesios,* 17).

42. 1 Cor. 7:29–32.

43. *Saṁyutta-nikāya,* XXII, 90 (in Warren, *Buddhism,* p. 165). This text will be the object of appeal and commentary on the part of Nagarjuna, in an effort to establish the truth *(dhamma)* of his *doctrina media,* the *mādhyamika.* Cf. *Mādhyamika Kārikā,* XV, 7 (in the edition by L. de la Vallée Poussin), as well as the text cited in n. 30, above.

44. Cf. the following traditional Christian propositions: *En agnōsia tēn peri autou ktōmetha gnōsin* ("In ignorance let us acquire knowledge of him"), Pseudo-Denis, *De Divinis Nominibus,* in Saint Maximinus, *Scholia in Lib. II de Divinis Nominibus,* PG, 4:216; *Agnōsia gar ginetai gnōstos ho theos"* ("For God becomes known by ignorance"), ibid.; *Kai dia gnōseōs ho theos gignōsketai, kai dia agnōsias"* ("God is known both through knowledge and through ignorance"), Pseudo-Denis, *De Divinis Nominibus,* VII, 3 (PG, 3:872). Saint Thomas embraces the same tradition when he repeatedly states that God *cognoscitur tamquam ignotus* ("is known as unknown"), *In Boethii De Trinitate, Proemium;* q. 1, a. 2, ad 1; *Hoc ipsum est Deum cognoscere, quod nos scimus ignorare de Deo quid sit* ("Knowing God consists precisely in this, that we know that we are ignorant of what God is"), *Commentarium in Dionysium,* VII, 14; or again, *Illud est ultimum cognitionis humanae de Deo quod sciat se Deum nescire* ("The highest degree of human cognition of God is to know that one does not know God"), *De Potentia,* q. 7, a. 5, ad 14; etc.

45. *Saṁyutta-nikāya,* XXII, 90. Cf. Mensching, *Geisteswelt,* p. 82.

46. "Work out your salvation with diligence," is the translation in Coomaraswamy, *Buddha,* p. 75, following the classic version of T. W. Rhys Davids: "When the Blessed One addressed the brethren and said, 'Behold now, brethren, I exhort you, saying, "Decay is inherent in all component things: Work out your salvation with diligence!" ' this was the last word of the Tathagata!" (*Mahāparinibbāna-sutta,* VI, 10, in *Buddhist Suttas,* 11:114; cf. *Mahāparinibbāna-sutta,* III, 66. "Strive onward vigilantly," we read in Rhys Davids' translation of *Dīgha-nikāya,* 156. "Strive diligently," is the translation of Radhakrishnan, *Dhammapada,* p. 32. *Appamadena saṁpādetha,* say the traditional words. The entire text is preceded by *vayadhammā saṁkhāra,* generally translated: "All composed things are bound to decay." Doubts have been expressed as to the authenticity of the *Mahāparinibbāna-sutta.* Silburn (*Instant,* p. 170), compares this passage (*En verité, ô disciples, toutes les énergies constructrices sont*

impermanentes, travaillez, efficacement sans relâche. . . . Soyez d'intention bien concentrée. Surveillez la pensée—"In truth, Disciples, all constructive energies are transitory; toil, efficaciously and without stint. . . . Be of a concentrated intention. Keep watch over thought") with the solemn words of Indra when the Buddha entered *nirvāṇa:* "Transitory indeed are the constructive energies *(saṁskāra),* underlying appearance and then disappearance. In the manner in which they are born, so they die; their quietus is well-being" (or felicity, *sukha*): *Dīgha-nikāya,* II (p. 157 of the Pali Text Society edition, 1889). See n. 20, above.

47. Hence the insistence on *kiriya* and *akiriya,* "what ought to be done" and "what ought not to be done." See, e.g., *Vinaya,* I, 235; *Aṅguttara-nikāya,* I, 62; *Saṁyutta-nikāya,* III, 208; etc.

48. Here compare the Pauline "Work with anxious concern to achieve your salvation" *(sotērian katergazesthe)* (Phil. 2:12). Diligence, constancy, patience—in a word, the verb *hupomenō,* which, as its very composition indicates, denotes perseverance, a persevering tension—constitutes a key concept for an understanding of the parallel attitude of the New Testament. "By patient endurance you will save your lives" (Luke 21:19); "If we hold out to the end we shall also reign with him" (2 Tim. 2:12); see also Matt. 24:13; Mark 13:13, etc. This same expectant perseverance has an important role in primitive patristic spirituality: see the index by Kraft, *Clavis,* under *hupomenō.* For a theological development of tolerance, see my "Pluralismus," pp. 118ff. To be sure, we must keep in mind the diversity of outlook of the Buddhist and Christian positions.

49. See, e.g., among many texts, *Majjhima-nikāya,* I, 486.

50. In Buddhism, *mādhyamika* would be the most characteristic example of this mentality.

51. See, e.g., von Glasenapp, "Buddha"; see also Glasenapp's discussion with Edgerton, "Buddha." Glasenapp believes he can assert that "the Buddha, just as the other teachers of his time, taught a determinate metaphysical system" (p. 46). Edgerton denies this, although recognizing that "premises" of a metaphysical order are to be found in the Buddha's position. What seems precarious in both studies is their manner of arriving at their conclusions. The response they seek to the aporias of the celebrated *avyākṛta vastūni* is a rational, if not rationalistic, one.

52. By way of an example of this practically endless scholastic theme, see the multivolume Ramirez, *Beatitudine.*

53. Cf. the medieval scholastic understanding of *existere: ex aliquo esse habere* ("to have being from someone/something"). See, e.g., Richard of Saint Victor, *De Trinitate,* IV, 12 and 19 (PL, 196:938, 942).

54. We have the same thought in the Christian tradition: *Hoc enim ipsum nomen, existentia, quasi extrastantia indicat* ("this very word 'existence' would mean something like 'standing outside'"), Meister Eckhart, *Liber Parabolorum Geneseos,* 29, 11, as cited by Vladimir Lossky, *Théologie négative et connaissance de Dieu chez Maître Eckhart* (Paris: Vrin, 1960), p. 124.

55. The Buddha's reaction against sacrifice and the caste system is perhaps due more to the need to tear up by the roots the creative act and the *status* of the preservation of creation than to motives of nonviolence *(ahiṁsā)* or social justice. See Vesci, "Heat," where, according to Brahmanic speculation, the origin of suffering is traceable to the pain instilled in the creative act itself, sacrifice.

56. I cannot refrain from citing, in extenso, but without commentary, the four noble truths of Saint John of the Cross, and I beg the reader's indulgence:

> In order to arrive at having pleasure in everything,
> Desire to have pleasure in nothing.
> In order to arrive at possessing everything,
> Desire to possess nothing.
> In order to arrive at being everything,
> Desire to be nothing.
> In order to arrive at that wherein thou hast no pleasure,
> Thou must go by a way wherein thou hast no pleasure,
> In order to arrive at that which thou knowest not,
> Thou must go by a way that thou knowest not.
> In order to arrive at that which thou possessest not,
> Thou must go by a way that thou possessest not.
> In order to arrive at that which thou art not,
> Thou must go through that which thou art not.
> When thy mind dwells upon anything,
> Thou art ceasing to cast thyself upon the All.
> For, in order to pass from the all to the All,
> Thou hast to deny thyself wholly in all.
> And, when thou comest to possess it wholly,
> Thou must possess it without desiring anything.
> For if thou wilt have anything in having all,
> Thou has not thy treasure purely in God.

In this detachment the spiritual soul finds its quiet and repose; for, since it covets nothing, nothing wearies it when it is lifted up, and nothing oppresses it when it is cast down, because it is in the center of its humility; but when it covets anything, at that very moment it becomes wearied [*Ascent of Mount Carmel,* ed. and trans., E. Allison Peers (Garden City, N.Y.: Doubleday-Image, 1958), pp. 72–73].

57. Cf. Matt. 10:39, 16:25; Mark 8:35; Luke 9:24, 17:33; John 12:25; etc.

58. "The idea of *anicca* does not, however, preclude the 'existence' of things, but only their duration. Similarly, the idea of *anattā* does not proclaim that there is no 'self,' but only that there is no unchangeably continuing self that would everlastingly persist as a separate unit. Actually it is precisely the notion of *anicca* that guarantees the possibility of the development and growth of the individual" (Govinda, *The Psychological Attitude,* p. 199).

59. Cf. *Aṅguttara-nikāya,* IV, 36 (against the existence of God), and *Udāna,* VIII, 1 and 3 together with *Itivuttaka,* 43 (against the "uncreated").

INTRODUCTION TO PART II

1. "One who no longer has any need of faith *(assadho),* who has arrived at a knowledge of the non-made (the uncreated, *akata*), who has severed every bond, who has destroyed every occasion [of good or evil], who has eliminated all desire within—such a one is in truth a superior *(poriso)* person" (*Dhammapada,* VII, 8 [97]). Unlike the Upanishads, where the vocable *puruṣa* also has a primordial meaning, the *nikāya*s rarely use the noun *purisa* (but see, e.g., *Saṁyutta-nikāya,* IV, 380). Cf. Pande, *Studies,* p. 489.

2. Considerations of space, time, and simplicity constrain me to omit not only a great number of texts, but a whole series of concepts, as well, such as *dharma, śūnya, prajñā,* etc., which in and of themselves ought to have been included. I can, however, assure the reader that their inclusion would not have changed my conclusions.

4. NAIRĀTMYAVĀDA

1. See above, chap. 2, nn. 27, 29, 30.

2. E.g., T. Stcherbatsky, V. Bhattacharyya, T. R. V. Murti, and others. For an introduction to the various schools of contemporary buddhology, see Regamey, "Buddhismus," 3:244–50.

3. E.g., Caroline Augusta Foley Rhys Davids, L. de la Vallée Poussin, and others. See the critique of this position in Murti, *Philosophy,* pp. 20–35.

4. This would seem to be Nāgārjuna's interpretation *Mādhyamika-Kārikā,* XVIII, 6) of the Buddha's ambiguity.

5. Frauwallner, for example, *Geschichte,* 1:225, thinks, as do others, that the question of the "I" is ignored because it distracts one from salvation as one's end, and that the "soul" is not denied, but only asserted to lie beyond the reach of concept.

6. See chap. 12 of the *Dhammapada.* In many verses, *ātman* is purely and simply the reflexive pronoun.

7. See von Glasenapp, *Vedanta,* p. 10.

8. See ibid.

9. See Frauwallner, *Geschichte,* 2:220.

10. This is the prevalent translation in works in English. It has the advantage of preserving the grammatical ambiguity of the Sanskrit pronoun/substantive.

11. See a survey of scholarly opinion in Pande, *Studies,* pp. 482ff.

12. See Murti, *Philosophy,* pp. 10ff.

13. Cf., e.g., the very texts I am about to present, which directly evidence both the difficulty of the question at issue, and the controversy surrounding it, from the very beginning.

14. Consider the colloquium held at Wooster College, in Ohio, at Easter 1965, on "The Self in Eastern and Western Thought." See also the report on this colloquium by B. Burkel and W. Norris Clarke in *International Philosophical Quarterly,* March 1966, pp. 101–9.

15. See Silburn, *Instant,* pp. 127ff.

16. Cf. a typical text of the *Mundaka Upanishad,* III, 2, 2, in which *krtātman* (the edification, or upbuilding of the *ātman*) seems to be the expression of perfection, which consists precisely in having completed one's own *ātman,* even though this *ātman* is then identified with the *brahman.* Of course the expression could also be translated simply as self-possession, minus any metaphysical pretensions.

17. A consequence whose importance, if only marginal for our own discourse, is considerable in itself. For the West, Parmenides' heir in this regard, perfection consists in being complete, "perfect" *(perfectum),* ultimate, rich. One must *don* virtue, knowledge, "perfections," even Christ. By contrast, in the typically Buddhist conception before us, positivity and the sublime are to be found in simplicity, in simplification, in a "stripping." This is an important observation, in view of the naive proposal by some of a cultural encounter on the basis of the presuppositions

offered by a technical conception of the world. See my *Intra-religious Dialogue,* chap. 5. Cf. also p. 187, n. 46; p. 192, n. 26.

18. If the subject changes, the Buddhist will say it is no longer the subject of the change but the change itself; if it does not change, then no real change is possible. And indeed this would be the conclusion that the vedantic *ātma-vāda* will be forced to draw.

19. Nāgārjuna's introductory prayer *(maṅgalācaranani),* at the beginning of his Kārikā, as handed down to us by Candrakīrti *(Prasannapadā,* XI, 13–16).

20. *Saṁyutta-nikāya,* III, 66 (Rhys Davids and Woodward trans., pp. 135–37).

21. *Dīgha-nikāya,* II, 64ff. (Rhys Davids and Charpenter trans., pp. 129–33).

22. This would of course be the Grecian king, Menander, who ruled over southern India in the middle of the second century B.C. According to legend it was Nāgasena himself who converted him to Buddhism. Although the text is a later one, the essential content very probably antedates the Christian era.

23. The concept of *puggala* seems to denote the subject of actions, although, as T. W. Rhys Davids notes, it may not as yet have had all of its later connotations. On the origin of the *puggalavāda,* see Pande, *Studies,* pp. 490ff.

24. *Milindapañha,* II, 1, 1ff.; or 251 in Trenckner's edition, pp. 25ff.

25. *Milindapañha,* II, 1, 1 (p. 40 in the Trenckner edition).

26. *Milindapañha,* III, 5, 6 (Trenckner, p. 71).

27. Cf., e.g., *Visuddhi-magga,* XVIII; *Saṁyutta-nikāya,* XXII, 85; IV, 54.

5. NIRVANA

1. Besides the bibliography I shall list, see also von Glasenapp, *Unsterblichkeit;* Obermiller, "Nirvana"; Thomas, "Nirvana"; Quiles, "Nirvana"; Altizer, *Nirvana*; S. Miyamoto, "Nirvana and the Limit of the Questioning," in *Indo-tetsugakuto-Bukkyo-no-Shomondai* (Tokyo: Iwanani Shoten, 1951), pp. 503–28.

2. Stcherbatsky, *Conception,* p. 27, offers the following resumé. For the primitive Buddhist schools, as well as for *vaibhasika, saṁsāra* und *nirvāṇa* are both real. For *mādhyamika, saṁsāra* and *nirvāṇa* are unreal in separation and distinction; for *sautāntrika, saṁsāra* is real and *nirvāṇa* unreal; for *yogācāra* or *vijnānavāda, saṁsāra* is unreal and *nirvāṇa* real. On the other hand there is no dearth of authors who question this framework: Dutt, *Aspects,* pp. 154ff.; Murti, *Philosophy,* pp. 272ff. These writers emphatically maintain that the Buddha asserted the existence of *nirvāṇa* and did not doubt its reality.

3. For B. Saint Hilaire, Pischel, and others, annihilation; for Max Müller, immortality; for T. W. Rhys Davids, holiness; for Coomaraswamy, transcendent rebirth; for Keith, state of absence, without being, nothingness; for de la Vallée Poussin (who maintains that the majority of Buddhist schools hold a nonnihilistic conception of *nirvāṇa*), perfect agnosticism. See de la Vallée Poussin, *Heritage;* Filliozat, *Inde,* pp. 2294–96; *Mus, Barabudur,* pp. 201–8; Law, "Nirvana," pp. 547–58. See also Slater, *Paradox.*

4. See, e.g., II, 72; VI, 15.

5. See, e.g., XIV, 543.

6. See *Majjhima-nikāya,* I, 4, 6.

7. See e.g. *Dīgha-nikāya,* I, 3, 19ff.

8. See Bareau, "Date," pp. 27–62; Dahlman, *Nirvana.* Tsukamoto, "Materials."

9. *Nirvāṇo'vāte,* according to the Panini grammar (VIII, 2, 50). *Vāta* means "wind" (cf. the Latin, *ventus*), and the root *va* means "to blow." Patanjali *(Bhāṣya)* gives a double example: *nirvāṇo'gnir vātena,* or fire blown out by the wind, and *nirvāṇah pradipo vātena,* a lamp blown out by the wind. But see another interpretation in n. 14, below.

10. "It is by ceasing our fires that the peace is reached," says Coomaraswamy, *Hinduism,* p. 63, in commenting on this particular. See also n. 13, below.

11. See n. 9, above. The same thing can be expressed by the Latin term *spiritus,* and the Greek *pneuma.* See n. 13, below.

12. See *nirvāṇa* in the Sanskrit dictionary compiled by Monier-Williams.

13. Would *nirvāṇa* be the wind of the spirit that blows whither it will, that comes one knows not whence (cf. John 3:8), and that consumes creatureliness, completing the inverse moment of the deed of creation—not of a creation issuing from nothing, but a creation that comes from God and that therefore returns to God divinized? Coomaraswamy translates *nirvāṇa* literally "expiration," as coming from *nir* (with the meaning of the Latin *ex*) and *vana,* "to exhale, to blow." In the texts of the Gita that I have quoted he translates "despiration in God" *(Hinduism,* p. 63). See later, in the same volume, references in the notes on p. 80. See also Campbell, *Hero,* p. 163.

14. See *Pali Text Society Dictionary,* 362a. The corresponding Sanskrit root would be *vṛ,* meaning "cover." Buddhaghosa *(Visuddhi-magga,* p. 239) connects the word with the root *vṛ,* "cover," coming to the same interpretation. See Dasgupta, *Development,* p. 185.

15. See chap. 3, n. 20, above.

16. See Rahula, *Buddha,* p. 41.

17. This mistake has vitiated more than one approach.

18. *Saṁyutta-nikāya,* I, 136.

19. Ibid., 210.

20. Ibid., 39.

21. Hatred, greed, disorder: *Saṁyutta-nikāya,* 43, 1, 2 (IV, 359).

22. A typical Buddhist expression. Cf., e.g., the introduction to the *Vairacchhedi-kā-sūtra (Prajñā-pāramitā-sūtra,* IX, in Goddard, *Bible,* p. 86 (although E. Conze's translation seems to me to be the best). See also *Aṅguttara-nikāya,* II, 24; IV, 13; IV, 160; *Itivuttaka,* 69; *Saṁyutta-nikāya,* IV, 175.

23. Cf. e.g. *Chandogya Upanishad,* VII, 26, 2; *Katha Upanishad,* II, 11; *Mundaka Upanishad,* II, 2, 6; *Prasna Upanishad,* VI, 8; *Maitri Upanishad,* VI, 21, 28, 30, etc.

24. *Saṁyutta-nikāya,* IV, 251–52. (Conze trans., p. 94).

25. See Introduction to part 2, n. 1, above.

26. These two words could stand as a symbol of the whole tension between Buddhism and Hinduism. Indeed, together they evince two tendencies inherent in human nature. The perfect, as the Latin and Greek words—*perfectum* and *teleios*—indicate, is the constructed, the created, the attained, the built, the developed, *saṁskṛta,* one tendency will say. The end to be attained is the nonconstructed, the uncreated, the one not-made, the not-manufactured, the nondeveloped, *akṛta,* the other will say. The sociological consequences, even in our day, seem to me to be enormous. See also chap. 3, n. 46, and chap. 4, n. 17, above.

27. Cf. *Dhammapada,* XXVI, 1 (p. 383), where the same *akatannū* (the unmade, the uncreated) appears as in VII, 8 (p. 97).

28. Cf., e.g., Matt. 11:15, 13:9, 43; Mark 4:9, 23; Luke 8:8, 14:35, etc. As we see,

it is not a matter of any one particular passage, and the assertion in question could, in my opinion, have surprisingly profound implications were it to be considered in the light of Buddhism. When all is said and done, not even the Master of Nazareth spoke clearly of the Father, and, despite the formulation in John 17:6, never actually uttered that Father's name.

29. Cf., in Christianity, John 1:2, Heb. 1:2, etc., as contrasted with Genesis 1:1 in the Hebrew tradition.

30. This is also the central idea of the asceticism of Saint John of the Cross, for example.

31. See *Dhammapada,* XXV, 9 (p. 368).

32. It is not my task to attempt a Christian hermeneutic of this whole problematic — although in so doing I should be able to extract a far deeper, and hitherto unsuspected, meaning — or to discuss whether the "undiscovered paradox of the gentiles" (de Lubac, *Surnaturel,* pp. 155–77) might be transcended in a theology that would take account of Buddhist reflection.

33. The variety of opinions among the various Buddhist schools apropos of the *asaṇkhata* is proverbial, and ranges from the recognition of one only in Theravada, for example, to the nine distinct "unconfected" *asaṇkhata*s in the doctrine of the *mahāsāṅghika,* and so on. A good review of the question appears in Bareau, *Absolu,* p. 260. Unquestionably, all schools acknowledge *nirvāṇa* as the *asaṃskṛta* par excellence.

34. See my *Myth,* chap. 2 and 3, for a layout of the problem with appropriate citations.

35. See Vesci, "Heat."

36. For Christian spirituality, see Louis Bouyer, *Le sens de la vie monastique* (Paris: Brepols, 1950), and the collective work, *Théologie de la vie monastique* (Paris: Aubier, 1961). See also Raimundo Panikkar et al., *Blessed Simplicity* (New York: Seabury, 1982).

37. Cf. Karl Rahner's expression, formulated in a different context from the Buddhist, but very close to the Buddhist intuition: "What, after all, does Christianity say? Really only this: The Mystery remains everlastingly Mystery: yet this Mystery seeks to communicate itself to the human spirit in absolute self-communication, in the midst of the experience of its finite void, as the Infinite, the Incomprehensible, as the Inexpressible called God, as self-bestowing Nearness" (*Schriften zur Theologie,* vol. 5 [Einsiedeln: Benziger, 1962], pp. 14–15). See also chap. 10, n. 209, below.

38. Cf., e.g., Heb. 9:11ff.

39. It is significant that this idea, so common and recurrent in the patristic texts — and so fertile for a dialogue between Christianity and other religions — has so often been left in obscurity out of a fear of pantheism. Cf., e.g.: "God's Logos has become human that humankind might be able to grasp how it can attain to being God" (Clement of Alexandria, *Protrepticus,* 1, 9). (It is instructive to recall that the word *theopoiein,* "to deify," used for the first time in the Christian tradition by Clement, in classical Greek meant "to manufacture idols," and in some cases "to apotheosize.") The expression, "human deification" *(theopoō anthrōpon — Protrep.,* XI), which Christian doctrine uses, is an echo of the gospel phrase "I have said, You are gods" (John 10:34, which in turn comes from Psalm 82:6), which Clement cites verbatim (*Stromata,* XIV, 146). With Saint Irenaeus the thought is all but a leitmotif: "The reason why the Word of God became human, and the Son of God the son of humankind, lies in the fact that humankind, joined to the Word of God

and receiving filiation, attains to being the son of God" (Irenaeus, *Adversus Haereses,* III, 19 — PG, 7:939). Sagnard's translation in *Sources Chrétiennes,* vol. 34, based on textual criticism, runs: *pour que l'homme entre en communion avec le Verbe de Dieu* ("that humankind may enter into communion with the Word of God"); cf. Irenaeus, *Adversus Haereses,* Preface (PG, 7:1120) as well as book 3, chap. 18, parag. 1 (PG, 7:937), etc. Saint Gregory the Theologian has a precise and daring formula: *Hina ginomai tosouton theos, hoson ekeinos anthrōpos* — "that I may become God to the extent that [God] became human" (Gregory of Nazianzen, *Oratio theologica,* III, 19 (PG, 36:100). Maximus the Confessor will call this formula "the beautiful transposition *(kalē apotrophē),* that humankind be deified and that God be humanized" *(anthrōpēsis).* Cf., finally: "The Word became human that we might be divinized" (Athanasius, *De Incarnatione Verbi,* 54 — PG, 25:192); "God became human so that humankind might become God" (Augustine, *Sermo 128* (PL, 39:1997); etc. For these and other texts, see Lemarie, *Manifestation,* pp. 145-60; Bouyer, *Spiritualité,* p. 334 and passim; Hausherr, *Direction,* p. 306 and passim; Gross, *Divinisation,* passim; etc.

40. See my *Mystère.*

41. See above, pp. 10f.

42. A number of authors have recently constructed a kind of systematic inventory of the various theories of *nirvāṇa.* Pande *(Studies,* pp. 443-540) comes to the conclusion that the prevailing modern opinion is contrary to both the agnostic and the nihilistic positions (p. 456). Welbon ("Understanding," 300-326) is also inclined to reject the total-nihilism theory (p. 322).

43. "But it would be a major heresy to wish to identify *nirvāṇa* with nothingness. No sect maintains this" (Regamey, "Buddhismus," p. 275).

44. See the series of studies by de la Vallée Poussin devoted to nirvana: *The Way to Nirvāṇa;* "Remarques sur le *Nirvāṇa";* *Nirvāṇa;* "Les deux Nirvana d'après la Vibhāṣā"; "Le Nirvāṇa d'après Āryadeva"; "Une dernière note"; "Musila et Narada." Stcherbatsky wrote his work upon realizing that he could not be satisfied with simply reviewing the 1925 book by de la Vallée Poussin.

45. *Visuddhi-magga,* XVI.

46. *Anupadiesāya nibbānadhātuyā.*

47. *Milindapanha,* III, 5, 10 (p. 73 in the Trenckner edition).

48. *Itivuttaka,* 43 (or II, 6 according to the other enumeration) (J. H. Moore trans., p. 56). See the same initial text in *Udāna,* VIII, 3.

49. *Udāna,* VIII, 1.

50. *Itivuttaka,* 44 (or II, 7) (J. H. Moore trans., p. 57).

51. The *Mādhyamika,* the source of the text here cited, cannot claim to relate the *ipsissima verba* of the Buddha. Nevertheless I cite it here, for it is perhaps among the clearest of those that maintain the total otherness of nirvana.

52. Or: If things are *being,* there is no passage from nonbeing to being, or vice versa. Such passage would mean that things are not being, in virtue of the very principle of noncontradiction, inasmuch as being is, and nonbeing is not. The argument proceeds *in infinitum.*

53. See almost the same words in *Laṅkāvatāra-sūtra,* 96ff.

54. Here the text begins to apply the classic schema of the *mādhyamika* with its four dialectical possibilities, based on the celebrated *catuṣkoti* of the Buddha's systematic negative responses to the four types of questions supposed to exhaust an inquiry.

55. See n. 32, p. 198.

56. *Mādhyamika-Kārikā* (Nāgārjuna's), XXV, 1–24. See (K. Inada trans., pp. 154ff.) Candrakīrti's comment, *Prasannapadā*, translated and annotated by Stcherbatsky, *Conception*, pp. 183–212. A good study for our purposes (in which the Buddha's silence is seen to culminate in Nāgārjuna's *śūnya*) is that of G. M. Nagao, "The Silence of the Buddha and Its Madhyamic Interpretation."

57. Scholars agree that the lost original Sanskrit of the *Laṅkāvatāra-sūtra* must belong to the first century of the Christian era, although its earliest Chinese translation dates only from the fifth century. Here I use, slightly abbreviated, the text constructed by Goddard, in his *A Buddhist Bible*, pp. 351ff., from the English translation from the Chinese by Suzuki, *Laṅkāvatāra*.

58. I present this text in so much detail because it constitutes a substantial resumé of a goodly number of philosophical schools, and demonstrates rather well the Buddhist conception of an ever-unconditioned *nirvāṇa*.

59. *Laṅkāvatāra-sūtra*, 12 (the chapter on *nirvāṇa*), according to the text cited by Goddard, *Bible*, pp. 351ff., following Suzuki.

60. Although I cannot offer an anthology of texts of the innumerable Buddhist schools, I here reproduce the Chinese text of the celebrated Hui-Neng, or Wei-Lang, the sixth *Ch'an* patriarch, very probably of the seventh century. (When the monk Bodhidharma, from the south of India, later considered to be the twenty-eighth patriarch after Śākyamuni, arrived in China, he came to be regarded there as the first of the Chinese patriarchs in the line of *Ch'an* Buddhism, which was eventually to be very important.)

61. "The Sūtra of the Sixth Patriarch," according to the English translation by Wong-Mou-Lam in Goddard, *Bible*, pp. 544–47. See also the (very eccentric) translation by P. F. and G. D. Fung, *The Sūtra of the Sixth Patriarch on the Pristine Orthodox Dharma*. The translation most to be recommended would be that of Wing-Tsit Chan, *The Platform Scripture*.

6. PRATĪTYASAMUTPĀDA

1. *Dīgha-nikāya*, II *(mahāpadāna sūtta); Saṁyutta-nikaya* I, 6, and the well-known *bokhikathā* in the *Mahāvagga*, I, 1, 1–3; etc. For other passages, see Pande, *Studies*, p. 413.

2. See any of the numerous biographies of the Buddha, or the resumé by Lamotte, *Histoire*, p. 17.

3. *Majjhima-nikāya*, I, 190–91, repeatedly cited in Buddhist literature. See, e.g., Candrakīrti, *Mādhyamika Kārikā Vṛtti*, p. 160. The text reads: *yo paṭiccasa-muppādam passati, so dhammam passati, yo dhammam passati so paṭiccasamuppādam passatīti.*

4. *Śālistamba-sūtra*, cited by Prajñākaramati, in the *Bodhicaryāvatārapañjikā* (ed. Bib. Ind.), in Murti, *Philosophy*, p. 7.

5. Cf. Murti, *Philosophy*, p. 7.

6. Apart from other works to be mentioned, see Oltramare, *Formule;* Barua, "Pratītyasamutpāda"; Law, "Formulation"; de la Vallée Poussin, *Bouddhisme.*

7. Following tradition, Nāgārjuna calls them *pratītyasamutpannadharman-irdeśakuśala*, "those capable of teaching interdependent production" (Nāgārjuna, *Mahāprajñāpāramitāśātra*, X, 14 (in Lamotte, *Histoire*, p. 349).

8. For a brief description, see Pande, *Studies,* pp. 407ff.

9. Candrakīrti, *Mādhyamika-kārikā-vṛtti,* 3, in Murti, *Philosophy,* p. 7.

10. Some examples: "production en dependence" (Lamotte, *Histoire,* p. 36, etc., and Silburn, *Instant,* p. 197, etc.); "production en consécution" (Filliozat, *Inde,* p. 540 [and 2238]); "entstehen in Abhängigkeit" (von Glasenapp, *Religionen,* p. 79); "Kausalnexus des abhängigen Entstehens" (idem, *Buddhismus*); "interdependent coexistence" (Casey, "Aspects," p. 2 and passim); "conditioned genesis" (Rahula, *Buddha,* 53); "generación condicionada" (Dragonetti, *Dhammapada;* p. 98); "dependently-coordinated-existence (of the elements)" (Stcherbatsky, *Conception,* p. 42); "dependent co-origination" (Streng, *Emptiness,* p. 58 and passim); "dependent origination" (Dasgupta, *History,* 1:92, etc.); "Lehrsatz von abhängigem Entstehen" (Frauwallner, *Philosophie,* pp. 27ff.).

11. T. W. Rhys Davids and others, including Coomaraswamy, are of the opinion that what we have here is the first formulation of the law of causality. For reasons that, it seems to me, ought to be evident to scholars of Buddhism, this interpretation might well constitute a *metabasis eis allo genos.* At all events we are surely not dealing with a substantialistic causality, nor indeed with a "cause" of being, but with a conception essentially distinct from the very idea of causality.

12. See Miyamoto, "Re-Appraisal."

13. *Pratītyasamutpāda* derives from *pratītya* and *samutpāda. Pratītya* is from *prati + i + ya:* from a prefix denoting dynamism, movement, proximity, "to" or "toward," "again," to make an appearance, etc. (cf. the Greek *pros*); then the root of the word for "to go," *ire;* then the gerund ending. Its literal meaning would therefore be: "going toward," "going for the purpose of." Dasgupta translates it "after getting" (*History,* 1:93), and Silburn "allant en fonction de" (*Instant,* p. 197). — *Samutpāda* is, again, a composite word, from *sam + ut + pāda* — a prefix signifying convergence, conjunction, union, intensity, the complete (cf. the Greek *syn-* and the Latin *cum, con-*), then the particle *ud,* denoting preeminence, "above," "above and beyond," etc., which, joined with the root *pad* of the verb for "to go" ("to fall," "to participate"), means "to produce," "to originate," "to give birth to," "to be produced," "to emerge," "to appear," "to become visible," "to cause," etc. Its literal meaning would be, then: "convergent production," "harmonious emerging," "conditioned generation," "conjoined appearance," "mutual origination," "germinating together," etc. Might we say, "epiphany"? — Thus *pratītyasamutpādā* comes down to something like "joint production realized in view of," "harmonious origination," the "way to conjoint emerging," "emergence in virtue of," etc. Let us simply note here both the meaning of going, proceeding — the meaning of the two roots — and the dynamic force of the prefixes. I may venture to describe it as "the epiphany of the ensemble of the totality," "the global manifestation of the dynamism of all things," or simply "the universal concatenation."

14. The word used to indicate the system of the various conditionings, sometimes called the theory of the twelve causes, is *nidāna:* connection, link, bond, tie. *Nidāna* comes from *ni + dāna,* and *dāna* comes from the root *dā* or *di,* meaning "to bind." The word is of ancient Vedic origin; see Renou, "Connection." Indeed it is a commonplace that the Buddha bestowed his own characteristic nuance on the concept of *nidāna,* renouncing the Upanishadic reliance on the *pratiṣṭhās.*

15. Tokurū Yamauchi lists three basic differences between the concept of *pratītyasamutpāda* and the "Western concept of causality": (1) Causality always operates from without, by way of *ex,* whereas the Buddhist concept operates by way

of *per.* (A child is born of a mother; something is on the right by virtue of something being on the left, and vice versa.) (2) Causality always precedes its effect, whereas the relationship of *pratītyasamutpāda* is always simultaneous. (3) Cause and effect are irreversible, whereas the Buddhist concatenation is mutual and reciprocal. See Yamauchi, "Problems," p. 7.

16. *Saṁskāra,* along with *dharma,* is "the most uncomfortable word to translate", says Silburn (*Instant,* p. 171), and goes so far as to assert that "the majority of the errors that have been committed with regard to Buddhism are owing to the fact that the verb *saṁskṛ* has not been grasped in its whole scope" (ibid., p. 200).

17. *Anityā sarve saṁskārā.*

18. *Udāna Vagga,* XIII, 5, 8.

19. *Mahāvagga Vinaya Piṭaka,* I, 6, 29.

20. Here it will not be out of order to recall the passage from the *Gospel According to the Egyptians,* as cited by Clement of Alexandria (*Stromata,* book 3, chap. 9, parag. 1 [452]): "Wherefore with reason, when the Word had spoken of the consummation [of the ages], Salome asked: 'How long will human beings die?' Whereupon carefully and ponderingly the Lord replied: 'As long as women give birth'—that is, as long as cupidities are at work. . . . For, by the natural necessity of the divine economy, death follows generation, and the conjunction of body and soul is followed by their dissolution." To be sure, life and creation in themselves are not an evil; it is only a matter of the course of nature, by which birth is invariably followed by death. See the interesting argumentation here, book 3, chap. 9 (452–54), which acquires an altogether new sense if considered in this Buddhist spirit.

21. Consider, by way of contrast, the thinking of a certain traditional Christian spirituality that exalts the dignity of human nature at the expense of the worth of other things—witness today's ecological catastrophes.

22. A comparative study of the Buddha's experience and that of Saint Benedict, who saw the entire world in the form of a single, closed globe (cf. Gregory the Great, *Vita Sancti Benedicti, Lib. II Dialogorum*), would surely provide abundant and promising material for a monograph. See, for Saint Benedict, A. Stoltz, *Theologie der Mystik* (Ratisbon: Pustet, 1936).

23. Another promising theme: a confrontation of the key notion of hierarchy in the cosmic vision of the Pseudo Areopagite (cf. *Hierarchia Caelestis,* PG 1:164–65) with Buddhism's universal concatenation.

24. A comparative study between the key concepts of the vision of modern physics with the Buddhist cosmology is still in its first beginnings. See, e.g., Capra, *Tao.*

25. It is significant that the Chāndogya Upanishad rejects the view that one thing would rest upon another in a mere undifferentiated circularity precisely because it would preclude the Buddha's conclusion: "I do not speak thus because otherwise one thing would be simply based on another *(anyohi anyasmin pratiṣṭhitaḥ)."* Things are reciprocally conditioned, but the total conditioning cannot be finite. *Pratiṣṭhita,* on which things are based, are founded, and rest, can be in no other thing, whether in linearity or in circularity, for this would entail a procession ad infinitum without any possible issue.

26. See certain passages: *Itivuttaka,* 43; *Udāna,* VIII, 3; 1, 480; *Majjhima-nikāya,* II, 173; III, 70; III, 145; etc.

27. See above, pp. 44–45, and below, p. 198, n. 132.

28. It is a cultural characteristic of India to set in confrontation a pluralism of

truths and a monism of reality. By contrast, Western culture is founded on a pluralism of realities "corrected" by a monism of truth. See my *Mystère,* pp. 37ff. This is the sense in which we must understand the assertion of Streng (*Emptiness,* p. 21, n.), to the effect that Nāgārjuna's expression, "ultimate reality," should be translated "ultimate truth."

29. Cf. *Saṁyutta-nikāya,* II, 48.

30. Silburn's thesis (*Instant,* pp. 193ff.), to the effect that the *pratītyasamutpāda* is situated in the same line as the sacrifices of the *brāhmana,* is worthy of consideration.

31. As von Glasenapp observes, the denomination of the Absolute as *das ganz Andere,*" the "utterly other," is more applicable to *nirvāṇa* than to the Christian God (cf. von Glasenapp, *Buddhismus,* p. 104). Strictly speaking, however, we should have to say that neither the Christian God nor *nirvāṇa* can be grasped, comprehended, in categories of equality and difference. God is not the other, but neither is *nirvāṇa*. We have no alternative but ontological silence.

32. See the celebrated distich, *na saṁsārasya nirvānāt kiṁcid asti viśesanam* ("There is no difference between *saṁsāra* and *nirvāṇa*)": in Nāgārjuna, *Mādhyamika-kārikā,* XXV, 19, cited above, p. 45.

33. *Majjhima-nikāya,* II, 32. Cf. practically the same words in *Saṁyutta-nikāya,* II, 28 and 65, as well as in the *pratītyasamutpāda-sūtra*. We are dealing with what H. Ui, appealing to tradition, calls *idaṁ-pratyayatā,* as he seeks to demythologize *pratītyasamutpāda-sūtra* and transform it into an explanation of all becoming and each existence. See Takeuchi, "Schweigen," pp. 12ff.

34. *Dīgha-nikāya,* II, 55; *Saṁyutta-nikāya,* II, 92 (12, 60).

35. Basham, *Sources,* p. 103, notes that, although Buddhism does not recognize the caste system in theory, one nevertheless discerns a certain caste mentality in passages like this one, in which the monk who has failed to grasp the message of the Buddha is in an inferior condition.

36. *Majjhima-nikāya,* I, 256ff. (Chalmers trans., pp. 19–20).

37. *Visuddhi-magga,* XVII.

38. Following is not the literal translation of a text, but a synthesis of the twelve bonds as customarily presented. It is a commonplace that even the descriptions given in the Pali canon contain important variants. Thus, for example, the *Mahānidāna-sūtta (Dīgha-nikāya,* XV, 1ff.) has a catalogue of just nine bonds, and there are other texts with six, seven, ten, or eleven. The basic texts are: *Vinaya-piṭaka,* I, 1; *Majjhima-nikāya,* III, 63; see *Saṁyutta-nikāya,* II, 1–4, for the etymology of *nidāna*. See also Williams, "Translation."

39. On this point as for others, see the important aspects brought into confrontation by Lamotte, *Histoire,* 1:39ff.

40. With characteristic German pithiness, von Glasenapp, *Religionen,* p. 79, translates and explains: "Driving forces forming the *karma,* which forces will determine the destiny of successive existence."

41. *Ṣaḍ āyātana* ("the six dominations") in Dragonetti's translation (p. 100); *bases,* in that of Lamotte, *Histoire,* 1:39ff.

42. Filliozat translates, with finesse: *la prise de contact* ("establishment of contact") (*Inde,* p. 2284).

43. Lamotte, ibid.

44. It has become classic to divide the twelve conditions into three temporal categories, past (1 and 2), present (3–10), and future (11–12). "Birth" obviously

refers to the future birth of those who have not yet been delivered from the chain of existences.

45. *Ánguttara-nikāya,* III, 60.

46. German translation and notes, Frauwallner, *Philosophie,* pp. 39ff., 409.

47. See Tucci, "Fragment," and the German translation in Frauwallner, *Philosophie,* pp. 48ff.

48. See de la Vallée Poussin, *Théorie,* pp. 68ff.

7. AVYĀKṚTAVASTŪNI

1. Other texts bearing on particular aspects of *avyāṛta* can be found in the following *suttas* of the *Dīgha-nikāya: Brahmajāla, Mahali, Potthapāda, Mahānidāna* (commonly numbered 1, 6, 9, 15); *Samyutta-nikāya,* III, 24 (called the *dittha samyutta*), pp. 213–24; Murti, *Philosophy,* p. 36, adds the following citations: *Majjhima-nikāya,* II, 229–38; *Milindapanha,* pp. 144ff.; *Abdhidarma Kósabhāṣya,* appendix *(Pudgala-viniścaya); Mādhyamika-kārikā* of Nāgārjuna, XXI, XXV, and XXVIII; *Aṣṭasāhasrikā-prajnāpāramitā,* pp. 269ff.; *Mahavyutpatti,* p. 64 (parag. 206); *Dharmasangraha,* p. 67.

2. See my *Māyā,* part 1, chap. 3 (pp. 71–98), as well as my *Spiritualità.*

3. See below, p. 89.

4. The threefold etymology of the word *deva* in traditional interpretations is instructive. A first interpretation derives the word from the root *div,* or better, from *di,* meaning "shining, flashing," so that in this derivation the gods are those luminous beings of refulgent splendor and loveliness. In a second interpretation, *deva* is from the root *dīv,* "to play, to amuse oneself," and the gods would be the beings who play and amuse themselves because they are not subject to the miseries of human life. Finally, a third etymology—much more contrived—relates the word either to *da* meaning "to divide, to share," or *da* meaning "to give." There is an interesting and illuminating play of words in the *Śatapatha Brāmaṇa* (XI, 1, 6, 7), where, playing with the root *div* ("to shine"), from which *dyu* ("sky," "day") is derived, and with the word *deva,* in the sense mentioned above, it is stated: "From his mouth came the *devas.* As soon as they appeared, they took possession of the sky. . . . And when Prajāpati had emitted them, it was as midday for him."

5. "In my opinion, there is not the slightest doubt that the Buddha and all his disciples believed in the real existence of these divinities" (von Glasenapp, *Buddhismus,* p. 23).

6. *Majjhima-nikaya,* 100 (II, 212). It would not be difficult to produce numerous other texts.

7. It seems to me that a monographic study of the different divinities in the various religions would be of importance and urgency for confronting the problem of contemporary "atheism." As a source with respect to Hinduism, see Gonda, *Observations.*

8. Cf. *Majjhima-nikāya,* I (I, 2); 49 (1, 329).

9. Cf. *Mahāprajnāpāramitāsāstra,* I, 141, in the French translation by Lamotte. This is the point certain moderns rely on for their emphasis on Buddhism's "scientific" character.

10. It is interesting that Christians were regarded as atheists during the first

centuries of their history, for they refused to acknowledge the gods of others, and their own had no temple.

11. In order properly to situate the Buddha's position, it will be in order to keep in mind the doctrine, of *vaiśeṣika* origin, but common to almost all the philosophies of India, of the four classes of *abhāva,* the absence or want of being: (1) *prāgabhāva,* the nonbeing proper to existence, rather like a garment before it is made; (2) *dhaṁsa,* successive nonbeing, that is to say, being having just ceased to be, like a vessel that has just been broken; (3) *atyantābhāva,* or impossibility, like the child of a sterile woman; and (4) *anyonyābhāva,* or reciprocal negation, such as water and ice (to give the traditional examples).

12. Although I follow my own interpretation of the celebrated tetralemma, it will still be useful to take cognizance of the bibliography on the problem. In addition to works cited above and below, the following articles are of interest: Robinson, "Aspects"; Nakamura, "Influence"; Schayer, "Antizipationen"; Organ, "Silence"; Nagao, "Silence."

13. See Robinson, "Nāgārjuna."

14. See the two studies by Staal, which, although not dealing exclusively with Buddhism, furnish abundant material for reflection: "Construction" and "Negation."

15. See Pandeya, *Logic.*

16. See ibid. and Murti, *Philosophy,* p. 130.

17. *Hēmeis de nun eilēphamen hōs adunatou ontos hama einai kai mē einai* ("We, however, say that it is impossible for anything simultaneously to be and not to be"); Aristotle, *Metaphysics,* II, 4 (1006a3–4).

18. *Esti gar einai, mēden hr'ouk estin:* "For being is, but nothing is not" (Diels, *Fragmente,* 6).

19. "Thus the self is to think and to be" (ibid., 3).

20. With A standing for proposition 1, ("A is B"), and B for the expression "is not my opinion."

21. In modern logic we have the familiar proposition of Sigwart (see his *Logik*), against the position of numerous others, on the negation of negation: "Not non-A = A." Without becoming a party to the dispute, which also involves a consideration of the principle of the excluded third, I hold the formula valid, provided A = A, which is indeed the case with the verb "to be." That is, the principle is not verified in "Not is-not is," as I have now made clear in the body of the text. After all, "To be" is said *pollakōs*—"in many ways," as Aristotle declares (*Metaphysics,* book 4, chap. 2 [1003a33, b5]).

22. A *is* and *is not* B.

23. A is *not (is and is not)* B.

24. Let us not become involved in the heated discussion as to whether Buddhist logic, and *mādhyamika* in particular, do or do not make use of the excluded third, although I am inclined to share the affirmative thesis. See R. Robinson, "Aspects"; Pandeya, *Logic*; Murti, *Philosophy*; Yamauchi, "Problems."

25. See a work whose study would shed a great deal of light on the problem of the application of the principles of human thought to the case under examination (a case not considered by the author, however, for he is concerned exclusively with the Western problematic): Morot-Sir, *Pensée,* esp. pp. 345ff.

26. *Caturdaśa avyākṛtavastūni,* tradition says. See Kasawara, *Dharma Saṁgraha.*

27. From *in-ex-plicare*, something that cannot be explicated, displayed, unfolded — something whose folds cannot be opened.

28. The root, *kṛ*, "to do, to make," is the basis of the word *a-vy-ā-kṛ-ta;* the initial *a-* is privative, so that *vy-akṛta* means "separated, divided, unwound, applied, exposed," hence also — very significantly — transformed, disfigured, changed. The verb *vyākṛ* means precisely "to unmake," and hence "to separate, to divide," and then "to declare, to explain," and finally "to foretell, to prophesy" — undoing the knot of time. Thus *a-vyākṛta* means "the unexplained."

29. I shall not venture to connect the Buddhist *avyākṛta* with the *avyakta* of *Katha Upanishad,* III, 11 (I, 3, 11); Bhagavadgita, VIII, 20–23; etc. The Upanishadic texts deal with the unmanifested, the undeveloped, the anterior-to-all. See a good commentary in Rawson, *Katha Upanishad,* pp. 129–43. *A-vy-akta* is composed of the negative *a-*, the particle *vy,* and the root *añj,* "to anoint." Hence *vyakta* means "adorned, beautiful, beautified"; but at once, as early as the *Rg Veda,* it assumes the meaning of "apparent, visible, manifest." To be sure, there is another root, *vi,* or *vya,* which means "to cover," and here *avyakta* would mean that which is discovered: "the manifest." The extent of the ties between the Immanifest of the Upanishads and the Inexplicable of the Buddha would constitute an engrossing research theme.

30. *Majjhima-nikāya,* 63.

31. Beginning here, I replace refrains with ellipsis.

32. Corresponding to the *vatica robusta.*

33. *Majjhima-nikāya,* I, 72, called the *Aggivacchagottasutta* (pp. 483–88), translated into French by Bareau, *Bouddha,* pp. 145–50; into English by Warren, *Buddhism,* pp. 123ff.; and into German by Frauwallner, *Philosophie.*

34. *Saṁyutta-nikāya,* 44 (IV, pp. 400–401) (Woodward trans., pp. 281f.).

35. Although this text makes no direct reference to the Buddha and is of relatively late date, it seems to me to be very characteristic of the spirit I seek to describe. Furthermore it is little known outside the learned world of scholars.

36. Vimalakīrti, "Discourse on Emancipation," chap. 7.

37. Here follow more than thirty opinions, which would fill more than six printed pages.

38. Vimalakīrti, "Discourse on Emancipation," chap. 9. I have followed the translation by H. Idumit, published in *The Eastern Buddhist,* 1925–27.

8. CHANGE OF HUMAN AWARENESS, THEN AND NOW

1. Psalm 39:14. The theme of this psalm, the vanity and hollowness of creation, is the focus of my own hermeneutic. Cf. Job 14:10; 7:8,21.

2. The effort of a Gandhi, for example, to show that the Buddha was not an atheist in the "negative" sense of the word, is typical. See his article in *Young India,* January 24, 1927, where he says of the Buddha: "He unhesitatingly said that law was God Himself. God's laws are eternal and not separate from God Himself. It is an indisputable condition of His very perfection. And hence the great confusion that Buddha disbelieved in God and simply believed in the moral law."

3. See, by way of an example from religious sociology, the interesting study by von Glasenapp, "Der Buddhismus in der Vorstellungsweit der Hindus," in his *Von Buddha zu Gandhi,* pp. 111–24.

4. See, among others, van der Leeuw, *Phänomenologie;* Brelich, *Introduzione.*

5. See Gen. 3:1-7. See also a revived appreciation of the value of this ancient and suggestive thesis thanks to the sensitivity generated by modern studies in the history of religions, in Zaehner, *Convergent Spirit,* pp. 63-95, etc.

6. See my *Mystère,* pp. 54ff.; Vesci, *Ambivalence.*

7. See my *Humanismo,* pp. 178-253; "La superación del humanismo," where I address the problem from a Christian viewpoint.

8. Protagoras, *Fragments,* 2:263. Cf. Plato, *Theatetus,* 151e.

9. Consider, e.g., *mīmāmsā* atheism.

10. Cf. Bartrhari, *Vakyapadīya,* I, 1.

11. Cf. Heraclitus, fragments 1, 2, 50, etc. Cf. Kelber, *Logos.*

12. John 1:1.

13. It is here that the theological current of the "death of God," in its more serious aspects, seems to me to be an unequivocal sign of the times.

14. Bareau, *Religionen,* 3:12-213, gives 560-480 B.C. as more correct dates for the life of the Buddha.

15. Generally regarded as *ksatrya,* although some continue to maintain that Gautama was of Brahmanic extraction.

16. Karl Jaspers' classic expression (*Ursprung,* pp. 14-31, dealing with the *Achsenzeit*).

17. See a development of the theme in U. M. Vesci, "Dio, Uomo, Salvezza in alcuni aspetti del rivolgimento spirituale del VII-VI sec. a.C. in Asia e in Grecia," thesis, University of Rome, Faculty of Letters and Philosophy, Institute of Historico-Religious Studies, 1962.

18. See Rosenberg, *Zeichen,* pp. 2ff.

19. See my *Myth,* chap. 1.

20. From this viewpoint—leaving political considerations altogether out of account—the new "fall of Jerusalem" in 1967 might be regarded as a key date in the historical consciousness of the Abrahamic traditions.

21. For an appreciation of the extent to which the West is impregnated with Judaism and Christianity, we might recall that even at the trial of Russian writers Andrei Sinyavsky and Juri Daniel, in Moscow in the 1960s, the prosecutor asked Daniel why, if he had not wished to make accusations against the Soviet people in his book, *The Call of Moscow,* he had said "Moscow" instead of "Babylon." See the account of the trial in *Encounter,* 26 (1966) 88.

22. Cf. 2 Kings 28ff.; Amos 5:21-27; etc.

23. Cf. Eccl. 35:1ff.

24. Isa. 1:16, Amos 5:24, Micah 6:8, etc.

25. Cf. Hos. 6:6, Amos 5:21, Jer. 6:20ff. See also Amos 8:4ff. and Micah 2:2,8.

26. For a development of the topic of the influence of worship in the formation of one's concept of God, see the address by U. M. Vesci, "Qualis cultus, talis Deus," delivered at the International Congress of History of Religions (IAHR) held in Stockholm in 1970.

27. Compare the preaching of Amos, Hosea, and Micah with that of Isaiah, who always tries to save the celebrated "remnant of Israel." See also the exceptional attitude of Elijah, who dies when the Philistines have captured the ark (1 Sam. 4:17ff.) because "the glory of God is over and done" as far as the immediate situation of the destruction the temple in 587 B.C. is concerned—although the catastrophe represents not Yahweh's defeat, but victory.

28. Cf. Isa. 37:16, 60:1ff., etc.

29. Cf. Isa. 19:23ff., 37:16, 45:14ff.; Jer. 10:10ff.

30. See, e.g., Kaufmann, *Religion,* particularly pp. 127ff. (Kaufmann emphasizes, perhaps excessively, the unique character of Israel's history and religion.) For a theology of all that I have been saying here, see Eichrodt, *Theologie,* vols. 1-2, esp. 1:53ff.; as well as von Rad, *Theologie des Alten Testaments,* vol. 2; Kraus, *Gottesdienst,* pp. 110ff.; etc.

31. There is disagreement on the era of Zarathustra's activity, from the hyperbolic date of 6000 B.C. given by many of his followers today, to immediately before the century under examination. See Widengren, *Religionen,* pp. 61, 376; Henning, *Zoroaster,* pp. 37ff., with its recent dating of ca. 1200 B.C. See also Burrow, "Proto-Indoaryans." Despite the fact that the data furnished in the last-named article are impressive, I am more inclined to share a synchronic interpretation that would place the Iranian prophet in the period in which a single breath seems to have breathed on humanity, and mostly in the same direction. Zarathustra's message, too, fits into the particular movement of this era. The idea that he anticipated, by some six to eight centuries, the movement under our examination here, so that he was a contemporary of Moses rather than of the Hebrew prophets, would make of him a unique phenonenon indeed. Of course if Henning's dating is correct, we are in the age of the attempted Egyptian reform of Pharaoh Akenatou, which, however, unlike Zarathustra's, enjoyed no lasting success.

32. See *Yasna,* XXIX, 6ff.

33. See Duchesne-Guillemin, *Zoroastre,* pp. 152ff.

34. See Zaehner, *Dawn.*

35. See *Yasna,* XXXIII, 14; XXXIV, 1ff.; XLVIII, 4ff.

36. On the translation of the name Ahura Mazda, see Pagliaro, "Idealismo gathico" and "Idealismo iranico."

37. See *Yasna,* XLVIII, 1; XLIV, 3ff.; XLVI, 9; etc.

38. See *Yasna,* III, 1ff.; Spenta Manyu and Angra Manyu, the principles respectively of good and evil, are twins, and proceed from one Lord.

39. See *Yasna,* XLIII, 5ff., especially the refrain: "I grasped that thou art holy, when. . . ."

40. See, by way of confirmation, Wang-Pi, author of a commentary on the *Tao-Te-Ching,* who adopted a position similar to that of Kuo Hsiang in his commentary on the *Chuang Tzu.* Both commentators say that Confucius entered into a mystical state—"the state of inward silence and quietude" (Bodde, *History,* 2:171). Wang Pi "presents the very silence of Confucius as a token of his higher knowledge. It is because Confucius identified himself with the higher sphere of reality, which is for Wang Pi the sphere of 'non being' *(u)*—as distinct from the realm of finite being *(yu)*—that the great sage said nothing about it" (Spencer, *Mysticism,* p. 107).

41. *Dialog.,* I, 4, 8.

42. See, e.g., *Tao-Te-Ching.* For a new interpretation, see Wu, *Chuang Tzu.*

43. See, e.g., Bodde, *History;* de Bary et al., *Sources.*

44. See Jaeger, *Theologie,* p. 29.

45. Aristotle, *Physics,* book 3, chap. 4, 4 (203b10), etc.; Simplicius, *Physics,* 24, 13ff.; 150, 23.

46. See Aristotle, *Metaphysics,* book 1, chap. 3 (948a5); Simplicius, *Physics,* 24, 26.

47. See Caird, *Evolution,* 1:58ff.; Kirk and Raven, *Philosophers,* pp. 103ff. Gadamer, *Begriffswelt,* with monographs on this theme.

48. See Jaeger, *Theologie,* the chapter devoted to Xenophanes, pp. 50–68.

49. See Aristotle, *Metaphysics,* book 1, chap. 5 (968b18).

50. Jamblicus, *Vita Phythagori,* 29, 72ff.; Plato, *The Republic,* book 10, 600b. See the testimony of Clement of Alexandria, *Stromata,* V, 11, 67, 3 (PG, 9:101b): "Pythagoras, too, desires for himself this five years' silence that he enjoins on his disciples". Likewise Clement regards a five years' noviceship in the spiritual life as appropriate.

51. See Empedocles, *fragments* 170/112; and, generally, Bignone, *Empedocle.*

52. Heraclitus, *Fragments,* B 1 and 2.

53. See Aristotle, *Metaphysics,* book 1, chap. 3 (983bff.); idem., *De Anima,* book 1, chap. 2 (405a19); book 1, chap. 5 (411a7); etc. See also Diogenes Laertius, 1, 24ff. Cf. Heraclitus's enigmatic expression: *bathos logos* "deep logos" (Diels, *Fragm.,* 68b, 45). Compare this *Ungrund-logos* with the *Ungrunden Gottes* of the New Testament (Rom. 11:33; 1 Cor. 2:10). Cf. the expression of Clement of Alexandria, *ta bathē tēs theias gnōseōs* (1 Clement, 40). Is it these depths of the divine knowledge that the Buddha would have us penetrate? (Cf., incidentally, Rev. 2:24, "depths of Satan"—*ta bathea tou Satana*), which the Vulgate translates "altitudines Satanae."

54. See various authors, *Mysteries,* in the Eranos series; Sabbatucci, *Saggio;* Pettazzoni, *Religione,* chap. 5; Kerény, *Apollon.*

55. Kerény, *Religion,* Jaeger, *Paideia;* Otto, *Gestalt.*

56. Tradition places Mahavira's *nirvāṇa* in 527 B.C. Another date proposed is 477 B.C. See Schubring, *Religionen,* 3:221; idem, *Jainismus;* della Casa, *Giainismo.*

57. See Vesci, "Heat," p. 442, as well as her book *Heat and Sacrifice,* where the internal continuity of the process is demonstrated. See also my *Vedic Experience.*

58. See my *Mystère,* pp. 62ff.

59. Cf. *Rg Veda,* X, 121; 129. "Great is the single Divinity of the Gods" *(mahad devānām asurtvam ekam), Rg Veda,* III, 55, 1, emphatically states.

60. This is especially significant inasmuch as the *brahman* was originally simply the formula, the prayer, recited at sacrifice. Its assumption to the status of First Principle is another aspect of the Upanishadic sublimation of sacrifice. See Gonda, *Brahman.*

61. See *Chāndogya Upanishad,* VI, 13.

62. See *Maṇḍaka Upanishad,* II; *Chāndogya Upanishad,* III, 14, 4; *Bṛhadāranyaka Upanishad,* II, 5, 1; etc.

63. See *Śatapatha Brāmana,* X, 5, 2, 20; *Muṇḍaka Upanishad,* III, 2, 9; *Chāndogya Upanishad,* VIII, 4, 3; *Maitrī Upanishad,* VI, 34; etc.

64. See *Taittirīya Samhitā,* V, 3, 12, 2; *Bṛhadāranyaka Upanishad,* I, 1, 1ff.; and *Bhāṣya,* in hoc loco.

65. *Śatapatha Brāmaṇa,* XI, 3, 1, 1ff.; *Chāndogya Upanishad,* III, 16, 1ff.

66. See *Kauṣītaki Upanishad,* II, 5.

67. "This is yourself" *(Chāndogya Upanishad,* VI, 8, 7; etc.).

68. "I am *brahman*" *(Bṛhadāranyaka Upanishad,* I, 4, 10).

69. Origen, in his *Peri Archon, (Treatise on Principles)* adjoins to the three traditional principles (God, world, and humankind) a fourth, as necessary for a complete conception of reality and a precise understanding of Christianity: revelation. See vol. 5 of the Berlin edition *(Griechische christliche Schriftstellen).*

70. Mus, in his *Barabuḍur,* p. 37, could write: "Śākyamuni's personal adventure is the archetype of revelation."

71. This important and difficult argument has been treated by me in an unfinished work, *Mysterium Crucis.*

72. See chap. 2, n. 15.

73. For a preliminary orientation on the subject, see the following works: Lübbe, *Säkularisierung;* Loen, *Säkularisation;* Gogarten, *Verhängnis.* For an evaluation of these works, and of the literature on the subject more generally, see Scheidt, "Säkularisierung": Newbegin, *Honest Religion;* Cox, *Secular City;* Mascall, *Secularisation;* Panikkar, *Culto;* Aubrey, *Secularism;* Meland, *Secularization;* Nichols, *History;* R. G. Smith, *Secular Christianity;* Spann, *Christian Faith;* Wilson, *Religion.* I expect to be able soon to publish a volume entitled *Sacred Secularity.*

74. "To know the divinity only as power and not as good, is idolatry," wrote Simone Weil (*Pensées,* p. 48). Indeed, the very claim to "know" God — in any way — is in and of itself idolatry. "If someone, seeing God, knew what he saw, he did not see God," said Denis the Areopagite (PG, 3, 1065a), and with him, the greatest part of Christian tradition.

75. See the so frequently cited expression of the Fourth Lateran Council (actually only a "pass" at the truth; of course, the divine object can be spoken of only *in obliquo*): "For it is impossible to observe a likeness between the Creator and the creature without there being noted an even greater unlikeness" (Denzinger-Schönmetzer, no. 806). Compare this with the prohibition in Judaism of uttering the name of Yahweh (Exodus 20:7) — as generally with the name of God in so many so-called primitive religions.

76. See the seventh and last proposition of Wittgenstein's *Tractatus logico-philosophicus:* "Concerning what one cannot speak of, one must keep silence".

77. This expression, taken from Matthew's Gospel (16:3), as used by John XXIII, acquired a very particular flavor.

78. A Friedrich Nietzsche, a Pierre Teilhard de Chardin, even an Aurobindo Bose, could be mentioned here, for all their diversity, as representative figures of this new situation.

79. See my "Technique," where I spell out more in detail, and exemplify, what I am saying here. Developments in these last decades seem to suggest that the negative aspect of technology is gaining the upper hand.

80. The current bibliography on atheism is simply overwhelming. I shall not attempt even a skeleton outline here. See *Ateismo contemporaneo.*

81. In India, the scope of the phenomenon of *cārvāka,* or materialistic philosophy, remains to be studied. It could have been equally important, had it not been stifled by tradition.

82. Here let us recall the etymological meaning of the Latin *credere,* "to believe," from *cor* and *dare,* to "give one's heart," to "set one's heart upon." The etymology of the Sanskrit word *śraddhā,* "faith," is the same. See my *Myth,* as well as p. 229, n. 109 of the present volume.

83. When certain religious groups do so — for example, Jehovah's Witnesses — they are regarded as "abnormal" and "fanatical" by "normal" persons.

84. The traditional Indian idea of the *iṣṭadevatā,* the divinity chosen to satisfy an individual's own need for adoration, amounts to a personalization, not a privatization, of religion.

85. Thus we have a reversal of the previous situation, in which it was the atheist who took a subjective view of religious behavior founded on objectivity. Now it is

no longer God who gives us to eat, but our own toil with machines, no longer Saint Barbara who protects us from lightning, but a lightning rod, and so on.

86. "There are two kinds of atheism, of which one is a purification of the notion of God" (Weil, *Pesanteur,* p. 132).

87. See my "Have 'Religions' the Monopoly on Religion?"

88. See chap. 1, n. 4, above. Note too that neither is the concept a New Testament one.

89. See Casper, *Phänomenologie.*

90. Lest anyone continue to deny that there is no religion in this attitude, I here transcribe, without commentary, Friedrich Nietzsche's "Dem unbekannten God" ("To the Unknown God"):

> Ere I stride ahead once more,
> ere I steer my gaze unto the fore,
> this one last time I lift my hands
> to thee, the one I flee,
> the one to whom, in my heart's remote recesses
> I consecrated solemn altars once—
> and beg that ever and again
> thy voice call to me.
>
> Upon thy holy table, writ deep, and glowing,
> I read: To the unknown God.
> Thine am I! Oh, true, till now
> Have I dallied in the gang of kings,
> and feel the serpents drag me to the fray
> and—ah, could I but flee!—constrain me
> to serve. Thee would I know,
> Unknown, plunged in my deepest soul
> like a storm, overwhelming my life.
> O Unseizable, like unto myself!
> I would know thee, nay, thee serve!

Cited by G. Siegmund, "Friedrich Nietzsche," in *Ateismo contemporaneo,* 2:265.

91. See Benz, *Das Bild.*

92. See, e.g., Psalm 39:6; Isa. 40:17. For the various texts of Christian scholasticism, see, e.g., Thomas Aquinas, *De Potentia,* q. 3, a. 3, ad 4; Śankara, *Brahmasūtrabhāṣya,* VII, 20, 2–3.

93. See, e.g., Karl Marx in so many of his typical expressions.

94. See Fabro, *Nozione metafisica.*

95. See my "Colligite Fragmenta" for an explanation of the significance of this cosmotheandric intuition.

96. See Preface to the Original Edition, n. 1, above.

97. See, e.g., the familiar ten oxherding paintings of several Zen masters since the twelfth century. There is a reproduction, with commentary, in Kapleau, *Three Pillars,* pp. 301–13.

98. See J. A. T. Robinson, *Honest to God,* p. 121.

99. See Dewart, *The Future of Belief,* with its almost desperate effort to dehellenize Christianity, beginning with its liberation from the equation God = being (which the author calls relative theism) in virtue of the fact that "God" is the reality present in all things and yet not exhausted by any of them. "The Christian

God is not both transcendent and immanent. He is a reality *other* than being who is *present* to being (by which presence he makes being to be)" (p. 139).

100. See Vahanian, *No Other God,* where the author makes the point that the "death of God," as a cultural phenomenon, cannot be erected into a new absolute.

101. It is not for nothing that Descartes is considered the father of modern philosophy.

102. See Dietrich Bonhoeffer, *Religion without Revelation,* p. 163, cited by John A. T. Robinson, *Honest to God,* p. 38. Bonhoeffer insists on the old hypothesis: *Etsi Deus non daretur* ("Even if there were no God . . .)." It is interesting to recall that Hugo Grotius, *De Jure Belli ac Pacis,* XI, sought, with the formula, *etsi daretur Deum non esse,* a kind of neutral ground where it would be possible for human life to develop as if God were a sectarian "hypothesis."

103. "The religion of flight is atheism"—G. van der Leeuw (*Phänomenologie,* p. 679)—an oversimplification, in my view. Then why not say, as well, "The religion of refuge is theism"? The German translation of J. Lacroix's *Le sens de l'athéisme moderne* (Tournai/Paris: Casterman, 1958), reads: *Der Atheismus ist der Anspruch auf Unschuld* ("atheism is the claim to innocence") (*Wege des heutigen Atheismus* [Tübingen: Mohr, 1956], p. 49).

104. See, e.g., the report on the Achilpa tribe in Spencer-Gillen, *Arunta,* 1:368. For the Achilpas, the sacred pole representing the "axis of the world" stands for the orientation of life, that which bestows meaning on life itself. Legend has it that the pole once broke in two, whereupon the tribe, after a period of aimless wandering, came to a place where they all collapsed on the spot and died. The elimination of the totem would mean chaos, the end of the world, and hence the end of life on earth.

105. See Harvey Cox, *The Secular City,* chap. 11: "To Speak in a Secular Fashion of God," pp. 241–68.

106. Consider the familiar observation that the answer to the question, "Does God exist?" is another question: "What if so?" If the practical consequences in terms of the questioner's behavior would be no different, then the existence of God is unnecessary for that individual (a superfluous hypothesis). Then God does not exist for that person, whatever be the theoretical answer. If, on the contrary, the inquirer's behavior would change, then that individual still has a personal "need" for God, and, for this particular person, God exists.

107. See above, pp. 62ff.

108. For a comprehensive evaluation of the controversy, see Comstock, "Theology"; Ogletree, *Controversy.*

109. As we know, Thomas J. J. Altizer was concerned with the history of religions, and devoted a number of writings to the thematic of oriental spirituality, for example, apropos of *nirvāṇa,* the volume cited above; *Mircea Eliade.* Other works by the same author on the subject in question are: *Gospel of Christian Atheism;* "Creative Negation in Theology"; "A Theonomy, in Our Time?"; and the anthology edited by him, *Truth, Myth, and Symbol.*

110. See Hamilton, *New Essence;* "Death of God Theology"; *Christian Man: Modern Reader's Guide to Matthew and Luke; The Modern Reader's Guide to John;* Hamilton and Altizer, *Radical Theology;* van Buren, *Secular Meaning of the Gospel;* Vahanian, *Death of God;* and, in a different direction, Sölle, *Stellvertretung.*

111. See my *Ontonomía de la Ciencia,* pp. 101–8.

112. See Rombach, *Substanz,* as an example of work in this now common direction.

113. It is instructive to observe the success of the philosophy of Alfred North Whitehead and his school, together with its application to the study of comparative religion.

114. See below, pp. 111ff.

115. See the text cited on our p. 76.

116. The cause lies "in the deviation of human thought due to the category of substance," writes Baumgartner, "Tranzendentales Denken," p. 48.

117. See Gulyga, "Atheismusstreit."

118. See below, p. 145, as well as chap. 8, n. 112.

119. See below, pp. 119ff.

120. "And this is what all call God," says Thomas Aquinas, concluding his own proofs. He has proved (on his premises) the existence of the *hoc,* but the problem today consists precisely in the identification of this metacosmological *hoc* with the theological God.

121. See below, pp. 114ff.

122. See Küng, *Existiert Gott?*

123. Although the problem was a different one, the case of Galileo was often cited in the conflict between Hans Küng and the Roman church (1979–1980). As of 1983 it seems that John Paul II has recognized the error committed by the church.

124. See Eccl. 3:11 in the Vulgate.

125. Without any "Buddhist contamination," Lacroix ("Sens et valeur," with discussion) arrives at a practical conclusion: "Perhaps it would be possible to find here a practical application of the distinction between *representation* and *visualization:* testimony cannot be wanting, but there are times that [Christ's] presence ought to be manifested in the silence in word and deed, and more luminously than ever" (pp. 61–62).

126. Paul Tillich adopted, if in something of a different context, the old medieval and mystical conception of "God above God" and "God beyond God." See *Courage to Be,* p. 186.

9. ONTOLOGICAL APOPHATICISM

1. Cf. Neill, *Faith,* p. 114.

2. Cf. Murthy, *Metaphysics,* pp. 23–24.

3. See below, p. 231 and nn. 130, 131.

4. Matt. 13:52.

5. For the traditional Christian position, see, e.g., Journet, *Dark Knowledge.*

6. See Panikkar, "Il superamento dell'essere nell'induismo e nel buddhismo," a course in the philosophy of religion given in the Faculty of Letters of the University of Rome in the academic year 1965–66.

7. "Curiously, in ancient times as today, philosophical systems opposing or not acknowledging Being have emerged as reactions to the tradition of Being, and have normally been regarded as heterodox, as heresies—things strange and different. Then, with the passage of time, even centuries, they have been reabsorbed. For example, Buddhism has almost completely disappeared in India, partly reabsorbed by the Śaṅkara reforms; in Mahāyāna it has returned as a theism. Christianity, regarded for centuries as an 'atheistic' reform, by virtue of its opposition to the traditional gods, has been gradually 'theicized,' apace with its theologization. The current materialistic, Marxist phenomenon is still too new to suggest a future resolution in the form of its absorption, but even here we begin to sense a demand

for the 'essentialistic,' or at least a 'nostalgia' for Being" [U.M. Vesci, a translator of the Italian edition].

8. See above, p. 10, and the references indicated there.

9. It was Plotinus, significantly, who recognized the possibility of knowing *that* a thing exists without knowing *what* it is. (*Enneads,* V, 5, 6).

10. See Meister Eckhart's conception of humankind as an adverb *(biwort)* of the verb *(wort),* and not as *esse.* Rather than an *ad-esse,* the human being would be an *ad-verbum.* E.g.: "Saint John asserts. 'In the beginning was the word,' and means that humankind in the presence of the *Verbum* was its adverb" *(Deutsche Predigten,* 9 [critical edition, Stuttgart, Kohlhammer], 1:155).

11. Cf. the similar "orthodox," or even commonsense, attitude of Renaissance Europe with regard to Copernicus's formulas, or Bruno's or Galileo's. As long as the intuition remained in the form of a theoretical, mathematical formula, it was accepted. When it came to applying it to the real, observable universe, it was condemned.

12. "It was only in Christianity and the speculation it engendered that an encounter was finally produced, and a lasting convenant struck, between the Being of philosophy and the God of religion" (Etienne Gilson, in his brilliant and profound study, "L'Etre et Dieu," p. 194).

13. See, merely by way of indication, Jaeger, *Theologie,* as well as the two-volume work by E. Caird, *The Evolution of Theology.*

14. Cf. the exciting problem long since posed by Xenophanes (texts and discussion in Jaeger, *Theologie,* pp. 55ff.).

15. See, e.g., above n. 12.

16. Heidegger, who managed a new state of the question from the viewpoint of his own philosophy, says, with his usual energy: "One who experienced theology, whether that of the Christian faith or that of philosophy, as a product of tradition, today prefers to keep silence about God in the domain of thought. The onto-theological character of metaphysics has become problematic, and not owing to any atheism" *(Identität und Differenz,* p. 45).

17. See the article cited just above: Gilson, "L'Etre et Dieu," pp. 181–202, 398–416.

18. The question has been posed thematically in our days: "How does God get into philosophy? And not only into contemporary philosophy, but philosophy as such?" (Heidegger, *Identität und Differenz,* p. 46). For a good critical study of Heideggerian exegesis, see Schuwer, "Intorno ai presupposti della demitizzazione."

19. See above, pp. 81f.

20. See, e.g., Gen. 1:26–27, as one of so many instances in which the religions of humanity place great emphasis on the kinship and likeness between God and human beings. Human beings are formed, on the one hand, of earth, and on the other, of the blood of the gods. Every god is a "father" of mortals, etc. See the materials and examples in Kristensen, *Meaning of Religion,* pp. 239–53.

21. To be distinguished from the personalism of the third moment, of which I have yet to speak.

22. Zoomorphism as well, which bestows on the divinity an animal form instead of a human one (anthropomorphism), is basically an anthropomorphic way of expressing the extrahuman.

23. See Hyatt, "Was Yahweh Originally a Creator Deity?"; Cross, Jr., "Yahweh and the God of the Patriarchs."

24. See Panikkar, *Vedic Experience,* passim; as well as S. Levi, *La doctrine du sacrifice dans les Brahmanas,* pp. 24ff., passim.

25. Note that I am speaking not of personification, but of the originally personal character of the divinities of the religions. "There is no personification, but only a depersonification," W. F. Otto rightly observes (*Mythos und Welt,* p. 261).

26. *Brahman,* strictly speaking, is not God, any more than is Aristotle's Unmoved Mover.

27. See Matt. 19:17, Mark 10:18, Luke 18:19.

28. *Sāda devā arepasaḥ* (*Sama Veda,* 442).

29. See, in order to preclude a "polytheistic" misinterpretation, Panikkar, *Die vielen Götter und der eine Herr,* pp. 43–51.

30. Ecstasy rightly connotes the loss of the subject — the sole condition for being able to "see" God "as God is." But then we no longer have either a human being to "see" God, or a God to "be seen."

31. See the authority of von Wilamowitz-Mollendorff, in Kerény, "Theos e Mythos," p. 39. As such, it did not have a vocative case (ibid.).

32. See the argumentation in Kerény, ibid., in its original version: "The content of the Greek word *theos* is clear: *ecce deus.* The same expression with the article, *ho theos,* means, in a context of worship, *illud deum,* the one known by its effects. . . . The content of the word *theos* is 'divine event' " (Kerény, "Theos e Mythos," p. 342).

33. See John 1:14.

34. See Panikkar, *The Vedic Experience,* part 6.

35. For Plato, too, the idea of the Good is found "beyond being" *(epekeina tēs ousias), The Republic,* 509B.

36. Aristotle, *Metaphysics,* A 8 (1704 b 1).

37. See Gilson, "L'Etre et Dieu," pp. 189ff.

38. Exodus 3:14.

39. See Panikkar, *Vielen Götter,* pp. 67–68, propounding four biblical meanings of the phrase: supratemporality, exclusivity, presence, and personality. (But nowhere is the God of Moses "Being.")

40. See Gilson, "L'Etre et Dieu."

41. For the exegesis of the exodus passage, sèe, among other studies, Dubarle, "La signification du nom de Yahweh"; Lambert, "Que signifie le nom divin YHWH?"

42. See the effort of Claude Tresmontant, *La métaphysique du christianisme et la naissance de la philosophie chrétienne.*

43. Consider the meeting of Christian theology and Marxist philosophy at Herrenschiemsee in 1966 (sequel to the Salzburg conference in 1965) organized by the Paulusgesellschaft. See especially Karl Rahner's contribution, "Christlicher Humanismus," later published in *Orientierung* (May 1966). See the complete acts published by Kellner, *Christentum und Marxismus heute.* (Here Rahner's contribution is entitled, "Christentum als Religion der absoluten Zukunft", pp. 208–13.)

44. See a very suggestive text: "T. Boman has shown . . . that *hajā* in Hebrew means 'to accomplish' rather than 'to be.' Yahweh says, then: I act as the one who acts, that is, according to 'salvation history.' I am the accomplishment of salvation history" (Cullman, *Heil als Geschichte,* p. 214).

45. Ibid., p. x.

46. See the works in Japanese of the director of the Japanese review, *Japanese Religions,* of Kyoto, Tetsutaro Ariga, who speaks of a *hayatheological* thinking, as

distinguished from an *ontological* manner of thought. The former would be the property of the Hebrew mentality, the latter of the Greek. See Abe, "Buddhism and Christianity."

47. See von Allmen, *Vocabulary,* "God," p. 144. Allmen cites 2 Kings 8:1, 1 Sam. 23:13, Exod. 33:19, and Ezek. 32:35 in support of this interpretation, which he accepts as true in part.

48. See n. 23, p. 109.

49. See the same principle at work in Brahmanic ritualism, which seeks to place God in the position of not harming others because of the possibility of self-harm (U. M. Vesci, "The Role of Heat," p. 417, where the problem is touched on; see Vesci's book, *Heat and Sacrifice,* offering further details).

50. The process is fraught with conflict. Consider the paradigmatic lot of Socrates, Galileo, Michael Servetus, Teilhard de Chardin, and others. Ultimately, however, religion accepts, indeed actually appeals to, the testimony of such individuals, who have made an effort to harmonize faith with reason.

51. See *Kena Upanishad,* III, 1ff. Here the process of harmonizing faith and intellect has perhaps not followed the same route of conflict as mentioned in the preceding note.

52. Cf. a modern attempt to preserve the scholastic identification of God with absolute Being through the utilization of the Heideggerian problematic (but not the Heideggerian solution): Johannes B. Lotz, s.v. *Gott,* in Fries, *Handbuch theologischer Grundbegriffe,* 1:573-79. Lotz devoted the best of his thought to an effort to reconcile the traditional scholastic idea of God and Being with the Heideggerian conception of Being. He is scarcely disposed, then, to renounce an identification of God and absolute Being, a renunciation regarded by Heidegger as essential. See Lotz, "Metaphysische und religiöse Erfahrung," in *Metafisica ed esperienza religiosa;* "Mythos, Logos, Mysterion," in Castelli, *Demitizzazione;* Lotz, "Geschichtlichkeit und Tradition," in *Hermeneutica e Tradizione.*

53. See one assertion among very many: "Hence the operation of the Creator extends to the innermost being of things more than does the operation of second causes" (Thomas Aquinas, *In Libro II Sententiarum,* d. 1, q. 1, a. 1, sol).

54. See, e.g., Radhakrishnan, *Indian Philosophy,* and *Philosophy of the Upanishads.*

55. Cf. the Old Testament God as described in the Psalms.

56. A Sufi legend recounts that Allah once addressed himself to a Sufi who was spending his life in a hermitage in the desert, heaped with honors and veneration by the local populace, who would supply him with food in return for his counsel. "Were I to tell the people what a great sinner thou art, no one would wish to have anything to do with thee any longer." "Yea, Lord," replied the Sufi, and added: "But were I to tell them how merciful thou art, neither would anyone wish to have anything more to do with thee." And so it was agreed that neither would betray their common secret.

57. Cf. a whole series of cosmogonic myths, of the kind, for example, called "of cosmogonic immersion" by Mircea Eliade ("Structure et fonction du mythe cosmogonique") in which God *does not know* that the one God sends to the depths of the waters to collect a bit of earth with which to build the world is precisely the devil. Thus God is not responsible for evil in the world, not even by virtue of "ignorance" and levity in making use of an insufficiently trustworthy agent. Even the "myth of original sin" claims to deliver God from responsibility for evil and suffering in the world, without thereby accusing God of mental cruelty, or of having

placed too much trust in humankind. See also Bianchi, *II dualismo religioso.*

58. Let us not forget that the destruction of the temple was an act of Yahweh's power, comporting no imputation of either weakness or evil.

59. The impact of the difficulty is felt from the very inception of Christianity. For example: "If God is good, knows the future, and can forestall evil, why did God permit humankind to fall? If this happens . . . God should not be believed to be good, or foreknowing, or powerful" (Tertullian, *Adversus Marcionem,* book 2, chap. 5 [PL, 2:288]). "Either God knew that humankind, placed in Paradise, would fall . . . or else God did not know. If God knew, the guilty one is not he who could not escape the divine foreknowledge, but the one who nevertheless [placed humankind in Paradise]. If God did not know, then the one whose prescience you deny, you deprive of divinity as well" (Jerome, *Adversus Pelagianos,* 2, 6 [PL, 33:575]).

60. The Christian answer is highly significant, especially in Greek patristics, but also in Latin patristics and even in scholasticism. All is justified by the grandeur of Christ, whose positivity submerges and overwhelms any possible guilt and suffering. See the texts in Galtier, *Les deux Adam,* pp. 74–94. Consider also the celebrated *felix culpa* of the liturgy. However, one difficulty remains: Why must the regal magnificence of Christ pass by way of suffering, misery, and sin? In the historical order, a more or less plausible answer can sometimes be given in terms of respect for human freedom. But this is not possible in an ontological order that identifies God with Being. Furthermore, even the redemptive act of Christ has left the evil of existence totally unchanged!

61. Cf. Śankara, *Brahmanùtrabhànya,* I, 1, 2, and my commentary in *Māyā e Apocalisse,* chap. 12.

62. "To this God can humanity neither pray nor sacrifice. Before the *Causa sui,* humanity can neither fall on its knees in fear and trembling, nor before this God make music and dance" (Heidegger, *Identität und Differenz,* p. 64).

63. In Sanskrit and Latin the incompatibility is more evident: it takes on grammatical expression. *Sat* and *esse* have no plural; to construct a plural, one must use another form (and in Sanskrit, the actual root): in Latin, *entes* (from *ens*); in Sanskrit, *bhūvan* (from *bhu,* to become).

64. To cite one example among many, Marx himself saw this. If God is Being, then there is no room for humankind. If we set up the dilemma in this fashion, it can be resolved only by sacrificing the weaker horn—which, evidently, is not humankind, but Being, and with Being, God. See Crespi, "Crisi del sacro," p. 76.

65. Cf. the whole problematic of a Hamman or a Jacobi, who declare themselves atheists as far as their reason is concerned, but believers in their feelings. See Panikkar, "Jacobi y la filosofía del sentimiento." From another viewpoint, consider the modern intuition: "It is a genuine contradiction. God exists. God does not exist. Where is the problem? I am altogether sure that there is God, in the sense that I am altogether sure that my love is not illusory. I am altogether sure that there is no God, in the sense that I am altogether sure that nothing real resembles what I can conceive when I pronounce this name. But what I cannot conceive is not an illusion" (Weil, *Pesanteur,* p. 132).

66. I am not using the expression here in the "primitive" and "naturalistic" sense of a certain interpretation pertinent to the history of religions.

67. See *Śvetasvatara Upanishad,* II, 7ff.

68. See Panikkar, *The Trinity and the Religious Experience of Man.*

69. The expression is from Martin Heidegger. See a good summary, introducing

a new distinction based on a personal communication from the author, in Müller, *Existenzphilosophie im geistigen Leben der Gegenwart*, p. 73: "(1) the *transcendental* difference, or ontological in the more narrow sense: the difference between the 'being' and its 'beingness.' (2) The difference *according to transcendence,* or ontological difference in the broad sense: the difference between the being with its 'beingness' and being itself. (3) The *transcendent* difference, or theological difference in the strict sense: the difference between God and the being, beingness, and being."

70. For a defense of the Heideggerian position that nevertheless preserves the Christian doctrine of God, see, in addition to the work by Müller just cited, Ott, *Denken und Sein,* pp. 129–57.

71. "Aristotle calls the science he is distinguishing, the science that considers being as such, 'first philosophy.' But it considers not only being in its 'beingness,' but also the being that purely corresponds to 'beingness'—the supreme Being. This Being, *to theion,* the Divine, is also called 'Being' [infinitive], by a strange ambivalence. First philosophy, as ontology, is at the same time theology of the True Being. It would be more accurate to call it theology. The science of Being as such is in itself onto-theological" (Heidegger, *Holzwege,* p. 179).

72. Paul Tillich follows the Heideggerian conception of Being as much as possible, veering away when Heidegger separates God from Being, from the Absolute. Consider, by way of indication and example: "The being of God is being-itself. The being of God cannot be understood as the existence of a being alongside others. If God is *a* being, [God] is subject to the categories of finitude" (*Systematic Theology,* 1:235). "Since God is the ground of being, [God] is the ground of the structure of being. [God] is not subject to this structure: the structure is grounded in [God]. [God] *is* the structure" (*Systematic Theology,* 1:238). "God is being-itself or the absolute" (ibid., 1:239). Tillich knew the objections of the personalists, and sought to respond to them with a book on the subject, *Biblical Religion and the Search for Ultimate Reality,* as well as with the second volume of his *Systematic Theology:* "No theology can suppress the notion of being as the power of being. One cannot separate them. In the moment in which one says that God *is* or that [God] has being, the question arises as to how [God's] relation to being is understood. The only possible answer seems to be that God is being-itself, in the sense of the power of being or the power to conquer non-being" (ibid., 2:11). As Heinrich Ott rightly observes: "Tillich was able to conceive and realize this project only because he treats the 'categories of being' as concepts of being in a metaphysico-ahistorical manner. In this sense the concept of being is considered here in a metaphysico-ahistorical manner. Tillich's construction of a doctrine of God as 'Being Itself' would be incapable of realization, indeed of projection, from the conception of Being as destiny, a conception that recognizes the 'categories' formed by destiny in every era" (Ott, *Denken und Sein,* pp. 151–52).

73. See Ebert, "Der Gott der Philosophen," for a good presentation of the problematic.

74. Protestant theology has always had less of a propensity than its Catholic counterpart to identify the God of metaphysics with the God of faith. See, e.g., Pannenberg, "Die Aufnahme des philosophischen Gottesbegriffs," p. 2.

75. For a presentation of the traditional Catholic effort, see de More-Pontigibaud, *Du fini à l'infini.*

76. See Panikkar, "Ṛtatattva," where I present an advaita-trinitarian view that

may offer a way out of the impasse. The *puruṣa* "is" the *I* (the Father) at the origin of the human *Thou* (the Son) at the heart of the World (Matter) in virtue of the power *(śakti, dynamis)* of the Spirit.

77. See above, p. 98, n. 111.

78. The philosophy of Alfred North Whitehead, with the whole current of "process philosophy," would be a suitable example. See the articles on "Mahāyana Buddhism and Whitehead," *Philosophy East and West,* 25:393–488.

79. "This thinking, which has taken no account of being, is the simple, all-vehiculating event, and therefore the enigmatic and unexperienced event, of Western history. . . . What is going on with Being? Nothing is going on with Being at all. Might not this be the essence of nihilism, hitherto so covered over and concealed?" (Heidegger, "Nietsches Wort, 'Gott ist tot,' " in *Holzwege,* p. 239).

80. See J. Habermas's inaugural lecture at the University of Frankfurt in 1965: "To dissociate values from facts means counterposing an abstract Ought to pure Being. Values are the nominalistic by-products of a centuries-long critique of the emphatic concept of Being to which theory was once exclusively oriented" (Habermas, *Knowledge and Human Interests,* pp. 303–4).

81. "The last blow against God and the suprasensible world consists in the reduction of God, the Being of being, to the supreme value" (Heidegger, *Holzwege,* pp. 239–40).

82. "Value and the valuable becomes a positivistic replacement for the metaphysical" (ibid., p. 120).

83. "The place that, metaphysically thinking, belongs to God, is the place of a causal action, and of the maintenance of being as 'created.' This place of God can remain empty" (ibid., p. 235).

84. Besides Max Scheler, and, in a certain sense Nicolai Hartmann, likewise the names of René Le Senne, Aloys Müller, and Fritz von Rintelen would deserve to be mentioned in this connection.

85. It cannot be denied that the alliance between the supreme Being and beings has obfuscated the very concept of Being, and that the celebrated Heideggerian *Seinsvergessenheit* touches a sore point both for Western speculation and for dialogue with other cultures: " 'Being' in Heidegger is no longer the highest concept had or produced by thought [Heidegger's reproach of Western tradition], but the condition of the possibility that there be thought at all. Being as such is an event of revelation, a destiny that imposes itself on thought" (Ott, *Denken und Sein,* p. 14). "The history of being begins, and necessarily, with the forgetfulness of 'being' " (Heidegger, *Holzwege,* p. 234). "Presupposing that all that is has to do with being, then the essence of nihilism consists in this, that Being itself has to do with nothing" (ibid., p. 245).

86. An adequate response to the question, why God willed, at least permitted, the "passion" of his own Son, and the entire redemption event, if God could have accomplished it without suffering and without the commission of sin on the part of the executioners, is possible only if we identify the divine justice with the intrinsic, immutable law of Being, which, by dint of a metaphysics of evil and by application of the principle of noncontradiction, has no choice but to accept that that "evil" be ontically opposed, and so on. God cannot do what God wishes. God is bound to the laws of Being. God's "justice," for example, demands something that, were God a person, would be counter to God's "love" and will, and so on.

87. "Being is not a product of thought. Rather, essential thought is an event of Being" (Heidegger, *Was ist Metaphysik?* p. 43).

88. "Accordingly, thought without God, thought that must give up the God of philosophy, God as *Causa sui,* is perhaps closer to the divine God" (Heidegger, *Identität und Differenz,* p. 71).

89. See Matt. 11:25; Luke 10:21; etc.

90. In 1802, in his *Glauben und Wissen.*

91. In 1882, in his *The Gay Science.* Consider the following passage, which I transcribe in extenso on account of its incomparable strength and beauty:

> *The Madman.* Have you not heard of that madman who lit a lantern in the bright morning hours, ran to the market place, and cried incessantly, "I seek God! I seek God!" As many of those who do not believe in God were standing around just then, he provoked much laughter. Why, did he get lost? said one. Did he lose his way like a child? said another. Or is he hiding? Is he afraid of us? Has he gone on a voyage? or emigrated? Thus they yelled and laughed. The madman jumped into their midst and pierced them with his glances.
>
> "Whither is God?" he cried. "I shall tell you. *We have killed him* — you and I. All of us are his murderers. But how have we done this? How were we able to drink up the sea? Who gave us the sponge to wipe away the entire horizon? What did we do when we unchained this earth from its sun? Whither is it moving now? Whither are we moving now? Away from all suns? Are we not plunging continually? Backward, sideward, forward, in all directions? Is there any up or down left? Are we not straying as through an infinite nothing? Do we not feel the breath of empty space? Has it not become colder? Is not night and more night coming on us all the while? Must not lanterns be lit in the morning? Do we not hear anything yet of the noise of the grave-diggers who are burying God? Do we not smell anything yet of God's decomposition? Gods too decompose. God is dead. God remains dead. And we have killed him. How shall we, the murderers of all murderers, comfort ourselves? What was holiest and most powerful of all that the world has yet owned has bled to death under our knives. Who will wipe this blood off us? What water is there for us to clean ourselves? What festivals of atonement, what sacred games shall we have to invent? Is not the greatness of this deed too great for us? Must not we ourselves become gods simply to seem worthy of it? There has never been a greater deed; and whoever will be born after us — for the sake of this deed he will be part of a higher history than all history hitherto."
>
> Here the madman fell silent and looked again at his listeners; and they too were silent and stared at him in astonishment. At last he threw his lantern on the ground, and it broke and went out. "I come too early," he said then; "my time has not come yet. This tremendous event is still on its way, still wandering — it has not yet reached the ears of man. Lightning and thunder require time, the light of the stars requires time, deeds require time even after they are done, before they can be seen and heard. This deed is still more distant from them than the most distant stars — *and yet they have done it themselves.*"
>
> It has been related further that on that same day the madman entered divers churches and there sang his *requiem aeternam Deo.* Led out and called to account, he is said to have replied each time, "What are these churches now if they are not the tombs and sepulchers of God?" [Walter Kaufmann, ed., *Existentialism from Dostoevsky to Sartre* (Cleveland and New York: World, 1956), pp. 105–6].

92. See Heidegger's study, "Nietzsches Wort 'Gott ist tot,' " in *Holzwege,* pp. 193–247.

93. "The phrase 'God is dead' means that the suprasensible world is without effective power. It bestows no life" (ibid., p. 200; see also p. 234).

94. See Heidegger's pertinent distinction: "To 'will nothing' does not at all mean to will the simple absence of all reality; it means rather to will reality, but to will it, in each instance and everywhere, as a nothing, and through this to will annihilation" (ibid., pp. 217–18). Consider Heidegger's own citation (ibid.) from Nietzsche: "Rather than not willing, it [the will] wills nothing" (Nietzsche, *Zur Geneologie der Moral,* 3. Abhandlung, A.1a [1887], Sämtliche Werke [Munich: Hauser, 1966], 7th ed., 1973, 2:839). It is not well known that Nietzsche had written, "I could be the Buddha of Europe; though admittedly an antipode to the Indian Buddha" (Montinais ed., VII, 1); see F. Mistry, *Nietzsche and Buddhism: Prolegomenon to a Comparative Study* (Berlin and New York: W. de Gruyter, 1981).

95. "It is never God who dies, but the representation made of God by a given religion when it permits the consciousness it has of itself to replace the sacred, which makes up its real substance" (Gilson, *L'Etre et Dieu,"* p. 408).

96. See, e.g., W. Strolz's work, *Menschsein als Gottesfrage: Wege zur Erfahrung der Inkarnation,* where, as the subtitle suggests ("Paths to the Experience of the Incarnation"), the question is polarized in anthropology, and anthropology is concentrated on the figure of Christ, the Man-God.

97. "If we reject everything modern atheism has to offer, to what extent do Catholics not part ways with reality, and save only an idea of God devoid of content and truth? On the other hand, if we embrace the values of atheism, to what extent do we perhaps compromise the purity of our own faith, with all its exigencies? No theoretical solution, no solution divorced from experience, can be offered in advance for a question this dramatic" (Lacroix, "Sens et valeurs de l'athéisme actuel," p. 61).

98. See, by way of example, del Noce, *Il problema dell'ateismo.*

99. See, e.g., C. Fabro, *Introduzione all'ateismo moderno,* where Descartes is "virtually an atheist" (p. 26), Kant "intrinsically and consciously an atheist" (p. 487), Hegel's system "a theism on the surface and an atheism in depth" (p. 154), and, naturally, in one way or another, Locke, Malebranche, Leibniz, Schelling, and others, as well. The argumentations prove, but perhaps a bit too well, in view of the fact that they can equally well be lodged against Saint Thomas and all of scholasticism. Where, indeed, does atheism not lie concealed? Were there no atheism at all, God would be a simple deus ex machina, a mere postulate of our mind. See, further, by the same author, *L'ateismo moderno.*

100. See Crespi, "Crisi del sacro, irreligione, ateismo."

101. See Metz, "L'incredulità come problema teologico," an analysis of the unbelief implicit in the believer's very act of faith.

102. See Rahner, in his introduction to vol. 23 of *Concilium (The Pastoral Approach to Atheism* [New York: Paulist, 1967]), p. 2; Dalmau, *Condemnats a creure.*

103. See an Indian example in *Ṛg Veda,* X, 121, 1ff.

104. See a *locus classicus,* again from India, ibid., I, 164, 46 (as well as X, 114, 5).

105. Gen. 15:1ff.

106. Gen. 32:25ff.

107. Exod. 32:11ff.; Num. 9:11; etc.

108. See the citations of Simone Weil on pp. 205, n. 74, and 206, n. 86.

109. See, by way of a meaningful example, the expression of the First Vatican Council: "In and of [the divine essence] most blessed, and ineffably exalted above all that exists outside [God] or can be conceived" (Denzinger-Schönmetzer, no. 1782).

110. See my contribution to the UNESCO Paris workshop in 1962, in "L'Athéisme, tentation du monde, révell des chrétiens," pp. 52ff.

111. "God is near us in his absence, just as he is luminous to us in his darkness," says the famous *Mirror of Simple Souls.*" "In the measure that their knowledge is renewed in bright darkness, in the presence of absence" (*Mengeldichten*, 17, Hadewijch of Antwerp, p. 133).

112. "Thus God does not know what God is, inasmuch as God is not 'something'; God is incomprehensible, then, in any regard whatsoever, to himself and to any intellect" (John Scotus Eriugena, *De Divisione Naturae*, II, 28 [PL, 122:589]), repeating the same doctrine almost immediately (2, 30) by calling God "pure nothing."

113. For the series of texts at the basis of both this statement and those that follow, see Panikkar, "Die existentielle Phänomenologie der Wahrheit," pp. 40ff., or the corresponding chapter in *Maya e Apocalisse*, pp. 241–89. See also Nicolas, *Dieu comme inconnu.*

114. "God cannot be comprehended by the mind, inasmuch as whatever can be comprehended of God is surely not God" (Evagrius, *De Octo Vitiosis Cogitationibus* [PG, 40:1275c]). See also Maximus the Confessor, *In Epist. Dionys.*, 1 (PG, 4:529a).

115. Consider the attitude of Meister Eckhart in many of his works, e.g., *Sermo XI*, 2 (§120).

116. See, e.g., in the area of Indian spirituality, *Rg Veda*, X, 129; *Śvetāśvatara Upanishad*, IV, 18; *Bhagavadgītā*, IX, 19; XIII, 12; *Arthava Veda*, IV, 1; (Brahman arising from being and nonbeing).

117. See *Kena Upanishad*, II, 2–3.

118. Evagrius Ponticus, *III Centuria*, 88. See Hausherr, "Ignorance infinie."

119. For the modern problematic, see two studies of rather different orientations. Hartshorne, *Anselm's Discovery*, and Warnach, "Zum Argument im Proslogion Anselms." For a useful anthology, from Anselm to the present, see Hick and McGill, *The Many-Faced Argument* (New York: Macmillan, 1967).

120. This does not mean that God exists, but only that the discussion between theists and atheists is meaningful.

121. We could summarize the three positions in three maxims: *Deus est: id quo maius cogitari nequit; id quod est maius quam id quod cogitari possit; id quod cogitari nequit* (God is: that than which nothing greater can be thought; that which is greater than what can be thought; that which cannot be thought).

122. "L'Etre est Amour," le Saux, *Sagesse hindoue*, p. 189; idem, *La rencontre de l'hindouisme et du christianisme*, p. 159.

123. "If I have not love, I am not" (1 Cor. 13: 2 — *agapēn de mē echō, outhen eimi):* without love I am not, I do not exist.

124. Exod. 3:14, according to the traditional interpretation.

125. See Panikkar, "Advaita e bhakti," for a development of the theme to which I merely allude here.

126. See Chuang Tzu (as translated by Thomas Merton, *The Way of Chuang Tzu* [New York: New Directions, 1965], p. 125):

This is the furthest yet! Who can reach it?
I can comprehend the absence of Nothing?
If now, on top of all this, Non-being Is,
Who can comprehend it?

127. "He is not here. He is risen" (*ouk estin, hōde, ēgērthē*—Matt. 28:6).

128. Cf.: All the things of the universe arrive at being from an origin in being; but being arrives at being from an origin in nonbeing"; or, as some translate, "nothing is the origin of all beings" (*Tao-te-ching* [Lao-Tzu], 40).

129. Cf. Mark 8:35, with abundant parallel passages.

130. See Panikkar, "Das erste Bild des Buddha," *Antaios,* 6 (1964), for examples to flesh out what I am saying here by way of mere summary.

131. Luke 7:47.

132. See 2 Cor. 5:21, and chap. 5, n. 34, above.

133. Creation is not self-sustaining, says Gregory the Great (*Moralia,* XVI, 37, 45): "For all of these things are, but principally they are not, for they by no means subsist in themselves, and if the hand of the one governing does not sustain them, in no wise can they be. For they all subsist in the one who has created them. Nor do living things move under their own power; rather the one who now bestows life, now does not, moves them all toward the extreme essence, and wondrously preserves them in their order." Or again: "All things would fall into nothingness, did not the hand of the almighty hold them" (PL, 75:1143). The property of creatures is nothingness, Thomas Aquinas repeats *(De Aeternitate Mundi):* "For that which pertains to a creature in se is within it prior to that which it has only from another. But a creature has *esse* only from another; left to itself, considered in itself, it is nothing: hence *nihil* is in it naturally before *esse.*" See idem, *De Potentia,* q. 5, a. 1, c.; *De Veritate,* q. 8, a. 16, ad 12. "The creature is darkness inasmuch as it is from nothing"; see also *De Veritate,* q. 18, a. 2, ad 5. See also the conciliar text: "[Deus] condidit creaturas: bonas quidem, quia a summo bono factae sunt, sed mutabiles, quia de nihilo factae "[God] has made creatures: good, surely, because they have been created by the supreme good, but unstable, because they have been made from nothing" (Concilium of Florence, *Decretum pro Iacobitis* [Denziger-Schönmetzer, no. 706]). This text is taken almost verbatim from Saint Augustine, *De Natura Boni,* 10 (PL, 554–55). See other texts, and a development of the subject from a strictly metaphysical standpoint, in the sections devoted to creatureliness and contingency in my book, *El concepto de naturaleza,* pp. 102–13, as well as in my *Myth, Faith and Hermeneutics,* chap. 3, and *Māyā e Apocalisse,* part 1, chap. 3.

134. This perspective allows for a more correct interpretation of numerous texts of the Christian scriptures seemingly so ridden with pessimism, but in actuality only seeking to lay out an ontological situation: the fact that positivity and truth reside only on the farther shore. In this view even the immolation of the Lamb, Christ, acquires a new meaning.

135. Whether Kierkegaard discerned something of this when he wrote in *Either/ Or* that "love for God has an absolute particularity, and its expression is repentance" (Sören Kierkegaard, *Aut/Aut* [Milan: Mondadori, 1960], p. 97), I shall not venture to say.

136. See John 1:29.

137. See *Śatapatha Brāmana,* I, 7, 2, 1ff.

138. See Luke 18:9-14, the only gospel to report the parable.

139. This would be the traditional Christian definition of sin ("a turning away from God and a turning toward creatures").

140. Cf. the liturgical *oratio* from the Common of a bishop and martyr in the Latin Rite of the Catholic Church: "Look graciously upon our infirmity, Almighty God; and, because the burden of our own actions weighs upon us heavily. . . ."

141. Cf. the famous *Dreifaltigkeitslied: Snick all mein ich in Gottes niht.* "I plunge my 'whole I' into the nothingness of God" (J. B. Porion, *Hadewijch d'Anvers,* [Paris, 1954] p. 137).

142. "Being is in nothing,
    and in being is no being.
    Then let fire surge within my soul
    and consume its being there!"
Djalaluddin Balki (Rumi), *Kolliyāt-é Sams-é Tabūzī* (Teheran: M. Darwish, 1962), 1:32; no. 67 in S. de Beaurecueil, *Le pain et le sel* (Paris: Cerf, 1965), p. 98.

143. See, as a single example, that precious jewel with splendors of the declining scholastic and the dawning Renaissance age, Nicholas of Cusa, *De Deo Abscondito,* no. 14, *Opera omnia* (P. Wilbert, ed., Hamburg, 1959), 4:3–10.

144. See a typical, representative text: Meister Eckhart's commentary on Acts 9:8, in which Saul, arising after his fall from the horse and the apparition on the road to Damascus, when he opens his eyes, *nihil videbat,* saw nothing: "It seems to me that this statement has a fourfold meaning. The first meaning is this: when he arose from the earth, he saw nothing with his eyes wide open, and this Nothing was God: for when he saw God, he called him a nothing. The second meaning: when he rose he saw *nothing but* God. The third: in all things he saw nothing but God. The fourth: when he saw God, he saw all things as a nothing" (Predigt 3 [J. Quint, ed., *Meister Eckhart, Deutsche Predigten und Traktate*] p. 329). See the same idea in Predigt 53 (ibid., pp. 400ff.).

145. Cf. the concept of *śūnya,* discussed in part 1 of the present volume.

146. "The wise, reflecting in the depths of their own hearts, seek the original connection *(bandhu)* between being and nonbeing *(asat)"* (Ṛg Veda, X, 129, 4).

147. We know the importance of the category of relationship in Christian scholasticism, owing to the trinitarian and christological problems confronting that philosophical current. Equally familiar is the awkwardness of the scholastic effort to fit all that the Christian faith sought to express into the Aristotelian framework. For a modern discussion of the problem of relationship in Saint Thomas, see Krempel, *La doctrine de la rélation.*

148. "No relation is a substance *secundum rem* [in concrete reality] in creatures" (Thomas Aquinas, *In 1 Sententiarum,* d. 4, q. 1, a. 1, ad 3). "But substance can itself be relative: witness the trinitarian doctrine of subsistent relations." See *Summa Theol.,* I, q. 28, a. 2.

149. Consider the etymology of the romance words for "thing": *cosa, chose.* They derive from *causa,* with its reference to utterance.

150. See studies on Hume and Buddhism.

151. This is precisely the Buddhist criticism of creationist systems. See von Glasenapp, *Buddhismus und Gottesidee,* p. 426, listing the corresponding passages. Even traditional Christianity felt this difficulty: see, e.g., Saint Augustine, *De Genesi ad Litteram,* V, 7 (PL, 34:328); VI, 6 and 10 (PL, 342–43, 346); and passim. Again: "God created heaven and earth and all within them at the same time, in their own state and plenitude, in perfect appearance and form and in the selection of

accidents, but they did not all appear together. Think of the farmer sowing different kinds of seed in the ground at the same time. One part [appears] after one day, another part after two days, yet another after three days, but all the seeds have been sown at the same moment" (Eckhart, *Expositio in Genesim [Lateinische Werke,* I, 54, no. 18]). "God speaks once, and does not repeat it" (Job 33:14), and other scriptural texts (as Ps. 61:12), which occasioned the traditional mystical interpretation. Or again: "God speaks once [Job 33:14]. God speaks in generating the Son, since the Son is the Word. God speaks again in creating creation. 'God spoke and they were made, God commanded and they were created' [Ps. 148:5]" (Eckhart, *Expositio in Genesim [Lateinische Werke,* I, 51, no. 7). Further he adds: "And this again is why another psalm asserts: 'God spoke once, I heard these two things.' Two, that is, heaven and earth, or rather these two: the emanation of persons and the creation of the world, which, however, he uttered once" (see below, n. 158).

152. See above, p. 53.

153. See above, p. 130.

154. *So bin ich ewig; denn ich bin* ("Thus I am eternal; for I am"), says Goethe in *Prometheus,* expressing the same intuition. In parallel fashion, the Buddha will say: " 'I am' not, for I am not eternal." If he were at all, he would be eternal. Whoever could live, for one moment, the "I am," would be outside time and outside contingency.

155. *Quid enim tam tuum quam tu?*
　　et quid tam non tuum quam tu,
　　si alicuius est, quod es?

("For what is so much 'yours' as you?/ and what is so much 'not yours' as you,/ if what you are belongs to someone else?" [*Tract. 29, in Ioann.,* Roman Breviary, feria III, dom. IV, Quadrag.]). See Panikkar, "The Threefold Linguistic Intersubjectivity," *Archivio di Filosofia,* 54 (1986) 593–606.

156. See *Bhagavadgītā,* IX, 9, 4–5, and, naturally, *tat tvam asi (Chāndogya Upanishad,* VI, 8, 7).

157. See the Upanishadic *ahambrahmāsmi (Bṛhadāraṇyaka Upanishad,* I, 4, 10), and the expression of the *Chāndogya Upanishad,* III, 14, 3: "This is my *ātman* within my heart, smaller than a grain of rice, or barley, or mustard, or millet, or the heart of the millet seed; this is my *ātman* within my heart, greater than the earth, greater than the atmosphere, than the sky and than these worlds." See also the traditional Christian affirmations: "More interior to me than my inmost recesses, and higher than what is highest in me" (Augustine, *Confessions,* III, 6); "God is within everything, for all things are in him; he is outside everything, since he is above all things" (idem, *De spiritu et anima,* chap. 14 [PL, 40:791]); "God is the proper and immediate cause of everything, and in some way more interior to it than it is to itself, as Augustine says" (Aquinas, *De Veritate,* q. 18, a. 16, ad 12; see also idem, *De Anima,* a. 12, ad 1).

158. See, by way of introduction to the argument, Nakamura, *The Ways of Thinking of Eastern Peoples.*

159. See, as a simple introduction to the topic, Kretschmar, *Studien zur frühchristlichen Trinitätstheologie.*

160. "Because with one action, he generates the Son who is heir, light of light, and creates the creature who is darkness, created, made, not the Son" (Eckhart, *Expositio in Ioannem (Lateinische Werke,* 3, 61, no. 73). See further the texts cited in n. 151, p. 219.

161. "As the Father is rightly said to know and utter himself and creatures with

the Word, so the Father and the Son [are rightly said to] love one another and creatures in the Holy Spirit" (Parente, *De Deo Uno et Trino*, p. 293). See also: "For God, knowing himself, knows every creature. Therefore the *verbum* conceived in the mind is representative of everything that is *actu* understood. . . . But because God knows himself and all things in one act, his one *Verbum* is expressive not only of the Father, but also of creatures" (Aquinas, *Summa Theol.*, I, q. 34, a. 3). See also ibid., q. 37, a. 2. Obviously neither Thomas's position, nor the one I maintain in the present work can be confused with any kind of pantheism. See further the liturgical expression: "Before me God was not formed, and after me God will not be" — Magnificat Antiphon, dom. III, Advent.

162. See, as an isolated reference, Kaliba, *Die Welt als Gleichnis des dreieinigen Gottes*.

163. I have had recourse to Christian terminology, but I could have used another language. The Trinity is not an exclusively Christian intuition.

164. "Forgetting what is behind, striving for what is ahead" (Phil. 3:13).

165. Cf. Heb. 11:27.

166. According to Evagrius (whose mysticism, holds Hans Urs von Balthasar, "Metaphysik und Mystik des Evagrius Ponticus," is more akin to Buddhism than to Christianity), God grants the beatific vision by denying it. See Gregory of Nyssa, *De Vita Moysis*, as I explain below.

167. See above, n. 164. See the synthesis by Jean Daniélou, *Platonisme et théologie mystique*, pp. 315–26. There is a second edition (1954), to which we owe the introduction of this concept into the scholarship of today.

168. Indeed, Gregory of Nyssa uses the word in a mystical sense only once.

169. Composed of *epi-*, which implies possession, and the divine immanence, *ek-*, which suggests emergence from oneself, and transcendence, and the root *-sta-*, which means precisely "to be here" — just to have a perfect *coincidentia oppositorum*.

170. See Hans Urs von Balthasar, *Présence et Pensée;* Völker, *Gregor von Nyssa als Mystiker*.

171. The simple mention of the word, without any exploration of the possibilities of the concept in comparative spirituality, is found in a work that I have cited, le Saux, *Sagesse hindoue*, pp. 239, 245.

172. None of the more commonly used theological or biblical dictionaries, as far as I have determined, list this word.

173. See the evidence for this in Völker, *Gregor*, pp. 202ff.

174. See a passage from *De Vita Moysis:* "O Moses, who have such desire to rush to the fore [*epekteinomenos tois hemprosthen*, an evident reference to Phil. 3:13], whose course has never known weariness, you should know that I [God, the speaker] have a space so great that you could never cross it. But in another way, this route is stability *(stasis)*. Indeed, I shall establish you on the rock. This is the most paradoxical thing *(paradoxotatou)* — that stability *(stasis)* and movement *(kinēsis)* would be the same thing. After all, ordinarily one advancing does not stand still, and one standing still does not advance. And yet the one who advances, by that very fact stands still" (PG, 44:405).

175. See Daniélou, *Platonisme*, p. 234.

176. This would be the minimalistic interpretation of certain patristic manuals. It seems to me, however, that many of the fathers were much more "Buddhistic" than is commonly imagined.

177. *De Vita Moysis* (PG, 44:376).

178. "The divine nature, then, is endless, and what is endless cannot be comprehended" (ibid., [PG, 44:401]).

179. Ibid. (PG, 44:376). The Migne Latin translation reads: *Quid oporteat de Deo cognoscere, quod quidem cognoscere nihil aliud est, quam nihil eorum esse Deum cognoscere, quae human mens potest cognoscere.* The Greek word is always *gignōskein.*

180. See ibid. (PG, 44:404).

181. See Daniélou, *Platonisme,* p. 318.

182. See the profound reflections in Hans Urs von Balthasar's commentary, *Présence,* p. 67.

183. *De Vita Moysis* (PG, 44:941).

184. We may think of Gen. 1:1 and John 1:1.

185. See *Ṛg Veda,* X, 129, 3; *Śatapatha Brāmaṇa,* VI, 1, 1, 1, etc.

186. See, e.g., Mircea Eliade, *The Myth of the Eternal Return.*

187. Cf. Luke 9:62.

188. Cf. Matt. 6:19.

189. Cf. Matt. 5:3.

190. The expression is from Gregory of Nyssa, and is used in Barsotti's *La fuga immobile.*

191. See such texts as Gal. 4:9; 1 Cor. 8:3, 13:12.

192. See, e.g., *Kena Upanishad,* 2, 3; *Tao-te-ching,* chap. 2, etc.

193. See *De Vita Moysis* (PG, 44:1).

194. See ibid. (PG, 46:97), and many other passages cited by Daniélou, *Platonisme,* pp. 320–21.

195. *De Vita Moysis* (PG, 44:1025).

196. See ibid. (PG, 44:404).

197. See the Buddhist expression that would have the "apparent movement" of the mystics depend on their gradual stripping themselves of their own thirst, attachment, desire.

198. "Indeed the divine precept forbids, before all else, thinking that anything you know were like unto God; indeed, any intellect that grasps at the divine nature through some kind of fantasy or conjecture does indeed form an image *(eidolon)* of God in the mind, but it does not know God" (PG, 44:376).

199. Romano Guardini, with his numerous works, would deserve particular mention here. See, e.g., *Gläubiges Dasein.*

200. See above, p. 99.

201. See the Indic position presented on p. 89.

202. Cf. 1 Sam. 3:9.

203. Cf. Gen. 32:29.

204. I refer to the six fundamental attitudes described above, beginning with "Anthropomorphism," p. 108ff.

205. Cf. *Dhammapada,* XX, 5–6, (277–78).

206. Cf. Pseudo-Hermes' beautiful definition, in his Book of the Twenty-Four Masters: "God is the only one whom words fail to express by reason of [God's] excellence, whom minds fail to comprehend by reason of [God's] dissimilarity" (Baeumker, ed., "Das pseudo-hermetische Buch der vierundzwanzig Meister," p. 36).

207. Cf. Gen. 3:24.

208. Here, as well, liturgical prayer carries an extraordinary impact: "That we who without Thee are unable to be, may become able to live according to Thee".

209. For another modern testimonial coming to us from the Christian side, see Paul Tillich's statement that an initiation to the religious problem of our time ought to be by way of "accepting the void which is the destiny of our period, by accepting it as a 'sacred void,' which may qualify and transform thinking and action" (Tillich, *Theology of Culture,* p. 65). See also n. 75, p. 205.

210. See Robinson and Edwards, *The Honest to God Debate;* Hochstafel, *Negative Theology.*

10. SILENCE OF THE BUDDHA

1. By the way of an example of what I mean to say, I might cite the statues of the Buddha that are to be found in a large room in Ellora. There are some twenty of them, all identical at first sight, all representing the Buddha in meditation, but each actually a bit more detached from the world than its predecessor in the series — until finally there is a quantum leap between the second last, with its maximal degree of perfection on "this side," and the very last, which is seen to have overcome, in peace and serenity, all mortal limits. See, e.g., Gupte, *Iconography,* tables 2c–2d.

2. See, e.g., the text with which I bring this work to a conclusion, below, pp. 175ff., with the corresponding n. 183.

3. Cf. a testimonial of Christian spirituality with a Buddhist flavor: "May it be, Lord, that humility, rather than consisting in a low, high, or middling opinion of myself, simply asks me to renounce having any opinion at all? . . . When all is said and done, I know nothing of what I am worth, nor shall I ever, here below" (Charles, *La prière,* p. 149).

4. Cf. the conditions for an authentic philosophizing as laid down by the Vedantic tradition, e.g., in Sankara: Panikkar, *Spiritualità indù;* Piantelli, *Śankara e la rinascita del Brahmanesimo.*

5. "Who are we? Where do we come from? Where are we going? What do we await? What awaits us?" (Bloch, *Das Prinzip Hoffnung,* 1:1). See also Wisd. 2:2 and parallel passages.

6. Let us consider — for it is less well known — gnosticism's basic question, and compare it with the Buddhist spirit. The difference will at once be evident. According to Jonas, *Gnosis,* 1/2:261, as cited by Cullmann, *Heil als Geschichte,* pp. 8–9, what gnosticism claims to tell can be summed up rather nicely in a sentence from Clement of Alexandria (*Excerpta ex Theodoto,* 78, 2): "Who we were, what we have come to be, where we were, where we have come, whither we plunge, whence we have been rescued, what birth and what rebirth."

7. Cf. the celebrated question put by the angel of the Lord to Manoah: "Why do you ask me my name?" (Judges 13:18, cf. Gen. 32:30, Exod. 3:13, Ps. 67:36; Isa. 9:6), and the interpretation of a Meister Eckhart, for example. See the excellent exposition by Vladimir Lossky, *Théologie négative et connaissance de Dieu chez Maître Eckhart,* in the first chapter, "Nomen innominabile," and the second, "Nomen omninominabile" (pp. 13–96).

8. Consider the political situation of a humanity threatened with nuclear death because two great powers seek to "save" the world.

9. See above, pp. 9ff.

10. See a parallel problematic in Ebert, "Der Mensch als Weg zu Gott," pp. 297–317. Consider also the difficulty Saint Thomas's followers have in defending the possibility of a knowledge of the existence of God in a context of the identification of God's "essence" and "existence." Must it not follow that, if we know God's

existence, we know God's essence; or else that, if we do not know God's essence, the "existence" that we know is not God's true existence?

11. *Saṁyutta-nikāya,* III, 189.

12. Ibid. See also the corresponding chapter in Panikkar, *Myth, Faith, and Hermeneutics:* "Silence and the Word: The Smile of the Buddha," pp. 257-76.

13. *Majjhima-nikāya,* III, 6.

14. Cf. the opposite attitude on the part of the Zoroastrian reform—more or less contemporary with that of the Buddha, as we have seen—where the Absolute appears, at least in name (Ahura Mazda, meaning "Thinking Lord"), as the sublimation of thought. See Pagliaro, "Idealismo gathico," and p. 86, above.

15. This would be precisely the *pratyavṛtti,* "reversal in the deepest seat of consciousness," according to the translation of Suzuki, *The Laṅkāvatāra-sūtra.*

16. *Saṁyutta-nikāya,* II, 17. See the text quoted above, p. 10.

17. "Man is neither angel nor beast, and the pity is that who seeks to play the angel, plays the beast" (Pascal, *Pensées* [Brunschvicg no. 358]).

18. See Sir. 7:16-19, where we find the same idea of a via media, and the invitation not to "go to extremes."

19. See above, pp. 117ff.

20. *Mahāvagga-vinaya-piṭaka,* I, 5, 2. Cf. *Majjhima-nikāya,* I, 167ff.; *Saṁyutta-nikāya,* I, 136; *Lalitavistara,* I, 390 and 395ff.; *Dīgha-nikāya,* II, 36; etc.

21. Cf. e.g., III, 32; IV, 40; VII, 3, 19; IX, 3; XII, 5; etc.

22. Cf. e.g., Matt. 7:13-14, 22:14; Luke 10:24, 13:23-24; etc.

23. As a simple example of the modern mentality, see Fontinell, "Reflections on Faith and Metaphysics." I do not know whether our author, the co-editor of the periodical *Cross Currents,* knows Buddhism—there is no mention of it here, and nevertheless he writes (p. 39): "Faith is *without* God. . . . The believer must be willing to work for values in the same way that he would just *as if* God did not exist. . . . The believer, I suggest, must act without God. And so must the atheist. They share the same existential situation." I am inclined to assume that he does not take religions other than Christianity into consideration, in view of the fact that the well-known text cited on page 40 (the torch to burn heaven and the water to quench hell) is not of Christian, but of Muslim (Sufi) origin, as far as we know (in the celebrated Rābi'a). See Anawati and Gardet, *Mistica Islamica,* p. 173, for the sources. Cf. Fontinell's latest book, *Self, God, and Immortality* (esp. pp. 132ff.), which, relying on W. James, goes in the same direction.

24. See Panikkar, *L'homme qui devient Dieu.*

25. John 9:38. Cf.: "I believe! Help me in my unbelief" (Mark 9:24).

26. *Taishō,* 45, 500b (in Chien, *Buddhism,* p. 358).

27. *Saddharmapundarika,* XV, 268-72.

28. Cf. John 16:7.

29. It is a common trait of all reforms—religious, social, political, or what have you—to challenge traditional religion in favor of a religion or spirituality of interiorized salvation. For the immediate intervention of the "idols" or God, one substitutes the authority of the community: the *Sampradāya* for Hindus, the sangha for Buddhists, the "people of God" for Jews, the church for Christians, the state for Marxists, the Umma for Muslims, etc.

30. The fifth sermon on the law, recommended by Aśoka for reading and meditation, is the *moneyasutta,* or discourse on silence, with the triple division there indicated. See *Dīgha-nikāya,* III, 220; *Anguttara-nikāya,* I, 273; *Itivuttaka,* 56.

31. I have the suspicion that, in different language, and with a different technique of composition, the "stopping the world" of the teachings of Don Juan, made famous by Carlos Castaneda, is precisely this "silence of thought" to which I am alluding. See Carlos Castaneda.

32. *Saṁyutta-nikāya*, III, 13.

33. *Suṣāgama Sutra*, in Goddard, *Buddhist Bible*, p. 263.

34. The bibliography on Buddhist prayer is immense. I refer readers to works listed in the Bibliography.

35. It is interesting to note that, with the revised approach to the sacraments initiated in Christianity by the Second Vatican Council, it was determined (June 1968) that, in the Catholic Church, the sacrament of priestly order be conferred in silence, by the simple imposition of hands.

36. For the next paragraphs, we follow the documented study of Renou, "La valeur du silence dans le culte védique"; as well as Levi, *La doctrine du sacrifice dans les Brahmanes,* esp. chap. 1.

37. Cf. *Aśv.,* I, 20, 11.

38. *Śabarasvamin,* ad 2, 2, 10 (in Renou, "Valeur du silence," p. 13).

39. See Renou, "Valeur du silence," p. 13.

40. See, e.g., *Śatapatha Brāhmana,* I, 7, 4, 4; *Aitareya Brahamana,* VII, 7, 2 (XXXII 1); *Gopatha Brāhmana,* II, 18; etc.

41. For an exposition of how such an identification came about, see Vesci, *Heat und Sacrifice.*"

42. See *Śatapatha Brāhmana,* VI, 4, 1, 6: "Then, having deposited [a piece of clay, representing Agni] on the skin of a black antilope—as the black antilope is the sacrifice . . . [the priest] spreads out [the skin] in silence, as the black antilope skin is the sacrifice and the sacrifice is Prajāpati and Prajāpati is ineffable."

43. See *Śatapatha Brāhmana,* I, 4, 5, 8-11, where we hear of the dispute between word *(Vāc)* and spirit *(manas)* as to which of the two had preeminence. The decision was referred to Prajāpati, who pronounced in favor of spirit. "Then word, thus contradicted, fell into consternation and dismay. Word then addressed Prajāpati: 'Never more shall I be thy vehicle of sacrifice, as thou hast outraged me thus.' Thenceforth any sacrifice offered to Prajāpati must be accomplished under one's breath, as word will no more serve as his vehicle of sacrifice" (ibid., v. 12).

44. See, e.g., *Pañcauiṁsa Brāhmana* VII, 6, 1: "Prajāpati desired: 'That I may be able to be more than one; that I may be able to reproduce myself'; he meditated in silence *(tūṣnīm)* in his own mind *(manasā)*; what was in his mind became the sacred formula *(bṛhat)*."

45. Cf. chap. 8, n. 66.

46. See *Śatapatha Brāhmana,* III, 2, 1, 38: "And when [the celebrant] withholds word, word is the sacrifice: herewith it bears the sacrifice within itself. . . ."

47. See *Aitareya Aranyaka,* III, 1, 6.

48. See *Aitareya Brāhmana,* II, 32, 4 (IX, 8): "Silent praise is the eye of the sacrifice"; *Śatapatha Brāhmana,* I, 4, 4, 10: "In silence do this offering, which is the root of the sacrifice; since indeed the root is silent and in it the voice does not sound."

49. See *Taittiriya Samhita,* II, 5, 11, 3: "Having repeated the *Samidhenis* formula, the Gods could not see the sacrifice. Prajāpati sprinkled the butter in silence. Then the Gods could see the sacrifice. The accomplishment of the sprinkling in silence [served] to illumine the sacrifice." See ibid., 6, 3, 7, 1-2, where it is as if

word covered or hid the sacrifice, comments Renou, ("Valeur du silence," p. 14), even immersed it in darkness.

50. See *Taittiriya Samhita,* III, 1, 9, 1: "He offers in silence . . . thus he gives the Gods divine glory."

51. See *Śatapatha Brāhmana,* VII, 2, 2, 14: "He plows . . . and he does so in silence, for what is silent is indeterminate, and the indeterminate is totality."

52. See *Taittiriya Brāhmana,* III, 2, 7, 3.

53. See *Taittiriya Samhita,* VI, 2, 7, 3.

54. *Pañcauimsa Brāhmana,* IV, 9, 10.

55. See *Śatapatha Brāhmana,* I, 9, 3, 22: "In silence . . . he ascends *(l'āhavanīya),* thinking: 'The sacrifice will be accomplished toward the East.' "

56. See *Śatapatha Brāhmana,* XII, 5, 1, 9: "In silence . . . he reverses it [in the spoon] but once, thus rendering it sacred to the ancestors."

57. See, e.g., *Śatapatha Brāhmana,* XII, 4, 2, 1: "And having boiled [the blood that has contaminated the milk of the offering], he offers it in silence in an indefinite manner, as Prajāpati is indefinite and the Agnihotra is sacred to Prajāpati; and the indefinite signifies totality, as well, and thus he makes expiation with totality."

58. See Renou, "Valeur du silence," p. 14: "According to the Brāhmanas, alongside the field of things 'expressed' *(nirukta),* which is that of the word, there is also a field of things 'inexpressible' *(anirukta),* not defined, not limited, uncertain *(anaddha).* . . . The *anirukta* characterizes, among other things, the duration of life, the future, the wind, and, especially, thought *(manas),* or its 'expression,' silence."

59. "Ritual silence taken generally may be of three kinds: the silence of waiting, sacramental silence, and unifying silence" (Otto, *Sünde und Urschuld,* "Sakramentales Schweigen," p. 185).

60. See, e.g., "The Lord [is] in his holy temple. / Let the earth keep silent before him" (Hab. 2:20); "Let all flesh keep still before the Lord, / for he has emerged from his holy dwelling" (Zech. 2:17). See further: Isa. 41:1; Ps. 75:9; Rev. 8:1.

61. Cf. in Christianity, as well, the ascetical expression, eventually to become so commonplace, of Anthony the First Hermit: "The prayer in which the monk comprehends either himself or what he recites [meditates, contemplates] is not perfect" (Cassian, *Collationes,* IX, 31 [PL, 49:808]).

62. "Silence belongs to mystery." Gregory of Nazianzus intimates this when, at the deathbed of his sister, Gorgonia, he says in his *Oratio . . .:* "Profound silence, and, as well, last, death" (Dölger, "Das heilige Schweigen," p. 49). See also the thesis of Odo Casel, advocate of the *Mysterien Theologie,* cited below, n. 165.

63. Panikkar, *Myth, Faith, and Hermeneutics,* pp. 270ff.

64. *Sutta-nipāta,* I, 2, 33 and 34. See *Udāna Vagga,* XXII: "Henceforth all experiences *(dhamma)* fail to touch me. I have renounced all; I am free of every fear *(bhaya)*" (Silburn, *Instant et cause,* p. 225). See also a modern example, in the short poem (1945) by the Japanese philosopher Kitarō Nishida appearing on the frontispiece of the English translation of one of his books: "The bottom of my soul has such depth; neither joy nor the waves of sorrow can reach it" (Kitarō Nishida, *Intelligibility and the Philosophy of Nothingness*).

65. The various *Paramam sukkham* found in so many Buddhist texts (see, e.g., *Majjhima-nikāya,* I, 508; *Digha-nikāya,* II, 94; *Dhammapada,* 15, 7-8 [203ff.]) repeatedly indicate the elimination of suffering as the door automatically opening out upon the greatest happiness. See *Anguttara-nikāya,* III, 442 and 354, etc. See

Pande, *Studies,* p. 480, and below in the present volume, n. 70.

66. See the study of Josef Pieper, *Glück und Kontemplation.*

67. See an interesting testimonial to this in the numerous papers of the Eleventh International Congress of the International Association for the History of Religions (IAHA) held in Claremont, California, September 1965. Consider too the antedeluvian myth of humankind (Gen. 2:8ff.), a myth shared, in one form or another, with most of humanity in its varied religions. See Campbell, *Hero.*

68. See the text cited in chap. 3, p. 46, above, where Indra treats the pacification of sorrow as happiness. See also Śantideva, *Bodhicaryavatāra,* VIII, 88: "Conducting himself at ease, without attachment, not being bound to anyone, he realized a joy that even Indra did not know how to achieve."

69. See n. 59, above.

70. *Dhammapada,* XV, 8 (204). See also n. 60, above.

71. See the monumental work of von Balthasar, *Herrlichkeit,* in which the author underscores the importance of this theme in great Western thinkers, and shows also how it came to be forgotten in scholastic and manual systemizations.

72. *Samyutta-nikāya,* V, 2. See also *Bṛhadāṇyaka Upanishad,* IV, 4, 4.

73. Ecclus. 24:19–21:

> You will remember me as sweeter than honey,
>> better to have than the honeycomb.
> He who eats of me will hunger still,
>> he who drinks of me will thirst for more.

74. See the text of Saint Augustine, *In Epistolam Johannis,* tractatus 4: "The entire life of a good Christian is a holy desire" (PL, 35:2008). See also Dan. 9:23 (Vulgate).

75. Cf. the traditional Christian criterion of distinction of desires: "Indeed, holy desires . . . mature in the waiting. If they diminish in the waiting, they have not been desires" (Gregory the Great, *Homiliae in Evangelia,* book 2, homily 25 [PL, 76:1190]). Cf. also the desire of deliverance (the *mumukṣutva)* in the Vedānta, e.g., Śankara, *Vivekacūdāmani,* passim.

76. See the very Christian and very Greek passage in Saint Gregory of Nyssa *(In Canticum Canticorum Homiliae,* 11 [PG, 44:1000a]), where we read that the desire to see is insatiable because whatever is seen is constantly more divine *(theioteron)* and greater than what has been expected.

77. Cf. the *Brahma-jijñāsā,* or desire to know *Brahman,* in the Hindu tradition. Cf. BS, I, 1, 1, and the commentaries by the various schools.

78. Cf. the intuition of Meister Eckhart, who considers the creature as a passive effect of the divine causality, and, accordingly, constitutively thirsting: "What is passive, ever thirsts, and when it drinks it thirsts for its proper active principle" (cited in Lossky, *Théologie négative,* p. 293). Beings have thirst because they are creatures, and creation is not an act of the past but the continuing conservation of existence. When Eckhart comments on the text of Sirach 24:21 (quoted above), he writes: "Let us stress that, in order to signify this truth of the analogy of all things with God, it is rightly said, 'Who eat of me will hunger still.' 'Eat,' because they are; 'will hunger,' because they are from another" (Lossky, ibid.). Being is "eating," "participating," "being created," "not yet being." It is the wellspring of Being.

79. See Matt. 5:6; etc.

80. See chap. 3, p. 46, above.

81. "Buddhahood is the state in which all our clinging to things is overcome, and there must be indifference to, or detachment from, even the ideal goal of becoming Buddha" (Tanabe, as cited in Y. Takeuchi, "Modern Japanese Philosophy," in *Encyclopedia Britannica,* 1966, p. 961).

82. See the preceding discussion on *nirvāṇa,* with the relevant texts cited there, above, pp. 73ff.

83. To avoid confusion, we might distinguish between the primordial *aspiration* for salvation (the Hindu *mumukṣutva*), and *desires* that are always an obstacle to salvation.

84. John 4:14: "Who drinks of the water I shall give him, will never more thirst, indeed, the water I shall give him will become in him a spring of water bubbling up for eternal life." See also John 6:35; 7:37; Rev. 7:16; 21:6; 22:17; Matt. 5:6; Ps. 61:3; 62:2; etc.

85. Cf. Hugo Rahner, *"Flumina de ventre Christi: Die patristische Auslegung von Joh. VII, 37–38,"* on which it would be fascinating to have a Buddhist commentary.

86. *"Nirvāṇa* exists, but the *nirvanized* subject by no means exists," is the translation by Lamotte, *Histoire,* p. 45, of the text I cited above, p. 41 (n. 45).

87. See Matt. 16:24; Mark 8:34; Luke 9:23.

88. Thomas Aquinas: "And thus the creature in God is the divine essence itself" (*De Potentia,* q. 3, a. 16, ad 24).

89. See the chapter with this title in Etienne Gilson, *La théologie mystique de Saint Bernard.*

90. Cf. 1 Cor. 15:28.

91. See Panikkar, "La Misa como 'consecratio temporis': La tempiternidad," where the ideas merely alluded to here are developed in a Christian perspective.

92. For the drop of water, see the traditional passages, *Mundaka Upanishad,* III, 2, 8; *Brahmasūtra* I, 4, 21. See also *Katha Upanishad,* IV, 14–15, and its Buddhist traits as studied by von Glasenapp, "Buddhism in the Kathaka Upanishad" (reprinted in his *Von Buddha zu Gandhi,* pp. 81–85), where Glasenapp offers numerous passages recalling the downward course of waters that finally plunge into the ocean.

93. See Panikkar, "L'eau et la mort."

94. Elsewhere (Intrareligious Dialogue, chap. 5) I have sought to show that in the West the paradigm of perfection is symbolized, from Parmenides onward, by the perfect, round, finite (finished) sphere, whereas in India the idea of perfection is represented by the point having no dimensions, qualities, or other determinations — infinite. Nevertheless we see the idea of the infinite to be applied to the universe, as well, as a sphere. See propositions 2 and 17 of *Liber 24 philosophorum,* cited above: "God is an infinite sphere, whose center is everywhere, and whose circumference is nowhere," and "God is a sphere with as many circumferences as there are points" (p. 31).

95. In Buddhist milieus the ideal of holiness is represented by the *arhat* and the *bodhisattva,* as in Hinduism by the *jīvanmukta* and in Christianity by the saint. See Rom. 8:19 and modern commentaries such as that of Romano Guardini or others. See also 2 Cor. 5:5, and Gal. 2:20.

96. See, e.g., Matt. 10:40ff., 25:31ff., and, for a commentary on "neighbor," Panikkar, "Sur l'anthropologie du prochain."

97. Luke 10:25–37.

98. "This question, to which the response is, 'Go thou and do likewise,' is not a

direct answer to the question that the scribe has just asked" (Nacar-Colunga's commentary on these verses); or again: "Instead of giving a theoretical response to the question he has been asked, Jesus goes directly to the concrete domain of facts" (Biblical Institute of Rome commentary on these verses).

99. See, e.g., James 2:15ff., 1 John 2:10–14; etc.

100. See Matt. 10:40, as well as 1 John 3:16, 4:12ff. (esp. v. 20); etc.

101. Cf. *Manauadharmas'astra,* II, 161; 6, 47–48; *Mahābhārata,* XII, 3880 and 5528; XIII, 5571; etc.

102. Cf. the parable used by the Japanese philosopher H. Tanabe (d. 1962), as reported by Y. Takeuchi in the above-cited article of the *Encyclopedia Britannica* (n. 76). A bodhisattva, after a long life, was prepared to join the Buddha, and set off to find him. Arriving at the Buddha's dwelling, however, he found it deserted. The Buddha had left his house to return to the world and redeem it. The bodhisattva understood, and returned to the world himself, to cooperate with the Buddha in the salvation of the cosmos.

103. Cf. *Dīgha-nikāya,* II, 196; III, 220. These four basic attitudes recommended by the Buddha are usually called *apramānacitta,* "infinite feelings," for they are directed toward a universal object having no exceptions or discriminations.

104. *Vinaya,* I, 301–2. This is a celebrated text, repeatedly cited and frequently represented in sacred art. See the references in Lamotte, *Historie,* p. 67; and any text on Buddhist art, as for example the one cited in n. 1, p. 223.

105. See Panikkar, *Myth, Faith, and Hermeneutics,* the chapter "Advaita and Bhakti," where this argument, with an analogous solution, is more amply treated (though in a context of advaita Hinduism rather than Buddhism).

106. See, e.g., Matt. 6:3: "When you give alms, let your left hand not know what your right is doing."

107. *Tao-te-ching,* 61ff., repeated in Chuang Tsu, XXII, 1, 8 (in Thomas Merton, trans., *The Way of Chuang Tzu,* p. 120). Cf. some relevant texts: "The *tao* that can be expressed is not the eternal *tao*" (*Tao-te-Ching,* 1); "The *tao* is always without a name. When for the first time attributes were attributed to it, for functional reasons, then it was given a name" (ibid., p. 32); see also ibid., p. 56. Further: "I do not think that I know it well, nor do I think that I know it not. Those among us who know it, [*brahman*] know it; what they do not know, is that they know not. Those who do not know it, know it. Those who know it, see it not. It is not understood by those who understand, it is understood by those who do not understand" (*Kena Upanishad,* II, 2–3). Cf. as well the religious, but also social, passage: "When, O Lord, did we give you to drink . . .?" (Matt. 25:37–39).

108. See the typical passage, Rom 1:20, with its innumerable commentaries.

109. Cf. a meaningful example: "If he faces the truth without panic he will recognize that there is no meaning to life except the meaning man gives his life by the unfolding of his powers, by living productively" (Fromm, *Man for Himself,* p. 45).

110. Cf. Isa. 45:15. See also Panikkar, "De Deo abscondito."

111. Cf. 1 Kings 8:12, where it is asserted that God dwells in the dark cloud. See also Ps. 18:12, 97:2; etc. Further: *Jaiminiya Brāhmana,* III, 20, 1, which speaks of the lair in which the divinity is shut up; or again, *Śvetasvātara Upanishad,* I, 1, 3, where we read that the power of the divinity is hidden in its qualities *(guna)*; etc.

112. Cf. the testimony of the Upanishads that could not but be lost. *Śankarācharya* refers to it when it says that Bāskali, questioned by Bhāva concerning the nature of the *brahman,* kept silent. When questioned a third time, he

decided to reply, lest he torment his disciple any further, he told him that he had already replied, but that the other had not understood. The response had been: the *ātman* is silence *(upaśāntoyam ātman).* See *Brahmasūtrabhaṣya,* III, 2, 17.

113. Pande (*Studies,* p. 294), on silence as a more eloquent expression of the ultimate reality, offers the following citations of the *Acyutagranthamālā* edition of the *Śatapatha Brāhmaṇa:* I, 3, 28, 53, 162–63, 624.

114. "Praise to thee keeps silence," is Jerome's translation of Ps. 61:2 (PL, 28:1174). Augustine, *Confessions:* "Let . . . be silent, and let the very soul keep its silence" (book 9, chap. 25). "And I kept silence amid bounty," says the Vulgate, Ps. 38:3. Whole volumes of bibliography could be cited on silence as a basic ascetical and mystical category. For examples: T. J. Bruneau, "Communicative Silences: Forms and Functions," *The Journal of Communication,* 23 (March 1973) 17–46; M. Baldini, *Il linguaggio dei mistici* (Brescia: Queriniana, 1986).

115. "God is honored by silence, not because nothing can be said or sought of God, but because we understand that God has made us by his knowledge" (Thomas Aquinas, *In Boeth. de Trinitate,* proem., q. 2, a. 1).

116. *Pañcauiṁsa Brāhmaṇa,* XX, 14, 2.

117. Cf. *Maitrī Upanishad,* VI, 22.

118. Ibid., VI, 23: "niḥśabdaḥ śūnya bhūtaḥ."

119. See Panikkar, *The Trinity and the Religious Experience of Man.*

120. [Christ] ". . . who is his Word, proceeding from silence," says Ignatius of Antioch, First Letter to the Magnesians, 8:2 (PG, 5:669).

121. ". . . the religious silence of the virgin [Mary] . . . concerning God's secret," says Rupert, *In Cantica,* I (PL, 168:844). She is "mute mother of the silent Word," according to the Santeuil hymn for the feast of the purification (de Lubac, *Méditation sur l'Eglise,* p. 260).

122. Cf. John 6:46; 14:8ff. But he has been "heard," and the *śruti* bears witness to this fact.

123. The same Word, within the divinity, is silent: "And note that those things [i.e., the things of creation] most perfectly and appropriately bless the Word of God, by which, in silence, without exterior word and above time, they ever praise and bless the Word that, in the silence of the Father's Intellect, is Verbum without word, or better, above and beyond any word" (Eckhart, *Expositio in Genesim* [*Lateinische Werke,* 1:62]).

124. Rom. 16:25. "The six words of the original text are almost untranslatable: *kata apokalupsin mystēriou chronois aiōniois sesigēmenou* ("according to the revelation of the mystery that had remained silent for eternal ages"). This is an idea that constitutes the main thread of Pauline theology on the mystery hidden from the beginning of the ages. See *Muṇḍaka Upanishad,* VI, 29; *Bṛhadarāṇyaka Upanishad,* VI, 3, 12; *Baghavadgītā,* 4, 3; 18, 67; etc.

125. Cf. Samuel Beckett's famous drama, *Waiting for Godot.*

126. Cf. the Upanishadic image of the human and divine fear of solitude in *Bṛhadarāṇyaka Upanishad,* I, 4, 1–2: "In the beginning this 'I' existed alone, in the form of a person. It reflected, and saw nothing but its 'I'. . . . It was afraid. This is why people have fear when they are alone. Then it thought: 'Nothing exists apart from Myself. Of what should I be afraid?'. . . . After all, it is from a second thing that fear arises."

127. Cf. the scriptural insistence on *timor Dei,* which is part and parcel of a consideration of God as a hidden, shadowy God. See nn. 105 and 106, above, as well as Ps. 18:10; 110:10; Prov. 1:7; 9:10; 14:27; Sir. 1:11,22,27; 19:18; 25:8; etc.

128. "The absurd arises from the confrontation between need and the irrational silence of the world" (A. Camus, *Il mito di Sisito,* p. 21; quoted in Friedman, *Problematic Rebel,* p. 469).

129. See, e.g., Kafka's *The Castle.*

130. Cf. Pascal, *Pensées,* 1:99: "The silence of the sidereal spaces terrify me"— although Pascal himself had also written: "In love, silence is worth more than discourse" (*Opuscule: Discourses sur les passions de l'amour,* p. 132). Silence without love terrifies.

131. Humankind "finds itself alone, aimlessly wandering through this monstrous silence, free and alone, without help and without excuses, condemned to decide, without support of any kind, condemned forever to be free" (the leitmotiv of J. P. Sartre's philosophy, as articulated at the beginning of his *L'age de raison* [Paris: Gallimard, 1945]).

132. The text of the *Bṛhadārāṇyaka Upaniṣhad,* I, 4, 1-2, cited above (n. 126, p. 230), continues: "[But] it was not happy [or: 'suffered from ennui'], and this is why a person is not happy when alone" (v. 3). For a commentary, see Panikkar, *Myth, Faith, and Hermeneutics,* chap. 3. Consider today's drama, where the anguish of long silences, and the uselessness of words, are employed to convey a lack of communication—e.g., the works of Ionesco, or of A. Campanile.

133. Neither are its homes, so often built one atop the other, any substitute for a good neighbor.

134. Consider the manic use of the radio, and the extravagant success of television.

135. *Majjhima-nikāya,* I, 161.

136. "Pāsamartho hy āryāṇām tuṣṇim bhāvaḥ," in *Prasannapada,* LVII, 8.

137. Candrakīrti's comment on chapter 25 of Nāgārjuna's *Treatise on Relativity,* XI, (539, 3ff.), as quoted by Stcherbatsky, *The Concept of Buddhist Nirvāṇa,* p. 210.

138. See, on this same experience, Vesci, "Dialogo e Mito."

139. "When you can say nothing more about it, then you shall see it, for the knowledge of God is divine silence, and the quiescence of all our sensation" (*Hermes Trimegistus,* X, 5). See also: "Thou art inexpressible, ineffable, and only with silence canst thou be embraced [comprehended]: receive the pure sacrifices that to thee are devoted, offered with words" (ibid., I, 31).

140. See above, n. 102.

141. See the discourse of Sarnath, given above, pp. 48-51.

142. "Indeed, the censure of silence is as it were a nutriment of the word," says Gregory the Great (*Homiliae in Ezechiel,* book 1, homily 40, no. 16 [PL, 76:907]). See further the three stages of the human discovery of the reality of God, in a text that would deserve to be cited in its entirety: "To great Moses, the divine epiphany occurs in a first moment by way of light; then [God] speaks *(dialegetai)* to him in the cloud; and finally, when he becomes higher and more perfect, Moses sees *(blepei)* God in the dark" (Gregory of Nyssa, *In Canticum,* homily 11 [PG, 44:1000c]). See Panikkar, "The Silence of the Word."

143. Cf. J. Ortega y Gasset, Martin Buber, J. Leclercq, and others.

144. It is to be noted, however, that, although official philosophy and theology continue to speak of the eclipse of God, and the secularized world complains that God "does not speak," in the popular world there are at least as many, if not more, "seers" who claim to have visions of God, the Madonna, or theophanies of all types, than in the past, and they publicize their message. For Italy, see Ferrarotti, *Studi;*

for Spain, Pascual, *Guía*. There are many essays on the contemporary scene in Castelli, *Le Sacré;* see too the issue of *Fondamenti,* 4 (1986), as also studies on the "apparition" at Casabanchel (Spain), Medjuorje (Yugoslavia), and elsewhere.

145. According to tradition, the Buddha once blurted out: [If God were to be introduced into human affairs] "human beings would be criminals, highway robbers, libertines, and liars; they would be possessed by greed, jealousy, error, and everything imaginable, by virtue of the 'creative will of God'!" (*Ánguttara-nikāya,* III, 61, 3 [vol. 1, p. 174]). See the same concern in Plutarch, *De Superstitione,* 10: "Is not that one perhaps more religious who believes that the Gods do not exist than the one who saddles them with unseemly behavior?" (cited by Kristensen, *The Meaning of Religion,* p. 250).

146. See Luke 12:14, where Christ is reported to have refused to allow himself to be drawn into a similar game: "Who has made me judge or referee over you?"

147. Let us recall that Hitler felt that he had been invested with a divine mission to protect the rights of a chosen race.

148. Cf., by contrast, an African myth, in which the "breach" that occurred was just the opposite: it was silence that injected itself into primordial sound. In the beginning was only sound, a continuous, and hence unseizable and incomprehensible, sound. Then sound was breached (here too is a form of the myth of a primordial "fall"), language was born, and with language, civilization. And surely the articulation of a sentence, and its comprehensibility by reason of its division into words, depends on the silence injected into the continuity of sound.

149. The principle of analogy, as Christian scholasticism saw it in better times (and not as certain modern critics have wished to understand and criticize it), representing as it does a solicitude to maintain due distance and separation between creator and creature, constitutes one of the finest attempts of the Western mind to approach the problem that concerns us here.

150. The original Spanish of the present volume provides the opportunity for a play on words that cannot be rendered in English: the possessive adjectives "your" (singular) and "his," "her," or "their," are, respectively, *tuyo* and *suyo* in Spanish, and *yo* means "I." I here (as also once above, chap. 9, n. 155) make a nonetymological pun and understand *tu-yo* to mean "your I," and *su-yo* "his I," "her I," or "their I." See above, p. 139.

151. My summary remarks here not only do not contradict, they may actually amplify, and in a way correct, the thesis of the I-Thou relationship that has acquired a certain currency since Martin Buber. See his *Das dialogische Prinzip,* a collection of his principal writings on this subject. See also Ebner, *Schriften,* vol. 1: *Fragmente, Aufsätze, Aphorismen — Zu einer Pneumatologie des Wortes.*

152. "That He [God] hides Himself does not diminish the immediacy; in the immediacy He remains the Saviour and the contradiction of existence becomes for us a theophany" (Buber, *Two Types of Faith,* p. 169).

153. It is significant that many of those who wish to have Buddhism accepted in the West, not excluding an A. K. Coomaraswamy, seek to present it in a positive, "ātmic" key. Cf. the attitude of a student who rejected the *anātma-vāda* as inauthentic on the grounds that "otherwise I could not have believed it."

154. "Verbal expression, so long as it is only a means of communication, serves only to alienate man from the Truth. Not to reveal is nearer to Truth and more loyal to the dharma." (Nagao, "Silence of the Buddha," p. 142).

155. The problem of God's inaccessibility — in Plato (cf. *Timaeus,* 28c) and

patristics (cf. Gregory of Nazianzus, *Orationes,* 27, 4 [PG, 36:32]) in the West, and in the Upanishads (cf. *Bṛhadārānyaka Upanishad,* II, 4, 13-14; III, 4, 12) in the East—seems to me to find a more profound explanation here than the one usually given.

156. "And therefore in the name of the Father and of the Son and of the Holy Spirit we confess one God, because [God] names a power [and not a property]" (*Fides Damasi,* Denzinger, 71).

157. Obviously the supreme cause cannot be its own cause. This would involve a *processio in infinitum,* and the latter is precisely the classic Buddhist objection to the existence of God. A typical example: "If asked 'How did Life begin' [the Buddhist] would ask in return: 'How did God begin' " (Malalasekera, "Buddhism and the Enlightenment of Man," as cited in von Glasenapp, *Buddhismus and Gottesidee,* p. 33).

158. "As the creature has its own *esse,* and its *esse*—for it to be—is to receive *esse;* so for God *esse* is to give *esse,* since for God *agere* or *operari* is always and only *esse*" (Eckhart, *Expositio in Genesi [Lateinische Werke,* 1:77, no. 146]), commenting on Gen. 2:2.

159. Cf., for Christianity, Pseudo-Denis the Areopagite: God "is not" (*De Divinis Nominibus,* I, 8 [PG, 3:388b]), because God is so far beyond affirmation or negation (*De Mystica Theologia,* I, 5 [PG, 3:1b, 3:1048]) and transcends all opposition between being and not being (*Epistolae,* 1 and 2 [PG 3:1065, 3:1068-69]). "God is beyond, inasmuch as *ens* and *non ens* is beyond *esse;* and all *esse* whatever is denied of God, for God is *esse* and beyond *esse*" (Eckhart, *Expositio in Exodum,* C, folio 46, 2, 1-7, as cited in Lossky, *Théologie négative,* p. 93).

160. See *Ṛg Veda,* X, 129, 1, etc., as Vedic testimony.

161. See ibid., X, 129, 3.

162. The Vedic hymn cited above is one of the most complete expressions of what the Vedas, Hinduism, Christianity, and other religions have sought to say with their respective myths of the "birth of the Creator."

163. Cf. the synthesis of the position of a Saint Gregory of Nyssa in Jean Daniélou, *Platonisme,* p. 317: "God and humankind both belong to the intelligible world. Now, spirit is of itself unlimited. In this, God and the soul are of the same order. But the essential difference is that God is infinite in act, whereas the soul is infinite in becoming. Its divinity consists in being transformed into God."

164. "The first production or emanation of the Son and Holy Spirit from the Father is from eternity; again, the general production or creation of the entire universe by one God is in time" (Eckhart, *Liber Parabolarum Genesis,* as cited in Lossky, *Théologie négative,* p. 52 [emphasis added]). See also *Tabula auctoritatum libri parabolarum genesis,* auctoritas 1, 1; in *Lateinische Werke,* 1, 457ff.

165. See the position of a father of the church like Gregory of Nyssa, as sketched by Louis Bouyer, *Spiritualité,* p. 437: "The discovery of God is accomplished a good deal less in any definable experience than in the gradually perceived need to transcend all experience." See also Casel, *De Philosophorum Graecorum Silentio Mystico;* Mensching, "Das heilige Schweigen."

166. Heiler (*Erscheinungsformen,* pp. 334ff.) distinguishes a magical silence of worship from religious silence of worship, an ascetical silence from a contemplative one, a theological silence from a metaphysical one.

167. "A being that thinks itself is not a simple being" (Plotinus, *Enneads,* VI, 7, 38).

168. Heiler (*Erscheinungsformen,* p. 339): "It is necessary for the Logos that at the foundation of the Logos be silence." See also *De Philosophia Chaldeorum* (Engl. edition, *The Chaldean Philosophy,* A. Jahn, ed. [Halle, 1891], p. 4).

169. The terms are reversed. For Philo, Plotinus, Proclus, God is the ultimate hypostasis, above silence. For the Buddha the divine is on this side of silence. See Heiler, *Erscheinungsformen,* p. 338, for the classic texts.

170. See Panikkar, "Gedankenfreie Meditation."

171. Consider one parable of Chuang T'su among thousands: The emperor has lost a precious pearl. He dispatches Action, Word, and Thought in search of it, but without result. Then he sends Nothing, and is astounded that Nothing succeeds in finding it (Allers, "Les ténèbres," p. 144). See Thomas Merton's translation, *The Way of Chuang Tzu,* p. 74. Only the cessation of all activity can enable us to discover truth. Cf. Matt. 13:45–46, where we hear not of the loss of a pearl, but of a quest for fine pearls (plural), and the discovery of a one precious pearl (singular) whose value is . . . everything. See also Prov. 8:11; Wisd. 7:9.

172. See p. 229, n. 102.

173. Cf., e.g., the legends of Kings Hauscandra and Vipaścit as recounted in the *Mārkandeya Purāna,* cantos 8; 13ff.; etc., according to which in one case the king chooses to stay in hell, in order to be with his family, and in the other with his sinful friends, rather than enter heaven alone. Cf. *The Mārkandeya Purāna* (Bibliotheca Indica), 1904. Repr., Delhi: Motilal Banassidan, 1969, pp. 38ff. According to other, probably later, versions (see le Saux, *La rencontre de l'Hindouisme et du Christianisme,* p. 226), the gods, edified by the king's love, and unwilling and unable to leave him in hell, have to empty hell and send all its captives to heaven. Consider Yudisthira, the hero of the *Mahābhārata,* who likewise desired to go to hell in order to remain with his family. See further, Papini, *Il diavolo,* so sensational in its time, which recounts a number of the more remarkable similar testimonials of Western tradition.

174. Cf. the decisive tone and anguished dilemma of the prophet of Israel when the people committed a grave sin by their own laws and cannot be pardoned: "Moses turned to Yahweh and said: 'This people has committed a great sin; it has fashioned itself a God of gold. But now, if thou wouldst forgive. . . . Otherwise, erase me from the book that thou hast written.' " (Exod. 32:31–32).

175. "Indeed, I should wish to be anathema myself, separated from Christ for the sake of my brethren, my relatives according to the flesh" (Rom. 9:3).

176. "The highest and most courageous thing a person can do is renounce God for God's sake. Saint Paul renounced God for God's sake — renounced everything he might have received from God, indeed everything God could give him, and everything that he could receive from God" (Eckhart, *Deutsche Predigten,* Predigt 13, pp. 214ff.).

177. See Lamotte's translation, *Le traité de la Grande Vertu de Sagesse.* It would make little difference for our purposes if this monumental work is not directly from the hand of Nāgārjuna, as more recent criticism is inclined to hold.

178. Ibid., 2:1112–13.

179. Many of the practical exercises of meditation have as their immediate aim the healing of the body, which at first might seem to represent the study of a utilitarian goal and an affirmation, rather than a negation, of matter.

180. Cf. *Visuddhimagga* XV, 68, according to the translation by I. B. Horner, in Conze, *Buddhist Texts,* p. 100 — although, as W. C. Smith notes in his "Religious

Atheism," p. 30, the word *dhamma* does not occur in the original, which reads *patipattiya vañjhabhavapajjanato.*

181. Cf., e.g., pp. 28ff.

182. *Majjhima-nikāya,* I, 304.

183. *Mahāparinibbāna-sutta,* VI, 5–7 (using the translation by T. W. Rhys Davids, pp. 113–14). J. Masson has pointed out to me that the monks then repented of having asked the Buddha nothing, and, as tradition narrates, a discussion ensued on the possible abrogation of the minor rules. Casuistry and chatter are human, as well.

BIBLIOGRAPHY

Abbagnano, N. "Quattro concetti di dialettica." *Rivista di Filosofia,* 49 (1958) 123–33.

Abe, M. "Buddhism and Christianity." *Japanese Religions,* vol. 3, no. 3, pp. 14ff.

Abhidhammattha-saṅgaha. Engl. trans. by S. Z. Aung and C. A. F. Rhys Davids. London: Pali Text Society Translations, 1910; repr. 1956.

Adhidarmakośa (by Vasubandhu). French trans. by L. de La Vallée-Poussin, 6 vols. Paris: Paul Geuthner, 1922–1931.

Aiken, C. F. *Bouddhisme et Christianisme.* Paris, 1903.

––––––. *The Dharma of Gotama the Buddha and the Gospel of Jesus Christ. A Critical Inquiry into the Alleged Relation of Buddhism with Primitive Christianity.* Boston, 1900.

Alfaric, P. "La vie chrétienne du Bouddha," *Journal Asiatique* (1917) 269–88.

Allen, G. F. *The Meaning of Mission,* London: SCM Press, 1943.

Allers, R. "Les ténèbres, le silence, et le néant." *Revue de Métaphysique et de Moral* (1956).

Allmen, J. J., von. *Vocabulary of the Bible.* London: Lutterworth, 1964.

Altizer, T. J. J. "Creative Negation in Theology." *Christian Century* (1965).

––––––. *The Gospel of Christian Atheism.* Philadelphia: Westminster, 1966.

––––––. *Mircea Eliade and the Dialectic of the Sacred.* Philadelphia: Westminster, 1963.

––––––. *Toward a New Christianity: Readings in the Death of God Theology.* New York: Harcourt, Brace and World, 1967.

––––––. *Nirvana and the Kingdom of God.* New York: New Theology, 1964.

––––––. *Oriental Mysticism and Biblical Eschatology.* Philadelphia: Westminster, 1961.

––––––. "A Theonomy in our Time." *Christian Scholar,* 46 (1963).

––––––, ed. *Truth, Myth, and Symbol.* Englewood Cliffs, N.J.: Prentice-Hall, 1962.

Anawati, G. C., and Gardet, L. *Mistica Islamica.* Turin: SEI, 1960.

Anderson, G. A. *Bibliography of the Theology of Missions in the Twentieth Century.* New York: Missionary Research Library, 1958.

Aṅguttara-nikāya. Engl. trans. by E. L. Woodward and E. M. Hare, *The Book of Gradual Sayings,* 5 vols. London: Pali Text Society Translations, 1932–1936; repr. 1960–65.

Appleton, G. *On the Eightfold Path.* New York: Oxford University Press, 1961.

Arvon, G. *Le Bouddhisme.* Paris, 1951.

Arvon, H. *L'Athéisme.* Paris: PUF, 1967.

Athanasius, St. *Opera,* Migne PG, vol. 25–28.

Aubrey, E. E. *Secularism. A Myth.* New York: Harper & Brothers, 1954.

Augustine, St. *Opera,* Migne PL, vol. 32–47.

Bahm, A. "Soul or no Soul? Why Buddha Refused to Answer." *Proceedings: The Self in East and Eastern Thought* (1966) 102ff.

Balthasar, Hans Urs, von. *Herrlichkeit.* Einsiedeln: Johannes, 1961.

———. "Meditation als Verrat." *Geist und Leben* (1977) 260–68.

———. "Metaphysik und Mystik des Evagrius Ponticus." *Zeitschrift für Aszese und Mystik,* 14 (1939) 31–47.

———. *Présence et Pensée. Essai sur la Philosophie religieuse de Grégoire de Nysse.* Paris: Beauchesne, 1942.

Bando, S., et al. *Bibliography on Japanese Buddhism.* Tokyo: Hokuseido Press, 1961.

Bapat, P. V. "Buddhist Studies in Recent Times," *2500 Years of Buddhism.* Delhi, 1956, pp. 380–442.

Bareau, A. *L'absolu en Philosophie bouddhique; Evolution de la notion d'Asamskrta.* Université de Paris, 1951.

———. *Bouddha.* Paris: Seghers, 1962.

———. *Die Religionen Indiens.* Stuttgart: Kohlhammer, 1964, 3:215ff.

Barr, J. *The Semantics of Biblical Language.* London: Oxford University Press, 1962.

Barsotti, D. *La fuga immobile.* Milan: Ed. di Comunità, 1957.

Barthelemy, S.-H. *La nirvana bouddhique.* Paris: Durand, 1875.

Barua, B. M. "Pratityasamutpada as Basic Concept of Buddhist Thought." *B. C. Law Festschrift.*

Bary, T., de, ed. *Sources of Indian Tradition.* New York: Columbia University Press, 1958.

Batthacaryya, B. "Mahayanic Pantheon." *The Cultural Heritage of India.*

Baumgartner, H. M. "Transzendentales Denken und Atheismus." *Hochland,* 56 (1963).

Beaurecueil, S., de. *Le pain et le sel.* Paris: Cerf, 1965.

Beckh, H. *Buddhismus, Buddha, und seine Lehre.* Stuttgart: Sammlung Gösschen, 1958.

Beckman, J. *Weltkirche und Weltreligionen.* Freiburg.

Bellini, A. "Buddhismo e Cristianesimo." *Atti del Quinto Congresso dell'Associazione "Ludovico Necchi."* Milan, 1938.

Bénoit, P. "La plénitude de sens des Livres Saints." *Revue Biblique,* 67 (1960) 161–96.

Benz, E. *Adam, der Mythus von Urmenschen.* Munich: Barth, 1955.

———. *Das Bild des Übermenschen in der christlichen Religionsphilosophie der Gegenwart.* Zurich: Rhein, 1961.

———. *Das Bild des Übermenschen in der europaischen Geistesgeschichte.* Stuttgart: Rhein, 1961.

———. *Buddhas Wiederkehr und die Zukunft Asiens.* Munich: Nymphenburger Verlagshandlung, 1963.

———. *Ideen zu einer Theologie der Religionsgeschichte.* Mainz: Akademie der Wissenschaften, 1960.

———. "The Present Meeting between Christianity and the Oriental Religions." *East and West,* 1 (1957).

Bergmann, G. *Jesus Christus oder Buddha, Mohammed, Hinduismus.* Gladbeck/Westf.: Schriften Mission Verlag, 1966.

Bernard, St. *Opera,* Migne PL, vol. 182–85.

Bertola, E. *Il pensiero ebraico. Studi e ricerche.* Padua: CEDAM, 1972.

Berval, R., de, ed. *Présence du Bouddhisme,* special issue of *France-Asie,* 1959.

Beth, K. "Gibt es buddhistische Einflüsse in den kanonischen Evangelien?" *Theol. Stud. Kritiken* (1916) 169–227.

Bhattacharaya, V. "Catuskoti." *Commemoration Volume.*

———. *The Foundations of Living.* Calcutta: University of Calcutta, 1938.

Bianchi, U. *Il dualismo religioso. Saggio storico ed etnologico.* Rome.

Biardeau, M. "Quelques réflexions sur l'apophatisme de Sankara." *Indo-Iranian Journal,* 3 (1959).

Biser, E. *Gott ist tot.* Munich: Kösel, 1963.

Bloch, E. *Atheismus und Christentum.* Frankfurt: Suhrkamp, 1967.

———. *Das Prinzip Hoffnung.* Frankfurt, 1958.

Bloch, J. *Les inscriptions d'Aśoka.* Paris: Les Belles Lettres, 1950.

Blyth, R. H. *Buddhist Sermon on Christian Texts.* Tokyo: Kokudoska, 1952.

Bodde, D., trans. *A History of Chinese Philosophy* (by Fung Yu-lan). Princeton: Princeton University Press, 1966.

Bodhisattvabhūmi (by Maitreyanatha Asanga), Sanskrit trans., U. Wogihara, 2 vols., Tokyo, 1930.

Bodhisattvabhūmi, French trans., C. Bendall and L. de la Vallée-Poussin, *Muséon,* n.s., 6 (1905) 38–52; 7 (1906) 213ff.; 12 (1911) 155ff.

Bodicarvāvatāra, French trans., L. de la Vallée-Poussin. Paris: Bloud, 1907.

Boman, T. *Das hebräische Denken im Vergleich mit dem griechischen.* 1959.

Botto, O. *Buddha e il Buddhismo.* Milan: Mondadori, 1984.

Bouquet, A. C. *The Christian Faith and Non-Christian Religions.* London: J. Nirbet, 1958.

Bouyer, L. *Le sens de la vie monastique.* Paris: Brepols, 1950.

———. *La spiritualité du Nouveau Testament et des Pères.* Paris: Aubier, 1960.

Brelich, A. *Introduzione alla Storia delle Religioni,* Rome: Ed. dell'Ateneo, 1966.

Brown, N. O. *Life against Death. The Psychoanalytical Meaning of History.* New York: Vintage, 1957.

Brunner, E. *Die Religion. Eine philosophische Untersuchung auf geschichtlicher Grundlage,* Freiburg: Herder, 1956.

Brunner, H. E. *Christusbotschaft im Kampf mit den Religionen.* Stuttgart/Basel: Evang. Missionsverlag, 1931.

Buber, M. *Dialogisches Leben.* Zurich: Müller, 1947.

———. *Das dialogische Prinzip.* Heidelberg, 1958.

———. *L'eclissi di Dio. Considerazioni sul rapporto tra religione e filosofia.* Milan: Ed. di Comunità, 1958.

———. *Two Types of Faith.* London: Routledge & Kegan Paul, 1951.

Buder, W. *Das Christentum und die anderen Religionen.* Stuttgart, 1927.

Buhr, M. *Wissen und Gewissen. Beiträge zum 200. Geburtstag Johannes Gottlieb Fichtes (1762–1814).* Berlin, 1962, pp. 205–23.

Burkel, B., and Clarke, W. N. "The Self in Eastern and Western Thought." *International Philosophical Quarterly,* March 1966.

Burnouf, E. *Introduction à l'histoire du Bouddhisme indien.* Paris: Imprimerie Royale, 1874; repr. 1876.

Burrow, T. "The Proto-Indoaryans." *Journal of the Asiatic Society* (1973) 123–40.

Burtt, E. A. *The Teachings of the Compassionate Buddha.* New York: Mentor, 1955.

Buston, *History of Buddhism*. Engl. trans. of Obermiller, *Materialen*.

Buu-Duong, T. "La béatitude d'après S. Thomas et d'après Sakyamuni." Diss., Faculté de Théologie de l'Université Catholique d'Ángers, 1943.

Cahari, C. T. K. "On the Dialectical Affinities between East and West." *Philosophy East and West*, 3 (Oct. 1953) 199–222.

Caird, E. *The Evolution of Theology in the Greek Philosophers*. Glasgow: MacLehose, 1958.

Campbell, J. *The Hero with a Thousand Faces*. Princeton: Princeton University Press, 1949.

Camus, A. *Le mythe de Sisyphe*. Paris: Gallimard, 1964.

Capra, F. *The Tao of Physics*, Boulder, Colo.: Shambhala, 1975.

Carpenter, J. E. *Buddhism and Christianity: A Contrast and Parallel*. London: Hodder & Stoughton, 1923.

––––––. "Buddhist and Christian Parallels: The Mythological Background." *Study in the History of Religions*, pp. 67–94.

––––––. "The Obligations of the New Testament to Buddhism." *Nineteenth Century*, 8 (1880) 971–94.

Carus, P. *Buddhism and its Christian Critics*. Chicago: Open Court, 1897.

Casel, O. *Das christliche Kultmysterium*. 3rd ed., 1948.

––––––. *De philosophorum graecorum silentio mistico*. Giessen: Topelmann, 1919.

––––––. *Mysterientheologie*. Regensburg: F. Pustet, 1986.

Casey, D. F. "Aspects of the Sunyata-absolute of Nagarjuna of the Second Century A.D." Diss., Harvard University, 1960.

Casper, B., ed. *Phänomenologie des Idols*. Munich: Alber, 1981.

Cassian, J. *Collationes Patrum*. Paris: Editions du Cerf, 1955.

Castaneda, C. *Viaggio a Ixtlan*. Rome: Astrolabio/Ubaldini, 1973.

Castelli, E., ed. *Mito e fede*. Padua: CEDAM, 1966.

––––––, ed. *Il Problema della demitizzazione (Archivio de Filosofia* [1961]).

––––––, ed. *Le Sacré*. Paris: Aubier, 1974.

Catuhstaka. French trans., P. Vaydya, *Etudes sur Arvadeva et son Catuhstaka*. Paris: Paul Geuthner, 1923.

Catuhstava (by Nagarjuna). French trans., L. de la Vallée-Poussin, "Les Quatres Odes de Nagarjuna." *Muséon*, 14 (1913) 1–18.

Chakkarai, V. *The Cross and Indian Thought*. Madras: Allahabad and Colombo Christian Literature Society for India, 1932.

Charles, P. *La prière de toutes des heures*. Brussels: Ed. Universelle, 1947.

Chien, K. *Buddhism in China: A Historical Survey*. Princeton University Press, 1964.

Cleman, C. "Buddhistische Einflüsse im Neuen Testament." *Zeitschrift für Urchristentum* (1916) 128–38; Engl. trans. *American Journal of Theology* (1916).

Clement of Alexandria. *Opera*, Migne PG, vol. 8–9.

Cobb, J. B. "Buddhist Emptiness and the Christian God." *JAAR*, 45 (1977) 11–25.

Commemoration Volume. Poona: Oriental Book Agency, 1937.

Comstock, W. R. "Theology after the 'Death of God.' A Survey of Recent Trends in Religious Thought." *Cross Currents*, 16 (1966).

Condon, K. "Word and Logos." *Irish Theological Quarterly*, 32 (1966).

Conze, E. *Buddhism. Its Essence and Development*. New York: Philosophical Library, 1951.

––––––. *Buddhist Texts through the Ages*. New York: Harper & Row, 1964.

––––––. *Buddhist Thought in India*. London: Allen & Unwin, 1962.

_____. "The Ontology of the Prajnaoaramita." *Philosophy East and West,* 3 (1953) 117–30.

Coomaraswamy, A. K. *Buddha and the Gospel of Buddhism.* London: Harrap, 1928; repr., Bombay, 1956.

_____. *The Essentials of Zen Buddhism.* New York: Dutton, 1962.

_____. *Hinduism and Buddhism.* New York: Philosophical Library, 1943.

_____. "Kha and Other Words Denominating 'Zero' in Connection with the Metaphysics of Space." *Bulletin of the School of Oriental Studies,* 7 (1933–1935).

_____. *Recollection, Indian and Platonic. On the One and Only Transmigrant.* Baltimore: American Oriental Society, 1944.

Coutourier, C. "Les religions, pierres d'attente ou d'achoppement." *Bulletin du Cercle St. Jean Baptiste,* 3 (1963).

Cox, H. *The Secular City.* London: SCM, 1965.

Crespi, F. "Crisi del sacro, irreligione, ateismo." *Rivista di Sociologia,* 3 (1965).

Cross, F. M., Jr. "Yahweh and the God of the Patriarchs." *Harvard Theological Review,* 55 (1961) 225–59.

Cullmann, O. *Heil als Geschichte.* Tübingen: Mohr, 1956.

Cultural Heritage of India, vol. 1. Calcutta: Ramakrishna Mission, Institute of Culture, 1958.

Cuttat, J. A. "Buddhische und christliche Innerlichkeit in Guardinis Schau." *Interpretation der Welt.*

_____. "Fait bouddhique et fait chrétien selon l'oeuvre du Père de Lubac." *Mélanges Henri de Lubac.*

Dahlman, J. *Condemnat a creure.* Barcelona: Edicions 62, 1977.

_____. *Nirvana. Eine Studie zur Vorgeschichte des Buddhismus.* Berlin: F. L. Dames, 1896.

Daniélou, J. *Le mystère du salut des nations.* Paris: Seuil, 1948.

_____. *Platonisme et théologie mystique. Essai sur la doctrine spirituelle de Saint Grégoire de Nysse.* Paris: Aubier, 1944; 2nd ed., 1954.

D'Arcy, M. C. *The Meeting of Love and Knowledge.* London: Allen & Unwin, 1958.

Dasgupta, S. *Development of Moral Philosophy in India.* Bombay: Oriental Longmans, 1961.

_____. *A History of Indian Philosophy.* England: Cambridge University Press, 1952–1955.

_____. *An Introduction to Tantric Buddhism.* University of Calcutta, 1957.

_____. "The Philosophy of Lankavatara." *B. C. Law's Buddhist Studies,* pp. 859–76.

Datta, D. M. "Identity, Contradiction, and Excluded Middle." *Phil. Quarterly,* 31 (1958–1959) 231–41.

David-Neel, A. *Le Bouddhisme, ses doctrines et ses méthodes.* Paris: Plon, 2nd ed., 1959.

De Jong, J. "Le problème de l'Absolu dans l'Ecole Madhyamika." *Revue Philosophique,* 140 (1950) 322–27.

De Kretser, Bryan. *Man in Buddhism and Christianity.* Calcutta, 1954.

Della Casa. *Il Giainismo.* Turin: Boringhieri, 1962.

De Silva, L. "The Problem of the Self—The Christian Solution in Relation to Buddhist Thought." *Church and Society* (1965) 13–19.

Dewart, L. *The Foundation of Belief.* New York: Herder & Herder, 1969.

_____ . *The Future of Belief: Theism in a World Come of Age.* New York: Herder & Herder, 1966.

Dewick, E. C. *The Christian Attitude to Other Religions.* England: Cambridge University Press, 1953.

Dhammapada (part of the *khuddaka-nikāya* of the *Sutta-Piṭaka*). Engl. trans., S. Radhakrishnan, London, 3rd ed., 1968; also, Narada Thera, London (Wisdom of the East Series), 1954; also, C. A. F. Rhys Davids, London (Sacred Books of the Buddhists), 1931.

Dhamma-saṅgani (part of *Abhidhamma-Piṭaka*). Engl. trans., C. A. F. Rhys Davids, *A Buddhist Manual of Psychological Ethics,* London: Pali Text Society Translations, 1900; repr. 1923.

Diels, H. *Fragmente der Vorsokratiker,* Berlin: Weidmann, 1951.

Dīgha-nikāka (of the *Sutta-Piṭaka*). Engl. trans., T. W. Rhys Davids and C. A. F. Rhys Davids, *Dialogues of the Buddha,* 3 vols., London (Sacred Books of the Buddhists), 1899–1923; repr. 1956–1966.

Dionysius the Areopagite. *Opera,* Migne PG, vol. 3–4.

Dölger, F. J. "Das heilige Schweigen und andere Rücksicht auf den heiligen Raum der Kirche." *Antike und Christentum,* 5 (1936) 47ff.

Dubarle, A. M. "La signification du nom de Yahweh." *Revue des Sciences Philosophiques et Théologiques* (1951).

Duchesne-Guillemin, J. *Zoroastre.* Paris: G. P. Maisonneuve, 1948.

Dutt, N. *Aspects of Mahayana Buddhism and its Relation to Hinayana.* London: Luzac, 1930.

Dutt, S. *Early Buddhist Monachism.* Bombay/Calcutta/London: Asia Publishing House, 1960.

Dvādaśamukhaśāstra (by Nagarjuna and an anonymous author). Engl. trans., Aiyaswami Sastri, *Visvabharati Annals,* 6 (1954) 165–231.

Ebert, H. "Der Mensch als Weg zu Gott. Selbstverständnis des Menschen und Gotteserkenntnis." *Hochland,* 57 (April 1965).

_____ . "Der Gott der Philosophen und der Vater Jesu Christi. Seinsverständnis und Gotteslehre." *Hochland,* 58 (Aug. 1966) 481–500.

Ebner, F. *Schriften,* vol. 1: *Fragmente, Aufsätze, Aphorismen. Zu einer Pneumatologie des Wortes.* Munich: Kösel, 1963.

Eckhart, M. *Deutsche Predigten,* critical ed. in *Deutsche Werke.* Stuttgart: Kohlhammer.

_____ . *Die lateinische Werke.* Stuttgart: Kohlhammer, 1936–

Edgerton, F. "Did the Buddha Have a System of Metaphysics?" *Journal of the American Oriental Society,* 79 (1952) 81–85.

_____ . "Jnana and Vijnana." *Festschrift Moriz Winternitz,* pp. 217–20.

Edmunds, A. J. *Buddhist and Christian Gospels Now First Compared from the Originals,* 2 vols. Philadelphia, 1908–1909.

Eichrodt, W. *Theologie des Alten Testaments.* Stuttgart: Klotz, Göttingen: Vandenhoeck & Ruprecht, 1959.

Eilade, M. "Images et symboles." *Essais sur le symbolisme magico-religieux.* Paris: Gallimard, 1952.

_____ . "Methodological Remarks on the Study of Religious Symbolism." *The History of Religions,* pp. 86–108.

_____ . *Mito e realtà.* Turin: Borla, 1966.

_____ . *Le mythe de l'éternel retour.* Paris: Gallimard, 1949. Engl. trans., *The Myth of the Eternal Return.* London: Routledge & Kegan Paul, 1955.

_____ . *La nostalgia delle origini, storia e significato nella religione.* Brescia: Morcelliana, 1972.

_____ . *Patterns in Comparative Religion.* London: Sheed & Ward, 1958.

_____ . *Il sacro e il profano.* Turin: Boringhieri, 2nd ed., 1973.

_____ . "Les Sept Pas du Bouddha." *Pro Regno, Pro Sanctuario.*

_____ . "Structure et fonction du mythe cosmogonique." *Naissance du Monde.*

Eliot, C. *Hinduism and Buddhism,* 3 vols. London: Arnold, 2nd ed., 1954.

Essays in East-West Philosophy. Honolulu: C. A. Moore, 1951.

Evdokimov, P. "Phénomenologie de l'athéisme." *Contacts,* 16, 47 (1964).

Faber, G. "Die Religionsgeschichte und das Problem einer gegenseitigen Beeinflussung buddhistischer und neutestamentlicher Erzählungen." *Der Geisteskampf der Gegenwart* (1914) 260–62.

Fabro, C. *L'ateismo moderno.* Rome: Studium, 1969.

_____ . *Introduzione all'ateismo contemporaneo.* Rome: Studium, 1964.

_____ . *La nozione metafisica di partecipazione secondo S. Tommasso d'Aquino.* Milan: Vita e Pensiero, 1939.

Farmer, H. *Revelation and Religion.* New York: Harper, 1954.

Fatone, V. *El Nihilismo Buddhista.* La Plata: Biblioteca de Humanidades, 1941.

Fernando, A. "The Four Noble Truths and the Christian." *Logos,* 6 (1965).

Ferrarotti, F. *Studi sulla produzione sociale del sacro,* vol. 1: *Forme del sacro in epoca di crisi.* Naples: Liguori, 1978.

Festschrift Moriz Winternitz. Leipzig, 1933.

Festugière, A. J. *L'idéal religieux des Grecs et l'Evangile.* Paris: Gabalda, 1932.

Filliozat, J.-L. *L'Inde classique,* vol. 2. Paris: Imprimerie Nationale, 1953.

Fontinell, E. "Reflection on Faith and Metaphysics." *Cross Currents,* 16 (1966) 15–40.

_____ . *Self, God, and Immortality.* Philadelphia: Temple University Press, 1986.

Foucher, A. *La vie du Bouddha d'après les textes et les monuments de l'Inde.* Paris: Payot, 1949.

Fox, D. A. *Buddhism, Christianity, and the Future of Man.* Philadelphia. Westminster, 1972.

Frauwallner, E. *Geschichte der indischen Philosophie.* Salzburg: O. Müller, 1953.

_____ . *Die Philosophie des Buddhismus,* 2 vols. Berlin: Akademie Verlag, 1956.

Freydank, B. *Buddha und Christus. Eine buddhistische Apologetik.* Leipzig, 1907.

_____ . *Kleiner buddhistischer Katechismus.* Leipzig: Buddhistische Missionsverlag, 1904.

Friedmann, *The Problematic Rebel.* New York: Random House, 1963.

Fries, H., ed. *Handbuch theologischer Grundbegriffe.* Munich: Kösel, 1962.

Fromm, E. *Man for Himself.* New York: Rinehart, 1947.

Fung, P. F., and G. D. *The Sutra of the Sixth Patriarch on the Pristine Orthodox Dharma.* San Francisco: Buddha's Universal Church, 1964.

Fung Yu Lang. *History of Chinese Philosophy.* Princeton University Press, 1953.

_____ . *A Short History of Chinese Philosophy.* New York: Columbia University Press, 1960.

Gadamer, H. G., ed. *Um die Begriffswelt der Vorsokratiker.* Darmstadt: Wissenschaftliche Buchgesellschaft, 1968.

Garaudy, *Dieu est mort. Etude sur Hegel.* Paris: PUF, 1962.

Garbe, "Contributions of Buddhism to Christianity." *Monist* (1912) 509–63.

———. "Postscript on Buddhism and Christianity." *Monist* (1912) 478.

———. "Was ist im Christentum buddhistischer Herkunft?" *Deutsche Rundschau* (1910) 73–86.

Gardet, L. *Expériences mystiques en terres non chrétiennes.* Paris: Alsatia, 1953.

Geffre, C. "Senso e non-senso di una teologia non-metafisica." *Concilium,* 8 (1972) 116–30.

Getty, A. *The Gods of Northern Buddhism.* Tokyo: C. Tuttle, 1962.

Giamblico, *Vita pitagorica.* Bari: Laterza, 1973.

Gilson, E. "L'Etre et Dieu." *Revue Thomiste,* 62 (1962).

———. *La theologié mystique de Saint Bernard.* Paris: J. Vrin, 1947.

Girardi, G., ed., *L'ateismo contemporaneo,* 4 vols. Turin: SEI, 1967–1970.

Glasenapp. H., von. *Brahma und Buddha. Die Religionen Indiens in ihrer geschichtlichen Entwicklung.* Berlin: Deutsche Buchgemeinschaft, 1962.

———. *Von Buddha zu Gandhi. Aufsätze zur Geschichte der Religionen Indiens.* Wiesbaden: O. Harrassowitz, 1962.

———. "Buddhism in the Kathaka Upanishad." *Von Buddha zu Gandhi.*

———. *Buddhismus und Gottesidee. Die buddhistischen Lehren von den überweltlichen Wesen und Mächten und ihre religionsgeschichtlichen Parallelen.* Mainz: Abhandlungen d. Akad. der Wiss. und der Lit., 1954.

———. *Entwicklungsstufen des indischen Denkens.* Halle: Max Niemeyer, 1940.

———. "Zur Geschichte der buddhistischen Darmatheorie." *Von Buddha zu Gandhi.*

———. "Hat Buddha ein metaphysisches System gelehrt?" *Von Buddha zu Gandhi.*

———. *Die nichtchristlichen Religionen.* Frankfurt: Fischer, 1957.

———. "Parallels and Contrasts in Indian and Western Metaphysics." *Philosophy East and West,* 3 (1953) 223–32.

———. *Unsterblichkeit und Erlösung in den indischen Religionen.* Halle: Niemeyer, 1938.

———. *Vedanta und Buddhismus.* Wiesbaden, 1950.

———. *Die Weisheit des Buddha.* Baden-Baden: H. Bühler, 1946.

Goddard, D. *Was Jesus Influenced by Buddhism?* Thetford, Vt., 1927.

———. *A Buddhist Bible.* London: Harrap, 1956.

Gogarten, G. *Verhängnis und Hoffnung der Neuzeit, Die Säkularisierung als theologisches Problem.* Stuttgart, 1963.

Gonda, J. *Change and Continuity in Indian Tradition.* New York: Humanities Press, 1966.

———. *Notes on Brahman.* Utrecht: J. L. Beyers, 1950.

———. *Some Observations on the Relation between "Gods" and "Powers" in the Veda apropos of the Phrase sunuh sahasah.* The Hague: Mouton, 1957.

Govinda, A. *Foundation of Tibetan Mysticism.* New York: Dutton, 1960.

———. *The Psychological Attitude of Early Buddhist Philosophy and its Systematic Representation according to Abbidhama Tradition.* London: Rider, 1961.

Graham. *Zen Catholicism—A Suggestion,* London: Collins, 1964.

Gregory of Nazianzen. *Opera,* Migne PG, vol. 35–38.

Gregory of Nyssa. *Opera,* Migne PG, vol. 44–46.

Grimm, G. *Buddha und Christus.* Leipzig, 1928.

———. "Christian Mysticism in the Light of the Buddha's Doctrine." *B.C. Law Buddhist Studies,* 26ff.

Gross, J. *La divinisation du chrétien d'après les Pères grecs.* Paris: Thovars, 1938.

Guardini, R. "Buddhistische und christliche Innerlichkeit in Guardinis Schau." *Interpretation der Welt.*

———. *Gläubiges Dasein.* Würzburg: Werkbund, 1951.

———. *Der Herr.* Würzburg: Werkbund, 1937.

———. *The Lord.* Cleveland: World Publishing, 1969.

Gulyga, A. W. "Der 'Atheismusstreit' und der streitbere Atheismus in den letzten Jahrzehnten des 18. Jahrhunderts in Deutschland." Buhr, *Wissen und Gewissen.*

Günther, H., von. *Das Seelenproblem im älteren Buddhismus.* Zurich: Rascher, 1949.

Gupte, R. S., *Iconography of the Hindus, Buddhists and Jains.* Bombay, D. B. Taraporevala Sons, 1972.

Haas, W. *The Destiny of the Mind.* London: Faber & Faber, 1956.

Habermas, J. *Knowledge and Human Interests.* Boston: Beacon Press. 1971.

Hadewijch of Anvers. *Hadewijch d'Anvers,* French trans., J. B. P. Paris: Seuil.

———. *Cinque Visioni.* Ital. trans., R. Guarnieri. Brescia: Morcelliana, 1947.

Hamilton, W. *The Christian Man.* Philadelphia: Westminster, 1956.

———. "The Death of God." *Playboy* (1966).

———. *The Modern Reader's Guide to John.* New York: Association Press, 1959.

———. *The Modern Reader's Guide to Mark.* New York: Association Press, 1959.

———. *The Modern Reader's Guide to Matthew and Luke.* New York: Association Press, 1959.

———, and Altizer, T. J. J. *Radical Theology and the Death of God.* Indianapolis: Bobbs-Merrill, 1960.

Hanayama, S. *Bibliography on Buddhism.* Tokyo: Hokuseido Press, 1961.

Harms. "Five Basic Types of Theistic Words in the Religion of Man." *Numen,* 13 (1966) 205-40.

Harṣacarita of Bana. Engl. trans., E. B. Cowell and F. W. Thomas. London: Cambridge University Press, 1897.

Hartel, H. "Buddhismus." *Die Religionen in Geschichte und Gegenwart.* Tübingen: Mohr, 1957, vol. 1, col. 1474-84.

Hartshorne, C. *Anselm's Discovery.* Lasalle, Ill.: Open Court, 1965.

Hauer, J. W. *Das Laṅkāvatāra-Sūtra und das Sankhya.* Stuttgart: Kohlhammer, 1927.

Hausherr, I. *La direction spirituelle en Orient autrefois.* Rome: Orientalia Christiana, 1955.

———. "Ignorance infinie." *Orientalia christiana periodica,* 2 (1936) 351-62.

Hegel, G. W. F. *Sämtliche Werke* (Jubiläumsausgabe). Stuttgart: Frommann, 1927.

Heidegger, M. *Identität und Differenz.* Pfüllingen: Neske, 1957.

———. *Holzwege.* Frankfurt: Klostermann, 1963.

———. *Was ist Metaphysik?* Frankfurt: Klostermann, 5th ed., 1949.

Heiler, F. *Die buddhistische Versenkung.* Munich: E. Reinhardt, 1922.

———. *Erscheinungsformen und Wesen der Religion.* Stuttgart: Kohlhammer, 1961.

———. *Die Religionen der Menscheit in Vergangenheit und Gegenwart.* Stuttgart: Reclam-Verlag, 2nd ed., 1962.

Heimann, B. "The Significance of Negation in Hindu Philosophical Thought." *B. C. Law Festschrift.*

Heinrichs, M. *Katholische Theologie und asiatisches Denken.* Mainz: Grünewald, 1963.

Held, H. L. *Deutsche Bibliographie des Buddhismus.* Munich/Leipzig, 1916.

Henning, W. B. *Zoroaster, Politician or Witch-Doctor?* London: Oxford University Press, 1951.

Henry, A. M. *Esquisse d'une théologie de la mission.* Paris: Cerf, 1959.

Heraclitus. *Frammenti.* Florence: La Nuova Italia, 1978.

———. *I frammenti e le testimonianze.* Milan: Mondadori, 1980.

———. *Testimonianze e imitazioni.* Florence: La Nuova Italia, 1972.

Hessel, E. "Christus, Buddha, und die Götter." *Evangelische Theologie* (1949) 43–48.

Hilliard, F. H. *The Buddha, the Prophet, and the Christ.* New York/London, 1956.

Hiriyanna, M. *Outlines of Indian Philosophy.* London: Allen & Unwin, 1956.

———. "What is Ananyatvam?" *Festschrift M. Winternitz,* pp. 221–24.

Hisimatsu, S. "The Characteristic of Oriental Nothingness." *Philosophical Studies of Japan,* vol. 2 (1960).

The History of Religions: Essays in Methodology. University of Chicago Press, 1959.

Hobogirin. *Dictionnaire encyclopédique du Bouddhisme d'après les sources chinoise et japonaise.* Paris, 1929–1937.

Hopkins, E. Washburn. *The Religions of India.* Boston: Ginn, 1895.

Horner, I. B. *Gotama the Buddha.* London: Cassel, 1948.

———. *The Middle Length Sayings,* 3 vols. London: Luzac, 1954–1959.

India Antiqua, Leiden: Brill, 1947.

Interpretation der Welt, Romano Guardini Festschrift. Würzburg: Echter, 1965.

Irenaeus, St. *Opera,* Migne PG, vol. 7.

Itivuttaka (part of the *khuddaka-nikāya* of the *Sutta-Piṭaka*). Engl. trans., F. L. Woodward. London (Sacred Books of the Buddhists), 1935.

Jadeswaranda, S. "A Christian Misunderstands Buddhism." *The Maha-Bodhi* (1942).

Jaeger, W. *Paideia: Die Formung des griechischen Menschen.* Berlin/Leipzig: De Gruyter, 1947.

———. *Die Theologie der frühen griechischen Denker.* Stuttgart: Kohlhammer, 1953.

Jasink, B. *Die Mystik des Buddhismus.* Leipzig: M. Altmann, 1922.

Jaspers, K. *Ursprung und Ziel der Geschichte.* Madrid: Revista de Occidente, 1968.

Jātaka (part of the *khuddaka-nikāya* of the *Sutta-Piṭaka*). Engl. trans., T. W. Rhys Davids, *Buddhist Birth Stories.* London, 1880. Also, E. B. Cowell et al., *The Jataka or Stories of the Buddha's Former Births,* 6 vols. England: Cambridge University Press, 1895–1907; repr. 1969.

Jayatilleke, K. N. *Early Buddhist Theory of Knowledge.* London: Allen & Unwin, 1963.

———. "The Logic of Four Alternatives." *Philosophy East and West,* 17 (1967) 69–83.

Jeanniere, A. "Atheism Today." *Cross Currents,* 16 (1966).

Jennings, J. G. *The Vedantic Buddhism of the Buddha.* London: Oxford University Press, 1948.

Jerome, St. *Opera.* Migne PL, vol. 22–30.

John of the Cross. *Obras Completas.* Burgos: El Monte Carmelo, 1959.

Jonas, H. *The Gnostic Religion. The Message of the Alien God and the Beginnings of Christianity.* Boston: Beacon, 2nd ed., 1967.

Journet, C. *The Dark Knowledge of God.* London: Sheed & Ward, 1948.

Jung, C. G. *Erinnerungen, Träume, Gedanken von C. G. Jung.* A. Jaffé, ed. Olten: Walter, 1972.

Justin, St. *Opera.* Migne PG, vol. 6.

Kaliba, C. *Die Welt als Gleichnis des dreieinigen Gottes. Entwurf zu einer trinitarischen Ontologie.* Salzburg: O. Müller, 1952.

Kapleau, P. *The Three Pillars of Zen: Teaching, Practice, and Enlightenment.* Tokyo: J. Weatherhill, 1965.

Kappstein, T. *Buddhismus und Christentum. Religionsgeschichtliche Parallelen,* Berlin, 1906.

Karatalaratna. Engl. trans. from Chinese and Tibetan, F. W. Thomas, "Hand Treatise," *JRAS* (1918) 264ff.

Karrer, O. *Das Religiöse in der Menschheit und das Christentum.* Freiburg: Herder, 1956.

Kasawara, K. *Dharma Samgraha.* Oxford: Clarendon Press, 1885.

Kathavatthu (of the *Abhidhamma-Piṭaka*). Engl. trans., S. Z. Aung and C. A. F. Rhys Davids, *Points of Controversy,* 2 vols. London: Pali Text Society Translations, 1915.

Kaufmann, Y. *The Religion of Israel.* University of Chicago Press, 1960.

Kawada, K. "Pratyatmadharmata—Methodischer Transzendentalismus." *Journal of Indian and Buddhist Studies,* 14 (Dec. 1965).

Keith, A. B. *Buddhist Philosophy in India and Ceylon.* Oxford: Clarendon Press, 1923.

Kelber, W. *Die Logos Lehre. Von Heraklit bis Origene.* Stuttgart: Uracchaus, 1958.

Kellner, E., ed. *Christentum und Marxismus heute.* Vienna: Europa Verlag, 1966.

Kerény, K. *Apollon und Niobe.* Vienna: Langen-Müller, 1952.

———. *La religion antique.* Geneva: Georg, 1957.

———. "Theos e mythos." Castelli, *Problema della demitizzazione,"* pp. 35–44.

King, W. L. *Buddhism and Christianity. Some Bridges of Understanding.* Philadelphia, 1962.

Kirfel, W. *Symbolik des Buddhismus.* Stuttgart: A. Hiersemann, 1959.

Kirk, G. S., and Raven, J. G. *The Presocratic Philosophers.* England: Cambridge University Press.

Kraemer, H. *The Christian Message in a Non-Christian World.* New York: Harper, 1938.

———. *Religion and the Christian Faith.* Philadelphia: Westminster, 1956.

Kraft, M. *Clavis Patrum Apostolicorum.* Munich: Kösel, 1964.

Kraus, H. J. *Gottesdienst in Israel.* Munich: Kaiser, 1954.

Krempel, A. *La doctrine de la relation chez Saint Thomas.* Paris: Vrin, 1952.

Kretschmar, G. *Studien zur frühchristlichen Trinitätstheologie.* Tübingen: Mohr, 1956.

Krishna, D. "Three Conceptions of Indian Philosophy." *Philosophy East and West,* 15 (1965).

Kristensen, W. B. *The Meaning of Religion.* The Hague: Nijhoff, 1960.

Küng, H. *Existiert Gott? Antwort auf die Gottesfrage der Neuzeit.* Munich/Zurich: Piper, 1978.

Kunst, A. "The Concept of the Principle of the Excluded Middle in Buddhism." *Rocznik Orientalistyczny,* 21 (1957) 141–47.

Lacroix, J. "Sens et valeur de l'athéisme actuel." *Monde moderne et sens de Dieu,* Semaine des Intellectuels Catholiques. Paris: P. Horey, 1954.

Lalou, L., and Przyluski, J. *Bibliographie bouddhique.* Paris, 1928.

Lambert, G. "Que signifie le nom divin YHWH?" *Nouvelle Revue Théologique,* 74 (1952) 897ff.

Lamotte, E. "Le Bouddhisme des laïcs." *Studies in Indology,* pp. 73–90.

———. *Histoire du Bouddhisme indien de l'origine à l'ère Śaka.* Louvain: Publications Universitaires, 1958.

———. *Lo spirito del Buddhismo antico.* Venice: Istituto per la collaborazione culturale, 1960.

Lánkāvatāra-sūtra. Engl. trans., D. T. Suzuki, *Lankavatara. A Mahayana Text.* London: Routledge, 1932.

La Vallée-Poussin, L., de. *Bouddhisme. Etudes et matériaux. Théorie des douze causes.* Gand: E. van Goethem, 1916.

———. *Bouddhisme. Opinions sur l'histoire de la dogmatique.* Paris: Beauchesne, 1909.

———. "Une dernière note sur le Nirvana." *Mélanges Linossier,* vol. 2 (1932).

———. "Les deux Nirvana d'après la Vibasha." *Acad. de Belgique Bulletin* (Dec. 1929).

———. *Le dogme et la philosophie du Bouddhisme.* Paris, 1930.

———. "Faith and Reason in Buddhism." *Proceedings of the Third International Congress for the History of Religions,* part 1, Oxford, pp. 32–43.

———. "The Madhyamakas and Tathata." *IHQ,* 9 (1933) 30–31.

———. "Musila et Narada, le chemin du Nirvana." *Mélanges chinoises et bouddhiques,* Brussels.

———. *Nirvana.* Paris: Beauchesne, 1925.

———. "Le Nirvana d'après Aryadeva." *Mélanges chinoises et bouddhiques,* 1 (1932).

———. "Remarques sur le Nirvana." *Studia Cattolica,* 1 (1924).

———. *The Way to Nirvana.* England: Cambridge University Press, 1917.

Law, B. C. Buddhist Studies. Calcutta: Thacker, 1931.

Law, B. C. Festschrift. Poona, 1946.

Law, B. C. "Aspects of Nirvana," *Indian Culture,* Calcutta, vol. 2, pp. 327ff.

———. *Buddhistic Studies.* Calcutta: Thacker-Sprink, 1931.

———. "Formulation of the Pratītyasamutpāda." *Journal of the Royal Society* (1937).

———. "Nirvana." *Cultural Heritage of India.*

Leeuw, G., van der. *Phänomenologie der Religion.* Tübingen: Mohr, 1956.

Lemarie, J. *La manifestation du Seigneur.* Paris: Cerf, 1957.

Le Saux, H. *La rencontre de l'hindouisme et du christianisme.* Paris: Seuil, 1966.

———. *Sagesse hindoue, mystique chrétienne.* Paris: Centurion, 1965.

Levi, S. *La doctrine du sacrifice dans les Brâhmanas.* Paris: Presses Universitaire de France, 1966.

———. "Maitrya, Le consolateur." *Mélanges Linossier,* vol. 2 (Paris, 1932).

Levy, P. *Amida.* Paris: Seuil, 1955.

———. *Aspects du Bouddhisme.* Paris: Seuil, 1959.

Lillia, A. *Buddhism and Christendom, or Jesu the Essene.* London, 1887.

Ling, T. O. *Buddhism and the Mythology of Evil.* London: Allen & Unwin, 1962.

Loen, A. E. *Säkularisation. Von der wahren Voraussetzung und angeblichen Gottlosigkeit der Wissenschaft.* Munich: Kaiser, 1965.

Loosky, N. "Christian versus Buddhist Mysticism." *Personalist* (1936), 256–77.

Lossky, V. *Théologie négative et connaissance de Dieu chez Maître Eckhart.* Paris: Vrin, 1960.

Lotz, J. B. "Geschichtlichkeit und Tradition," Castelli, *Ermeneutica e Tradizione,* pp. 289–300.

_____ . "Gott." Fries, *Handbuch.*

_____ . "Metaphysische und religiöse Erfahrung." *Metafisica ed esperienza religiosa (Archivio di Filosofia* [1961] 79–121).

_____ . "Mythos, Logos, Mysterion." Castelli, *Problema della demitizzazione,* pp. 117–28.

Lubac, H., de. *Aspects du Bouddhisme.* Paris: Seuil, 1950.

_____ . "La charité bouddhique." *Bulletin de la Faculté Catholique de Lyon* (May-June 1950) 14–44.

_____ . *Le fondement théologique des missions.* Paris: Seuil, 1946.

_____ . *Meditation sur l'Eglise.* Paris: Aubier, 1953.

_____ . *Le mystère du surnaturel.* Paris: Aubier, 1965.

_____ . *La rencontre du Bouddhisme et de l'Occident.* Paris: Aubier, 1952.

Lübbe, H. *Säkularisierung.* Freiburg: K. Alber, 1965.

Luttge, W. *Christentum und Buddhismus.* Göttingen, 1916.

Madhyamakaratnapradīna (by Bhāvaviveka). Tibetan trans. analyzed by S. Schayer, "Notes and Queries on Buddhism," *RO,* 11 (1935) 206–13.

Madhyamakāyatāra (by Candrakirti). French trans., L. de la Vallée-Poussin, *Muséon,* 7 (1907) 249–307; 10 (1910) 271–358; 11 (1911) 236–328.

Mahāprajñāpāramitāśāstra (anonymous). French trans., E. Lamotte, *Le traité de la Grande Vertu de Sagesse,* 2 vols., Louvain, Bureaux du Muséon, 1944–1949; repr. 1966–1969.

Mahāvastu. Engl. trans., J. J. Jones, *Mahavastu Translated from the Buddhist Sanscrit,* London (Sacred Books of the Buddhists), 1949–1957.

Mahāyānasamgraha (by Asaṅga). French trans., E. Lamotte, *La Somme du Grand Vehicule d'Asanga,* 4 vols., Louvain, Bureaux du Muséon, 1938–1939.

Mahāyānavlmśaka (by Nagarjuna and an anonymous author). Engl. trans., S. Yamaguchi, "Nagarjuna's Mahūyāna-Vimśaka," *EB,* 4 (1926) 56–72, 169–76. Also, V. Bhattacharyya, *Visvabharati Studies,* vol. 1, Calcutta, 1931.

Maitreyasamiti (anonymous). Germ. trans., Tokharian, *Maitreyasamiti, das Zukunftideal der Buddhisten,* Strasbourg, 1919.

Majjhima-nikāya (of the *Sutta-Piṭaka*). Engl. trans., R. Chalmers, *Further Dialogues of the Buddha,* 2 vols., Oxford (Sacred Books of the Buddhists), 1926–1927.

Malalasekera, G. P. *Dictionary of Pali Proper Names,* 2 vols. London: J. Murray, 1937–1938.

_____ , ed. *Encyclopedia of Buddhism.* Colombo: Government of Ceylon, 1961.

Mallman, M. T., de. *Introduction à l'étude d'Avalokitećvara.* Paris: Civilisation du Sud, 1948.

March, A. C. *A Buddhist Bibliography.* London, 1935.

Margiaria, A. *La concezione buddhista del cosmo.* Turin: SEI, 1968.

Mariano, R. *Cristo e Buddha e altri Iddii dell'Oriente.* Florence, 1900.

Maritain, J. *La signification de l'athéisme contemporain.* Paris: Desclée de Brouwer, 1949.

Mascall, E. L. *The Secularisation of Christianity.* London: Darton, Longman & Todd, 1965.

Masson-Oursel, P. "Foi bouddique et foi chrétienne." Congrès d'Histoire du Christianisme. *Jubilé Alfred Loisy, Annal. d'Histoire du Christianisme,* vol. 3, Paris, 1928.

Masuda, H. "Some Reflections on the Buddhist Conception of Voidness *(Sunyatā)* in the Prajñā-pāramita-sūtra and in Nāgārjuna." *Religion East and West* 35 (1963).

Masure, E. *Devant les religions non chrétiennes.* Lille: Ed. Catholicité, 1945.

Masutani, Fumio. *A Comparative Study of Buddhism and Christianity.* Tokyo: CIIB Press, 1959.

Maximo, St. *Opera.* Migne PG, vol. 90–91.

Meland, B. E. *The Secularization of Modern Cultures.* New York: Oxford University Press, 1963.

Mélanges Henri de Lubac. Paris: Aubier, 1964.

Mensching, G. *Die Bedeutung des Leidens im Buddhismus und im Christentum.* Giessen, 1930.

––––––. *Buddha und Christus.* Bonn, 1952.

––––––. *Buddhistische Geisteswelt. Von historischen Buddha zum Lamaismus.* Darmstadt: Holle, 1955.

––––––. *Das Christentum im Kreis der Weltreligionen.* 1928.

––––––. Das heilige Schweigen. Giessen: Topelmann, 1926.

––––––. *Tod und Leben im Buddhismus und im Christentum.* Giessen, 1931.

Merkel, R. F. "Buddhismus und Neues Testament." *Jahrb. fur die Evang. Luth. Landeskirche Bayerns* (1915) 36–49.

Merton, T. *The Way of Chuang Tzu.* New York: New Directions, 1965.

Messina, G. *Cristianesimo, Buddhismo, Manicheismo.* Rome: N. Ruffolo, 1947.

Metz, J. B. "L'incredulità come problema teologico." *Concilium* (Sept. 1965) 72–92.

Milloue, L., de. *Quelques resemblances entre le Bouddhisme et le Christianisme.* Paris, 1908.

Miyamoto, S. *The Fundamental Truth of Buddhism.* Tokyo: Sanyosha, 1957.

––––––. "Nirvana and the Limit of Questioning." *Indotetsugakuto-Bukkyo-no-Shomondai.* Tokyo: Iwanani Shoten, 1951, pp. 503–28.

––––––. "A Re-Appraisal of Pratītya-Samutāda." *Studies in Indology,* pp. 152–64.

Monier-Williams, M. *Buddhism. In Connection with Brahmanism and Hinduism and its Contrast with Christianity.* Varanasi: Chowkhamba, 1964.

––––––. *Buddhism and its Connection with Brahmanism and Hinduism and its Contrast with Christianity.* London: J. Murray, 1889.

Mookerjee, S. *The Buddhist Philosophy of Universal Flux.* University of Calcutta, 1935.

Moore, C. A. "The Meaning of Duhkha." *Atti del XIII Congresso Internazionale di Filosofia.* Florence: Sansoni, 1960.

––––––, and Radhakrishnan, S. *A Source Book in Indian Philosophy.* Princeton University Press, 1957.

Moreno, M. "Mistica mussulmana e mistica indiana." *Annali Lateranensi,* 10 (1946) 156–61.

More-Pontgibaud. *Du fini a l'infini. Introduction à l'étude de la connaissance de Dieu.* Paris: Aubier, 1957.

Morot-Sir, E. *La pensée négative.* Paris: Aubier, 1947.

Mulamadhyamakakārikās. Engl. trans., chap. 1–25, T. Stcherbatsky, *The Concept of Buddhist Nirvana.* Petersburg, Academy of Sciences of the U.S.S.R., 1927.

Mulamadyamakakārikās (by Nagarjuna) and *Prasannapadā.* Sanskrit text, with commentary by Candrakirti, L. de la Vallée-Poussin, Petersburg, 1930–1931; repr. 1970.

Müller, E. *Existenzphilosophie im geistigen Leben der Gegenwart*. Heidelberg: Kehrle, 2nd ed., 1958.

Müller, F. M. *Lecture on Buddhist Nihilism*. New York: Asa K. Butts, 1869.

Munby, D. *The Idea of a Secular Society*. London: Oxford University Press, 1963.

Murthy, K. S. *Metaphysics, Man, and Freedom*. London: Asia Publishing House, 1960.

Murti, T. R. V. *The Central Philosophy of Buddhism. A Study of the Madhyamika System*. London: Allen & Unwin, 1955.

Mus, P. *Barabudur*. Hanoi: Imprimerie d'Extrème Orient, 1935.

Nagao, G. "The Silence of the Buddha and its Madhayamic Interpretation." *Studies in Indology*, pp. 137–51.

Nakamura, H. "The Influence of Voidness on Hetu-vidya Logic." Miyamoto, *Fundamental Truth*.

———. *The Ways of Thinking of Eastern Peoples*. Honolulu: East-West Center, 1966; rev. ed., University of Hawaii Press, 1971; repr. 1985.

Neill, S. *Christian Faith and Other Faiths*. London: Oxford University Press, 1961.

Neuner, J. *Christian Revelation and World Religions*. London: Burns & Oates, 1967.

Newbegin, L. *Honest Religion for Secular Man*. London: SCM, 1966.

Nicholas of Cusa. *De Deo Abscondito*. Hamburg: P. Wilbert, 1959.

Nichols, J. H. *History of Christianity 1650–1950. Secularization of the West*. New York: Ronald Press, 1956.

Nicolas, J. H. *Dieu comme inconnu. Essai d'une critique de la connaissance*. Paris: Desclée, 1966.

Nietzsche, F. *Opera*. M. Montinari and G. Colli, eds. Milan: Adelphi, 1968.

Nishida, K. *Intelligibility and the Philosophy of Nothingness*. Tokyo: Maruzen, 1958.

Nishitani, K. "Der Buddhismus und das Christentum." *Zeitschrift für Kultur und Geschichte Ostasiens*, 88 (1960) 5–31.

———. "On Sartre's Existentialism." *Psychologia* (June 1962).

Noce, A., del. *Il problema dell'atheismo. Il concetto di ateismo e la storia della filosofia come problema*. Bologna: Il Mulino, 1964.

Nola, A. M., di. "Buddha." *Enciclopedia delle Religioni*. Florence: Vallecchi, vol. 1, 1970, coll. 1232–78.

———. "Buddhismo." Ibid., coll. 1278–1311.

Northrop, F. S. C. *The Meaning of East and West*. New York: MacMillan, 1946.

Nyamatilona. Die Rede des Buddhas aus dem A. N. Übersetz, 5 vols. Munich.

Nyāyasūtras (by Gautama). Sanskrit text and Engl. trans., Satis Chandra Vidyabusana, *Nyaya Sutras of Gotama*, Allahabad (Sacred Books of the Hindus), 1913. Also, Ganganatha Jha, "The Nyaya of Gautama, with the Bhasya of Vatsyayana and the Vartika of Uddyotakara," *Indian Thought*, 4 (1912) and 11 (1919).

Obermiller, E., ed. *Materialen zur Kunde des Buddhismus*. Heidelberg, 1931–1932.

———. "Nirvana according to Tibetan Tradition." *Indian Historical Quarterly*, 10 (1934) 211–57.

———. "The Term Śūnyatā and its Different Interpretation Based Chiefly on Tibetan Sources." *Journal of Greater Indian Society*, 1 (1934) 105–17.

———. "A Study of the Twenty Aspects of Śūnyatā Based on Haribhadra's Abhisamayālamkārāloka and the Pañcavimsatisāhasrikā." *Indian Historical Quarterly*, 9 (1933) 170–87.

Ogletree, T. W. *The "Death of God" Controversy.* London: SCM, 1966.

Oldenberg, H. *Budda, sein Leben, seine Lehre, seine Gemeinde.* Munich, 13th ed., 1961.

———. "Der Buddhismus und die christliche Liebe." *Deutsche Rundschau,* 84, pp. 380–89.

———. *Die Lehre der Upanishaden und die Anfänge des Buddhismus.* Göttingen: Vandenhoeck & Ruprecht, 1923.

Olschki, L. "The Crib of Christ and the Bowl of Buddha." *Journal of the American Oriental Society,* 70 (1950) 161–64.

Oltramare, P. *La formule bouddhique de douze causes. Son sens originel et son interprétation théologique.* Geneva: Georg. 1909.

Omodeo Sale, M. *Venticinque secoli di Buddhismo.* Milan: Giunti-Martello, 1957.

Organ, T. W. "The Silence of the Buddha," *Philosophy East and West,* 4 (July 1954) 125–40.

Orsenigo, C. *Buddhismo e Cristianesimo.* Monza, 1908.

Ott, H. *Denken und Sein.* Zollikon: Evangelischer Verlag, 1959.

Otto, R. "Sakramentales Schweigen." *Die christliche Welt* (1920).

Otto, W. F. *Die Gestalt und das Sein.* Darmstadt: Wiss. Buchgesellschaft, 1974.

———. *Mythos und Welt.* Stuttgart: Klett, 1962.

———. *Sund und Urschuld.* Gotha: L. Klotz, 1929.

Pagliaro, A. "L'idealismo gathico." Rome, *Studia Indologica Internationalia,* 1 (1954).

———. "L'idealismo iranico." *Umanesimo e mondo precristiano.* Rome, 1959.

Pande, G. C. *Studies in the Origins of Buddhism.* University of Allahabad, 1957.

Pandeya, R. C. *The Logic of Catuskoti and Indescribability.* Banaras University.

Panikkar, R. "Advaita e bhakti." *Humanitas,* 20 (1965) 991–1001.

———. "Sur l'anthropologie du prochain." *Actes du VIII Congrès des Sociétés de Philosophie de Langue Francaise,* 1956, pp. 228–31.

———. "Das erste Bild des Buddha. Zur Einführung in den buddhistischen Apophatismus." *Antaios,* 6 (1965) 373–85.

———. "Che accade all'uomo quando muore?" *Bozze,* 80 (1980) 117–36.

———. "Colligite fragmenta; for an Integration of Reality." *From Alienation to At-oneness,* Proceedings of the Theology Institute of Villanova University, 1977.

———. "El Concepto de naturaleza." Madrid: *CSIC,* 2nd ed., 1972.

———. *Culto y secularisación.* Madrid: Marava, 1979.

———. "De Deo Abscondito." *Arbor,* 9 (1948) 1–26.

———. "L'eau et la mort." *Archivio de Filosofia* (1981) 481–502.

———. "Die existentielle Phänomenologie der Wahrheit." *Philosophisches Jahrbuch der Görresgesellschaft,* 64 (1956) 27–54.

———. "La foi, dimension constitutive de l'homme." Castelli, *Mito e Fede,* 17–44.

———. "Gedankenfreie Meditation oder seinserf ülte Gelassenheit?" In *Munen Mysō. Ungegenst ändliche Meditation,* a festschrift for Hugo M. Enomiya-Lassalle, S. J., on his 80th birthday.

———. "Have 'Religions' the Monopoly on Religion?" *Journal of Ecumenical Studies,* 11 (1974) 515–17.

———. *Intra-religious Dialogue.* New York: Paulist, 1979.

———. "F. H. Jacobi y la filosofia del sentimiento." *Sapientia,* 3 (1948) 23–59.

———. *Kerygma und Indien.* Hamburg: Reich, 1964.

———. *Kultmysterium in Hinduismus und Christentum. Ein Beitrag zur vergleichenden Religionstheologie.* Freiburg: Alber, 1964.

_____ . "La metafisica de los textos hindues sobre la creación." *Atlantida,* 1 (1963) 86–90.

_____ . *L'homme qui devient Dieux.* Paris: Aubier, 1970.

_____ . *Māyā et Apocalisse: L'incontro del Induismo e del Christianesimo.* Rome: Abete, 1966.

_____ . "La Misa como 'consecratio temporis.' " *Actas del V Congreso Eucaristico Nacional,* Zaragoza, 1961, pp. 75–93.

_____ . *Le Mystère du culte dans hindouisme et le christianisme.* Paris: du Cerf, 1970.

_____ . *Myth, Faith, and Hermeneutics.* New York: Paulist, 1979.

_____ . *Ontonomia de la Ciencia. Sobre el sentido de la Ciencia y sus relaciones con la Filosofia.* Madrid: Gredos, 1961.

_____ . "Pluralismus, Toleranz, und Christenheit." *Pluralismus, Toleranz, und Christenheit.* Munich: Abendländische Akademie, 1961, pp. 117–42.

_____ . "Relation of Christians to their non-Christian Surroundings." *Indian Ecclesiastical Studies,* 4 (1965).

_____ . *Religione e Religioni.* Brescia: Morcelliana, 1964.

_____ . "Rtatattva: A Preface to Hindu-Christian Theology," *Jeevadhara,* 49 (1979) 6–63.

_____ . "The Silence of the Word: Non dualistic polarities," *Crosscurrents,* 24 (1974) 154–7.

_____ . *La spiritualità indù.* Brescia: Morcelliana, 1975.

_____ . "La superación del humanismo." *Humanismo y cruz,* pp. 178–253.

_____ . "Technique et temps: La technochronie." Castelli, *Tecnica e casistica,* pp. 195–229.

_____ . *The Trinity and the Religious Experience of Man. Icon, Person, Mystery.* London: Darton, Longman & Todd, 1973.

_____ . *The Vedic Experience. Mantramanjan.* Berkeley/Los Angeles: University of California Press, 1977.

_____ . *Die vielen Götter und der eine Herr.* Freiburg: Barth, 1963.

Pannenberg, W. *Grundfragen systematischer Theologie.* "Die Aufnahme des philosophischen Gottesbegriffs als dogmatisches Problem für frühchristliche Theologie." Gottingen: Vändenhoeck & Ruprecht, 1971, pp. 296–346.

Papini, G. *Il diavolo.* Florence: Vallecchi, 16th ed., 1967.

Parente, P. *De Deo Uno et Trino.* Rome: Institutum Graphicum Tiberinum, 1938.

Pascal, B. *Pensieri, Opuscoli, Lettere.* Milan: Rusconi, 1978.

Pascual, C. *Guía sobrenatural de l'Espana.* Madrid: Al-Borak, 1976.

Pettazzoni, R. *Miti e Leggende,* 4 vols. Turin: UTET, 1948–1959.

Philip Hyatt, J. "Was Yahweh Originally a Creator Deity?" *Journal of Biblical Literature,* 86 (1967) 369–77.

Phillipidis, L. J. *Das Liebesprinzip im Buddhismus und Christentum.* Athens: Pyrsos, 1938.

_____ . *Religionsgeschichte als Heilsgeschichte in der Weltgeschichte, Mitteilung an die XI deutsche Jahrestagung für Religionsgeschichte.* Bonn, 1952.

Phillips, B. *The Essentials of Zen Buddhism — Selected from the Writings of Daisetz T. Suzuki.* New York: Dutton, 1962.

Piantelli, M. *Sankara e la rinascita del Brahmanesimo.* Fossano/Cuneo: Ed. Esperienze, 1974.

Pieper, J. *Glück und Kontemplation.* Munich: Kösel, 1957.

_____ . *The Silence of St. Thomas.* New York: Pantheon, 1957.

The Platform Scripture (by Hui-neng). Engl. trans., W. T. Chang. New York: St. John's University Press, 1963.

Plato. *Opere complete,* 9 vols. Bari: Laterza, 1971.

Plotinus. *Enneadi,* 3 vols. Bari: Laterza, 1973.

Prasannapada (by Candrakirti). *See Mūlamadhyamakakārikās.*

Prater, S. *Das Christentum und die ausserchristlichen Religionen.* Dresden, 1935.

Pro Regno, Pro Sanctuario, Festschrift Van der Leeuw. Nijkerk: G. F. Callenbach, 1950.

Prümm, K. *Der christliche Glaube und die altheidnische Welt.* Leipzig: J. Hegner, 1935.

Przyluski, J. *Le Bouddhisme.* Paris: Rieder, 1932.

Puech, H.-C. "La ténèbre mystique chez le Pseudo Denys l'Aréopagite et dans la tradition patristique." *Etudes carmélitaines,* 23 (1938) 33–53.

Quiles, I. "Nirvana y esperiencia metafisica." *Memorias del Congreso Internacional de Filosofia,* Mexico City (Sept. 1963), vol. 4, pp. 263–68.

Rad, G., von. *Theologie des Alten Testaments,* vol. 2: *Die Theologie der prophetischen Überlieferungen Israels.* Munich: Kaiser, 4th ed., 1965.

Radhakrishnan, S. *Indian Philosophy,* vol. 1. London: Allen & Unwin, 1929.

_____ . *The Philosophy of the Upanishads.* New York: MacMillan, 1966.

_____ . *The Principal Upanishads.* New York: Harper, 1953.

_____ . "The Teaching of the Buddha by Speech and Silence." *Hibbert Journal,* 32 (April 1934).

Raguin, Y. *Théologie missionaire de l'Ancien Testament.* Paris: Seuil, 1947.

Rahner, H. *Symbole der Kirche.* Salzburg: O. Müller, 1964.

Rahner, K. "Christentum als Religion der absoluten Zukunft." Kellner, *Christentum und Marxismus.*

_____ . "Christlicher Humanismus." *Orientierung* (May 1966).

_____ . "Über die Moglichkeit des Glaubens heute." *Schriften zur Theologie,* vol. 5, Einsiedeln: Benziger, 1962.

_____ . *The Pastoral Approach to Atheism.* New York: Paulist, 1967.

Rahula, W. *What the Buddha Taught.* New York: Grove, 1963.

Rājataraṁgini (by Kalhana). Engl. trans., E. Hultzsch, "Extracts from Kalhana's *Rajataraṁgini,"* *Indian Antiquary,* 18 (1889) 65–73.

Raju, P. T. "The Buddhist Conception of Negation." *Prof. M. Hiriyanna Commemoration Volume,* Mysore, 1951, pp. 162–70.

Ramírez, J. M. *De hominis beatitudine.* Madrid: CSIC, 1944.

Ratnāvali (by Nagarjuna). Engl. trans., G. Tucci, "The Ratnavali of Nagarjuna," *JRAS* (1934) 307–25; (1936) 237–52, 421–35.

Ratzinger, J. H., and Fries, H. *Einsicht und Glaube.* Freiburg: Herder, 1962.

Rawson, J. N. *The Katha Upanishad.* Oxford University Press, 1934.

Regamey, C. "Der Buddhismus Indiens." *Christus und die Religionen der Erde,* Freiburg: Herder, 1951.

_____ . *Buddhistische Bibliographie.* Bern, 1950.

_____ . *Buddhistische Philosophie.* Bern: Franck, 1950.

Renou, L. "Connexion en Védique, cause en Bouddhique." C. Kuhnan Raja, *Presentation Volume.*

_____ ."La valeur du silence dans la culte védique." *JAOS* (1949).

_____ , and Filliozat, J. *L'Inde classique.* Paris: Imprimerie Nationale, 1953.

Retif, A. *Foi au Christ et mission d'après les Actes des Apôtres.* Paris: Cerf, 1953.

Rhys Davids, C.A.F. *A Manual for Buddhism for Advanced Students.* New York: MacMillan, 1932.

————. *Sakya, or Buddhist Origins.* London: Kegan Paul, 1931.

————. *What Was the Original Gospel in Buddhism?* London: Epworth Press, 1938.

Rhys Davids, T. W. "Buddhism and Christianity." *Inter. Quarterly* (1903).

————. *Buddhism. Its History and Literature.* New York: Putnam's, 1896; 5th ed., 1962.

Richard of St. Victor. *Opera.* Migne PL, vol. 11.

Robinson, J. A. T. *Honest to God.* London: SCM, 1963.

————, and Edwards, D. L. *The Honest to God Debate.* London: SCM, 1963.

Robinson, R. H. "The Classical Indian Axiomatic." *Philosophy East and West,* 17 (1967) 139–54.

————. "Did Nagarjuna Really Refute All Philosophical Views?" Seminar, "Vedanta and Buddhism," Banaras Hindu University (March 1966).

————. "Some Logical Aspects of Nāgārjuna's System." *Philosophy East and West* (June 1957) 291–309.

Robinson, R. *The Madhyamika in India and China.* University of Wisconsin Press, 1967.

Rombach, H. *Substanz, System, Struktur.* Freiburg: Alber, 1966.

Rommerskirchen, P. *Bibliografia missionaria.* Rome: Pontificia Università di Propaganda Fidei, 1960.

Rosenberg, A. *Zeichen am Himmel. Das Weltbild der Astrologie.* Zurich: Metz, 1949.

Rosenberg, O. *Die Probleme der buddhistischen Philosophie.* Heidelberg, 1924.

Roustang, F. *Une initiation à la vie spirituelle.* Paris: Desclée, 1963.

Ruben, W. "Indische und griechische Metaphysik." *Zeitschrift für Indologie und Iranistik,* 8 (1931) 147–227.

Rupert, St. *Opera.* Migne PL, vol. 167–69.

Sabbatucci, D. *Saggio sul misticismo greco.* Rome: Ed. dell'Ateneo, 2nd ed., 1979.

Samyutta-nikāya (of the *Sutta-Piṭaka*). Engl. trans., C. A. F. Rhys Davids and F. L. Woodward, *The Book of Kindred Sayings,* 5 vols., London: Pali Text Society Translations, 1907–1925; repr. 1951–1956.

Sanders, J. A. *Union Seminary Quarterly Review,* 21 (1966).

Sangharkshita, B. *A Survey of Buddhism.* Bangalore: Indian Institute of World Culture, 1966.

Śantideva. *Bodhicaryavatāra. Introduction à la pratique des futurs bouddhas.* Paris: Bloud, 1907.

Sartre, J. P. *Essere e nulla.* Milan: Il Saggiatore, 2nd ed., 1980.

————. *Le parole.* Milan: Il Saggiatore, 4th ed., 1980.

Saunders, K. J. "Buddhism and Christianity." *The Chinese Recorder* (1927) 416–21.

————. "The Christ and the Buddha." *Atlantic Monthly* (1927) 182–88.

————. *Christianity and Buddhism.* New York, 1927.

————. "Christianity and Buddhism." *International Missionary Council* (1928) 1–20.

Schayer, S. "Altindische Antizipationen der Aussagenlogik" *Bulletin International de l'Académie des Sciences et des Lettres* (1933).

————. "New Contributions to the Problem of Prehinayastic Buddhism." *Polski builetyn orientalistyczny,* 2 (1937).

Scheidt, J. "Säkularisierung. Odysee eines Begriffs." *Hochland* (Aug. 1966).

Schlötermann, H. *Mystik in den Religionen der Völker.* Munich: Reinhardt, 1958.

Schlunk, M. *Die Weltreligionen und das Christentum.* Frankfurt: Anker, 1951.

Schmidt, W. *Ursprung und Werden der Religion.* Münster: Aschendorff, 1930.

Schomerus, H. W. *Buddha und Christus. Ein Vergleich zweier grosser Weltreligionen.* Halle, 1931.

Schrader, O. *Über den Stand der indischen Philosophie zur Zeit Mahaviras und Buddhas.* Leipzig, 1902.

Schroeder, L., von. "Buddhismus und Christentum. Was sie gemein haben und was sie unterscheidet." *Leopold von Schroeder, Reden und Aufsätze,* 1913, pp. 85–127.

Schubring, W. *Der Jainismus. Eine indische Erlösungsreligion.* Berlin: A. Häger, 1925.

Schulemann, G. *Die Botschaft des Buddha,* Freiburg: Herder, 1937.

Schuon, F. *De l'unité transcendante des religions.* Paris: Gallimard, 1948.

Schuster, H. *Der christliche Glaube und die Religion der Völker.* Frankfurt, 1951.

Schuwer, L. "Intorno ai presupposti della demitizzazione: 'Wie kommt der Gott in die Philosophie.' " E. Castelli, *Archivio di Filosofia* (1961) 129–46.

Schweinitz, H., von. *Buddhismus und Christentum.* Basel/Munich: Reinhardt, 1955.

Scott, A. *Buddhism and Christianity. A Parallel and a Contrast.* Edinburgh: David Douglas, 1890.

Scotus, Duns. *Opera.* Migne PL, vol. 122.

Schweitzer, A. *Christianity and the Religions of the World.* London: Allen & Unwin, 1923.

Seidenstücker, K. B. "Christentum und Abend-land." *Die buddhistische Welt* (1909) 29–33.

Seydel, R. *Das Evangelium von Jesu in seinem Verhaltnisse zu Buddha und Buddha Lehre.* Leipzig, 1882.

Shōjun, B., and Shōyu, H. *A Bibliography on Japanese Buddhism.* Tokyo, 1958.

Sigwart, C. *Logic.* New York: MacMillan, 2nd ed., 1895.

Silburn, L. *Instant et cause. Le discontinu dans la pensée philosophique de l'Inde.* Paris: Vrin, 1955.

Simon, G. *Auseinandersetzung des Christentums mit den ausserchristlichen Mystik.* Gütersloh: C. Bertelsmann, 1930.

Slater, R. L. *Paradox and Nirvana. A Study of Religious Ultimates with Special Reference to Burmese Buddhism.* University of Chicago Press, 1951.

———, and Tun Hla, U. "The Christian Approach to Buddhism." *Nation. Christian Council Rev.* (1921) 586–95.

Smith, F. H. "The Sutta and the Gospel. An Inquiry into the Relationship between the Accounts of the Supernatural Births of Buddha and Christ." *The Church Quart. Rev.* (1921) 305–24.

Smith, R. G. *Secular Christianity.* New York: Harper & Row, 1966.

Smith, W. C. *The Faith of Other Men.* New York: New American Library, 1965.

———. *The Meaning and End of Religion.* New York: Scribner's, 1967.

———. *The Question of Religious Truth.* New York: Scribner's, 1967.

———. "Religious Atheism? Early Buddhist and Recent American." Charles Strong Memorial Lecture, 1966.

Sobczak, R. *Licht und Schatten. Zwiegespräch zwischen einem Christen und einem Buddhisten.* Breslau, 1914.

Söderblom, N. "Buddha und Christus." *Die Religionen der Erde* (1905) 47–63.

Sölle, D. *Stellvertretung. Ein Kapitel Theologie nach dem "Tode Gottes."* Stuttgart: Kreuz, 1965.

Spann, R. J. *Christian Faith and Secularism.* New York: Abingdon, 1948.

Speer, R. E. "Points of Contact with Christianity in the Heresies of Siamese Buddhism." *Princeton Theological Quarterly* (1916) 62–71.

Spencer, S. *Mysticism in World Religions.* Baltimore: Penguin, 1963.

Spencer-Gillen, B. *The Arunta.* London: MacMillan, 1927.

Staal, J. F. "The Construction of Formal Definition, Subject and Predicate." *Philosophical Transactions* (1960) 89–103.

———. "Negation and the Law of Contradiction in Indian Thought. A Comparative Study." *Bulletin of the School of Oriental and African Studies,* 25 (1962).

Stählin, W. *Symbolon. Vom gleichnishaften Denken.* Stuttgart: Evangelischer Verlagwerk, 1958.

Stange, C. "Buddhismus und Christentum." *Zeitschrift für systematische Theologie* (1953) 414–23.

Stcherbatsky, T. *The Central Conception of Buddhism and the Meaning of the Word Dharma.* London, 1923.

———. *The Concept of Buddhist Nirvana.* The Hague: Mouton, 1965 (reprint of the 1st ed., Petersburg, 1927).

Steiner, "Buddha and Christ." *Anthroposophy,* (1926) 279–305.

Stix, H. S. *Christus oder Buddha? In Parallelstellen aus dem Neuen Testament und den heiligen Schriften Indiens dargestellt.* Leipzig, 1900.

Stolz, A. *Theologie der Mystik.* Regensburg: Pustet, 1936.

Streeter, C. R. H. *The Buddha and the Christ. An Explanation of the Meaning of the Universe and the Purpose of Human Life.* New York, 1932.

Streng, F. J. *Emptiness. A Study in Religious Meaning.* New York: Abingdon, 1967.

Strolz, W. *Menschsein als Gottesfrage.* Pfüllingen: Neske, 1965.

Strong, D. M. *The Metaphysic of Christianity and Buddhism. A Symphony.* London: Watts, 1899.

Studies in Indology and Buddhology in Honour of Prof. Susumu Yamaguchi Kyoto: Hozokan, 1955.

Study in the History of Religions Presented to Crufford Howel Toy, 1912.

Sutta-nipāta (part of the *khuddaka-nikāya* of the *Sutta-Piṭaka*). Engl. trans., R. Chalmers, *Buddha's Teaching or Discours Collection,* Cambridge, Mass. (Harvard Oriental Series), 1933; also, E. M. Harc, *Woven Cadences of Early Buddhism,* London (Sacred Books of the Buddhists), 2nd ed., 1948.

Suzuki, D. T. *Essence of Buddhism.* London: The Buddhist Society, 1947.

———. *Mysticism, Christian and Buddhist.* London: Allen & Unwin, 1957.

———. *Outlines of Mahayana Buddhism.* Chicago: Open Court, 1908.

———. "Reason and Intuition in Buddhist Philosophy." *Essays in East-West Philosophy,* 17–48.

———. *Studies in the Laṅkāvatāra-Sūtra.* London: Routledge, 1930.

———. "The Zen Sect of Buddhism." *Journal of the Pali Text Society* (1906–1907) 13ff.

Takakusa, J. *The Essentials of Buddhist Philosophy.* Honolulu/Calcutta: Chan and Moore, 1956.

Takeuchi, Y. "Modern Japanese Philosophy." *Encyclopedia Britannica,* 1966.

———. "Das Schweigen des Buddha." Yearbook of the University of Kyoto, Faculty of Letters, 1965.

Tamura, K. "The Concept of Absoluteness in Buddhism." *Religion East and West,* 38 (Jan. 1965).

_____ . "Some Developments of the Buddhist Approach to Reality." *International Philosophical Quarterly,* 1964.

Taymans D'Eypernon, F. *Les paradoxes du Bouddhisme.* Brussels: L'Edition Universelle. 1947.

Tertullian. *Opera.* Migne PL, vol. 1–3.

Theragāthā (part of the *khuddaka-nikāya* of the *Sutta-Piṭaka*). Engl. trans., C. A. F. Rhys Davids, *Psalms of the Sisters,* London (Pali Text Society Translations), 1935.

Therīgāthā (part of the *khuddaka-nikāya* of the *Sutta-Piṭaka*). Engl. trans., C. A. F. Rhys Davids, *Psalms of the Sisters,* London (Pali Text Society Translations), 1909.

Thomas, E. J. *The History of Buddhist Thought.* London: Routledge & Kegan Paul, 2nd ed., 1963.

_____ . *The Life of the Buddha, as Legend and History.* New York: Knopf, 1933.

_____ . "Nirvana and Paranirvana." *India Antiqua,* 294ff.

Thomas, O. C. "Being and Some Theologians." *Harvard Theological Review,* 70 (1977) 107–60.

Tillich, P. *Biblical Religion and the Search for Ultimate Reality.* University of Chicago Press, 1955.

_____ . *The Courage to Be.* New Haven: Yale University Press, 1955.

_____ . *Religion and the Protestant Era.* University of Chicago Press, 1948.

_____ . *Systematic Theology,* 3 vols. University of Chicago Press, 1951.

_____ . *Theology of Culture.* New York: Oxford University Press, 1959.

Tisdall, C. W. "Mahayana Buddhism and Christianity." *Journal of Victoria Inst.* (1915) 253–76.

Tokuru Yamauchi. "Problems of Logic in Philosophy East and West." *Japanese Religion,* 3 (Aug. 1963).

Tomomatsu, E. *Le Bouddhisme.* Paris: F. Alcan, 1935.

Toynbee, A. J. *Christianity among the Religions of the World.* New York: Scribner's, 1957.

_____ . *An Historian's Approach to Religion.* New York: Oxford University Press, 1956.

Tresmontant, C. *La métaphysique du christianisme et la naissance de la philosophie chrétienne.* Paris: Seuil, 1961.

Tsukamoto, K. "Materials for the Date of Buddha's Nirvana." *Religion East and West,* 33 (March 1960).

Tucci, G. *Il Buddhismo.* Foligno, 1926.

_____ . "A Fragment from the Pratītyasamutpāda of Vasubandhu." *Journal of the Royal Asiatic Society* (1930) 611–23.

_____ . *Teoria e pratica del Mandala.* Rome: Astrolabio/Ubaldini, 1949.

_____ . "Un traité d'Aryadeva sur le Nirvana des Hérétiques." *T.P.,* 24 (1925) 16–31.

Udāna (part of the *khuddaka-nikāya* of the *Sutta-Piṭaka*) with *Itivuttaka.* Engl. trans., F. L. Woodward, *Verses of Uplift,* London (Pali Text Society Translations), 1935.

Ünderweg-Geyer, *Die patristische und scholastische Philosophie.* Tübingen, 1951.

Unesco, C. I. *L'athéisme, tentation du monde, réveil des chrétiens.* Paris: Cerf, 1963.

Ut, H. *The Death of God.* New York: Braziller, 1961.

_____ . "Maitreya as an Historical Person." *Indian Studies in Honour of Charles Rockwell Lanman.* Cambridge: Harvard University Press, 1929, pp. 95ff.

_____ . Research on Indian Philosophy, vol. 2–4, Tokyo, 1925–1927 (in Japanese).

Vahanian, G. *No Other God.* New York: Braziller, 1966.

_____ . *Wait without Idols.* New York: Braziller, 1964.

Van Buren, P. *The Secular Meaning of the Gospel.* New York: MacMillan, 1963.

Venkata-Ramanan, K. *Nagarjuna's Philosophy as Presented in the Mahā-Pajñāpāramitā-Sāstra.* Tokyo: Harvard/Yenching Institute, 1966.

Vereno, M. *Von Mythos zum Christos.* Salzburg: O. Müller, 1958.

Vesci, U. M. "Die Beziehung Gott-Mensch in der Spiritualität Indiens." *Meditations* (1978) 114ff.; (1979) 27ff.

_____ . "Dialogo religioso per la scoperta del mito al centro del proprio credo." *Conoscenza religiosa* (Sept. 1978).

_____ . "Dio, Uomo, Salvezza in alcuni aspetti del rivolgimento spirituale del VII/VI secoli a.c. in Asia e in Grecia." Tesi di perfezionamento, University of Rome, Faculty of Letters, 1962.

_____ . *Heat and Sacrifice in the Vedas.* Delhi: Motilal Banassidass, 1985.

_____ . "The Role of Ritual Heat in Vedic Sacrifice. The Place of Pain in the Act of Creation." *Bijdragen,* 39 (1978) 399–423.

Vicedom, G. F. *Die Mission der Weltreligionen.* Munich: Kaiser, 1959.

Vigrahavyavārtanī. Engl. trans., G. Tucci, "Pro-Diññaga Buddhist Texts on Logic from Chinese Sources." *GOS,* 49 (1929).

Vimalananda, T. "The Influence of Buddhism on the Greek System of Thought and on Christianity." *The Maha Bodi* (1939) 549–55.

Vinaya-Piṭaka, Engl. trans., T. W. Rhys Davids and H. Oldenberg, 3 vols., Oxford (Sacred Books of the East), 1881–1885.

Völker, W. *Gregor von Nyssa als Mystiker.* Wiesbaden: F. Steinert, 1955.

Wadia, A. R. "Philosophical Implications of the Doctrine of Karma." *Philosophy East and West,* 15 (1965).

Warnach, V. "Zum Argument im Proslogion Anselm von Canterbury." *Ratzinger-Fries, Einsicht und Glaube.*

Warren, H. C. *Buddhism in Translations.* Cambridge, Mass.: Harvard University Press, 1922.

Watsuji, T. *The practical philosophy of primitive Buddhism.* Tokyo, 1927 (in Japanese).

Waymann, A. "The Buddhist 'not this, not this.' " *Philosophy East and West,* 11 (Oct. 1961) 99–114.

Weil, S. *Pensées sans ordre concernant l'amour de Dieu.* Paris: Gallimard, 1962.

_____ . *La pesanteur et la grace.* Paris: Plon, 1948.

Weinrich, R. *Die Liebe im Buddhismus und im Christentum.* Berlin, 1935.

Welbon, G. R. "Comments on the Max Müller's Interpretation of the Buddhist Nirvana," *Numen,* 12 (Sept. 1965).

_____ . "On Understanding the Buddhist Nirvana." *History of Religions,* 5 (1966) 300–326.

Widengren, G. *Die Religionen Irans.* Stuttgart: Kohlhammer, 1965.

Wijeyesekera, D. E. *Buddhist and Christian Philosophy.* Colombo, 1928.

Williams, D. M. "The Translation and Interpretation of the Twelve Terms in the Paticcasamuppāda." *Numen,* 21 (April 1974) 35–63.

Wilson, B. R. *Religion in a Secular Society.* London: Watt, 1966.

Windisch, *Mara und Buddha.* Leipzig: S. Hirzel, 1895.

Wing-Tsit, Chan. *The Platform Scripture.* New York: St. John's University Press, 1963.

Winternitz, M. *Geschichte der indischen Literatur.* Leipzig, 1920. Engl. trans., *History of Indian Literature,* 2 vols., Calcutta University Press, 1927–1933; repr., Delhi, Motilal Banassidass, 1963.

Wisse, S. *Das religiöse Symbol.* Essen: Ludgerus, 1963.

Witte, J. *Die Christusbotschaft und die Religionen.* Göttingen, 1936.

––––––. "Die Einwirkung des Buddhismus und Religions-wissenschaft." *Zeitschrift für Missionskunde und Religions-wissenschaft* (1914) 289–301, 353–74.

Wittgenstein, L. *Tractatus logico-philosophicus,* London: Routledge & Kegan Paul, 1922.

Yamauchi, T. "Problems of Logic in Philosophy East and West." *Japanese Religions,* 3 (Aug. 1963).

––––––. *Studies in Indology and Buddhology.* Kyoto: Hozohan, 1955.

Zaehner, R. C. *The Convergent Spirit.* London: Routledge & Kegan Paul, 1963.

––––––. *The Dawn and Twilight of Zoroastrianism.* London: Widenfeld & Nicolson, 1961.

––––––. *At Sundry Times.* London: Faber, 1958.

Index of Concepts

Index of Names

Index of Sacred Texts

BUDDHIST

CHRISTIAN

HINDU

Aitareya Brāhmana		*Pañcauimsa Brāhmana*		*Śatapatha Brāhmana*	
II, 32	*225n48*	VII, 6	*225n44*	I, 4	*225n42*
		XX, 14	*165*	I, 9	*226n55*
Brhadarānyaka				III, 2	*225n46*
Upanishad		*Rg Veda*		VII, 2	*226n51*
				XII, 4	*226n59*
I, 4	*230n126*	X, 129	*219n146*	XII, 5	*226n56*

JEWISH

Genesis		*1 Samuel*		61:2	*230n114*
32:29	*145*	3:9	*145*		
Exodus		*Psalms*		*Lamentations*	
32:31–32	*234n174*	39:14	*201n1*	3:28	*182n71*

ZOROASTRIAN

Yasna	
XLIII, 5	*203n39*